OLD OREGON UNDER THE SHADOW OF THE ALMIGHTY

THE UNADULTERATED HISTORY OF THE AMERICAN WEST

STUART DICK

MATTESON SCHOOL HOUSE PUBLISHING
PENDLETON, OREGON

Copyright © 2009 Stuart Dick

All rights reserved. No part of this publication may be reproduced,
stored in a retrieval system, or transmitted in any form or by any means,
electronic, mechanical, photocopying, microfilming, recording,
or otherwise, without permission of the author.

Printed in the United States of America

Library of Congress Control Number
2009923241

International Standard Book Numbers
978-0-615-2347-1-7 (softcover)
978-0-615-27365-5 (hardcover)

The author thanks David Manuel for granting permission to reprint his paintings in this book.
His permission does not constitute an endorsement of the book. In addition the owner of the
Manuel Collection, Kyle Mussman, has also granted permission for use of the oil paintings.
The collection is available to be viewed at no charge at the Marcus Whitman Hotel
and Conference Center in Walla Walla, Washington.

Published by

Matteson School House Publishing
14 SE Isaac Ave.
Pendleton, OR 97801

Printed by

Marquette Books LLC
5915 S. Regal St., Suite 118B
Spokane, Washington 99223-6970
509-443-7057 (voice) / 509-448-2191 (fax)
books@marquettebooks.com / www.MarquetteBooks.com

To my father, Ed Dick

TABLE OF CONTENTS

PREFACE, vii

ACKNOWLEDGMENTS, ix

SYNOPSIS OF CHAPTERS, xi

CHAPTERS

1. Under the Shadow of the Almighty, 1
2. The Spanish Empire: The First Lord of the Pacific, 4
3. Challengers on the Horizon, 8
4. The Fabled Northwest Passage, 13
5. Stewards of the Land, 17
6. The Columbia Plateau Indians, 19
7. Overland Quest for Oregon, 25
8. The Golden Age of the Free Trappers, 33
9. The Hudson's Bay Company, 38
10. Columbia Plateau Indians and the First Wave of White Men, 41
11. The Spiritual Battle for Liberty and Freedom in Oregon, 44
12. American Missionaries, 52
13. The Clash Between Protestants and Roman Catholics in Oregon, 63
14. The Difference Between Jesuit and Catholic Priests and Their Impact in Oregon, 67
15. The Whitman Mission, 69
16. Whitman's Ride Across America, 74
17. The Oregon Question, 81
18. Westward Ho, 85
19. The Controversy over the Whitmans — Ethnocentrically Biased? 98
20. The Advent of the Jesuit/Catholic Priests, 110
21. The Whitman Massacre: The Final Act of the Oregon Territory, 114
22. Eyewitness Accounts of the Whitman Massacre, 125

23. Protestantism According to Father Brouillet, 139
24. The Testament of the Protestant Church and the Oregon Government Concerning Romanism in Oregon, 154
25. The Nez Perce Indians: Great Patriots for America and Oregon, 163
26. Chief Joseph's Historic Speech to America, 169
27. Manifest Destiny and the Native American Indians, 192
28. Indian Reservations, 196
29. The Bridge Between the Protestant Almighty and the Indian Great Spirit Chief, 202
30. The Confederated Tribes of the Umatilla, Walla Walla and Cayuse and the Peace Treaty of 1855, 206
31. The Tutuilla Presbyterian Church, 214
32. Happy Canyon, 223
33. Matteson School House Pioneers, 228
34. Irish Catholics Discover Eastern Oregon, 235
35. The Emergence of the Confederated Tribes of the Umatilla, 239
36. The Resurrection of the Umatilla River, 250
37. The Destruction of the Columbia River: The Fabled Northwest Passage, 254
38. Give Therefore Thy Servant a Discerning Heart, 260
39. A Controversy with the Inhabitants of the Land, 265
40. The Third Great Awakening, 271

BIBLIOGRAPHY, 281

INDEX, 285

ABOUT THE AUTHOR, 290

PREFACE

This book began as a history of the Matteson School House, the last remaining evidence of the pioneer forefathers of the Heppner District of the Blue Mountains of eastern Oregon. As I researched the letters, newspaper articles and personal stories of the original pioneers who attended and supported the Matteson School House I realized the research had to begin one step deeper with the Cayuse Indians. This small but powerful tribe held dominion throughout the Blue Mountains before the first white men arrived on the scene. As I researched the Cayuse Indians an astounding story of stewardship of the magnificent natural resources of the Pacific Northwest begged to be documented, but the Native American Indians left no written records. To my annoyance I began to realize the research had to begin with the first European documented history of the Pacific Northwest. Three hundred fifty years of documented history beginning in the 15th century was a hefty assignment, but I figured a few chapters would provide sufficient introduction to allow the story to progress. Those few chapters turned out to be thirty-two chapters introducing an incredible story now titled *Old Oregon—Under the Shadow of the Almighty*. Our Indian forefathers go back farther than the 15th century, but that is where the documented history of Old Oregon begins, so in like manner that is where the story must begin. For the purposes of this history the term Old Oregon refers to the land of the original Oregon Territory encompassing the entire Pacific Northwest from the Rocky Mountains to the Pacific Ocean, as far as San Francisco to the south and Canada to the north.

It is a joy for me to tell this story, not so much because it has been on my heart for decades but rather because the research reveals a poignant story of a magnificent heritage common to all Americans, especially the Native Americans.

I have established one abiding standard for this work: to tell the truth, the unadulterated truth. I am not bound, constrained or motivated to satisfy any ideology, or repeat previously politically or religiously correct versions of the history of the West, or meet the restraints of any publisher, or win a respected university's approval. I am committed to telling the story of Old Oregon, without compromise, exactly as it happened according to the writings and eyewitness accounts of those individuals who carved the heritage of the West.

To illustrate my motivation to tell this story I will rephrase an old proverb attributed to Abraham Lincoln. You can please some of the people all of the time and all of the people some of the time but you can never please all of the people all of the time. It was never my purpose or intention, but I am sure in the course of this research I will have documented something that will offend individuals of every political and religious persuasion including Protestants, Catholics, atheists, environmentalists, liberals, conservatives, Republicans, Democrats, Native Americans, and on and on.

I will admit from the outset that I have a bias. The truth is all authors have a bias, whether they admit it or not. The recognition of personal bias does not release historians from their responsibility to be unbiased in their disposition of the truth. My personal bias is my faith in God. I believe in an Almighty God who created the world and gave mankind the Bible that we might know Him. Even if I did not have a faith bias, my research would have convinced me beyond a shadow of a doubt that the Creator of the universe had a plan and a purpose for Oregon long before civilization, Native American or European, reached the shores of the Pacific. I will leave it to the reader and the Almighty whether I have correctly handled this sacred disposition of the truth.

The original testimonies, resolutions, memoirs, diaries, and the excellent scholarship of historians of the 19th century have produced a portrait filled with astounding courage framed with fractured schisms that remain to the present hour. The passion to sustain the true testimony of the history of Oregon has become bittersweet. Great confusion has been caused by historians and theologians/religious leaders who pressed their personal agendas through positions of political power to rewrite and re-craft Oregon's history to fit a preconceived political, religious or cultural position. The result of this re-crafting of history has produced a template that remains to the present hour casting a veil over the real history of Oregon. The spiritual imprint and cultural/political impact of this veil continues to mold the cultural, religious and political heritage of the lands and peoples of Old Oregon in a negative manner and blinds the people to their true heritage.

George Otis Jr., in his book *Informed Intercession*, has documented the impact of faith in God on multiple western civilizations of the present age. Historical truth that includes God's sovereign purposes can be framed in a spiritual map that allows the reader to "see things that were previously undetectable with our natural eyes." (Otis, George Jr., *Informed Intercession*, Renew Books, Ventura, Calif., 1999, p. 81) Otis writes, "Western Christianity has been clinging to its millpond discriminations of reality so tenaciously that it has nearly lost all ability to recognize the spiritual dimension." (p. 80) The purpose of this research is to document a spiritual and cultural map of Old Oregon that allows the citizens of historic Oregon to have an accurate knowledge of their true political, cultural and religious heritage. The great statesmen of America have recognized the spiritual dimension of historical truth since the birth of the Republic. Shortly before his assassination in 1865, American president Abraham Lincoln wrote: "That the Almighty does make use of human agencies, and directly intervenes in human affairs, is one of the plainest statements of the Bible. I have had so many evidences of his direction—so many instances when I have been controlled by some other power than my own will—that I cannot doubt that this power comes from above." (Federer, William, *America's God and Country*, Amerisearch, Inc. St. Louis, MO, p. 390)

Some of the historical findings and documents of this research will be considered controversial. John F. Kilkenny at the beginning of *Shamrocks and Shepherds* pleaded with his Irish friends: "Well knowing your penchant for sharp-tongued invective, I am also aware of your tolerance. Please withhold the sting of your tongue, while exploring the breadth of your clemency." (John F. Kilkenny, *Shamrocks and Shepherd, The Irish of Morrow County,* Glass-Dahlstrom Printers, Portland, Oregon, 1969, p. 2) Please read the whole of the story of Old Oregon before developing any stinging invectives and even then I plead with John Kilkenny for the breadth of your clemency. A true unbiased historiography of any subject has a way of turning villains into heroes and vice versa. This is one story that must be followed through to the conclusion to glean the gold. The true story of the American West, of cowboys and Indians, wagon trains and pioneers, has a message of hope and inspiration for every nation and goes to the heart of every culture.

Enjoy!

ACKNOWLEDGMENTS

This book is dedicated to my Father, L. E. (Ed) Dick Jr., whose heritage dates back to the Revolutionary War. Harmon Dick, progenitor of the Dick clan in America, was born in Loch Lomond, Scotland in 1756. As a young man he emigrated to Hesse Castle, Germany, where he joined the Hessian Army under orders to subdue the American colonists under the command of Hessian Colonel Rahl. General George Washington crossed the Delaware River on ice and surprised the Hessian Army celebrating Christmas festivities at Trenton, New Jersey. One thousand Hessian prisoners were taken to Valley Forge. Among those prisoners was a 6-foot-2 man who weighed 253 lbs and went by the name of Harmon Dick. Harmon immediately took the oath of allegiance to the United Colonies and became a staunch friend and ally of George Washington and was ever loyal to the American cause. He became a Federalist at the organization of the American government. He lived and died as a Christian, committing his soul into the hands of Almighty God through Jesus Christ his savior.

L. E. Dick Jr. is 91 years old and still ever loyal to the American cause and a stanch ally to the divine purpose of Old Oregon. He fought to save the multiple natural resources of the National Forests of the west and he served for over five decades on almost every city, community, and county board that guided the heritage of Eastern Oregon during the 20th century. He sacrificed his time, his money, his business and his reputation to provide a voice of integrity, vision and purpose so the heritage of freedom and liberty in Old Oregon would prosper into the next century. This book is dedicated to his memory and the fellow pioneers that shared his allegiance to the American cause.

In addition I wish to express appreciation to the following individuals that helped make this book possible. Members of the Faith Center Four Square Church in Pendleton, Oregon have been invaluable in supporting me during the multiple years of researching and preparing the text. Joan Pfaff and D-Ann Pahl helped edit the text. Pastor Ray O'Grady and his wife Julie have been ardent supporters and trusted confidants.

In addition I wish to include one living pioneer of the Matteson School House, Dorothy Matteson Scott, in the list of those that made this book possible. Dorothy represents the hearty spirit and unquenchable love of our common pioneer heritage in Old Oregon. I promised Dorothy I would write a history of the Matteson School House. I did not know at that time it would only be one small chapter of forty to ultimately include the entire heritage of Old Oregon.

My wife Julie and my daughter Taryn Suchy have been a source of great encouragement. Tayrn shares my love of history as a professor of history at Columbia Basin Community College in Pasco, Washington. Dr. Dave Demers, editor of Marquette Books LLC in Spokane, Washington, has provided expertise and astute advice in every area of formatting and publishing this manuscript. Without Dr. Demers' gracious and diligent assistance, this book would never have been properly completed. I give thanks to God to all these individuals and many more unnamed for making this manuscript possible.

Synopsis of Chapters

Chapter 1
Under the Shadow of the Almighty

Three hundred ships from seventeen different nations throughout nearly three hundred years searched for the Northwest Passage, the mighty Columbia River, yet without explanation the prize remained hidden until the American Robert Gray discovered the river of the West in 1792. Did providence play a sovereign role? This chapter explores the mystery of how the great river of the West that emptied the entire Pacific Northwest into the Pacific Ocean remained hidden from the great mariner nations of the world for nearly three centuries.

Chapter 2
The Spanish Empire: The First Lord of the Pacific

By the middle of the sixteenth century, Spain controlled all of the Americas from the 40th parallel in North America to the southernmost tip of South America. Nevertheless, every attempt by the legendary Spanish conquistadors to conquer the Indian nations of the Pacific Northwest, whether by land or sea, ended in dismal failure. Did providence once again play a sovereign role?

Chapter 3
Challengers on the Horizon

The mighty mariners of the multiple nations of the storied Age of Discovery were romantically aware of the fabled Northwest Passage because Spanish sailor Martin de Aguilar actually discovered and documented the Columbia River in 1598. He called the passage the Straight of Anian. For nearly two centuries every world power of the Western world attempted to find the legendary land British novelist Jonathan Swift would call the land of Brobdingnag. According to the journals of these legendary mariners, the ancient foe of the human race always blinded or befuddled their most stalwart attempts to claim the greatest sweepstakes of the modern era. Was the Oregon Territory protected under the shadow of the Almighty?

Chapter 4
The Fabled Northwest Passage

British Captain George Vancouver met American Captain Robert Gray near the mouth of the Columbia River in 1792 and assured Gray there was no break in the coast line. Vancouver sailed away and Gray sailed directly to the mouth of the "Northwest Passage" and discovered the mighty river of the West for the emerging nation of the United States of America. Four nations would immediately claim ownership—Great Britain, Spain, Russia and the United States—yet none had even a single inhabitant on the ground in the land that would become known as the Oregon Territory. In actual fact, the land was already owned and occupied by the indigenous tribes of the American Indians that had occupied the Pacific Northwest for centuries.

CHAPTER 5
STEWARDS OF THE LAND

The Columbia River was the focal point of Indian civilization along the entire Pacific coast of North America. The indigenous American Indians of the Pacific Northwest were organized into multiple nations and tribes and had developed a highly sophisticated civilization that accentuated stewardship of the land and resources in contrast to European civilizations that emphasized industrial progress that required consumption of resources.

CHAPTER 6
THE COLUMBIA PLATEAU INDIANS

The Cayuse Indians ruled the vast terrain of the 1.4 million acre forest known today as the Blue Mountains. The Nez Perce Indians ruled the vast Snake River basin to the east. These two Indian nations were central to every major act in the history of the Pacific Northwest because Western civilization was destined to traverse through their land. The temperament, character and spiritual disposition of these and related Columbia Plateau Indians were largely in unity with the first Americans drawn to the Oregon Territory, and the relationship between the two races was positive and productive until sabotaged by the tragic events of the WHITMAN massacre.

CHAPTER 7
OVERLAND QUEST FOR OREGON

At the turn of the 19th century, multiple nations had aspirations to claim the vast Oregon Territory including the United States of America, which was in the least favorable position to claim the prize. France commissioned the first overland expedition in 1728. The British commissioned a second expedition in 1766, but King George III rejected the attempt. In 1793, Englishman Alexander MacKenzie crossed the continent and reached present-day Vancouver and claimed the Pacific Northwest for Britain. Thomas Jefferson had learned of the land of the Oregon Territory from John Ledyard (who sailed with Captain Cook) while in France and commissioned the Lewis and Clark Expedition in 1803 after he became president of the United States. Britain took Fort Astor by force in the War of 1812, establishing dominion of the Pacific Northwest despite losing both wars with America.

CHAPTER 8
THE GOLDEN AGE OF THE FREE TRAPPERS

One of the great romantic epics of American history was staged upon the pristine wonders of the Wild West of the Pacific Northwest. The fur trappers, mountain men and explorers were a special breed of men and women and their exploits were legendary yet almost always unsuccessful. The successive American overland exploration parties after Lewis and Clark would have all perished without the benevolent support and grace of the indigenous Indians of the Pacific Northwest. The world clamored for the "brown gold" of the beaver pelt at this hour and the rich veins of the mighty Columbia River were their greatest natural habitat. The stage was set for the "joint occupancy" of the region between Great Britain and the United States, but in historical reality the Union Jack ruled with no challenge to their absolute authority.

CHAPTER 9
THE HUDSON'S BAY COMPANY

Great Britain's control of Fort Astor in 1812 initiated over three decades of virtual British rule in the Pacific Northwest. Their essential line of communication was the Columbia River. The Hudson's Bay Company ruled their vast empire as a trading monopoly under the astute leadership of John McLoughlin. McLoughlin governed the vast Oregon Territory with more absolute sovereignty than most monarchs in Europe and his kingdom was larger than every European state. No power or authority in the world threatened the complete autonomy of the Hudson's Bay Company under McLoughlin.

CHAPTER 10
COLUMBIA PLATEAU INDIANS AND THE FIRST WAVE OF WHITE MEN

In the beginning, the Columbia Plateau Indians supported the advent of white men into their territory. They welcomed the first fur trappers and traded and prospered from their interchange. They did not see these white mountain-men as a threat to their culture. For the most part the Hudson's Bay Company exploited the Indians for beaver furs but the trade actually enhanced their wealth and did not undermine their freedom.

CHAPTER 11
THE SPIRITUAL BATTLE FOR LIBERTY AND FREEDOM IN OREGON

In 1832, four Nez Perce and Flathead Indians undertook an expedition to the East to obtain the "white man's Book of Heaven" that would forever change the history and heritage of the Oregon Territory. The Columbia Plateau Indians were a reverential, spiritual people and when they heard of the Bible that contained the written word of the Great Spirit who created the world they pursued this truth at the cost of every life save one on the expedition. The American Indian quest for truth initiated the great missionary movement to the Pacific Northwest that brought Protestant and thereafter Jesuit missionaries. The great world religious schism caused by the Protestant Reformation in the 16th century and Catholic Counter Reformation thereafter would have a monumental and tragic result in the Oregon Territory.

CHAPTER 12
AMERICAN MISSIONARIES

When the first Protestant missionaries arrived in the Pacific Northwest, the Oregon Territory was hopelessly outside the political grasp of the American government. Until that hour every American endeavor to claim and establish a foothold in the Territory ended in dismal failure. The advent of the Protestant missionaries, or more precisely the Protestant missionary wives, changed everything. Hudson's Bay Chief Factor John McLoughlin had an answer for every American challenge except American women who were willing to give up their homes, comforts and heritage in the East to minister the Gospel in the West and start families in the Territory.

CHAPTER 13
THE CLASH BETWEEN PROTESTANTS AND ROMAN CATHOLICS IN OREGON

The global impact of the Protestant missionary ministry in the Oregon Territory reached all the way to the Vatican in Rome. Roman Catholicism held sway with the dominion of the Hudson's Bay Company but now that dominion was being severely challenged by the missionaries, especially the Whitmans. The history of the clash between the two great Christian faiths went back to the Protestant Reformation in 1532 and the subsequent Catholic Counter Reformation led by the Jesuits under Ignatius Loyola. Great religious wars and persecutions had followed the Protestant Reformation wherever it went and the Oregon Territory would be no exception. The Whitmans wrote often of their great agitation over the growing threats of the "Papists" who insidiously began to undermine their work and ministry.

CHAPTER 14
THE DIFFERENCE BETWEEN JESUIT AND CATHOLIC PRIESTS AND THEIR IMPACT IN OREGON

Most historians do not differentiate between Jesuit and Catholic Priests in relationship to the missionary movement in the Pacific Northwest and that has become a grave error in respect to historical integrity. This chapter documents the history of the Catholic Counter Reformation as it relates to the course of the missionary movement in Old Oregon. The Society of Jesuits had a significantly different mission and purpose, at least in part, than the Catholic Church and they would ultimately clash with the Protestant missionaries for control of Old Oregon.

CHAPTER 15
THE WHITMAN MISSION

The Whitman Mission near Walla Walla became the center of the spiritual and political battle for Oregon. The Whitmans have been widely criticized by contemporary historians for exploiting the Indians, undermining their culture, stealing their land and mistreating their heritage. Narcissa Whitman has been highly criticized for being haughty and insensitive to the needs of the Indians. This chapter documents the actual written record of the Whitmans and their contemporaries, including both friends and foes. The chapter also includes the work of sister Protestant missions in Spokane and Lapwai and documents the truth of history regarding the Whitman Mission.

CHAPTER 16
WHITMAN'S RIDE ACROSS AMERICA

One of the most inspirational events in American history was Marcus Whitman's winter ride across America in 1842-43. Unfortunately, revisionist historians have spuriously but nonetheless successfully shed doubt on the historical, spiritual and political reasons for this amazing five-month crossing of the continent. The confusion of the historical revision of the purpose of Whitman's ride across America remains to the present hour. For this reason the cause that Whitman risked his life for and the destiny of the Protestant mission to Oregon continues to be shrouded in dark clouds of mystery. Whitman rode across the continent in the dead of winter to save the Oregon Territory for the American Union and the purposes of the Almighty. Secretary of State Daniel Webster and President John Tyler were about to yield Oregon to the British because they had been deceived to believe Oregon was useless and uninhabitable. Whitman's amazing sojourn through virtually impossible hindrances across the snow-packed Rockies saved the day for Oregon and the Union of American States.

CHAPTER 17
THE OREGON QUESTION

The "Oregon Question" was the focal point of controversy in the nation's capital. The "joint occupancy" of the Oregon Territory had been a brewing teapot for over two decades. Most Americans in the eastern states did not want a third war with Great Britain. Unfortunately, no one in Washington, D.C. knew anything about the Oregon Territory because no statesman had ever set eyes on the fabled land west of the Rocky Mountains. Whitman's advent in Washington in the spring of 1843 changed everything. James Polk won the presidency of the United States in 1844 with a campaign to win Oregon for the Union. His campaign slogan for the presidential election was "54' 40' or fight."

CHAPTER 18
WESTWARD HO

The westward wagon train migration of American pioneers to the Oregon Territory and California was one of the great migrations of history. The re-crafting of the saga of wagon trains to fit revisionist historians' vision of America's "manifest destiny" leaves out the essential role and prominence of Marcus Whitman on the maiden voyage of the Oregon Trail in 1843. At this hour in American history there was only a withering hope, with no clear vision, to settle Oregon with Americans. The first migration across America would never have succeeded without the authorship, inspiration, direction and expertise of this frontier missionary doctor. When Whitman was forced to leave the first pioneers in the Grande Ronde valley (Eliza Spalding was near death in Lapwai), Cayuse Indian Stickus led the first American wagon train over the formidable Blue Mountains.

CHAPTER 19
THE CONTROVERSY OVER THE
WHITMANS — ETHNOCENTRICALLY BIASED?

One of the great tragedies of America's heritage has been the success of revisionist historians who have re-crafted history in order to remove the Protestant missionaries and the Whitmans from their central place as founders and authors of the American nation's heritage in Oregon. This chapter exposes the deceit, deception and ignorance of most twentieth-century historians with regard to the purpose and ministry of the Whitmans and their rightful place in American civilization. The re-crafting of history continues to the present hour, undermining the purposes of the Almighty for the Pacific Northwest and the mission of the Protestant Church and the vast majority of American Indians who remain to this hour separated from their rightful Christian heritage.

CHAPTER 20
THE ADVENT OF THE JESUIT/CATHOLIC PRIESTS

The first Jesuit priest to arrive in the Oregon Territory was Father Blanchet in 1838. He established his mission in the Willamette Valley near Mt. Angel. The first Jesuit to minister to the Columbia Plateau Indians was Father Pierre-Jean De Smet beginning in 1839. Many historians incorrectly identify these "black-robed" priests as Catholic Fathers, but this chapter documents that all the first missionaries were Jesuits commissioned directly by Jesuit General Father Roothaan in Rome. General Roothaan governed the military wing of the Jesuit order and commissioned a vicariate-apostolic in Oregon to oversee the vast Pacific Northwest. The actual Jesuit mission was not established until the fall of 1847, initiating the bloodshed of the Whitman massacre. Prior to this new Jesuit dominion in the Pacific Northwest there was only one Jesuit vicariate-apostolic in America located in Chicago.

CHAPTER 21
THE WHITMAN MASSACRE: THE FINAL ACT OF THE OREGON TERRITORY

The Whitman massacre was the watershed event of Oregon and Pacific Northwest history. The Whitman massacre ensured that Oregon would become a state of the American Republic. The causes and events that led to the Whitman massacre are documented from the diaries, letters, correspondence and testimony of the Protestant missionaries, Jesuit priests, and Hudson's Bay employees. The drama of the hour has been recreated in this chapter to allow the reader to feel the temper of the hour and understand why the Protestant missionaries and their family would not abandon their post even though they knew their lives were in imminent and mortal danger from the grieving Indians deceived by the "Papists" to believe the Whitmans were poisoning them.

CHAPTER 22
EYEWITNESS ACCOUNTS OF THE WHITMAN MASSACRE

The survivors of the massacre developed diaries and testimonies of the atrocities and the complicity of the Jesuit priests and Catholic co-conspirators. The massacre continued for nearly two weeks after the murder of the Whitmans, and the Jesuit priests had full liberty to come and go in the midst of the slaughter. Some of the Cayuse Indians involved in the atrocities actually cried after they committed the brutal murders. All the survivors of the Massacre refuted the testimony of Father Brouillet.

CHAPTER 23
PROTESTANTISM ACCORDING TO FATHER BROUILLET

Jesuit Vicar General Brouillet came under intense examination in the newspapers of the hour in the Oregon Territory because of his complicity in the Whitman massacre, primarily in Portland. Father Brouillet wisely did not respond to the accusations of the survivors of the massacre but temporarily left the Territory and later sent a rebuttal attached to an 1855 Congressional report submitted by J. Ross Browne. Browne had been commissioned by Congress to issue a report on the causes of the Indian Wars in the West. By submitting his rebuttal three thousand miles away from Oregon, Brouillet skillfully had his interpretation of the Massacre approved as a Congregational Report. In his rebuttal, Brouillet accused the Whitmans of oppressing the Indians, seeking worldly profit and ministering violence against the natives.

CHAPTER 24
THE TESTAMENT OF THE PROTESTANT CHURCH AND THE
OREGON GOVERNMENT CONCERNING ROMANISM IN OREGON

The Protestant Church in Oregon was a healthy vigorous body of believers during the later half of the 19th century. The Protestant Church maintained a strong and consistent witness against the abuses of Romanism that led to the Whitman massacre and the subsequent Indian Wars. The Protestant churches of the Willamette Valley issued a number of statements to document what they called the "truth of history." Some 30,000 Christians signed these accords, well over a third of the population of Oregon at the time.

CHAPTER 25
THE NEZ PERCE INDIANS:
GREAT PATRIOTS FOR AMERICA AND OREGON

The Nez Perce Indians remained loyal to the Americans during the Indian Wars after the Whitman massacre. The Nez Perce warriors actually captured the Cayuse Indians guilty of killing the Protestants at the Whitman Mission. The early Oregon military commanders documented that the Americans would have been routed had the Nez Perce joined their fellow American Indians on the warpath. Much credit was ascribed to the Protestant teachings of the Spaldings for causing the Nez Perce to remain loyal to America. When the American government demanded the Columbia Plateau Indians yield their freedom and move to government reservations, Chief Joseph of the Nez Perce refused to comply. This chapter documents the betrayal of the American government with regard to the Nez Perce Indians.

CHAPTER 26
CHIEF JOSEPH'S HISTORIC SPEECH TO AMERICA

The peace treaty of 1855 established reservations for the Columbia Plateau Indians to live on, separated from white culture. Chief Joseph refused to sign the accord of 1855 or the new accord of 1863 that reduced the Nez Perce reservation by 90 percent. Chief Joseph was promised the Wallowa Valley by the American government but the discovery of the lush valley by American settlers caused the government to renege on their promise. Chief Joseph the younger was forced to flee his homeland and embark on a 1,700-mile, four-month trek seeking freedom in Canada. The Nez Perce demonstrated superior skill, military tactics and horsemanship against four of the best-mounted cavalries America had to offer. In the end, Chief Joseph had to surrender to save his freezing and starving women and children. All the promises the American generals made were broken and all the Cayuse ponies that had ridden circles around the cavalry were shot. Chief Joseph's speech to America still reverberates across the conscience of America.

CHAPTER 27
MANIFEST DESTINY AND THE NATIVE AMERICAN INDIANS

Did the "manifest destiny" of the American Republic include the American Indians? Were the American Indians of the East treated like the Nez Perce? In 1823, the Indian nations of the South took their grievances to the Supreme Court. The Supreme Court of the United States ruled the Indian right of occupancy was subordinate to the United States' right of discovery. Since the Indians were not considered equal to the white man in a court of law they had no liberty or justice in American courts. Even when the Supreme Court, at the request of Protestant missionaries, ruled in the Indians' favor President Andrew Jackson (of fame as an Indian fighter) refused to enforce the ruling. The result was that the Southern Indian nations were uprooted and forced to march to their new reservations in Oklahoma. In the legendary Cherokee "Trail of Tears" forced march, nearly a third of the nation died.

CHAPTER 28
INDIAN RESERVATIONS

The grand American plan for the American Indians was to remove them from their land and heritage and liberty and confine them on reservations. The Indians, without exception, languished on these reservations. The Columbia Plateau Indians did better than most because they were allowed to stay on ancestral grounds for the most part. This chapter documents Chief Seattle and his speech to Governor Stevens before the era of Indian reservations in the west began.

CHAPTER 29
THE BRIDGE BETWEEN THE PROTESTANT ALMIGHTY
AND THE INDIAN GREAT SPIRIT CHIEF

The Second Great Awakening began in the Northeast in the early part of the 19th century under the preaching of zealous men of God like Charles Finney. These Protestant ministers preached against the oppression of slavery and corresponding social injustice toward Indians and called the nation to return to the covenant America's forefathers made with God. The Protestant ministers were charged with the mission of bridging the cultural and spiritual gap between the Almighty God of the Bible and the Great Spirit Chief of the Native American Indians.

CHAPTER 30
THE CONFEDERATED TRIBES OF THE UMATILLA,
WALLA WALLA AND CAYUSE AND THE PEACE TREATY OF 1855

This chapter chronicles the history of the Confederated Tribes of the Umatilla. The American people through unjust laws and economic policies of deception systematically stole most Indian reservation land. The Confederated Tribes of the Umatilla were treated better than most, but multiple laws that were passed over seven decades to help the Indians were nearly always twisted to steal more land. By the hour of America's Great Depression in the 20th century the American Indians had lost 90 percent of their reservation land and they were languishing as a people. The Great Depression engulfed the whole nation. As the Indians, forced onto reservations, had no jobs or trading partners, now America had no jobs or trading partners. Was the Great Depression a judgment on America from God? The Indian Restoration Act of 1934 restored the fortunes of the Indians and in like manner America gradually rose out of the Great Depression.

CHAPTER 31
THE TUTUILLA PRESBYTERIAN CHURCH

This chapter documents an unpublished manuscript written by Dr. J. M. Cornelison, a Presbyterian missionary who followed in the footsteps of Dr. Marcus Whitman after an interim period of 50 years. Dr. Cornelison, in his manuscript *The Seed of the Martyrs*, answered the question that historians never bothered to ask. What happened to the church and the Christian faith of the Cayuse/Columbia Plateau Indians after the Whitmans were martyred? Dr. Cornelison continued the ministry, birthed by the Nez Perce warriors seeking the Word of God, at Tutuilla near Pendleton for 43 years. This church continues to minister the Word of God first preached in 1837, making it the oldest continuous church (Protestant or Catholic) in the Pacific Northwest.

CHAPTER 32
HAPPY CANYON

Happy Canyon was the brainchild of Roy Raley. Raley was an Eastern Oregon businessman, banker, surveyor, cattleman and promoter of Pendleton and the West. He envisioned a grand pageant that included Indians and cowboys working together. He called his invention the "Pageant of the West—An Outdoor Dramatic Production Symbolizing the History and Development of the Great West." Happy Canyon began with a picture of what the Oregon Territory was like before the white man came. Some local Indians did not take part in the pageant because they felt they were being exploited. Nonetheless, the Pendleton Round-Up and Happy Canyon became a rousing success. The cooperation and industry between the two races has been sustained for almost one hundred years.

CHAPTER 33
MATTESON SCHOOL HOUSE PIONEERS

The Matteson School House chapter documents the story of the first pioneers of the Blue Mountains south of Heppner, Oregon. These pioneer families were the first families to live in the Blue Mountains year-round. Their heritage was centered, like most frontier communities, around the School House. Education was central to their culture. The School House was a church, a dance hall, a pie social and a meeting place. These pioneers lasted six decades until the Great Depression finally pushed them back to the city, in this case Heppner.

CHAPTER 34
THE IRISH CATHOLICS DISCOVER EASTERN OREGON

The Irish were instrumental in the heritage of Eastern Oregon and Morrow and Umatilla Counties. These influential immigrants brought their Catholic culture and values to the West. What impact, positive or negative, did these Irish immigrants have on the heritage of Eastern Oregon?

CHAPTER 35
THE EMERGENCE OF THE CONFEDERATED TRIBES OF THE UMATILLA

By the middle of the 20th century the Confederated Tribes of the Umatilla finally began to exercise self-rule. There was a learning curve but through trial and error the Tribes began to make progress. In time, U.S. dollars became available through grants and the Education Assistance Act. By 1992 the Confederated Tribes were strong enough to hire an executive director to enforce and articulate policy. Significant financial resources became available through the establishment of a gambling casino/resort. The Tribes wisely applied much of their newfound wealth to restoring natural resources. The Tribes drew from their ancient heritage of firsthand knowledge to restore the mountains and forests and rivers that had become sick and polluted, decimated by decades of abuse and greed. For the first time since the advent of white men the Confederated Tribes had the power and resources to begin the process of restoring their heritage.

CHAPTER 36
THE RESURRECTION OF THE UMATILLA RIVER

No salmon returned to the Umatilla River from the time of the Great Depression until the turn of the 21st century because the Umatilla River ran dry in the summer. Forest abuse, overgrazing of livestock, and ecologically insensitive irrigation practices virtually sucked the river dry in the summer. The Confederated Tribes of the Umatilla could sue the government over violation of treaty rights or they could seek redress through diplomatic and pragmatic solutions. The Tribes (consistent with their nature) wisely chose the latter and through skillful negotiation and a consortium of conservation allies they established the Umatilla River Project that replaced Umatilla River water with pumped water from the Columbia River. The precedent was reestablished for the American people to fund salmon restoration through tax dollars. The first salmon runs on the Umatilla River in over half a century occurred in 1998. The Tribes had established a precedent for salmon and river restoration that could restore the whole Columbia basin watershed.

CHAPTER 37
THE DESTRUCTION OF THE COLUMBIA RIVER:
THE FABLED NORTHWEST PASSAGE

The Columbia River was the greatest, coldest and purest river in America when Lewis and Clark first viewed salmon in over twenty feet of crystal clear waters. In less than a century and a half of American rule the Columbia River had become one of the most polluted rivers in the world. By 1960 Hanford had released more radioactive toxic waste into the Columbia River than released by Chernobyl, yet the American government to this hour has yet to establish minimum reference levels for radionclide (plutonium, cesium) concentrations in the water. Thirteen pulp mills that continue to release toxins into the Columbia River have become the primary source of funds for the Oregon Department of Environmental Quality (DEQ), the state agency established to regulate clean water standards. No power or agency is better positioned to stop this ecological disaster than the Confederated Tribes. The question of the hour is: Will they use their political and economic power to stop the destruction of the Columbia River?

CHAPTER 38
GIVE THEREFORE THY SERVANT A DISCERNING HEART

The issue of stewardship of the multiple and vast resources of the Pacific Northwest has become an issue of great controversy and growing concern. The primary pressure points of this controversy are water rights, hunting rights and salmon restoration. This controversy pits Indian against white, landowner against sportsman, industrialist against conservationist, and irrigators against advocates of salmon restoration. Resolution of these issues will require the wisdom of Solomon. According to Indians and conservationists, the source of the solution will always be found in restoration of mountain forest habitat, aquifers and watersheds. The historic mountain aquifers and watersheds have been compromised by abusive logging practices and excessive road building; however, the greatest threat to the waterways of the Pacific Northwest has been indiscriminate and unregulated industrial pollution. The Christian church must extend the Gospel message to include social justice and stewardship of God's creation.

Chapter 39
A Controversy with the Inhabitants of the Land

The Almighty has a controversy with the inhabitants of the land because the Maker's creation of forests, watersheds, fish and game are sick and polluted. The Almighty has a controversy with the inhabitants of the land because God's people and God's creation are being destroyed for lack of knowledge of the truth. The Almighty has a controversy with the Christian Church because the Church has not accepted or sustained the biblical mandate for moral and ecological justice or sustaining the knowledge of God in the land. The Pacific Northwest has become the most un-churched area of America. This chapter summarizes the historical manifold natural resource blessings of the Pacific Northwest and the responsibility of the inhabitants of the land to exercise justice and stewardship. Why have the lands of Old Oregon, so blessed by the Almighty, become so closed to the knowledge and statutes of God? The Pacific Northwest has become the most un-churched region in the entire Republic.

Chapter 40
The Third Great Awakening

The lands and peoples of the Pacific Northwest are languishing. Most of the rivers are polluted, the mighty Columbia River is sick and the fish are largely inedible. At the beginning of the 21st century the American Republic is morally, politically and economically languishing as well. The challenge and purpose of the research of this book is to initiate a "third great awakening." The call of the Almighty is for mighty men and women of all races of God to initiate a third great awakening and finish the purposes of the Almighty for the Pacific Northwest and America. The world is entering into a time of great travail. The Bible calls this time the "hour of tribulation." Does the land of Old Oregon have a role to play in this great end-time drama? Will the church answer the final call to complete the purposes of the "Old Oregon, under the shadow of the Almighty?" This final chapter poses this great challenge to the "Sons of Oregon" in the Pacific Northwest and throughout the world.

Chapter 1

Under the Shadow of the Almighty

Did the Almighty play a sovereign hand in the settlement of the Pacific Northwest? Was the vast Oregon Territory that stretched from the Rocky Mountains to the Pacific Ocean bounded by the present nation of Canada to the north and consuming nearly half of the state of California to the south divinely protected and preserved for the American peoples? The historical record documents that many maritime nations coveted dominion over the riches and territorial domain of the Pacific Northwest and the fabled Northwest Passage beginning in the 16th century. By this time, the American Indians had already established rich, albeit nomadic, empires throughout this land. According to Oregon historian Stephen D. Beckham, as many as 300 ships from 17 countries had explored the Pacific Northwest coast during the Age of Discovery. (*Oregonian*, "Branding Oregon," January 5, 2004) The great Spanish Empire had consolidated dominion of all the Native American nations of South America and Latin America, and the North American continent was at her command long before the Pilgrims arrived at Plymouth Rock early in the 17th century. Spain was the dominant sea power, controlling the vast majority of the West Coast of the Americas for most of the 16th, 17th and 18th centuries, yet every endeavor to penetrate farther north into the Pacific Northwest inevitably ended in failure. Russia, Portugal, France, and as many as a dozen other nations made efforts to lay claim to the great prize of Oregon as well. Ill fortune in the form of treacherous Indians or violent storms or national misfortunes always thwarted every effort to claim the great prize of Oregon.

Even more mysterious were the romanticized tales of the search for the fabled Northwest Passage. The most brilliant and knowledgeable maritime sailors of the contending nations of the world throughout the three centuries of the Age of Discovery missed the great and mighty Columbia River, one of the most powerful river systems of the world and the dominant river on the entire west coast of the Americas. The vast Oregon Territory appears to have been hidden under the wings of the Almighty waiting for a time and a people worthy of the land's high calling.

The Oregon Territory was strategically, economically and politically the haven of great treasures ardently sought by the great world powers for over three centuries. The rivers of the Pacific Northwest were teeming with virtually unlimited supplies of fur-bearing animals coveted by the merchants of the world during the 17th and 18th centuries. The massive conifer forests of the Pacific Northwest were unequalled in the world in size, quality, quantity and sheer magnificence. These seemingly inexhaustible forests were readily accessible, and it would have been impossible for the maritime nations of the world not to survey these forests from the sea.

Aerial picture of the mouth of the Columbia River

Gold was the insatiable driving force that moved the contending world powers to seek and ravage and plunder New World empires for greater spoil. Gold was the great treasure that moved the daring and fearless captains of the high seas to explore every land, every nation, and every possible source for this great treasure. Indeed, rich gold veins were waiting to reward the first occupants of the hidden wonderland of Oregon, especially when the undiscovered gold reserves of Northern California were included in this unclaimed prize.

The streams of the Northwest were teeming with fish, and runs of steelhead and salmon filled the Columbia and its tributaries. There was so much native food in the form of berries, other fruits, nuts and roots that the indigenous Indian populations did not need to cultivate the land for their own food supplies. Wild game was readily available, especially deer and elk. Given the passion and energy and ardor of the Old World conquistadors, it is a mystery that the Oregon Territory remained unconquered through the 16th century. But the great prize of the Oregon Territory did last indeed, not only through the 16th century, but inexplicably through the 17th and most of the 18th centuries as well.

Defying reason, the greatest and most daring mariners and fearless conquistadors of the great empires of the civilized world throughout the Age of Discovery did not discover or lay claim to the Oregon Territory and the mighty Columbia River. The hidden land of Oregon was one of the great wonders of the world, yet twentieth-century historians have hardly seemed to raise an eyebrow at the mystery of its divine seclusion.

How could this wonderland, overflowing with treasures coveted by the contending powers of the world, have been missed, overlooked and/or neglected for three centuries by the contending maritime nations of the world? The student of history must probe very diligently to establish a plausible rationale how the multiple contending world dominions missed the great prize of the Pacific Northwest and the golden passage of the Columbia River for over THREE CENTURIES!

The treacherous shifting sand bar at the mouth of the Columbia River, which funnels the massive water volume like a fire hose, has made entry into the treasured land perilous. Since the discovery of the "River of the West," 2,000 large ships have been lost crossing the bar. Nevertheless, it wasn't the danger of crossing the Columbia River bar that kept the nations at bay. The very first mariner who attempted to cross the treacherous bar was successful. From the latter portion of the 16th century, the great mariners of the age, whether they were seeking the mystical straits of Anian or the equally mysterious Northwest Passage, simply miscalculated, misjudged or were somehow blinded when they approached the mighty Columbia River. Even when the estuary of the Columbia River was discovered by Spaniard Don Bruno de Heceta in 1775, the prize still remained unclaimed. Heceta "described and mapped it [the mouth of the Columbia River]. This was August 17, 1775. He named it Bahia de la Asuncion." (Cross, Francis E. & Parkin, Charles M. Jr., *Captain Gray*, Maverick Production, Bend, Oregon, 1987, p. 18)

The mariners of the age carried the hydrographical and geographic documents of previous voyages of the time as standard procedure. They had accurate instruments to determine latitude and longitude. "At that time, altitude observations of the sun, stars, or moon, for determining a ship's position, were obtained by John Hadley's or Thomas Godfrey's reflecting quadrant." (Cross, Parkin, p. 42) This instrument, known as the "pigyoke" or "hogyoke," came into use around 1730 and was standard until outmoded by the sextant two centuries later. Before the discovery of the Columbia River, an invention known as the chronometer effectively corrected the errors of navigation commonly made during the age of discovery. "Thenceforth, observations (sights) of celestial bodies could be depended upon. For now navigators could quickly and accurately compute the hour angle and thus obtain the correct longitude." (Cross, Parkin, p. 43)

The exact longitude and latitude of the hidden Columbia River were known to all nations nearly twenty years before it was discovered. American Captain Robert Gray did not even have a chronometer aboard the *Columbia* on his historic voyage of discovery in 1792. Were the vast lands of Oregon kept under the shadow of the Almighty to protect the Native American nations until the advent of the free men of the emerging and developing United States of America in the 19th century? Were the free men of the emerging American Republic destined by providence to possess this wonderland, hidden from the rest of the world? Did the Almighty play a sovereign hand in Oregon for such a people?

This study will look at that historical record: journals, legal and Congressional records, government documents, diaries of frontiersmen, missionaries and immigrants, letters, newspapers and the chronicles of historians to find answers to these questions. If Providence has kept the Oregon Territory under the shadow of the Almighty for a peculiar people of free men under the banner of the American Republic, then it behooves that people to comprehend and earnestly endeavor to fulfill their providential destiny. First and foremost, the historical case must be carefully established relating to the mystery of Old Oregon if in fact the Almighty had kept this treasured land for providential purposes yet to be fully revealed. At least five world powers actively sought to gain control of the Oregon Territory during the 16th, 17th and 18th centuries: Spain, England, Portugal, France and Russia. This study will examine each world dominion in the order in which they appeared to establish answers for the questions posed by this research.

Chapter 2

The Spanish Empire: The First Lord of the Pacific

Christopher Columbus gave birth to the great Spanish maritime kingdom at the end of the 15th century. Once Columbus demonstrated the world was spherical rather than flat, uncharted new worlds and vast unlimited riches were provocatively waiting to be claimed. Spain commenced with fervor to extend her power and sovereignty around the world. In less than a generation, the Spanish captain Vasco Núñez de Balboa discovered the great South Sea, the previously unknown Pacific Ocean, the largest ocean in the world. The Spaniards swiftly, methodically and ruthlessly established military control of their vast Pacific domain. By 1521, Hernán Cortés, with a small force of five hundred armed men, had conquered all of Mexico. The Spaniards quickly exploited a highly organized Aztec civilization based at Tenochtitlan (modern-day Mexico City), one of the world's largest cities at that time. These Spaniards called this elaborate metropolis the "Venice of the New World" because of the sophisticated system of water canals and lavish temples and royal palaces. The Spanish brutal treatment of the native Aztecs caused Montezuma II to rebel, and most of the Spaniards died in the canals in their retreat weighted down by stolen gold. Cortés cunningly was able to subdue the Aztecs by gathering Native American allies using superior weapons of iron, steel and gunpowder. Cortés callously reduced the Aztec culture to slavery, forcing them to labor in Spanish estates and gold mines. When news of the rich gold treasures of the New World reached the European kingdoms, the Old World was ablaze with tales of wonder and intrigue, of fortunes and treasures waiting for the plunder.

In 1520, the Spaniard Ferdinand Magellan, in command of five war ships, sailed around the world on a monumental cruise that lasted 533 days and further entrenched the Kingdom of Spain as the dominant power around the world. Ten years later, another Spanish conquistador, Francisco Pizarro, discovered an Indian Empire in Peru "so much richer than Mexico as to turn Cortés green with jealousy." (Lyman, Vol. 1, p. 181) Pizarro, with a small army of 180, was able to conquer an empire of 5 to 10 million subjects because the Inca civilization worshipped a creator god called Viracocha whom they disastrously considered Pizarro to incarnate. This fabulously wealthy, highly politically evolved civilization, which practiced advanced medicine and maintained its society through a sophisticated system of transportation, was reduced to forced labor and slavery to its new European masters, virtually overnight.

In 1542, another Spaniard, Hernando de Soto, marched across North America from Florida to the Mississippi River as high as the 40th parallel in search of other Indian empires to plunder. Fortunately, the Native American Indians of North America did not hold their Spanish conquistadors in reverential awe, as had their Latin American counterparts, and De Soto found no rich Indian kingdoms in North America to plunder.

Before the midpoint of the 16th century, Spain exercised sovereignty in America from the 40th parallel in North America to the southern tip of South America. The Spanish language, culture and especially the Catholic religion were pressed upon the Americas with no rival to contest their will or dominion. Columbus had the courage to prove the earth was a sphere and thereby unlocked the oceans of the world to future maritime powers, and the Spaniards established initial mastery of the New World. The Spanish were more than eager to press their advantage. The discovery of vast treasures of gold, at an hour when the world was sorely pressed for gold reserves, added fervor to their intoxication for greater conquest. In like manner, the Spaniards under the authority the edict of Pope Alexander VI in 1494 to rule the world from Rome aggressively established religious sovereignty over the new domain. Catholic priests and nuns were sent to win converts to the faith and build a Roman Catholic empire in their new kingdom.

The Native American Indians were brutally converted to the militarily superior religion of their conquerors, won by sheer military prowess. The Spanish conquistadors were driven by an unquenchable lust for extracting priceless treasures from the Inca, Mayan, Aztec and lesser American empires. With no rival in sight, the Spaniards found it easy to build, explore, consolidate and subdue their immense new kingdom. Beyond a shadow of a doubt, the tiny nation of Spain ruled the New World, and her culture and religious persuasion faced no credible opponent in the 16th century. So powerful was their New World domain and sovereignty that by the power of sheer momentum it lasted through the 17th and 18th centuries. Although the world power of Spain declined, the Catholic faith and Spanish language still dominated in most of Latin and South America at the turn of the 21st century.

At the onset of the emerging world power and influence of Spain, a monumental schism of the Catholic religion rocked the Western world. This revolution would have significant religious, political and military repercussions in the New World. The focal point of the history of the 16th century, indeed the watershed event of modern world history, was the schism of the Catholic Church initiated by the Protestant Reformation. This social, economic, religious and spiritual revolution changed and energized the world and the impact of that reformation has continued to the present hour (see Chapter 7). The great mystery of the Spanish Empire, which quickly and ruthlessly conquered all the Americas below the 40th parallel, was the utter failure of every attempt to reach and conquer the Oregon Territory. Not only Spain but also every contending power of the world in three centuries of intense and systematic exploration and discovery somehow missed, foolishly discounted or lacked the strength to pursue the great prize of Oregon.

At the epicenter of the Spanish zest for conquest and expansion was the thirst for gold. Europe was in the midst of an economic crisis brought on by debased money caused by overextended credit. The world is facing a similar crisis in 2009. Middle-century financiers did not have credit cards, but they had nonetheless developed an overtaxed and discredited financial policy that made paper money virtually worthless. Since the beginning of history, gold has been the world's true money standard, and in times of great inflation the value of gold has historically multiplied. "The total stock of gold of the world, available at that time in Europe, is estimated at but little over $150,000,000." (Lyman, Vol. 1, pp. 183-4) At the same hour in Europe the Catholic Pope had initiated building the great St. Peter's Basilica in Rome at the unprecedented astronomical cost of $80 million. To finance this massive project, the Pope conceived the Papal edict of selling indulgences as a requirement to pardon the Catholic sinner from the punishment of sin. The plan backfired with the Protestant Reformation explosion in Germany that rocked the world.

The lavish and spectacular discoveries of gold treasures in the New World of the Americas energized the Western world. The fact that these gold treasures belonged to the indigenous American empires was of no consequence to these Spanish conquistadors and the pirates and thieves that would follow in their footsteps. The thirst for gold and plunder knew no restraint under Spanish world sovereignty. The onset of white European civilization in America devastated and destroyed the wonderfully developed American civilizations of the Inca, Mayans, Aztecs, and every people and tribe that the conquistadors' lust fell upon. These Spanish mercenaries were searching up and down the Americas for new empires to crush and treasures of gold, silver, precious jewels and artifacts to confiscate. The Old World was energized by the infusion of the treasures of America.

The kingdom of Spain, under Charles V, grew in proportion to the plunder and soon consolidated the kingdom's authority to become emperor of Germany. No European nation dared to challenge Spanish authority. The source of the Spanish wealth was the Americas and the Spanish emperor developed a Pacific Ocean manifesto that brought all the islands and shores of the world's greatest ocean under their domain for nearly three centuries. The Spanish juggernaut in the Americas was finally politically penetrated in 1819 when Spain was forced to abdicate Florida, the first of their many titles, to the United States. Until that Spanish concession, the bustling Spanish Empire controlled trade commerce between Acapulco, Mexico in America and Manila in the Philippines and Macao in China, making the world a very cosmopolitan place from the middle of the 16th century.

Had Spain ruled her vast kingdom with equality and justice for all men the whole world could have conceivably been dominated by the Spanish language and Spanish culture. The dominion of the Pope and the Catholic Church would have encompassed the world. The world was ripe for the whim and fancy of the Spanish Empire. The great Pacific Ocean was an unknown and uncharted New World of unlimited potential. The invincible character of the Spanish conquistadors was the source of their victory and tragically the source of their demise. The very capacity of the Spanish that made them conquistadors also rendered them impotent to generate new productivity and industry in the New World. "They were like the Romans, a predaceous people....Wealth did not appear to them, except as first created or extracted by some other people." (Lyman, Vol. 1, p. 215) The Spanish controlled the New World but they did not develop or cultivate or nurture their New World kingdom. They reduced their new subjects to slaves, working as forced laborers in gold and silver mines and on Spanish agricultural estates.

The Spanish were consistently looking for new empires to spoil, hence rivalries and power struggles developed from within, stifling their strength and compromising their new initiatives. The New World came under the bondage of Spain much as the Old World once owed her allegiance to Rome. The growth of power in Mexico in the beginning developed into a threat to the old country home rule in Spain. In response, retrogressive and repressive policies were established to keep the local spirit and industry arrested. A compliant indolent populace was encouraged. To ensure that no Spaniard became powerful in the New World, no Spanish citizen was allowed to immigrate without express permission from the king. Foreigners were forbidden by Spain to navigate in the New World. Spain would rule her new domain for the exclusive benefit of the mother country. Freedom of thought and the radical Protestant ideas of liberty of conscience, free expression, public schools and vocational mobility were denied in the New World. The unbridled growth of the Protestant Reformation in the Old World was fervently oppressed in the New World under the authority of Spain and the Pope. The Pope would use Spanish military authority to ensure no seed of the Protestant rebellion would set root in the New World and their new subjects would bow to the victor of God, the Catholic Pope.

The great prize of Oregon, waiting for the first flag to be planted on her abundant soils, remained beyond the grasp of the Spanish Empire. The Spanish conquistadors had discovered no great Indian empires with lavish treasures to plunder to the north. It could easily be argued that no act of providence was required to protect Old Oregon from the predacious Spaniards. Still, even the Spanish needed to explore into Oregon if only to protect her vast empire from potential enemies to the north. Álvar Núñez Cabeza de Vaca, with two Spaniards and a Moor, had spent nine years crossing the North American continent from Florida to California more than two and a half centuries before Lewis and Clark. These Spanish explorers brought testimony of great nations to the north that energized the Spanish conquistadors. Indeed, Spain sent expeditions under the command of Francisco Coronado through present-day Arizona, New Mexico and as far north as Colorado, but no rich or powerful empires were discovered. In 1542, de Soto explored the vast Mississippi River basin yet once again no fabled treasures were found to plunder. Cortés himself sent not one but four expeditions to explore the Pacific coast to the north yet misfortune beset each and every endeavor until he gave up the quest to the north.

By the middle of the 16th century, Spain owned by right of discovery the vast North American continent from Florida to California. These military conquistadors could find no new Indian civilizations worthy of merit and no treasures to confiscate and therefore discarded their northern discoveries. Spain turned her limitless energies to the known treasures of commerce where she was mistress of the seas. The lucrative trade routes flourished under Spanish dominion, establishing the interchange of silk, porcelains, spices, fabrics, gold, and silver from the New World, the Pacific islands, China and India to the Old World of Europe.

Chapter 3

Challengers on the Horizon

Given the notoriety of the excessive wealth plundered by the Spanish conquistadors and the inherently repressive and self-defeating policies of home rule, it was only a matter of time before new European maritime kingdoms began to test the rich waters of the great Pacific Ocean. An English satirist, Jonathan Swift, introduced to the world the delightfully improbable *Gulliver's Travels* in 1726, adding spice to the tasty morsel of intrigue the fabled Northwest Passage had become. Dr. Gulliver charmed his way into the world's priceless collection of great literary creations. Gulliver visited new worlds, humorously lampooning the smug ways of 18th century Europe. The mythical land of Brobdingnag with massive tall pines "so lofty that he could make no computation of their altitude" (Lyman, Vol. 1, p. 379) and gigantic food crops for an empire of giants comprised a mystical kingdom that could only exist in the unconventional and fertile mind of Swift. Still, the prodigious quantities of gold plundered by the conquistadors from New World empires gave merit to the wildest of uncharted magical kingdoms, inciting the spirit and imagination of 17th and 18th post-Renaissance European society.

Certain fables of the New World were repeated so often they became "fact" by their sheer weight of redundancy. The eastern terminal of the fabled Northwest Passage was actually planted on North American maps of that age. Oregon historians George Bancroft and Robert Greenhow documented that "a Portuguese navigator, Gaspar Cortereal, had sailed through a narrow channel westward from the coasts of Labrador into another sea, communicating with the Indian Ocean. It was called by him Anian." (Lyman, Vol. 1, p. 222) Swift's imagery and the mystical land of Brobdingnag were now on the map!

The fact that the fabled Northwest Passage through the nonexistent Straits of Anian moved and enticed the world of visionary maritime explorers from as early as the early 16th century only added to the mystique of Old Oregon and the mystery of a great river no "foreign" power could find. The nation that would claim the Northwest Passage would have clear title to the great unexplored northland, and that threat gave Spain grave concern. Many a romantic and heroic testimony of discovery of such a nonexistent passage was passed down throughout the span of these empire-building centuries, creating a mystique that defied reason.

As early as 1588, a century and a half before Brobdingnag, credible accounts were documented by a Portuguese sailor, Captain Lorenzo Ferrer de Maldonado, who inaccurately laid the foundation for the legend of the Northwest Passage. Another significant account was the report of Captain Juan de Fuca, a Greek mariner sailing for the viceroy of Mexico on an expedition to discover the Strait of Anian in 1592. De Fuca, in an account written by Englishman Michael Lock, testified discovering a broad inlet between the 47th and 48th latitude. He boldly exulted "that he saw some people on land in beasts' skins; and that the land is very fruitful and rich of gold, silver, pearls, and other things like Nova Spania." (Lyman, Vol. 1, p. 234)

One can only imagine the impact these reports had on the kingdoms of the Old World. The Oregon Territory and the real Northwest Passage of the Columbia River was the romanticized and mythical great unknown and uncharted wonder of the world during this budding Renaissance age of splendor as the world burst out of the Dark Ages. Even the greatest writer of the entire epoch, William Shakespeare, referenced the temper of the time with passages reflecting the sailors' lingo, the unquenchable spirit of exploration, and the mystique of new worlds to discover. Shakespeare's last and arguably greatest play "The Tempest" was set on one of these Pacific islands. The historical documents of the Age of Discovery clearly testify that the Old World was romantically aware of Oregon and the fabled Northwest Passage nearly two centuries before it was finally discovered.

Given the central place of the literary genius manifesting in Great Britain during the Age of Discovery, it should come as no surprise that the first nation to actively dare to challenge the sovereignty of Spain and by proxy the authority of the Pope was England. The papacy had divided the world into two spheres to be controlled by Portugal and Spain. Queen Elizabeth I encouraged her maritime sailors, known as free traders or buccaneers, to take liberty on the open sea. If the Spanish conquistadors could plunder the empires of the New World with no restraint or license, then the buccaneers could return the favor on the open sea. These buccaneers celebrated the intrepid spirit of the British during this oft-romanticized era resulting in perpetual warfare on the high sea.

The legendary Sir Francis Drake was the most skilled and charming knight for the irrepressible Queen. He departed from England in 1577 with five ships. His mission was nothing more than to plunder the maritime dominion of King Philip of Spain, in particular the gold galleons of the Pacific. Drake indeed pirated the riches of the Spanish ship, Our Lady of Conception, off the coast of Callao de Lima in the Pacific. "Drake, like others was seeking the mystical straits of Anian." (Cross, Francis, E. & Parkin, Charles M., *Captain Gray*, Maverick Publications, Bend, Oregon, 1987, p. 18). Drake continued north attempting to find the Northwest Passage to the Atlantic Sea in an attempt to evade Spanish galleons to the south. Cold weather and the burden of the weight of the plunder forced Drake to seek refuge in the Pacific Northwest harbor of Nova Albion (British Columbia) where Drake staked the first claim for the name of Queen Elizabeth. (Steber, Rick, *Where Rolls the Oregon*, Bear Wallow Publishing Co., Union, Oregon, 1985, p. 26) Other than the dashing legend Sir Francis firmly polished for the would-be buccaneers of the age, no lasting political advantage was gained by Drake's foray into the Pacific Northwest.

The heart and soul of future British sovereignty in North America would not be secured through the exploits of dashing sea pirates. Of far greater significance to the ultimate destiny of the Pacific Northwest was the British effort to chart and explore the northern and western reaches of Hudson's Bay that would lead to the operations of the Hudson's Bay Fur Trading Company, the first governor of the Oregon Territory. Nonetheless, the Spanish Empire was shaken by the British encroachment into her Pacific domain and responded accordingly. King Philip III of Spain in 1598 commissioned an expedition to the Pacific Northwest in search of the Strait of Anian to protect the northern front of their Pacific empire. Martin de Aguilar sailed the Fragata to the 43rd latitude and sighted land he named Cape Blanco, the first known site on the shores of Oregon. Aguilar documented a broad and powerful river, which proved impossible to navigate. "It is supposed that this river is the one leading to a great city...and that it is the Strait of Anian, through which the vessels passed, in sailing from the North Sea (Atlantic) to the South Sea (Pacific)." (Lyman, Vol. 1, pp. 202-3)

Martin de Aguilar had indeed discovered the mighty Columbia River, the so-called fabled Northwest Passage. Old Oregon, indeed the entire Pacific Northwest, was waiting for the Spanish conquistadors to claim their prize. The relentless energies and conquistador passion of the Spanish nation now had a new empire to plunder and exploit. The rich trade routes empowered Spain and provided even greater incentive to protect the New World kingdom and secure the vast empire of the Oregon Territory on the northern border of their Pacific kingdom. The great prize of Oregon was now at the beck and call of the mighty Spanish Empire with no challenger on the horizon to contest or even impede the irresistible momentum of the conquistadors. Sebastián Vizcaino was charged with an expedition that left Acapulco in 1602 to proceed north and establish the first known landing in Oregon. As with every previous Spanish endeavor to access Oregon, save Aguilar's, this expedition was beset with trouble from the beginning. The Spanish navigator believed the natural enemies of the expedition were in league with the evil one: "He speaks of the 'chief enemy,' the North West Wind, which was raised up by the foe of the human race, in order to prevent the advance of the ships, and to delay the discovery of those countries, and the conversion of their inhabitants to the Catholic faith." (Lyman, Vol. 1, p. 201) Oregon historian Horace Lyman candidly offered, "Possibly the Providential purpose was quite as much to let the country and its inhabitants wait for another race of people, to whom the deserts and the northwest winds would be no enemy." (Lyman, Vol. 1, p. 201) Was the hand of the Almighty actively engaged in the affairs of mankind, as President Abraham Lincoln affirmed? Would any nation or power claim sovereignty in Oregon before the advent of the free men of the new American Republic?

Whether the Almighty intervened in the affairs of the Spanish in their endeavor to conquer Oregon can be debated. Every Spanish endeavor, by land or sea, to claim the great prize of the Pacific Northwest met with failure. The national fortunes of Spain fell into gradual decline as well after the defeat of the Spanish Armada in 1588 to Great Britain. Spain's maritime power lost its position, making it virtually impossible to protect her vast Pacific empire from encroachments, especially from the pirates of the sea. Despite Spain's decline on the high seas, the nation remained the dominant military power in the New World and much of the Old World. Catholic historian J. H. Pollen attributed Spain's decline to a stubborn refusal to remedy the causes of the destruction of the Spanish Armada. Pollen identified four sources for the decline of the great Spanish maritime kingdom: "Slave labor with attendant corruptions in the colonies, want of organization and want of free government, joined with the grasping at power abroad." (*Catholic Encyclopedia*, "The Spanish Armada," J. H. Pollen, Vol. 1, Robert Applegate Company, 1907) So monumental and devastating was the decline of Spain's authority and confidence that no new expeditions were commissioned for 160 years to verify and possess Aguilar's Oregon discovery. Spain instead determined to fortify her colonization with Catholic missions with a northern perimeter terminating in the San Francisco Bay area of present-day California. The Columbia River and the Oregon Territory had been discovered, but Spain could not summon the spirit or strength to claim her great prize.

The prize of the Oregon Territory was waiting patiently for 160 years for any of the multitude of world contenders to break Spain's tenuous, yet still unbroken power on the Pacific coast of America. Martin de Aguilar's documentation of the Columbia River, "a broad and powerful river" at the 43rd parallel was impossible to hide from the great maritime nations of the 17th and 18th centuries.

Did the contending maritime powers of the world go into a deep slumber regarding the quest for Oregon in the very midst of the Age of Discovery? There is no question that the Protestant Reformation radically changed the European cultural, political, social and religious environment. The quest for discovery was supplanted by the quest for order and power in light of the new age of reformation. Nevertheless, would not even one of the great world and maritime powers of the age muster the resolve, energy or purpose to successfully pursue and validate Aguilar's discovery of the Columbia River and the vast land of Oregon?

Political unrest and incessant wars in Europe caused primarily by new power structures initiating from the Protestant Reformation undermined the resources and energy required for discovery and exploration through much of the 17th century into the 18th century. Still, it is not accurate to imply the world went into slumber regarding Aguilar's discovery. This political turmoil in Europe created a vacuum, which in due course opened the door for new nations to enter the fray for the prize of Oregon and the Northwest Passage.

The intrepid British were hardly disinclined to aggressively contend for the empire Spain had created in her Pacific domain. England had developed a policy that the simple fact of discovery could not be regarded as title to any country unless followed up by actual colonization and occupation. Providentially, this policy would backfire against the British when the dispute over final possession of the Oregon Territory was settled in the middle of the 19th century.

In 1724, Peter the Great of Russia commissioned Danish naval officer Vitus Bering to explore the northeast coast of Russia. "Bering and his men traveled by dog team, suffering from the cold and hardship of dragging cables, rigging and anchors across 2,000 miles to the coast of Siberia." (Steber, p. 33) Bering launched the *Gabriel* in 1728 and claimed on his return, "there really does exist a Northwest Passage." (Steber, p. 33) On Bering's last voyage in 1740, Empress Anne commissioned two ships. Bering, commanding the *St. Peter*, was separated by a storm from the *St. Paul*, commanded by Alexei Tchirikof and sailed as far south on the Pacific coast as the 46th latitude approaching the mouth of the Columbia River. He altered his course to land northeast on the shores of the present American state of Washington. The discovery of the shores of the Oregon Territory in mid-July afforded ample opportunity for the Russians to explore the entire Pacific shores to the Spanish colonies at San Francisco. Bering "now old and enfeebled by the voyage...imbued with an old man's caution...refused to allow any of his men on shore...gave orders that the 'St Peter' steer away for Kamchatka." (Lyman, Vol. 1, p. 284) The golden opportunity for the Russian czar to expand his empire to include the great prize of Oregon was forever lost.

The journal of the German surgeon, Georg Steller, demonstrates the glamour and adventure of such a monumental voyage hardly equated with the terror and misery these courageous sailors endured. "The general distress and mortality increased so fast that not only the sick died but those who pretended to be healthy, when relieved from their post, fainted, or fell down dead; of which the scantiness of water, the want of biscuits and brandy; cold, wet, nakedness, vermin, and terror, were not the least causes." (Lyman, Vol. 1, p. 284) Tchirikof also reached the Pacific coast near Prince Wales's archipelago and unlike Bering sent an exploratory boat ashore. The team never returned, so he sent a second boat to investigate. In like manner the second boat never returned, so the *St. Paul* gave up the discovery of the Pacific and returned home.

Bering did not survive his fated voyage. However, his maritime explorations initiated a Russian fur trading industry that established trading colonies all along the north Pacific coast as far as the 60th latitude. The hearty Russians attempted to proceed farther to the warmer and more productive lands to the south, but every such endeavor met with similar ill fortune in league with the Spanish to the south. The Russians never penetrated beyond 60 degrees into the Oregon Territory.

Once again the student of history must consider each and every plausible explanation why the Russians would not have great incentive to proceed south to the warmer and more bountiful treasures of the Oregon Territory. There were no Spanish armies or outposts to inhibit their approach. The Native American Indians of the Columbia River, especially inland tribes, were neither organized nor particularly hostile to the white men. Lewis and Clark and the first European explorers into the Oregon Territory would never have survived without the benevolent care of the native Indian tribes. The Russian experience with Pacific Coast Indians was not so positive. Once again the only plausible conclusion, consistent with the central thesis of this work, is that the Russians were confronted with the shadow of the Almighty and could progress no farther than the northern border of the Oregon Territory.

In 1799, a Russian fur company, the Russian-American, successfully established control of the lucrative fur industry on the Pacific coast from the 55th latitude north. The chief American agent, Alexander Baranoff, exercised a typical shrewd, bold, yet coarse and severe Russian temperament and held sway over the fur trade in North America for twenty years. It was a marriage of convenience, as the Japanese and Chinese would not trade with the Russians whom they considered treacherous. They trusted the Americans who required the fur-gathering connections of their northern counterparts.

By the latter portion of the 18th century, the European nations had great incentive to renew their enthusiasm for control of the north Pacific motivated by the lucrative fur trade and the promise of a Northwest Passage to make a strong effort to extend their borders to the Pacific Northwest. The veil of slumber over the Oregon Territory for three centuries was about to be pierced, and Spain summoned the energy and resources to once again attempt to claim the great river and solidify control of the Pacific coast of America. Remarkably, the great prize still remained for the Spanish Empire after 175 years of neglect!

In 1775, the Spanish reached the Oregon Territory, this time sailing to the 54th parallel, but foolishly the Spanish captain refused to trade for the sea otter the Indians offered in abundance. A second expedition, the Sonora, under Bruno Heceta, was weakened by scurvy. Indians killed a boarding party of sailors seeking fresh water and berries and Heceta was forced to return to Mexico. On August 17, 1775 Heceta wrote in his journal, "On the evening of this day I discovered a large bay, to which I gave the name Assumption Bay….The currents and eddies were so strong that, notwithstanding a press of sail…cause me to believe that the place is the mouth of some great river, or some passage to another sea…" (Steber, p. 28) Heceta's crew was reduced to five able-bodied seamen and a cabin boy and therefore he determined not to explore the mouth of the "great river."

Once again Spain had made a good showing but had failed to finish the job and claim the prize, and the mysterious "great river" continued to flow unbounded by the sovereignty or occupation of any of the contending empires of the Age of Discovery. There can be no historical question that ill fortune, foolish decisions, and miscalculations were the rule in every Spanish attempt to claim the Oregon Territory. Nevertheless, the great prize of Oregon remained unclaimed after nearly 300 years.

CHAPTER 4

THE FABLED NORTHWEST PASSAGE

England emerged from the political unrest in 18th century Europe through the legendary exploits of Captain James Cook as the mistress of North America and future mistress of India and the uttermost parts of the earth. "Wherever he touched, in New Zealand or Australia, he claimed the soil for the English Crown. The records which he published not only woke the interest of Englishmen in these far off islands...but familiarized them more and more with the sense of possession, with the notion that this strange world of wonders was their own, and that a new earth was left in the Pacific for the expansion of the English race." (Lyman, Vol. 1, p. 256) Most certainly this great and thoroughly scientific mariner of the Age of Discovery would not succumb to the foolish miscalculations of the Spanish and Russians and would finally discover and set the Union Jack on the "great river" of the Pacific Northwest for the expansion of the English race.

Indeed, the fabled Captain Cook was commissioned by the Crown to lay claim to the great prize of the Northwest Passage. Cook meticulously charted the Pacific coast of Oregon and sighted and named Cape Foulweather, indicative of the tempestuous weather the Oregon expedition afforded. The British, the greatest mariners of the hour, were aggressively and diligently seeking the fabled passage, a prize worth 20,000 pounds of sterling, but alas all Captain Cook found was a boatload of sea otter skins the Indians induced him to trade for. Cook found the Arctic ice impenetrable on his excursion to the north and was forced to return to England via China. By good fortune the Chinese purchased the sea otter skins for superlative prices and the mission was a success. Unfortunately, Captain Cook was killed on the Sandwich Islands, clubbed to death by natives, on the return voyage. When the news of the unexpected yet wildly profitable sea trade with China reached England the new age of fur trading had begun with fervor. The maritime success and growing power of the British Crown, an empire so extensive that the "sun never set on her shores," regrettably initiated a similar system of repression that stifled the Spanish Empire.

England claimed the Pacific Northwest from San Francisco to the Russian settlement above the Straits of Fuca (British Columbia), yet failed to ratify their claim by discovery of the great Columbia River. Britain suppressed the records of Cook's voyage of discovery because the English hope of a Northwest Passage was dashed and the north coastline, instead of breaking down at the 65th parallel, actually rose in stature and turned westward.

Other British explorers fared no better, including Captain John Meares who lamented, "We can safely assert that there is no such river as that of St. Roc exists, as laid down in the Spanish charts." (Steber, p. 35) Once again the Almighty thwarted the British and Captain Meares as he approached the mighty Columbia River with a string of rough breakers, foul weather and heavy fog.

The nation that gained the greatest advantage from Captain Cook's last voyage was the infantile nation of the still emerging United States of America. Fortunately and most providentially for the emerging American states, a young American officer accompanied Captain Cook, a Mr. John Ledyard. Ledyard turned out to be a keen historian and a fearless adventurer who will later enter into the story at a most propitiously fortunate hour for American destiny on behalf of the Oregon Territory and the Lewis and Clark voyage of discovery. Ledyard visited France, where he not only impressed King Louis XVI but more importantly American ambassador Thomas Jefferson. Jefferson turned out to be a keen historian as well and Ledyard's documentation of Cook's ill-fated voyage to the Pacific Northwest found a receptive heart and mind.

John Ledyard

Consequently, France joined the maritime competition for the prize of Oregon miraculously still waiting for any foreign civilization to claim. It was a mystery that France had waited until the last generation of the 18th century to enter into the fray. Until 1764, France held unquestioned control of Canada, and the Oregon Territory that lay hidden beyond the Shining Mountains (Rocky Mountains) was open to her exploration. The vast Louisiana territory that also bordered Oregon belonged to France for a season as well. Perhaps historian Horace Lyman best penned the reason of the late French appearance: "Composed of Gaul and Norman under Roman ideas, and with a romantic language, they have developed such clearness of thought and keen power of expression as to be content with little action." (Lyman, Vol. 1, p. 300)

A French expedition under Captain La Perouse, which left in 1785, was equipped with the finest scientific equipment of the age to win for France what Cook had missed. La Perouse repeated what the vast majority of mariners invariably accomplished on the Pacific shores of the Oregon Territory. He duplicated the course of previous failures and therein fell in lock step with the fatal blunders that protected the discovery of the great Columbia River from every Old World empire. The prize of the Oregon Territory required a mariner or explorer with the courage and conviction to chart his own course and not follow in the safe footsteps of his predecessor. Would men that had the courage and conviction to sail around the world in an age when medicine had no foolproof answer for scurvy and science had no answer for obtaining fresh water at sea be intimidated by the shores of the Oregon Territory? Could the mystery of the shadow of the Almighty have obscured the clear minds of these veteran seamen?

The upstart Yanks from Boston, the new kids on the block, would enthusiastically enter into the fray. In 1787, two ships were commissioned by Boston entrepreneurs, the *Columbia Rediviva* under John Kendrick and the *Lady Washington* under Robert Gray. After a successful maiden voyage, the *Columbia* returned three years later, this time under Captain Robert Gray. John Kendrick and the *Lady Washington* never returned. Kendrick met an untimely death in 1794 due to many unauthorized engagements abroad. One may not believe in providence, but after three centuries of the futility of the Age of Discovery to find the Columbia River, it appears providence rode with Captain Gray. A young Hawaiian boy, Attoo, had agreed to an act of treachery that would have sealed the doom of the *Columbia* crew. At the last moment the boy renounced his treachery, which would have been rewarded with his becoming a chief, gaining a wife and receiving other favors, and warned Captain Gray of a sinister plot to kill the entire crew. The Americans were outmanned by a ratio of thirty men to one man and the Indians were well armed. On the same voyage the Indians, instead of attacking the scurvy-weakened sailors, as had been their manner, gave them fresh berries and crabs.

Captain Gray met British Captain George Vancouver as the two ships met off the coast of Oregon near the Columbia River. Vancouver's journal narrated his position directly at the confluence of the Columbia River with the Pacific Ocean: "On reference to Mr. Meares description of the coast south of this I was first induced to believe it Cape Shoalwater: but on ascertaining its latitude I presumed it to be that which he calls Cape Disappointment, and the opening south of it Deception Bay. This cape was found to be in latitude 46', 19', by 236', 6'. The sea now changed from its natural to river colored water; the probable consequence of some streams falling into the bay, or into the ocean north of it, through the low land. Not considering this opening worthy of more attention, I continued our pursuit to the northwest, being desirous to embrace the advantage of the breeze and pleasant weather, favorable to the examination of the coast." (Lyman, Vol. 1, p. 341)

The evidence of river-colored water at so great a distance that the shore line was obscured to hide a mighty river should have been an "opening worthy of more attention." Vancouver's search for the "great river" was even documented by Heceta at that very latitude, a fact a seaman as astute as Captain Vancouver must have known. Incredibly, Vancouver, like every mariner before him, found no credible evidence of the existence of a mighty river. "Under the most favorable circumstances of wind and weather I have found the whole coast to be one compact and nearly straight barrier against the sea." (Steber, p. 38)

Captain Vancouver had been commissioned by the British government to survey and map the Pacific coast from 30 degrees to 60 degrees after the famous Nootka Convention in 1790 established a truce between Spain and England to counter the impending rise of Napoleonic France. The crown was aggressively fortifying her new authority in the North Pacific with concrete possession. No Englishman was better suited for this task than Vancouver, a veteran seaman having sailed with Caption Cook on his final voyage. His ship contained both a scientific and literary department as well as the finest maritime equipment of the hour. He was charged "to ascertain particularly the number, situation, and extent of the settlements of civilized nations within these limits; and especially to acquire information as to the nature and direction of any water passage which might serve as a channel of communication between that side of America and the territories of the Atlantic side of America..." (Lyman, Vol. 1, p. 336) Vancouver worked his way methodically up the Oregon coastline. This captain and crew were not intimidated by the fabled mystique of the shores of Oregon. All the mighty mountains of the Oregon Territory—Baker, Ranier, St. Helens and Hood—were not only charted but named by Vancouver and his crew as well as Puget Sound and Hood's Canal.

To add greater intrigue to this great mystery of the quest for the Northwest Passage, American Captain Robert Gray made contact on the high seas of the Pacific Ocean with Vancouver within a few days of his mis-discovery of the Columbia River. Gray even attempted to convince the veteran captain that he had indeed been at the mouth of a great river exactly where Heceta documented, 46 degrees 10 minutes. Vancouver refused to believe the upstart Boston captain and defiantly sailed south. Captain Gray sailed north to his destiny, and the "great river of the north" was uncovered from the hand of the Almighty where it had been hidden for three centuries from the maritime empires of the world. The discovery of the Columbia River would prove to be a vital anchor in the subsequent battle for Oregon and the free men of the emerging United States of America.

The infant nation of the United States had virtually no interest in the discovery of the great prize of the age, the Northwest Passage. Captain Robert Gray was the greatest mariner the United States of America had produced. He boldly raced his ship *Columbia Rediviva* across the previously impenetrable bar and established the American claim for the mystical land of Oregon. In the "Remarks" column of the ship's log, under the date of May 19, "Captain Gray gave this river the name of Columbia's River…" (Cross, Parkin, p. 157) By the time Robert Gray died in 1806 he had become a forgotten man. The young nation did not esteem or appreciate the value of Gray's momentous discovery. His wife and four daughters were reduced to poverty and a request was made to the United States Congress to provide a $500 per annum stipend for Mrs. Gray. Congress had no appreciation or sympathy for the widow of the greatest American mariner of the age and the stipend was rejected. A second attempt to obtain relief for the dependents of Robert Gray failed as well, most likely because by the time it was considered they had all perished.

If the leaders of the infantile American Republic had no vision for the land of Oregon, did the Almighty play a decisive hand on behalf of the emerging Union? The foundation of the United States' claim to the Pacific Northwest was grounded on a visionary American sea captain who became the first sailor to cross the bar and claim the river that he would name Columbia's River in honor of his ship.

Captain Vancouver hastily retreated when word reached him of Gray's discovery. He was unable to cross the bar and left Lieutenant W. R. Broughton, the commander of the *Chatham*, to explore the mighty river. Broughton worked his way up to the Willamette River and in 1792 claimed possession of the Columbia River and all its drainage for the Crown of Britain.

The great Northwest Passage, the mighty river of the North, the future British line of communication, was now revealed to the wonder of the world. No less than four great empires laid instant claim to the Oregon Territory: Russia, Spain, Great Britain and almost in spite of itself the United States of America. Not one world power had a solitary occupant representing a national authority living in the now fabled land. Still, the great mystery of the ages had finally been unlocked and the world was ablaze to know more about the land of giants of *Gulliver's Travels*.

The multiple Indian tribes of the Oregon coast and the Columbia Plateau Indians of the Blue Mountains understood no historical or cultural precedent to comprehend how or why any nation could possibly lay claim to their historical possession. No indigenous native tribe of the Pacific Northwest had any worldly understanding or teaching that would allow them to understand the drainage of the Columbia River was one of the last great unclaimed treasures of the world.

One powerful fact of history remained to be discovered by the contending nations of the world. The drainage of the great river was indeed already possessed by a nation of individual Indian tribes that knew little about the multiple white civilizations and contending religions drawing careful aim on the riches of the Pacific Northwest. The stage was set for a historical drama of unprecedented significance that would have an impact around the world. The Native Americans of Old Oregon ruled the vast land of the Pacific Northwest with a sovereignty that did not include the Western concept of land ownership. As the rugged Pacific coast had helped protect Oregon for three centuries from encroachment from the West, the Rocky Mountains and the formidable Blue Mountains formed an equally protective barrier sheltering the "noble red man" from the Old World conquerors from the East.

CHAPTER 5

STEWARDS OF THE LAND

The prevailing opinion regarding the origin of the Indians of the Pacific Northwest "is that our Indians are a branch of the Turanians or Tartars, of Northern Asia." (Lyman, Vol. 1, p. 76) These Indians kept no written records; scientific conjecture postulates that these tribes migrated eastward along the Pacific Coast of East Asia. In time these peoples developed the skill necessary to cross the Bering Straits and begin a gradual migration southward along the west coast of North America to the Columbia River. The extensive size of the Columbia River, which accommodated transportation and fisheries and the rugged Oregon coastline to the south with few sheltered harbors, caused subsequent migration to turn eastward. Anthropologists differ regarding the length of time these Indians inhabited Oregon; however, "we may say with Gatchet many hundreds of generations." (Lyman, Vol. 1, p. 159) Samuel Gatchet was an ethnologist with the Smithsonian Institute in the 19th century. For the purposes of this book it is significant to note "the lower Columbia River was initially the point of settlement of the entire Pacific coast of North America." (Lyman, Vol. 1, preface)

These courageous and bold Indian explorers found a previously unknown and untouched wonderland rich in salmon, elk, deer, abundant roots, nuts and berries. They had no need to build cities or cultivate the land because the vast expanse of the Pacific Northwest supplied their every need. Old Oregon was a domain larger than this Indian civilization would ever develop the organization to control. "The very fact they were not a civilized race—using the term strictly as meaning a race accustomed to city life and its arts—made them a people much more useful in assisting the settlement and in influencing the mind of the present American people." (Lyman, Vol. 1, p. 75) One of the developing themes of this research on the providential destiny of two distinct races of free men will be the impact and extent of the influence and assistance of the first (American Indians) on the settlement of the second (American immigrants). The spiritual heritage and culture of the Native American Indians of the Columbia Plateau was crucial to the ultimate destiny of the Oregon Territory becoming part of the United States of America.

The first stewards of the Pacific Northwest were predisposed by providence "to give whatever they had to their white brothers who might come." (Lyman, Vol. 1, p. 163) Certainly there were Indian massacres that established egregious exceptions to the positive reception afforded to the white intruder. The massacres of Spanish, English and Russian sailors were the exception in the Oregon Territory and most often under the surface there was invariably a reason for hostility. For example, "of all the whites ever visiting the Columbia, except on two or three occasions, and for special reasons they were treated with perfect friendliness and consideration, and without fear or surprise, by the Chinook and Clatsop." (Lyman, Vol. 1, p. 174)

Certainly the same claim can be made for most initial confrontations between the native New World people and the European nations that led the world in explorations. In the course of time, major hostilities invariably broke out between the Europeans and Native Americans throughout the Americas. The Native Americans of the Oregon Territory were the exception to the rule and even a few notorious historical hostilities, such as the Whitman massacre, will under the scrutiny of primary research illustrate mitigating factors that instigated the hostility. Native American Indian culture has always given precedent to submission and worship of the "Great Spirit," which led to an affinity of spirit with the first white expedition of Lewis and Clark. The Native American Indians, particularly those of the Pacific Northwest, as documented by European written records, had been a devotedly spiritual people.

The Columbia Plateau tribes, particular the Cayuse, were a taciturn people, strong and well skilled in warfare, never lacking in courage and well named as "braves." Nonetheless, "their first reception of whites was almost invariably friendly, and extended hospitality according to their customs and ability." (Lyman, Vol. 1, p. 59) Instead of resenting or fearing the superior manifestations of white man's civilization, in particular iron weapons, "the Indians were eager from the first to learn and acquire them, and understood at once the benefits to be derived from trade and commerce and education, and even from white man's religion." (Lyman, Vol. 1, pp. 59, 60)

This is not to imply that the Indians were predisposed with the wisdom and grace to comprehend the significance of white man's inventions or superior military power from the beginning of intercourse with the white man. A close study of the developing relationship between the two races will demonstrate a providential number of circumstances over three centuries in duration that continued to propitiously occur to facilitate mutual respect and accommodation. Were the first white American explores and settlers, the vanguard of the free men of the emerging nation, merely the fortunate benefactors of this progressive good will? The reader will have ample opportunity to discern whether this continual providential refrain was a curious act of natural and random evolution or yet more evidence that the Oregon Territory from its inception has been under the shadow of the Almighty for a purpose yet to be realized.

Certainly, the Native American Indians evolved from a common stock, probably Tartar; however, by the time of interaction with white Europeans beginning in the 15th century they had evolved into a number of distinct tribes with distinct and separate dialects. "There were perhaps a dozen very distinct tribes among the Oregon Indians." (Lyman, Vol. 1, p. 62) For the purposes of this work there were two dominant stocks of Indians that interacted positively with the European intruders for nearly three centuries. The Chinook stock included the Clatsops, Kathlamets, Wahkiahkums, Wascos, and to a lesser degree the Chehalis, Cowlitz, Tillamooks, and Nisquallies. The great Indian family of the upper Columbia Basin was called Sahaptin and incorporates the Cayuse, Walla Walla, Umatilla, Nez Perce, Flathead and even the Molallas and the Snoquallamies. These Sahaptin tribes "are among the brightest and most powerful of the native people, and have taken an active part in the history of Oregon." (Lyman, Vol. 1, p. 63)

To accomplish the greater purpose of understanding the multi-leveled, many textured layers of the unfolding destiny of the Oregon Territory, the enormous role of the Native Americans must be placed in historical perspective. "History will show that the possession of Oregon by Americans, and the selection of a government by free men, was the action of a long succession of men's choices....The opportunity was given to every nation in the civilized world to own this immense shore, but like Esau's birthright it was traded away." (Lyman, Vol. 1, p. 51) To the great blessing of the Native Americans of the Pacific Northwest, neither the brutal Spanish conquistadors, nor the harsh Russians, nor the unpredictable French, nor the pragmatic British became their suppressors and conquerors.

CHAPTER 6

THE COLUMBIA PLATEAU INDIANS

The Cayuse Indians were predisposed by providence to occupy one of the most strategic and majestic natural barriers in all of North America. The Blue Mountains were a formidable ruggedly forested barrier presently organized into a 1.4 million acre national forest carved out of land reserves established by Congress at the turn of the 20th century. The Cayuse Indians ruled this vast domain centuries before the white man set foot on the lands of the Pacific Northwest.

The Cayuse "were involved in, if not epicentral to, every important act in the drama of the Pacific Northwest." (Brown, John A., & Ruby, Robert H., *The Cayuse Indians, Imperial Tribesmen of Old Oregon*, University of Oklahoma Press, Norman, Oklahoma, 1989, p. xi) The fact that the Oregon Trail traversed across their domain and the Columbia River bordered their territory ensured that the Cayuse would play a central role in the history of the West. Providence could not have chosen a more imperial tribe of Indians to play such a pivotal role in the cataclysmic merging of two divergent races of nations. "Never in the history of the United States has so small a tribe wielded so great an influence over so many years and at so great a cost to the white government as the Cayuse Nation." (Brown, Ruby, p. ix) This work will examine in depth the great influence the Cayuse have wielded on the American people, especially the emerging culture and heritage of the immigrants of Oregon and the Pacific Northwest. Brown and Ruby write about the great cost of the Cayuse upon the white government; however, it would be fair to document as well the great blessing the Cayuse and their respective Sahaptin tribes have been to the white immigrants.

The Cayuse called themselves Waiilatpus. They lived in mat houses in the summer and mud-covered semi-subterranean houses in the winter. Like most Pacific Northwest Indian tribes they subsisted by hunting and fishing and gathering roots and berries. Early in the spring they would search the foothills for wild carrots, wild onions, bitterroot wild berries and most importantly camas root. The Indian women would dig the camas root with digging sticks often made of yew wood. The bulbs were eaten raw, roasted over an open fire or beaten into cakes that were boiled.

The Cayuse were hardier and more aggressive than their neighboring Indian tribes and by the turn of the 18th century dominated the vast terrain between the Columbia River and the Snake River. Their domination was accentuated by their rapid adaptation to a most startling discovery. According to Cayuse tradition, sometime before the year 1750 spies were dispatched to the Malheur River to gain information on enemy Snake Indians. What they reported brought great fear upon the tribe. "The Snakes appeared to be riding either elk or deer." (Brown, Ruby, p. 7) Wisely the Cayuse negotiated a truce and came home with a pair of horses, descendants from the Spanish entry earlier in the century. The Cayuse prized their new possessions and very rapidly mastered the art of horsemanship. The horse enabled the Cayuse to traverse the vast expanse of the

Blue Mountains. Their ability to ride, hunt and cover vast distances greatly expanded their dominion. Soon the foothills of the Blue Mountains were covered with spotted ponies. The Cayuse did not need corrals, or fences, or barns. The horses roamed freely just as the Indians did. The foothills produced excellent bunchgrass to nourish these mounts.

The Cayuse freely traversed the Blue Mountains hunting deer, rabbit, mountain sheep and elk and fishing for salmon, steelhead and trout. They perfected a method of hunting by encircling their prey, a maneuver greatly facilitated by the addition of the horse. They worked the tributaries of the Columbia River: Rock Creek, Willow Creek, and the Umatilla River and its tributaries, particularly Butter Creek and Birch Creek, as well as the vast John Day river system.

The Cayuse shared a common boundary to the east with the Nez Perce, and every July they would rendezvous with peaceful Shoshone bands (Snakes) and Nez Perce in the Grande Ronde valley. The Grande Ronde valley provided rich pasture for their horses and camas roots, a staple for their diet. The Cayuse acted as middlemen in these Indian gatherings. The Snakes would bring elk and buffalo meat and hides and receive from the Cayuse dried salmon and shells from the Columbia tribes.

The Walla Walla valley provided yet another lush wonderland to rendezvous with the Shahatian (a variant spelling of Sahaptin) Indians from the north and the Nez Perce from the east to engage in trade and athletic competition. The Cayuse excelled in horse training and physical contests. The Cayuse were the first to own and train horses on the Columbia plain and that prized possession allowed them great prominence with their neighbors. The Nez Perce in time surpassed the Cayuse in their expertise in horse breeding, a skill that made them preeminent among all North American Indians. The Cayuse nevertheless sustained their dominion of the Blue Mountains by shrewd horse dealing, particularly as middlemen in the flourishing trade between the slave-holding tribes of the northwest coast and the tribes of the plains to the East.

The Cayuse have been described as cold, taciturn and high-tempered. These characteristics made them a formidable enemy on the battlefield. Neighboring Indian tribes respected their territorial domain and therefore they fought more for booty and glory than for territory. Among the Cayuse, status was grounded in individual possessions and family groups rather than tribes or bands, and young warriors soon learned that bringing home captured women, children and horses brought honor and prominence. At the turn of the 19th century, the measure of the power of the tribe could be demonstrated in the affluence of prominent Cayuse owning up to two thousand horses for hunting, raiding, trading, travel or recreation. (Brown, Ruby, p. 18)

The Cayuse were meticulous in their appearance, especially in the care and attention to their hair and clothing. The women adorned themselves with grease, paint and different types of decoration. The Cayuse practiced polygamy; primarily men of status would enhance their position by taking several wives. Perhaps because warriors died in battle the Cayuse also practiced levirate, where a widow married her husband's brother, and sororate, where a man could wed his living wife's sister.

At the turn of the 19th century the Cayuse ruled the vast plateau. Their power was stable, their borders were secure and they had escaped the ravages of the smallpox epidemic that devastated the tribes of the Columbia River during the latter portion of the 18th century. They were indeed imperial tribesmen rich in domain, horses, prestige and power to the extent of exacting tribute from the associated tribes of the Columbia. Based on their sovereignty and mobility due to horsemanship it was surprising their nation was relatively small in number, around five hundred at the turn of the 19th century. (Brown, Ruby, p. 17). Raids by hostile Snake River tribes were the only real threat to their power and families.

Providence could not have provided a more positive Indian tribal dominion for the advent of the first American explorers, mountain men and fur trappers through the Blue Mountains. Because the Cayuse had escaped the smallpox plague they had no reason to feel challenged by the first exposure to the white man.

The first documented meeting between the two races occurred with the advent of the Lewis and Clark "Tour of Discovery" which will be examined in greater depth later.

For the purposes of developing a deeper appreciation of the Cayuse nation we will allow their story to progress through a few Native American accounts verbally passed on to priests and fur trappers that recorded their reactions. There are no written Indian records of their first impression of the white intruders.

One of the first significant accounts was written by Father Daste for the *Western Wonderland* in 1900, recounting the story of an old Flathead Indian woman named Agnes. The Flathead were a kindred Sahaptin tribe of the Cayuse and it is highly possible word of the positive encounter with Lewis and Clark reached the Cayuse before the explorers. This account documents that the Native American peoples watched and studied the white explorers at a distance without exposing their presence. These strange white men puzzled them for a number of reasons. Lewis and Clark rode with no blankets, something Indians never did. There was a strange Black man (York) who further confused them. "When they came to the open prairie he [old Chief Three Eagles] noticed that they traveled slowly and unconcerned, all together, the two leaders going ahead and looking around, as if surveying the country and consulting their men....From the easy and unconcerned way the strange beings were traveling the Indians inferred that they had no intention of fighting or doing them injury." (Lyman, Vol. 2, pp. 174-5)

The Flathead Indians not only welcomed the strange white intruders but also gave each of the white party two of their best buffalo robes, accorded them safe passage through their domain, and showed them the best way to the Nez Perce country. Why did the Flathead accord such generous treatment when they had no cultural precedent for allowing an unknown civilization and strange race of people into their domain? Their culture not only allowed stealing the prized horses of any intruder, but also required such defensive action. The answer remains a historical mystery. The two races enjoyed great fellowship on their monumental first encounter: "Cutting some of their own tobacco, gave it to the Indians, telling them to fill their pipes with it. But it was too much for them, who had never tried American weed, and all began to cough, with great delight to the party. Then the two leaders asked for some Kinnekanick, mixed it with the tobacco, and gave again the prepared weed to smoke. This time the Indians found it excellent, and in their way thanked the men, whom they now believed a friendly party. On their side the whites, seeing the friendly disposition of the Indians, decided to camp right there..." (Lyman, Vol. 2, p. 175)

The two races camped together! What a historic night for the Oregon Territory and American history. There was no law to protect them and no historical precedent to bind them. Both races were armed, as men of war should be. They trusted each other to the point they could sleep in the same camp. Put yourself in their place for that first night and only then can one appreciate the divine providence that accorded this historic first encounter between two races and two nations that still share a common American heritage.

A Nez Perce missionary, Miss Kate Macbeth of Lapwai, wrote the second significant account for the *Oregon Historical Quarterly*. In this instance the Lewis and Clark party surprised a great company of Nez Perce Indians and were at the mercy of a nation that did not welcome armed intruders into their domain. The story begins with a Nez Perce woman, Watkuese, taken captive by an enemy tribe and transported into an eastern land where she met the white man. In time she escaped from her captors and "met with much kindness from the whites, which she called So-yah-po, or the Crowned Ones (because of the hat)." (Lyman, Vol. 2, p. 181)

When Lewis and Clark first encountered the Nez Perce they were working their way down the Lolo Trail and startled a great company of Indians on their best camas ground. These Nez Perce Indian warriors had no opportunity to observe the friendly unconcerned nature of the Lewis and Clark party. The Indians chiefs made immediate plans to kill the strange intruders. An old and diseased Nez Perce woman who lay dying in her tent heard about the advent of the white intruders and plans to kill them. "She at once began to plead for them saying, 'Do not harm them, for they are the crowned ones who were so kind to me; do not be afraid of them; go near to them.'" (Lyman, Vol. 2, p. 182) Watkuese had miraculously made her way back to her people in time to save the American expedition. She died the same day, and Lewis and Clark never knew how close their monumental voyage of discovery came to ending as another great tragedy akin to the Whitman massacre.

We have no written Indian record of their first encounter with the expedition so we must rely on the journals of the American party. The journals of the expedition indicate the Nez Perce Indians guided the expedition into the domain of the Cayuse down the Clearwater River to the Snake and finally to the great Columbia. Most fortunately, friendship with the Nez Perce opened the vast Blue Mountain domain of the Cayuse to the expedition. Had Lewis and Clark surprised the regal Cayuse, even the intervention of a deathbed testimony may not have saved the day. The Nez Perce, the strongest Columbia Plateau nation, proved to be a great friend of the American nation dating back to this first encounter. The lone aberration, the rebellion of Chief Joseph, cannot be blamed upon the historically reliable and faithful Nez Perce, but rather on the shameful lack of integrity exercised by the American Republic. That story will be chronicled later.

Although Lewis and Clark do not specifically mention meeting Cayuse Indians, they did document meeting an Indian chief called Yelleppit whom they found a "handsome well-proportioned man" with a "bold and dignified countenance." (Brown, Ruby, p. 22) According to J. B. Tyrrell, editor of "David Thompson's Narrative," Chief Yelleppit was Cayuse Chief Allowcatt. David Thompson was an English-Canadian fur trader, surveyor and map-maker that first crossed the Rockies in 1807. Over his career he mapped over 3.9 million square kilometers in North America. Lewis and Clark gave Chief Yelleppit a number of gifts below the confluence of the Big River (Columbia) and the Little River (Snake River) and promised to meet again on the return journey. On the second visit Lewis and Clark provided an ointment for the eyes called eyewater and other medications and in return Chief Yelleppit provided crucial supplies including horses and canoes as well as essential food reserves. The two groups were able to communicate because Sacagawea was able to interpret through a Snake prisoner in the Indian camp. Lewis and Clark learned Chief Yelleppit was "a man of much influence, not only in his own but in the neighboring nations" (Brown, Ruby, p. 23), perhaps because he was able to draw together a group of Indians for a fiddle-accompanied dance.

There can be no question the Cayuse knew and were impressed with the weapons and medical power of the white men of the Lewis and Clark expedition. The enticement of white man's goods was powerful, and the Cayuse had what white men needed, horses and know-how to survive in the wilderness. There was no documentation that liquor, a great stumbling block for the Indian people, had yet been offered to the Cayuse. The most powerful attraction for the Cayuse to the white man was the wonder of the powder and ball, a weapon the Cayuse cherished. Certainly the outcome would have been different had the Cayuse nation resisted the American encroachment from the beginning, as they most probably resisted every other encroachment on their territory up until that hour in history. Had Lewis and Clark and their men treated the Native Americans like the Spanish conquistadors or even the British patrons of the Union Jack, it is highly doubtful the mountain men, fur traders, missionaries and immigrants that followed would have been so warmly greeted.

On June 8, 1806, Nez Perce Chief Cut Nose approached Lewis and Clark with twelve braves, two from the Cayuse band, "which (people) we have not yet seen." (Brown, Ruby, p. 23) The discovery expedition documented of a band of Indians of "250 souls living in thirty-three lodges under the 'southwest' (Blue?) Mountains on a 'small river' (Grande Ronde?)." (Brown, Ruby, p. 23) The Indians traded desperately needed horses to the expedition from their bands, which one member wrote in his journal "to have been the most numerous he had ever seen in the same space of country." (Brown, Ruby, p. 24) The fellowship between the American expedition force and the Nez Perce and Cayuse Indians was extraordinary. The weary Americans spent a memorable day running foot races, playing games and dancing to the melody of a fiddle with their Indian guests. Sergeant Patrick Gass was moved to write in his journal these Indians were "an honest, ingenious and well disposed people," in sharp distinction from the "'rascally, thieving set' from the Cascades of the Columbia to the coast." (Brown, Ruby, p. 24)

These Indian nations had no way to understand the full extent of white man's ways. They did not understand that American (Boston) immigration meant an unrelenting usurpation of their territorial dominion and traditional way of life. The Cayuse warriors coveted the white man's arms (axes, knives), and the women were taken with kettles, awls, needles, blue beads, rings and blankets. White man's goods were a double-edged sword. Fur trader Alexander Ross carefully observed the Indians' apparently insatiable need for trade goods. "They require but little, and the more they get of our manufacture the more unhappy they will be, as the possession of one article naturally creates a desire for another, so they will never be satisfied." (Ross, *Adventures of the First Settlers*, pp. 130, 131)

In the summer of 1811 over a thousand Cayuse, Nez Perce and Walla Walla encamped along the Walla Walla River near the columned bluffs of the Columbia River when fur traders of the John Jacob Astor Pacific Fur Company approached from the east. The Indians were imperially dressed with buffalo robes, white deer-skin shirts and leggings with porcupine quills. Thousands of horses grazing on the nearby hillsides framed the picture brought into perfect focus by the guns with which the Indians were now armed.

The die had now been set. The regal tribes of the Columbia Plateau had welcomed the white explorers and fur traders with gusto. White man's manufactured goods had magnified their standard of living. The entrepreneurial skills of the plateau Indian tribes were a perfect fit as middlemen to the competing fur traders of Boston men (America) and King George men (Britain). It was the grand age for the Columbia Plateau Indian nations, but it was not to be long-lived.

These Columbia Plateau Indian tribes had no historical foundation to develop wise discernment to understand the ramifications of the New World battlefield that would soon engulf their historical domain. The magnificent prize to the victor was the scepter to the Oregon Territory now that the Columbia River had been made known to the world. The Plateau Indians, particularly the Cayuse, did not understand in the beginning their aboriginal Oregon Territory heritage was the great prize that some in the subsequent waves of white immigration would covet. The Cayuse were strategically located and providentially disposed to play a critical and in fact pivotal role in the ultimate outcome of this international drama once American missionary Marcus Whitman set his camp in their midst.

This research must take temporary leave of the regal and imperial Cayuse as they ruled their Blue Mountain kingdom with pomp and majesty. If those Blue Mountains could talk, what a story they would tell. A tale of Cayuse horses roaming freely amidst deer, elk, mountain sheep, bear, bobcats, cougars and rabbits with over 200 species of forest and bird life and especially the prized beaver. A magnificent and unbridled Columbia River and powerful tributaries were teeming with trout, steelhead and salmon easily viewable in the crystal clear waters of the Columbia up to twenty feet. Not one proud Ponderosa Pine or Douglas fir had yet been felled by the iron teeth of white man's industry. The forests abounded with berries and seeds and roots, facilitated by the Indian burning practices. A very few pioneer forefathers are yet alive who were blessed to witness these majestic Blue Mountain forests still prospering at the turn of the 20th century.

We shall return to the Cayuse when their missionary friends Marcus and Narcissa Whitman take center stage in the final dramatic act of the Oregon Territory. This research will next examine the overland quest for Oregon for the control of the Northwest Passage, the mighty Columbia River, initiating a bold new chapter in the Pacific Northwest. If the Almighty could hide Oregon and its mighty Columbia River for three centuries, protecting the Native American nations within her borders, would the Almighty also protect these noble Red men from the inevitable confrontation of the immigrating free men of the Republic?

Chapter 7

Overland Quest for Oregon

With the discovery and opening of the mighty Columbia River by the end of the 18th century the west coast of the vast North American continent had been well mapped and a flourishing trade with coastal Indian tribes was beckoning maritime nations throughout the world. Precious little was documented regarding the vast interior, and tales of the mighty river draining the vast expanses of the west was the source of the romanticized unknown throughout the civilized world.

The casual student of American history could easily assume once the thirteen colonies declared independence from Britain and became the sovereign United States of America it was only a matter of time until the national boundaries extended to the Pacific Ocean. In actual fact no political, historical, cultural or military precedent at the turn of the 19th century worked in favor of the so-called "manifest destiny" of the United States to expand westward. The infantile nation had no army or navy and no mandate from the public to expand its borders. No fewer than four European powers had national designs on the rich and limitless wealth of the unclaimed lands west of the Allegheny Mountains and all were politically and economically better endowed to pursue their national ambitions than this neophyte republic known to the world as the United States of America. Had it not been for political intrigue and sabotage in Europe these upstart Americans may never have won their independence from Great Britain in the first place.

The political reality at the turn of 19th century was: 1) France had acquired from Spain the vast Louisiana Territory that controlled migration and commerce across the North American continent, and France under Napoleon had designs on ruling the world; 2) England controlled Canada to the north and claimed all unoccupied lands to the south including the Oregon Territory; 3) Spain claimed and occupied vast tracts of the North American continent from present-day Texas to California and aspired to add to their American empire the Oregon Territory; 4) Russia continued to forge into the Oregon Territory and owned and occupied the Pacific coastlands to the north, including Alaska; 5) the Federalist Party held political sway in the United States, and they favored no vision for national expansion; 6) multiple sovereign and powerful Native American tribes already controlled the vast Pacific Northwest and the bordering lands to the east of the Rocky Mountains.

If indeed the Oregon Territory was preserved under the shadow of the Almighty for the manifest destiny of the emerging United States of America, then providence would once again be called upon to work some mighty miracles of the same monumental proportion of hiding the Columbia River for three centuries from the Age of Discovery. Before we examine these political realities and the series of propitiously fortunate events that inevitably always favored the free men of the United States, let us set the stage for the overland conquest of the Oregon Territory.

The first nation to attempt to discover the vast uncharted depths of the West interestingly was France. The French were not an 18th century sea power and their colonial empire paled compared to those of Britain and Spain. Nonetheless, in 1728 France directed the colonial government in Montreal to commission an overland expedition across the North American continent to find and claim the great river and its drainage. Pierre Caultier de Varennes de la Verendrye, an experienced Indian trader and explorer, reached a mighty snowcapped range of mountains he called the Shining Mountains (Rocky Mountains). Local Indian tribes told of a mighty river to the west that flowed to the Pacific Ocean. Verendrye was not willing or prepared to attempt to cross this mighty snowcapped mountain range. Subsequent maps of the North American interior largely based on fiction and romance showed a powerful river draining the uncharted western slopes of the Shining Mountains into the Pacific Ocean. The Seven Years War with Britain ended the French dominion of Canada in the mid-18th century and France faded from the picture in the north.

In 1778, two years after the birth of the United States of America, Jonathan Carver of Connecticut wrote a book titled *Travels Through the Interior Parts of North America* that enhanced the mystique of the unknown, unconquered and uncharted drainage of the "River of the West." Carver wrote, "Four great rivers take their rise within a few leagues of each other, nearly about the center of this great continent; The River Bourbon which empties into Hudson's Bay; the Waters of the Saint Lawrence; The Mississippi; and the River Oregon, or the River of the West…" (Steber, p. 44)

Carver was the mapmaker for an unsuccessful expedition in 1766 to locate the Northwest Passage. British Major Robert Rogers, the governor-commandant of Fort Mackinac at the head of Lake Michigan, commissioned the expedition. Major Rogers had attempted to head an overland expedition force of 200 men to find the fabled Northwest Passage under the authority of the Crown. King George III of Britain had a golden opportunity to lay claim to land west of the Mississippi three decades before President Thomas Jefferson commissioned the Lewis and Clark expedition. In light of the fervor with which the British sought to consolidate their vast North American colony and the competence of Major Rogers to undertake this mission, it is surprising King George III rejected the endeavor. It is significant to note the route described by Major Rogers called for an expedition "from the Great Lake towards the Head of the Mississippi, and thence to the River called by the Indians Ouragon, which flows into the Pacific Ocean…" (Steber, p. 44)

Here we have the origin of the name that would identify the vast territory of the coveted Pacific Northwest. Major Rogers named Ouragon—the "River of the West"—most likely from the local Indian dialect. Carver refined the name of the river to Oregon and the famous American poet William Cullen Bryant after the triumphant return of the Lewis and Clark expedition fastened the attention of the literate world on this now mystical land. The vanguard of this romanticized legend was concisely framed in one succinct line from his literary masterpiece "Thanatopsis": "Where rolls the Oregon and hears no sound, save his own dashing." (Steber, p. 44) The pearl of great price now had a name, a name that thereafter would excite the heart of free men throughout the literate world.

Alexander Mackenzie was a fearless British fur trader of the North West Company of Montreal. He explored northern Canada extensively and determined there could be no northwest passage across North America. In the fall of 1792, with ten seasoned men he ascended the Peace River and found refuge in the Rocky Mountains. He reached the Pacific Ocean near present-day Vancouver at the mouth of the Bella Coola River on July 22, 1793. Mackenzie's monumental feat established the British claim to the riches of the vast Pacific Northwest in the name of the Crown.

In hindsight it is a clear geological and historical reality that the destiny and political survival of the emerging United States of America would be dependent on the westward expansion of the nation. The politically and economically fragile nation had defeated the mighty British army, but by no means did their union and territorial power extend very far beyond the thirteen States at the beginning of the 19th century. Spain, although political reverses had forced relinquishment over the vast Louisiana Territory, still held power from present-day Texas to California and the Spanish were ever seeking to expand their borders to the north of Mexico. The British Crown had staked a claim to the Pacific Northwest through the discoveries and explorations of Alexander Mackenzie. Westward expansion for the infantile United States was only a pipe dream at the turn of the 19th century.

Once again providence extended a propitious hand toward America. France had experienced a series of humiliating defeats throughout the 18th century, forcing her to yield all of her colonial control in the New World and Asia. The spectacular rise of Napoleon Bonaparte at the turn of the 19th century restored French imperial prestige, but there was a price required to sustain the conquest of Europe. An essential piece of the puzzle for the westward expansion of America was the Louisiana Territory. Fate could not have smiled more propitiously upon America. No American statesman could take credit for this incredible twist of history in America's favor. In actual fact, American President Thomas Jefferson was greatly alarmed at Napoleon's imperial designs and even considered alliance with America's bitter enemy England. He wrote to the American minister in France: "The cessation of Louisiana and the Floridas by Spain to France works sorely on the United States….It completely reverses all the political relations. There is on the globe one single spot the possessor of which is our natural and habitual enemy. It is New Orleans. It is impossible that France and the United States can continue friends when they meet in so irritable position." (Lyman, Vol. 2, p. 125)

Only those who understand how greatly Jefferson admired France and feared the Anglican power of Britain can appreciate how grievously the position of Napoleon's ascendancy endangered America. It was no secret that Napoleon desired to subjugate all of North America and indeed rule the world. Jefferson had already unsuccessfully attempted to purchase New Orleans from Spain; in a desperate attempt to sustain a positive relationship with France he commissioned James Monroe to attempt to purchase New Orleans from Napoleon. In one of the greatest mysteries of all time, not only did Monroe secure New Orleans but also he purchased the entire Louisiana Territory for the paltry sum of $15 million! Certainly Napoleon needed financial resources to sustain his European conquest. However, $15 million would hardly be a drop in the bucket for this emperor's dreams of world domination.

Napoleon had greater designs than money for this monumental acquiescence of the priceless Louisiana Territory without the drop of one ounce of American blood: "I know the full value of Louisiana, and I have been anxious to repair the fault of the French minister who abandoned it in 1762…but if it escapes from me it shall one day cost dearer to those who oblige me to strip myself of it than those to whom I wish to deliver it. The English have successfully taken from France Canada, Cape Breton, Newfoundland, Nova Scotia, and the richest portions of Asia. They shall not have the Mississippi which they covet….This accession of territory strengthens forever the power of the United States; and I have just given England a maritime rival that will sooner or later humble her pride." (Lyman, Vol. 2, pp. 127-8)

At the hour the burgeoning yet still fragile nation was looking to the east, not west, and the Federalists in Congress vehemently opposed wasting precious resources on western territories, the great Napoleon Bonaparte, would-be emperor of the world, virtually gave the vast Louisiana Territory to America. In one gift of monumental proportions, a gift that cannot be credited to aspirations of the free men of the Republic, the four great foes of the manifest destiny of America—France, Spain, Russia and the Federalists—were all dealt a fatal blow, and Britain was no better than a wounded lion.

Let us not so elevate Napoleon's gift to diminish the political strategic ingenuity exercised by Thomas Jefferson, truly a man of vision before his time. He defied the prevalent sentiment of the nation and with the stroke of a pen doubled the size of the nation with a check for $15 million. The world wondered at this transaction and Great Britain was incensed, but America's manifest destiny had providentially received the strategic realty essential to consolidating the Atlantic with the Pacific.

Was the Oregon Territory, now fully exposed to the westward migration of the infantile nation, under the shadow of the Almighty for the express purpose of the manifest destiny of the American Republic? Let the discerning reader ponder that question. The drama for the prize of Oregon had now entered into the overland phase. The crucial question yet to be resolved centered on the inevitable clash between two completely different races, multiple divergent white European cultures and the separate Native American red tribes in the lands of the Pacific Northwest.

At this point in history the clash of emerging empires of the Old World with the Native Americans of the New World throughout the Age of Discovery was invariably a sad story of exploitation and subjugation by the militarily superior Old World civilization. Spain had conquered and enslaved every Native American civilization her conquistadors had discovered. Russian fur explorers had brutally exploited every Native American tribe in her way to the lucrative fur resources of the coasts of the North Pacific. Britain and France had consistently exploited the Native Americans of Canada and eastern North America for economic and military purposes. We have already documented how the relentless explorers of the Age of Discovery had most fortunately somehow missed the Native Americans of the Pacific Northwest.

The attention now shifts to the indigenous American Indians, the stewards of the Pacific Northwest. What kind of culture, civilization and military prowess had these Native Americans developed? Would these sovereign American Indians hinder, frustrate and more dangerously thwart the manifest destiny of the new American Republic? These Native Americans of the Pacific Northwest were not totally ignorant of the so-called superior civilizations of the Old World. The Oregon coast Indians had traditions of shipwrecked Spanish intruders with iron weapons that date to the 17th century. The Pacific Northwest Indians acquired their Cayuse ponies from the Spanish. The plains Indians, especially the Blackfoot, had learned white man's ways and some treachery from the French and British. Even the idealistic English colonists who would put into practice the principles that led to the Declaration of Independence were nonetheless capable of self-seeking and treachery in their dealings with the Native Americans. Certainly there must have been rumors of intrigue and wonder and doubtless great concern that reached even the most insulated tribes of the interior of the vast Pacific Northwest. After all, one of the most momentous events in the history of modern nations, the rise of the United States of America, was occurring on the same continent.

Who were these free men of the emerging American Republic and what was the source of their powerful convictions for liberty of heart, conscience and action? They were certainly Englishmen contending for the rights of all Englishmen, rights the British Crown suppressed to bring the American colonies under control. "They were pre-eminently the believers in the liberal principles of the Magna Charta, of the protectorate of Cromwell, and the Revolution of 1688." (Lyman, Vol. 2, p. 45) These free men believed in the right of private ownership of property, that taxes were a free gift and not a requirement to their rulers, and that they had a free right to address their grievances. Fortunately the architect of the policy for the American treatment of the Native Americans of the Pacific Northwest was one of the great souls of the American Revolution, Thomas Jefferson. On behalf of the future of race relations between the Native Americans of the Pacific Northwest and free men of the United States of America, Thomas Jefferson was providentially educated and predisposed to one day be elevated to the position of president at the turn of the 19th century.

The stage was now set for one of the most auspicious and courageous frontier expeditions of all time, the Voyage of Discovery captained by Meriwether Lewis and William Clark and commissioned by American President Jefferson. This expedition would establish the first contact between the white and red races of North Americans and the consequences of that first meeting, either positive or negative, would be monumental. Every precedent established by initial contact of the Lewis and Clark expedition with each of the multiple Native American nations would initially establish, with allowance to historical variables, the subsequent relationship between the two races.

No man was culturally, spiritually or historically better predisposed to accomplish this task to the mutually beneficial reward of both races than Thomas Jefferson. The question of the hour was, how could a New World man who really preferred the Old World elegance he enjoyed in France know anything about the frontier Indians of the Oregon Territory? How could this man or any man be expected to frame a policy to the benefit of a race of Native Americans virtually nobody knew anything about? Could the ideals of liberty and justice of the new nation be preserved and honored and somehow be transferred with equality to the primitive "savages" of the West without compromising the sacred ideals of the Declaration of Independence? The third president of the Union of States was going to need some divine insight to solve this dilemma.

By coincidence, such a man who could provide providential insight and knowledge appeared at the most opportune hour in history. John Ledyard, a native of the state of Connecticut, was a New World man who attempted great feats with a highly irregular and romantically tireless energy, yet paradoxically never achieved a single prominent goal in his life. He started out to be a missionary to the Native Americans and somehow found himself a mate to an Englishman, Captain James Cook, on his monumental voyage to the Pacific Northwest. He met the Indians of his calling by accident at the opposite end of the continent and his soul was moved: "All the early emotions incident to natural attachments and early prejudices played around my heart, and I indulged them….They are bold and ferocious, shy and reserved; not easily provoked, but revengeful; we saw no sign of religion and if they sacrifice, it is to the god of liberty." (Lyman, Vol. 2, pp. 67, 69)

The British Crown suppressed the results of Captains Cook's voyage, in part because he failed to find the Northwest Passage. Cook's voyage was repressed, but not the irrepressible John Ledyard. In Ledyard's attempt to set up a fur trading enterprise to return to the Pacific coast, the ever adventurous and ambitious American characteristically made his way into high-society France. It was there that Ledyard, by his own admission "damned to fame," met among other luminaries John Paul Jones, Marquis de La Fayette, and the American ambassador to France, Thomas Jefferson. The renowned statesman actually encouraged Ledyard to attempt to reach the Oregon Territory via Russia when all other efforts failed: "In 1786, while at Paris, I became acquainted with John Ledyard, of Connecticut, a man of genius, of some science and of fearless courage and enterprise." (Lyman, Vol. 2, p. 78) Ledyard never reached Oregon, failing in his overland attempt to cross Russia, and died on an expedition to the Nile. However, he had nonetheless passed his passion on to Jefferson. One of Jefferson's biographers recounts the significance of Ledyard's impression on the third president: "He was convinced, therefore, of the propriety of its [the Oregon Territory] being explored by a citizen of the United States, and regretted the failure of Ledyard's attempts in his own country to engage in a voyage before the same thing had been meditated anywhere else. These views were deeply impressed on the mind of Jefferson and in them originated the journey of Lewis and Clark, twenty years afterwards, which was projected by him, and prosecuted under his auspices." (Lyman, Vol. 2, pp. 75, 76)

Ledyard had passed on more than his vision for a historic voyage of discovery to Oregon. He had passed on his soul and passion for the noble red man who ruled the regal empire of the Pacific Northwest to a fellow visionary. The extraordinary care that Jefferson exercised choosing the men for this historic overland voyage and the fervent spiritual zeal for the warfare of the Native American natives was birthed in the missionary zeal of John Ledyard.

It will not be the purpose of this work to examine in detail what the prominent historians and anthropologists of the hour have brought to the American public regarding the Lewis and Clark Tour of Discovery. This research will focus on the aspects of the expedition that support the supposition that the Almighty ordained through Thomas Jefferson that the free men of the United States of America extend their vision of liberty and justice for all men, including the free men of the Indian nations of the fabled land of Oregon.

Many biographies and documentaries have illustrated the undaunted courage and propitious providential good fortune that continually graced the Tour of Discovery into the mystical land of Oregon. In terms of the destiny of the burgeoning United States of America, the overland expedition to the Pacific Ocean was more than the sum of all the triumphant testimonies that documented the journey. The expedition accomplished even more than President Jefferson had hoped for, eventually establishing precedent for inclusion of the Oregon Territory into the United States of America. It was not the first overland crossing of the North American continent, but it was the most important expedition ever undertaken by this nation of free men birthed for such a purpose.

It is significant to note the first American endeavor to be commissioned to attempt an overland expedition across the North American continent failed. The American Philosophical Society, under the leadership of none other than Mr. Thomas Jefferson, commissioned a French botanist, André Michaux, to lead the exploratory force and a young army officer by the name of Meriwether Lewis was chosen to accompany him. With the addition of Lewis the excursion would have able leadership, but unknown to Jefferson, Michaux was a French spy. Fortunately, the mission was abandoned when the French Minister of the Interior sent a courier who overtook the party in Kentucky with a message that redirected Michaux to a less dangerous endeavor. Was the shadow of the Almighty safeguarding once again the destiny of the infant union of States?

This same irregularly educated Meriwether Lewis was appointed private secretary to Thomas Jefferson in 1800. When Jefferson initiated plans to explore the vast interior, his private secretary once again was commissioned for the task, a task he was providentially destined to lead, not once, but twice. Jefferson's commission was to find "…an intelligent officer, with ten or twelve chosen men, fit for the enterprise and willing to undertake…might explore the whole line, even to the Western Oregon…While other civilized nations have encountered great expense to enlarge the boundaries of knowledge, by undertaking voyages of discovery, and for other literary purposes, in various parts and directions, our nation seems to owe to the same object, as well as to its own interests, to explore this the only line of easy communication across the continent, and so directly traversing our own port of it…" (Steber, p. 46)

Lewis and Clark were commissioned for a monumental voyage of discovery to enlarge the boundaries of knowledge for the purpose of enhancing other literary purposes and a direct line of communication across the continent. They were not commissioned to gain political advantage over the aspirations of the British to the north or the Spaniards to the south; nonetheless, the expedition became a vital link to right of title to Oregon. They were not commissioned to lay claim to the financial riches of the fur trading commerce of the Pacific Northwest; however, American entrepreneurs soon boldly entered into the fray. They were not commissioned to make claim to the lands of the native Indian tribes, but succeeding waves of immigrants were willing to bear unknown and mostly undocumented suffering to occupy such lands.

Jefferson commissioned his Voyage of Discovery to enlarge the boundaries of knowledge hidden in the great-uncharted wilderness. The expedition of discovery was blessed from the very beginning because the fundamental motive was noble and virtuous. At an hour in history when the Native Americans were commonly referred to as savages and barbarians and most generously as Indians, Jefferson commanded his emissaries to deal with the indigenous people as sovereign nations of the West and equals with the new American nation of free men. With respect to the indigenous Native American nations Jefferson wrote, "Treat them in the most friendly and conciliatory manner…make them acquainted with the position, extent, character, peaceable and commercial dispositions of the United States, of our wish to be neighborly, friendly, and useful to them…" (Marshall, Manuel, p. 325) Jefferson had medallion medals made as presents to the Native Americans. These medallions bore the inscription "Peace and Friendship" with clasped hands designating the unity of the two races and nations. Jefferson rightly understood these so-called uncivilized Native American nations were governed by the same ideals of liberty, justice, mutual good will and respect as the framers of the Declaration of Independence. If Jefferson had been wrong about these indigenous natives his Tour of Discovery would never have made it to the Columbia River, let alone complete the monumental task with the loss of only one man in two and a half years in the wilderness.

The chronicles of the journals of the Lewis and Clark expedition testify that the men of the voyage of discovery would have perished in the wilderness were it not for the benevolent and gracious hospitality and oft times courage continually afforded by the native Indian tribes. The vast majority of indigenous Indian tribes had little or no knowledge of the white man, as previously noted, yet they seemed to have been providentially predisposed to receive the strange pale-faced explorers.

The only exceptions to the favorable treatment the expedition received from the Native Americans were invariably due to miscalculations, mistakes or unavoidable surprises on the part of the Americans and Indians alike. At the beginning of the tour, when the expedition crossed into the territory of the Teton Sioux, Lewis and Clark invited five Sioux chiefs to board their keelboat. The chiefs gladly accepted glass beads and trinkets and the quarter-glass portions of whisky they were generously offered. "The chiefs consumed the potion in one gulp and, amazed at the result, suddenly grabbed the bottle away from the hosts. Tilting it to their lips, they passed it to one another until it was empty and obstreperously called for another." (Marshall, Manuel, p. 325)

The fellowship quickly deteriorated, and Clark and three men judiciously rowed the chiefs back to shore. On shore the chiefs confronted and encircled Clark with drawn bows. Clark's men drew back the hammers of their rifles. The fate of the expedition had been compromised by a bottle of whisky, and the collective heritage of America held its breath. Providence shined on the expedition that day and the Sioux relented. That was a mistake the captains wisely did not repeat, but only after being reproved by the Aricaras Indians after once again offering liquor. These Native Americans of the plains had seen the impact of liquor on their people and rebuked the captains, responding they "were surprised that the Great Father should present them a liquor that made them fools. [They also adverted to the affair again, saying that no man could be] really a friend who would lead them into such folly." (Lyman, Vol. 2, p. 146)

It would appear the captains learned their lesson, because we read of no further incidents where the American party offered liquor to cement their new friendship. It appears the Native American Indians of the western portion of the continent had not developed alcoholic beverages as part of their culture. In addition, unlike other indigenous natives of the Americas to the south, the Indians of the Pacific Northwest exercised no pagan practice of human sacrifice. Even the common custom of the age, flogging, practiced by the American expedition, made the Aricaras chief cry aloud.

We must be careful not to elevate the indigenous American Indians onto a pedestal that other historical records would quickly topple. The continual wars among their tribes were caused by the same vices that undermine all societies: theft, revenge, mindless feuds, superstition and murder. Most tribes practiced the same system of slavery that led to the horrors of the Civil War. Given these fundamental carnal truths common to all men, it is still fair to say that Jefferson's positive position regarding the noble character of the red man was the underlying principle that made the Voyage of Discovery successful. In the quest for the Pacific Northwest for the American Republic, even the wisest most astute acts of mankind and the finest impulses of the champions of nobility such as Thomas Jefferson would not have fully succeeded, save for divine intervention.

The addition of Sacajawea, a 16-year-old Shoshone Indian purchased as a slave by a French-Canadian named Toussaint Charboneau, is another case in point. Sacajawea not only consented to accompany and interpret for these culturally diverse pale-faced men, she traversed the rugged uncharted frontier with an infant child. What would move an Indian slave woman to risk her life and the life of her precious infant child to traverse the unknown with a race of men she knew not? To be willing to accompany and translate for this tour of discovery required suffering, privation and physical hardship unknown to the world today and she did it carrying an infant baby! At the very least the impartial student of history must concede Sacajawea's inclusion established the providential provision that ensured success for America's first Tour of Discovery.

It is not the intent of this study to fully document and chronicle the nation-changing exploits of the Lewis and Clark expedition. Distinguished historians have written about this expedition at great length, especially with the Tour of Discovery approaching a two-hundred-year celebration at the turn of the 21st century. This research and the wonderful interpretive centers all along the Lewis and Clark trail will help all Americans appreciate the prodigious price that has been paid for our heritage. The expedition was blessed because the cause was just. The party was protected from harm and calamity because they conducted their commission with honor. They were victorious because they were wholly committed to the challenge. No significant evil befell these men and only one man out of 43 died in a perilous journey over four thousand miles taking two years, four months and ten days. Two Spanish armed regiments were formed to find and kill these men and destroy their mission and the knowledge that would open the West to the United States. Those well-equipped and fortified fresh Spanish troops were inexplicably never able to find the often exhausted explorers, and the success of the latter meant the United States of America would have first claim to the lands drained by the mighty Columbia River.

The Native American nations of the Pacific Northwest, because of the Lewis and Clark expedition, established a concrete understanding of their white brothers from the civilization of the "Great White Father." They had seen with their own eyes the individual fiber and strength of the white American men, their gunpowder and rifles, and their courage and the peaceful nature. The way had been molded for future generations of white Americans (not always as peaceful and as exemplary as the first white party) to enter into the great Pacific Northwest with the blessing and assistance of the Indian nations that ruled this vast domain. These Indian nations chose to accept their white brothers, and the reputation of American forbearance of Lewis and Clark among these Indian nations grew as their exploits were shared around the Indian campfires. Unfortunately, Meriwether Lewis did not live to return to Washington, D.C. He was either killed by his guide or a tavern keeper or committed suicide because he was suffering from syphilis and/or depression. William Clark lived to become governor of Missouri, where he would once again play a crucial part in the continuing saga of *Old Oregon, Under the Shadow of the Almighty*.

Chapter 8

The Golden Age of the Free Trappers

The Lewis and Clark expedition opened the doors to one of the great romantic epics in American history, the age of the vaunted explorers, mountain men, missionaries and immigrants of the West. It was to this stock of common men that the sons of Oregon owe their origin. The true story about this romantic era in the Pacific Northwest, which comprised the first half of the 19th century, did not bode well for America's manifest destiny for the Oregon Territory. Most everything these bold, yet ill-prepared, Americans attempted failed and usually failed miserably, especially for the first explorers and fur trappers. Nevertheless, failure did not seem to daunt the free-spirited explorers and zealous fur trappers who followed.

The first mercenary fur trappers into the new western theater seemed to set the mold for those who would follow. A good example was Ezekiel Williams, who honored Lewis and Clark's pledge to escort Mardan chief Big White safely back home from his trip to Washington, D. C. Williams and his men took advantage of the golden opportunity and proceeded into Blackfoot country with twenty armed mountain men to trap in the Yellowstone. After a series of confrontations with the Blackfoot (a brave evidently got caught in one of William's traps), the Crow, and the Sioux, only three very fortunate men, including Williams, returned alive.

The initial American fur trading endeavors into the Pacific Northwest did not fare much better than did Ezekiel Williams. The first Boston merchants to attempt to trade and settle the mouth of the Columbia were the Winship brothers. Their ship was aptly named the *Albatross*. The Chinook Indians easily relieved the poorly financed merchants of most of their wealth and they returned home empty-handed. They were fortunate to return home at all.

John Jacob Astor had a bolder vision and the finances to make him the first American merchant prince of the Pacific Northwest. Sadly, he lacked the discernment and wisdom that Thomas Jefferson exercised for the Oregon Territory. He may have still succeeded had his pursuit valued integrity as much as it valued profit. Despite the rash, arbitrary and thoughtless leadership of the maritime captain of the Astor expedition, Jonathan Thorn, who lacked not only temperance but also skill, the first American settlement was miraculously planted on the Columbia in 1811. Thorn's egotism and ignorance about the Chinook Indian culture led to a tragic confrontation in which the besieged ship blew up, killing the whole crew along with most of a village of Indians.

Duncan McDougal, captain of the second Astor ship, rashly overreacted to Thorn's disaster. He employed fear and deception to protect his men from the altogether faithful and friendly Clatsop Indians. He gravely informed them he had vials of smallpox which he would disperse should need be. He became known, unfortunately in circles well up the Columbia River, as the "Great Small Pox Chief." With the men Astor handpicked, hereafter known as "Boston men," exercising American leadership in the Pacific Northwest, it is no wonder that the British fur companies soon dominated the lucrative fur trade of the Pacific Coast.

Despite the foolhardy leadership exercised by the first wave of Boston men, it was the undocumented courage of the common men, the unknown sailors, fur traders, missionaries and explorers who cast their lot for a new life in the untamed West who largely determined the destiny of America for the Oregon Territory. In particular it was these pioneer fur traders, explorers and mountain men of the West, in spite of the foolish mercenary policy of those who financed the fur industry, who established the first true American presence on the ground in the Oregon Territory. The inflated exploits of the mountain men were revered and embellished in the East to make them the most fearless, independent and dauntless breed of men to ever walk the face of the earth. The fact that these Americans almost invariably failed in their multiple endeavors to gain some monetary profit hardly tarnished their growing fame. Only the resourceful and most cunning survived, and the strongest kept pushing west when civilization approached. These men were in part the product of the "roarers" in Kentucky and "river men" of the opening of the Mississippi.

Consider for a moment the typical day in the life of one of these early Americans soon to be dubbed a free trapper. The nearest game could be days away and the nearest countryman many months to the east. Some Indian tribes had become hostile and treacherous to the point of tracking a man like an animal because of years of hostile relations with white men in the east. The French and British in Canada had soured them on white men. Grizzlies were so prominent that it was not uncommon to see fifty or sixty in a day, and the key to living another day was dependent on seeing them first. The grizzly would attack a man as it would any other animal of prey and only a well-placed lead ball in the heart or head could stop this vicious predator. A grizzly could break the back of a horse with a swipe of its paw. The only advantage of contending with the grizzly over hostile Indian nations was that the trapper knew all grizzlies were deadly.

"Brown gold" drew these hardy men to the wilderness where constant danger waited around every ravine. Around the turn of the 19th century the world had developed an insatiable desire for fur clothing, especially hats, coats and muffs. Everybody who was anybody in the "civilized" world had to have a wardrobe rich in precious brown fur. The sea merchants of the world had over-harvested the easily accessible sea otter. Until the hour of the mountain men of the West the nocturnal beaver was richly insulated in the far reaches of the wilderness of the tributaries of the great rivers of the West. They were only a marginal prey to the snares of the Indian but they would not escape the iron trap of the mountain man.

The lucrative fur market brought America (Boston men) into contention with the Crown of Britain (King George men). The Revolutionary War had not settled the destiny of the North American continent between these two foes. That confrontation was only the first chapter in a continuing battle that raged for the first half of the 19th century. The British Hudson's Bay Company was firmly entrenched in Canada with established trading posts and positive relations with the indigenous Indians, and the lucrative fur trade drew them into the rich Columbia River highway.

The British North West Company had developed a rival stronghold in the Pacific Northwest as well, illustrating the growing dominant presence of the British Crown on the ground in the Pacific Northwest. John Jacob Astor, a wealthy New England entrepreneur, determined with typical Yankee gusto to compete with the fur monopoly of the Hudson's Bay Company. In 1810 he was granted a charter to form the Pacific Fur Company and sent two expeditions, one by land and one by sea, to the Pacific Northwest to set up trading posts. Despite Captain Thorn's dismal failure, the first permanent settlement in Oregon by Astor's crew on the Columbia River would mark the trail for Oregon's future claim to statehood. The Astor overland ascent for Oregon did not fare much better than the maritime expedition; nevertheless, the impact on the Oregon

Territory was firmly imprinted. The first American immigrants had arrived in the promised land, but only thanks to the grace and kindness of the Columbia Plateau Indians.

Organizing and outfitting an overland crossing of the continent was no small feat. The Lewis and Clark expedition, just five years previous, required over two years and only succeeded because of a continuous string of good fortune and the full support of the President of the United States. Wilson Price Hunt, the leader of the Astor party, had no experience as an explorer or expedition leader in stark contrast to Lewis and Clark. It should come as no surprise that this purely mercenary fur trading enterprise did not meet with the providential good fortune of the Lewis and Clark expedition. The fact that any members of the Hunt party survived their overland trek was a miracle. No wonder the legendary Daniel Boone wisely turned down the persuasive and well-financed Hunt as his party prepared to leave St. Louis.

Daniel Boone could certainly have warned Hunt's party of the growing violent nature of the Sioux nation. John Colter, a member of the Lewis and Clark expedition, was also at St. Louis. His fur trapping expedition into the wilderness barely escaped by sustaining a 120-mile forced march after killing two Sioux warriors. The highly spirited and splendidly built Sioux had grown callous under the corrupt influence of the French and British fur trappers to the north. They had acquired horses, firearms and most dangerously liquor and now they were pushing their hereditary enemies to the west and south. The equally warlike Blackfoot and Crow nations had killed American intruders from the Ezekiel Williams party and the bloody die was cast for future American explorers and fur traders who attempted to pass through these Indian nations' domain to reach the Oregon Territory. The Sioux, Blackfoot and Crow nations were not ignorant of the lucrative fur trade. They had experienced the treachery and deception of the British and French who had used them as vassals and paid them in worthless trinkets for the brown gold flourishing in their rivers. Now these Indian nations would use the lessons they had learned from their former Old World masters against both the whites and the more peaceful Shoshone and Nez Perce nations to the West. It was no idle rumor that the British fur companies encouraged such treachery against the Americans, and they were anxious to purchase these Indians' mostly stolen furs.

The fact that Hunt's party successfully passed through the Sioux, Blackfoot and Crow domain and somehow reached the breakage of the Columbia River was due mostly to pure blind luck and the good will the Lewis and Clark party established. The Hunt expedition's good luck was sorely tested when they reached what is now known as Hells Canyon. Hunt made a regrettable choice to turn loose his 180 horses and his men attempted to canoe down the Snake River to the Columbia. Perhaps Hunt gave the canyon its name. The party was forced to head overland with no animals to pack, no map of the land and only five days' supply of food. By the time the first remnants of the Astor party of 60 reached the Blue Mountains winter was upon them and they were reduced to a sorry straggling ragtag band of desperate survivors. Included in the party was the pregnant wife of Pierre Dorion, who delivered a baby on the plateau of the Powder River Valley; the Dorion baby died and was buried in the snow in the Blue Mountains. Hunt made the heart-wrenching decision to leave John Day and Ramsey Clark behind because they were too weak to keep up. It was a miracle that any of the party survived the ill-conceived trek, and that only because of the mercy of the Cayuse, Shoshone and Nez Perce Indians.

On February 15, 1812 Hunt and most of his party finally reached Fort Astoria, built by the sea expedition of the American Fur Company on the ocean-facing banks of the Columbia River. They could only lament the fate of John Day and Ramsey Clark. One can only imagine the grief that must have filled Hunt's heart at the point of leaving Day and Clark behind, too weak to continue. Three months later a group of fur traders led by Robert Stuart found the emaciated Day and Clark at an Indian village at the mouth of the Umatilla River. John Day and Ramsey Clark were left with a small party of Snake Indians that soon ran out of food and departed. Day and Clark were so weak they could hardly travel. Winter was upon them so they attempted to build a wigwam for shelter from the cold. In their compromised state they allowed their fire to die and with no water or food they would soon experience the same fate. The diary of Clark poignantly fills in the missing pieces of two fur trappers hopelessly lost in the wilderness of Oregon: "But Providence is ever kind. Two straggling Indians, happened to come our way, relieved us. They made us a fire, got us some water, and gave us something to eat, but seeing some roots we had collected for food lying in the corner, they gave us to understand that they would poison us if we ate them. If we had a fire, those very roots would have been our first food, for we had nothing else to eat; and we can tell but by the hand of a kind and superintending Providence was in all this?" (Steber, p. 69)

The Indians spent the better part of two days assisting the white foreigners and left two pounds of venison. "On the same day, after the Indians had left us, a very large wolf came prowling about our hut, when John Day, with great exertion and good luck, shot the ferocious animal dead, and to this fortunate hit I think we owed our lives." (Steber, p. 69) Day and Clark ate or dried every edible part of that wolf. They dried the flesh. They feasted upon the skin and they even pounded the bones into meal to use to be eaten as a broth, "which in our present circumstances we found very good." (Steber, p. 69) For two months Day and Clark stumbled about in the Blue Mountain wilderness in the latter part of the winter. By good fortune they chanced upon the drainage of the Umatilla River (Umatallow) and slowly and painfully worked their way toward the Columbia River. "Our clothes being torn and worn out, we suffered severely from the cold; but on reaching this place, the Indians were very kind to us. One man, an old gray-headed Indian called Yeckatapam, in particular treated us like a father." (Steber, p. 69)

The Indians encouraged Day and Clark with the news that white men had gone ahead to the mouth of the Columbia and the two Americans followed by canoes given to them by the Indians. Near the Great Falls, Indians once against surrounded Day and Clark. After receiving such wonderful hospitality from the plateau Indians they were not suspicious when the Columbia Indians handled their guns. They were soon surrounded, stripped of weapons, ammunition and clothing and after much disputing among the Indians allowed to retreat, bare-naked. After four days and four nights they finally reached a solitary wigwam where they received fish, broth and roots to eat. They finally made it back to the Umatilla and their "good old friend Yeckatapam." (Steber, p. 70)

The courage and persistence of Day and Clark in the face of impossible circumstances was indicative of the type of men and women who would forge their identity and passion on the face of the emerging Oregon. The names of these courageous men still bear their imprint on Oregon's heritage, especially John Day whose name now autographs one of the mighty rivers draining the Blue Mountains into the Columbia River. Without the mercy and compassion of the Columbia Plateau Indians these names would have been erased before they ever reached the Columbia River, never to be etched in the halls of Oregon history.

The War of 1812 between Great Britain and the United States once again changed the perimeters of the conflict for the Oregon Territory. The Crown had commissioned the British warship *Raccoon* to lay claim to the Oregon Territory, Astoria, and all the outposts owned by the Pacific Fur Company. Fort Astoria became Fort George and the power of the Union Jack very nearly snuffed out the light of America's candle ignited by Lewis and Clark's voyage of discovery. America won the second major war with Great Britain thanks to Old Hickory, the brilliant, legendary and at times ruthless Andrew Jackson, but the peace accord called the Treaty of Ghent did not settle the battle for the Pacific Northwest. In 1818 the two foes signed a treaty of "joint occupation" for the disputed territory, virtually leaving the destiny of Oregon in the hands of these independent, yet mostly inept, American fur traders, explorers and mountain men. They were no match for the mighty British and the iron-fisted monopolistic fur industry of the Crown. The joint occupation treaty in actual fact empowered the status quo of British sovereignty on the ground in the Pacific Northwest under the control of the Hudson's Bay Company. In reality the American Republic offered little competition.

"It was agreed that any country that may be claimed by either party (the United States or Great Britain) on the northwest Coast of North America, westward to the Stony Mountains, together with its harbors and creeks, and the navigation of all rivers with the same, be free and open for the term of ten years from the date of the signature of the present convention, to the vessels, citizens, and subjects of the two powers, it being well understood that this agreement is not to be construed to the prejudice of any claim which either of the two high contracting parties may have in said country." (Lyman, Vol. 2, p. 344)

Britain may have lost the War of 1812, but the news never reached the Oregon Territory. The joint occupation treaty actually sustained British control of the Columbia River and in essence gave Oregon to the Crown. The prevailing opinion in the United States, as evidenced by Oregon historian Robert Greenhow as late as 1846, was that the land west of the Shiny (Rocky) Mountains was unfit for settlement. "These countries (Oregon and parts further north) indeed contain lands in detached portions which may afford to the industrious cultivator the means of subsistence, and also, in time procuring some foreign luxuries; but they produce no precious metals, no cotton, no coffee, no rice, no sugar, no opium....Capital invested in agriculture, pasturage, cutting timber, fishing, and other pursuits…can yield but slender returns." (Lyman, Vol. 2, p. 345)

The American Republic may have won the first two wars between Britain and America, but the die was cast in favor of the Union Jack in the battle for the Oregon Territory. Was the Almighty once again hiding a trump hand in favor of the free men of the Republic? Let us next examine the power and autonomy of the British Hudson's Bay Company in the Oregon Territory.

CHAPTER 9

THE HUDSON'S BAY COMPANY

The Hudson's Bay Company was granted a charter by King Charles II in 1670. This meant they had the exclusive right or monopoly of the entire waters, land and tributaries of the great Hudson's Bay. They acted as their own government. They built forts, maintained an army, and defended their possessions and privileges against all challengers. As Oregon historian Bancroft aptly concluded, "All great monopolies are unjust and injurious; men combine and monopolize for no other purposes than to exclude others having equal rights." (Lyman, Vol. 2, p. 306) The monopoly was extravagantly profitable. The Native Americans were induced to trap or plunder other tribes' stocks of fur in exchange for worthless trinkets. The success of the Hudson's Bay Company brought competition, primarily French, and forced aggressive expansion mostly to the richer domains to the West. The Native American nations in the path of British and rival French expansion were exploited, corrupted with alcohol, and ultimately demoralized and treated as European vassals.

By 1763 Britain had successfully prosecuted the French and Indian War, ousting the French; all Canada was now controlled by the Hudson's Bay monopoly. With no rival in sight profits again exploded, further degrading the American natives who were treacherously exploited to sustain the supply of brown gold. Cortés and his Spanish conquistadors would have been jealous to see how easy it was to mine the natives for brown gold compared to forcing the Indians to dig for real gold. With no foreign rival, the British landlords became the conquistadors of the north and "desired only that the status quo of savagery in North America should never be altered." (Lyman, Vol. 2, p. 309)

It should come as no surprise that it was only a matter of time until the lavish profits of the aristocratic shareholders of the Hudson's Bay Company were challenged from within the Crown. Actually it was the demoralization of the Native Americans that led to reduced profits that induced the Northwest Fur Company to challenge the mighty Hudson's Bay. The aggressive Northwest Fur Company was the first to occupy the great Columbia River fur system, the largest supply of furs in the world. This monopoly moved rapidly when news of Astor's settlement on the Columbia reached the fur barons of Europe. Their mission had the full authority and might of the British Crown, whose fleet entered the Columbia and captured Astor's settlement and expelled Astor's fur company from the Pacific Northwest in 1812. The Oregon Territory for over the next 30 years was ruled by the Union Jack through their monopoly fur companies. Britain claimed the Oregon Territory based on the discoveries of Captains Meares and Vancouver, and the Northwest Fur Company ruled Oregon for the first ten years of the British dynasty.

The British had no competitors on the ground in the Pacific Northwest. It can be argued that, were it not for the stubborn British old-world aristocracy that suppressed the free spirit in man, the British Crown most likely would still rule Oregon today. These King George men were not free men but rather servants of the monopoly. It should not come as a surprise that many of these British subjects would in time join forces with the American free men trappers and mountain men who competed with the Crown for the brown gold. After all, the free men of Oregon largely came from the same British heritage of the Magna Charta and the Protestant Reformation.

The British sovereigns had a different spirit from the spirit that moved the men of the Reformation and they feared the freedom of the Yankee free trappers. Fur trading was a commercial endeavor of British aristocracy, first and foremost. For ten years the rival British fur companies, the Northwest Fur Company and the Hudson's Bay Companies, were so consumed waging a war for supremacy they initially didn't bother with the pesky American fur traders. The indigenous Indians must have been bewildered to watch the King George men murder each other and burn down their rival trading posts. The British resorted to time-tested policies of corrupting and winning the allegiance of the Native American nations. "In one two-year period, nearly 200,000 gallons of liquor were expended to the Indians by the rivals." (Steber, p. 73) The exploitation, corruption and demoralization policies of the British Crown inevitably caused great suffering among the previously insulated Indians of the Columbia River. The good will carefully crafted by Lewis and Clark and those free men of similar spirit who followed was methodically and ruthlessly destroyed.

The British continued to consolidate their vast Pacific empire. The two warring fur companies finally merged under the Chief Factor of the Columbia District, Dr. John McLoughlin, the man acclaimed by historians as the "Father of Oregon." John McLoughlin ruled the British Empire in the Pacific Northwest with more power and authority than most sovereign kings in the Old World. There was no landed gentry or privileged aristocracy or papal powers that could compromise his power. McLoughlin's power extended beyond the imaginary border of California to the south and Canada to the north, with no restraint on his authority save that he continue to send literally millions of dollars to the Crown in the form of brown gold. Fortunately, very few men have ever been vested with such absolute power in the history of mankind. The results have usually been disastrous for civilization and individual liberty. For this reason history has recorded the axiom that absolute power corrupts absolutely. It would appear on the surface the fabled heritage of the indigenous American Indians in the Pacific Northwest would not survive this British autocracy, especially from a monopoly steeped in oppression and exploitation.

Once again it seems the hand of the Almighty intervened on behalf of the heritage of the free men of the Pacific Northwest and the ancient pursuit of liberty by the Native Americans. John McLoughlin proved to be the very finest the British Empire had to offer. He was a mountain of a man, some say over six foot six, with a massive chest that matched the broad width of his countenance. There would be no exploitation of the noble red man under McLoughlin's autocratic rule. Liquor was not allowed to be sold to the Native American Indians. Even the intrepid American free traders were treated with tolerance under McLoughlin's regime. The Native Americans were afforded justice with dignity and their affairs were handled forthrightly. Oregon had a British sovereign who adhered to the same timeless principles that inspired Thomas Jefferson to envision and charter the Lewis and Clark expedition.

McLoughlin most astutely built Fort Vancouver, near the confluence of the Willamette and Columbia Rivers, dedicated in 1825. Fort Vancouver soon became the hub of fur trading from as far as San Francisco in the south to the Russian outposts in the north and the entire massive Columbia River inland outpost system controlled by the Hudson's Bay Company. The momentum for British control of the vast Oregon country was seemingly impossible to resist. It was the golden hour of the British Pacific Empire.

To enforce sovereignty of the Crown, Peter Skeen Ogden was appointed Chief of the Snake River Trapping Expedition. His force of 71 men and 372 horses left the Bull River of Montana in 1824 on the first Hudson's Bay trapping expedition. The inevitable confrontation of King George trappers and Yankee mountain men was indicative of the underlying competition that was invisibly battling for the greater prize of the Oregon Territory. The inevitable confrontation between the free trappers of the American empire and the armed authority of the all-powerful British Crown appeared on the surface to be a mismatch. In documented confrontations, strange things happened when these mountain men were challenged that invariably set the tenor for the future of the Oregon Territory in favor of the free men.

"The journal of the first expedition was lost but it is known they camped in Bear Valley (Idaho) and while there a small group of American trappers set their camp alongside. They hoisted an American flag, openly passed a jug and called invitation to the freeman trappers among the Company men to join them." (Steber, p. 77) The British had learned to harness the Indian tribes through whisky and trinkets. They had gained control of the fur trade commerce through the wise governorship of John McLoughlin. They had solved their own inner battle for control through a forced truce. They had in effect solved every challenge save the freemen mountaineers from the upstart union of states from the east. Twenty-eight of Ogden's men deserted his expedition to join the unquenchable freemen, severely undermining the task. The golden age of the fabled mountain men of the West was in full bloom.

A British trapper, Captain Benjamin Bonneville, competed with these freemen and left a testimony of their fabled temperament. "The wandering whites who mingle for any length of time with the savages, have invariably a proneness to adopt savage habitudes; but none more so than the free trappers….You cannot pay a free trapper a greater compliment, than to persuade him you have mistaken him for an Indian brave; and, in truth, the counterfeit is complete. His hair, suffered to attain to a great length, is carefully combed out, and either left to fall carelessly over his shoulders, or plaited and tied up in otter skins, or parti-colored ribbons….A blanket of scarlet, or some other bright color, hangs from his shoulders, and is girt round his waist with a red sash, in which he bestows his pistols, knife, and the stem of his Indian pipe, preparations for peace or war….They come and go, when and where they please; provide their own horses, arms and other equipment, trap and trade on account, and dispose of their skins and peltries to the highest bidder…" (Steber, p. 78) The proud day of the American mountain man had finally arrived.

These brass intrepid freemen had a spirit the British could not contain. It was so winsome that the like-minded Hudson's Bay indentured trappers were quickly won over. Why trap for King George when the brown gold was free for the taking? Many of the original sons of Oregon arose from these intrepid free trappers. It was their unbridled spirit that defined a true Oregonian. For the purpose of this work Oregonians refer to all the heirs of the Native American and American pioneers of the original lands of the Oregon Territory. An Oregonian is one who sustains the love, convictions and pursuit of liberty illustrated by the original Indians, free trappers and courageous immigrants. By this definition the first courageous and free-spirited Native Americans were indeed the first of the Oregonians. The fact that the free trappers were complimented to be mistaken for Indian braves further defines the true Oregonian. The Native Americans were the original Oregonians. The Native Americans of the Pacific Northwest were driven by the same love of liberty to win their rightful place as the first Oregonians before the advent of white men. It should come as no surprise that the first free traders had an affinity with the Native Americans that was reciprocated.

The final destiny of the Oregon Territory will be achieved when the American immigrants and original Native American peoples are fully merged into one nation with one common purpose and one common heritage. The common historical trait of the prevailing American and Indian nations was the powerful need to be free men. The vast rugged terrain of the Pacific Northwest all the way to the Rocky Mountains was the habitat of the beaver, the brown gold of sophisticated society around the world. The Indians who possessed this previously uncivilized domain were soon to be caught in the middle of a battle that they knew not. Let us roll the camera back once again and examine anew the noble red man embodied by the Cayuse of the Columbia Plateau.

Chapter 10

Columbia Plateau Indians and the First Wave of White Men

Monumental worldwide economic and political pressures were bearing down from all angles on the pristine wonders that provided the habitat for the beaver of the Pacific Northwest. The indigenous Indian tribes of the Columbia Plateau were initially receptive to the intrusion of multiple nationalities that found their way into the Indian domain. "The Cayuse and their neighbors were bewildered by the curious assortment of strangers in their land: daring French-Canadians, patient Owyhees from the Sandwich (Hawaiian) Islands, and treacherous Iroquois brought from the East to encourage the Northwest Indians in the fur trade." (Brown, Ruby, p. 36)

On January 8, 1812 in the dead of winter the Cayuse witnessed in wonder the "fatigued and enfeebled" Wilson Price Hunt-led Astor expedition straggling down the Umatilla River near MacKay Creek. (Brown, Ruby, p. 27) The Cayuse traded beaver and dried venison to the beleaguered white men on the Columbia for tobacco. The Cayuse probably felt pity for these impoverished white sojourners. Hunt was impressed with the Cayuse civilization. "They do not eat dogs or horses; nor will they permit the flesh of animals to be brought into their lodges." (Brown, Ruby, p. 27) The foreign intruders did not understand that the beaver were prominent in Columbia Indian mythology; the Cayuse believed they had commenced from the heart of the beaver. Nonetheless, they were not averse to snaring the harmless mammal, although fur trading was "only fit for women and slaves." (Brown, Ruby, p. 30)

An early Astor fur trader, Robert Stuart, crossed the Cayuse nation in 1812 and noted the land contained "incredible multitudes of the Furr'd race…in their bosom." (Brown, Ruby, p. 30) In the beginning the Cayuse welcomed the white fur traders to come into their domain. They even made a trip to Fort Vancouver to encourage fur trade; however, they made it clear that the white man was welcome to hunt for beaver only. The deer and elk and ancestral hunting grounds were sacred. The Indians' enthusiasm was tempered when Astorian John Clarke hanged an Indian for stealing a silver goblet. The white fur traders were on edge as well when an Indian war party killed members of Astorian John Reed's expedition during the winter of 1812 near the Boise River.

There were no rules to protect the divergent cultures from unavoidable and sometimes tragic clashes. The indigenous Columbia tribes had time-honored rules and customs for bartering, passing through neighbors' land, hunting and fishing. Most of the white men followed rules consistent with their own cultures and considered the Indian tribes uncivilized and barbaric for the most part. Both cultures looked for economic gain essentially from the brown gold of the beaver. It was not uncommon for the Indian braves to confront the white traders once they broke Indian protocol. In these situations it was not unusual for violent confrontation to commence when white fur traders violated Indian procedure. In one instance where two Indians were killed when the white fur traders failed to honor Indian river trade rules, the Indians responded with tempered grace instead of revenge. "After a three-hour negotiation the whites paid for the two dead bodies, according to Indian custom, and took their leave in peace and safety, and this ended the disagreeable affair." (Brown, Ruby, p. 34)

The Columbia Plateau Indians must have realized the white man had greater designs than acquisition of the harmless beaver when the foreign intruders began building a trading post near the confluence of the Walla Walla and Columbia Rivers. This was no ordinary trading post. By 1818 the fur trade was so profitable that the British Crown ordered the construction of Fort Nez Perce. In typical British pomp and ceremony this fort had nothing in common with its namesake. For a Nez Perce Indian to enter this stronghold he would require a special invitation to pass through the outer fortress of sawed planks twenty feet long, two and a half feet wide and six inches thick. Within the fortress were weapons of modern warfare including hand grenades, sixty stands of muskets and bayonets, twenty boarding pikes and one- to three-pound ordinance. Rising high in the sky as a symbol of sovereignty over the Pacific Northwest was the Union Jack, causing the British to boast of her, "energy and enterprise, of civilization over barbarism." (Brown, Ruby, p. 42)

The most significant problem the British were facing was the continuing warfare between the Snake and Cayuse. It was imperative for the British to maintain peace between the tribes to ensure the safety and profitability of the fur trade. In 1824 over 2,000 beaver pelts were brought to the fort. By 1826 the count had been reduced to 800. There were a number of factors influencing the decline in beaver collection. The most significant problem was disease and mortality primarily through smallpox and measles among the Columbia Plateau Indians. The British further degraded the plight of the Plateau Indians in an effort to encourage greater fur production with rum and tobacco, against the rules of Chief Factor McLoughlin. Perhaps most troublesome was the British indiscreet amours with the indigenous Indians. Hudson's Bay Company superintendent George Simpson noted, "9 Murders out of 10 Committed on Whites by Indians have arisen through Women." (Brown, Ruby, p. 48)

The overriding imperative of the Hudson's Bay Company was sustaining business along the Columbia River and its tributaries by whatever means. A productive relationship with the Columbia Plateau Indians was mandated, not for the benefit of the Indians but to sustain the lines of communication. The Cayuse controlled the trade routes whereby the fur brigades worked across the Blue Mountains on their seasonal tour to the domain of the Snake Indians. The Cayuse were known to range as far south as Sacramento as they refined their entrepreneur bartering skills with the powerful use of their Cayuse ponies.

It was only a matter of time until the enterprising Americans would one day dispute the supremacy of the British Hudson's Bay Company. Nathaniel J. Wyeth made two trips across the continent to establish trading posts to challenge the mighty Hudson's Bay. The always vigilant McLoughlin countered Wyeth's every endeavor, building rival trading posts at Wapato Island (Sauvie Island) and in like manner establishing Fort Boise downstream from Wyeth's Fort Hall on the Snake River. Dr. McLoughlin was a man of great integrity but nonetheless was a formidable opponent. He knew a successful American trading post would undermine the sovereignty of the Crown in the Oregon Territory. The sagacious chief factor probably understood the harmless beaver was only a passing fancy, dependent on the fickle whims of fashion. The pristine and untarnished habitat that produced the beaver was priceless. Wyeth eventually capitulated.

An industrious and enthusiastic colleague of Wyeth, Captain Benjamin Bonneville, did not fare much better in his pursuit of a fur trading empire. Bonneville's fur expedition of 110 men was the first to take oxen-pulled wagons over the continental divide in 1832. Bonneville was fearless and pushed the fur trading potential of the Pacific Northwest to the limits, driving his men through the Wallowas, the Imnahas and the Blue Mountains. When his Indian guides cautioned him that the route was impassable Bonneville replied, "My friends, I have seen the pass and have listened to your words; you have little hearts. When troubles and dangers lie in your way, you turn your backs. That is not the way with my nation. When great obstacles present, and threaten to keep them back, their hearts swell, and they push forward. They love to conquer difficulties." (Steber, p. 116)

Dr. McLoughlin knew full well the bravado of Americans like Captain Bonneville. He also knew how to defeat the intrepid Yanks: cut off their supplies. He ordered the trading posts to refuse to supply the Americans. The Union Jack would have nothing to do with the upstart Yankees. They may have been victorious in the first two battles but the vast Pacific Northwest was another world, a world the Union Jack firmly controlled.

Captain Bonneville yielded his fur-trading dream and returned to the U.S. Army. He left a lasting testament to the Cayuse whom he noted to be "mild, playful, laughing people, devout, rigidly observing religious ceremonials." (Brown, Ruby, p. 57) Bonneville documented the same strong devotional feelings among the Flathead and Nez Perce and attributed these values to have been "cultivated by some 'resident personages' of the Hudson's Bay Company." (Brown, Ruby, p. 65) It is significant to record that Bonneville also noted the Indians' religious observance of Sunday and the traditional holidays of the Roman Catholic faith. Dr. McLoughlin may have been a formidable and at times ruthless opponent for the Americans, but he promoted adherence to the Catholic faith at the British trading post. The Plateau Indians had demonstrated to Bonneville a form of worship that exhorted "good conduct and right living, to which the latter, at the end of every admonitory sentence, responded in unison with one word, the equivalent of 'amen,'" (Brown, Ruby, p. 65) This is not to imply all the Columbia Plateau Indians were adhering to the principles of the Christian faith. Bonneville noted often the religious ceremonies, "not even on Sunday could prevent the Indians from racing horses at full speed or gambling in every corner of the camp." (Brown, Ruby, p. 65) Wyeth informed Bonneville there were Indian prophets who "by captivating the people with their mysterious knowledge, the seers often took command of tribes or split them themselves as independent chiefs and shamans." (Brown, Ruby, p. 66)

Nevertheless Captain Bonneville's overall opinion of the Cayuse people was that they were a spiritual people, devout in attending religious ceremonies. This could hardly be said about the white men who were drawn to the Pacific Northwest in pursuit of the brown gold of the beaver. From the journals of Lewis and Clark to the diaries of mountain men and fur explorers and traders there is scant mention of religious faith. With the notable exception of Jedediah Smith there is little record of any spiritual predilection. A contemporary observer noted, "They had little fear of God, and none at all of the devil." (Marshall, Manuel, p. 333)

The Columbia Plateau Indians encouraged the white men to enter their land for more than the powder and ball, trinkets, kettles, tobacco and rum. These Indians were seeking something more substantial from the white man than material goods. Little were they to understand, especially the Cayuse, that they were destined to become the central players in a titanic battle between two world powers and two world Christian religious faiths for the prize of the Pacific Northwest and its flagship, Oregon. The age of the beaver was coming to a close. The fur trappers and Indians were running out of mountain streams to explore when the fickle tastes of the fashion world were fortunately turning to silk. A new and powerful thrust initiated by the Columbia Plateau Indians' thirst for the white man's "Book of Heaven" was about to upset the all powerful Hudson's Bay monopoly. The plot was beginning to thicken.

Chapter 11

The Spiritual Battle for Liberty and Freedom in Oregon

"Whatever the opinion of the intelligent individual as to the objective reality of religious opinion, it cannot be ignored by the historian that there is no other such universal sentiment as religious faith. From the time that Mahomet preached the return to Mecca, or Peter the Hermit preached the recovery of the Cross, or Luther preached for an unchained book, or Robinson preached for a New World, every great popular movement has been accompanied by a religious awakening..." (Lyman, Vol. I, p. 131)

The Holy Roman Catholic Church under the absolute dominion of the Pope was the sole proprietor of the Christian faith until the advent of the Protestant Reformation ignited by Martin Luther with his "95 Theses" in 1517. The Protestant Reformation was arguably the greatest revolution of the modern age and a turning point in the history of mankind. Prior to the Reformation there was no nation in the world where freedom or liberty could find universal expression. The Roman Catholic Church dictated not only the rules of the Christian faith whereby mankind could find eternal life in heaven but ruled the empires and nobility of the Western world as well. The religious unity of the Roman Catholic world was ruled by the unassailable edicts of the Pope. In order to be saved all men were obligated to belong to the Catholic Church and abide by the edicts of the Pope. The church alone had the authority to read and interpret the Bible.

The Protestant reformers objected to the Catholic belief system known as the Mass or Eucharist. Their objection centered on the Mass itself, known as transubstantiation, which meant that Jesus Christ's death on the cross was a perpetual sacrifice. The substance of the bread and wine of the Eucharist were "actually changed into the body and blood (of Christ), the 'real presence' by the priest." (Semlyen, Michael de, *All Roads Lead To Rome?*, Dorchester House, Norwich, England, 1993, p. 36.) The Protestant reformers believed the Mass to undermine and in effect cancel the price Jesus Christ paid on the cross to purchase once and for all time the redemption of mankind. Particularly odious to the reformers was the Catholic system of indulgences whereby the common people were required to purchase temporal pardons for sins.

According to the reformers, the result of Roman Catholic religious and political oppression and corruption was the Dark Ages, when personal and collective liberty and freedom did not exist. For those who lived during this dark era there was no principle of freedom of conscience or freedom of worship or freedom of the press. Mankind was stifled during the Dark Ages under this oppressive Roman Catholic government. Dissenters or dissidents who spoke out or disobeyed the edicts of the church were persecuted and oft times martyred.

In the interest of unbiased objectively it is necessary at this point in the narrative to interject that spiritual and theological tables have a way of turning 180 degrees. The "good guys" can become the "bad guys." For instance at the turn of the 21st century it is the Catholic Church that is calling America back to the nations' biblical roots and adherence to the word of God especially in regards to the sanctity of life and marriage between one man and one woman. This research will document in the concluding chapters of the book why historians must be careful not to make heroes or villains of any religion, race or culture. All men, religions and cultures are flawed, and a diligent and forthright historian must allow the truth to come to surface no matter how painful the results may be to those whose heritage history may uncover. Sadly, history has oft times demonstrated that when even zealous reformers gain power, that power can corrupt. The Almighty often uses previous adversaries of the Gospel, in this case the Catholic Church, to bring the reforming church back to a righteous standard. No church or culture has a copyright on the truth.

The turning point in contemporary history, since the fourteenth century, in the age-old battle between liberty and oppression came with the monumental work of Englishman John Wycliffe in the 14th century. Wycliffe was a Roman Catholic priest and teacher at Oxford University. He shook the foundation of the Catholic system when he declared that the people had the right to read the Bible and that individuals had the right and the authority to interpret the Bible for themselves. To complete the revolution in freeing man's individual soul for religious liberty Wycliffe translated the Bible from Latin to English. Once the Bible, the book the Columbia Plateau Indians called the "white man's Book of Heaven," reached the heart and soul of the populace, freedom and liberty from Roman Catholic oppression could not be suppressed.

Martin Luther was the Father of the Protestant Reformation. He was a German Catholic monk who earned a doctor of divinity at the prestigious University of Wittenberg. He was grieved by the impious and unscriptural abuses of the church, and after a tumultuous personal spiritual battle he posted the revolutionary "95 Theses," calling the attention of the world to the subversion of the Catholic Christian faith by the Pope and Catholic clergy. After Luther's "95 Theses," powerful and fervent preachers brought the concept of liberty and freedom in Christ to the common people. The Roman Catholic Church exercised its political power to silence the treasonous threats against its authority. Rebellious priests were ordered to recant or die by public execution. Scores of Bible-believing Catholic Christians were burned at the stake in defense of their newfound faith.

Dr. John Huss of Bohemia preached the liberty of the Bible so convincingly after Luther's proclamation at the beginning of the 16th century that the Pope convened a council to silence his ministry. "When the fagots were piled up to his very neck, the duke of Bavaria was so officious as to desire him to abjure. 'No, (said Huss) I never preached any doctrine of an evil tendency, and what I taught with my lips I now seal with my blood.'" When the Bishop denounced Huss, "Now we commit thy soul unto the devil," Huss responded, "But I do commend into thy hands, O Lord Jesus Christ! My spirit, which thou hast redeemed." (*Fox's Book of Martyrs*, ed. William Forbush, p. 143).

The fire kindled by the persecution and martyrdom of the saints of Christ was fanned by the revolution of the printing press. When the written word of God found in the Bible reached the hands of common man, the passion of the Protestant Reformation spread like wildfire. The political and ecclesiastical power of the Roman Catholic Church was severely wounded. Tradesmen, peasants, nobles, princes and kings declared independence from the Roman Catholic Church and Roman Catholic emperors. Protestant movements began to spring up throughout Europe under the protection of like-minded nobles and kings. These reformers boldly declared that they were anointed by the spirit of God to minister liberty and freedom through Jesus Christ alone. Their fervor ushered a new age in which man could find salvation outside of the Roman Catholic

Church through the teaching found in the Bible whereby "the just shall live by faith" (Romans 1:17) and a personal commitment to Jesus Christ as personal Lord and Savior.

The Protestant Reformation virtually exploded in Europe. The climate for a spiritual revival and new and innovative ecclesiastical church organizations could not have been more conducive for growth and productivity. In virtually every European state a healthy and vibrant reformed church rose from the rigid and binding pontifical corruption of the Roman Catholic Church. The personality, worship forms and doctrinal distinctions of the reformed church assumed a separate character according to the predispositions of the national heritage and the doctrinal beliefs of the church leader. Prominent reformers were John Calvin of France, Huldrych Zwingli of Switzerland, and John Knox of Scotland, but in truth the Reformation kindled a renaissance not only in religion but also in the arts, science, commerce, exploration and human productivity that cannot be adequately addressed in the context of this endeavor. It would be an understatement to conclude the United States of America as well as Australia and New Zealand would be the direct recipient of the blessing of religious freedom and personal liberty conceived by the Reformation.

The Roman Catholic Church responded to the Protestant declaration of independence by sponsoring the Counter Reformation, which found its most powerful expression under the leadership of the Jesuit movement. The Catholic Church initiated a number of reforms to reestablish political and ecclesiastical sovereignty in Europe as well as the uttermost parts of the earth at the Council of Trent (1545-1563). The Reformed movement endured a vicious counterattack from the Roman Catholic Church spearheaded by the brilliant and brutal military leadership of the Jesuit movement, which ruthlessly crushed the leaders of the Reformation in most of Europe and virtually saved the papacy from ruin. We will examine the Jesuits and the Council of Trent in detail in chapter thirteen.

For the purposes of this research the two great forces of Western civilization, the Protestant Reformation and the Counter Reformation of the Catholic Church, were destined to collide in the wilderness of the Pacific Northwest. That monumental conflict would trap and engulf and embroil the Native American Indians in a world struggle pitting liberty against papal monarchy that would ultimately determine the fate of the Oregon Territory.

The climate of unrest and discord in Europe forced the Reformed Church to seek and find liberty and religious freedom in the new world of America. The colonization of North America represented an invigorating break from the established order in Europe. Because the New World had no structure or rigid system of religious tradition, the new colonies were developing exciting, innovative, unexpected and unprecedented modes of expression and worship. "Among other things, they had become the most thoroughly Protestant, Reformed, and Puritan commonwealths in the world. Indeed, Puritanism provided the moral and religious background of fully 75 per cent of the people who declared independence in 1776." (Ahlstrom, Sydney, *A Religious History of the American People*, Vol. 1, Doubleday & Co., Garden City, NY, 1975, p. 169)

The spiritual foundation and driving force of the American Revolution was the Protestant Reformation. The bedrock of the wellsprings of liberty expressed in the freedom to worship, freedom of conscience, and freedom of thought in the Constitution of the emerging United States of America was birthed by the Protestant Reformation. The contending values of the established order of the monarchies of the Old World were pitted against the inalienable rights of free men of the American Revolution who rebelled against King George III. These same opposing spiritual forces would ultimately and violently clash in the battle for the crown jewel of the American Union, the Oregon Territory.

The American Indians had only a surface understanding of the laws, religion and European cultural diversity of the "Great White Nation." They had no worldly understanding that at least four world powers were coveting their ancestral homeland and two, Great Britain and the United States of America, had signed a treaty in 1818 establishing the conditions whereby one of those nations would assume sovereignty over the land. More significantly, they had no understanding that the Christian religion of the white man was actually divided into two major contending belief systems as well as multiple contending denominations. Most confusing to the Indians was that some of the contending "Christian" belief systems were fundamentally untenable, especially the Protestant versus the Roman Catholic, and had led to centuries of violent and bloody confrontations and wars in Europe. The worldwide schism of the Roman Catholic Christian faith in the 16th century that birthed the Protestant Reformation made the Bible available to the common man. The Cayuse Indians, guardians of the Blue Mountains, were propelled into the centerpiece of this providential and usually bloody historical drama.

In 1832 the entire northwest, from the Russian settlements to the north to the Spanish colonies of California to the Rocky Mountains in the east, were under the "absolute and undisputed control of the Honorable Hudson's Bay Company; and the said company claimed and exercised exclusive civil, religious, political and commercial jurisdiction." (Gray, W. H., *A History of Oregon*, H. H. Bancroft and Company, Portland, Oregon, 1870, p. 106) In actual fact the British Crown ruled the vast Oregon Territory with virtually no opposition from any previously contending world power.

The joint occupation for the Oregon Territory originally signed between Great Britain and the United States in 1818 in actual fact "placed British sovereignty over every foot of all Oregon, and British commerce over all the Pacific from San Diego to Bering's Straits, and to the Sandwich Islands; and to the United States nothing but disaster." (Lyman, Vol. 2, p. 131) The legislative representatives in the American government in favor of extending American sovereignty to the shores of the Oregon Territory were in marked minority in Congress. The strategic location of the Oregon Territory, vital to the manifest destiny of the new American Republic, was not a significant issue to the majority of those vested with political position in the new government. John Quincy Adams embodied the prevailing eastern view of Oregon in 1818 with his closing instructions regarding the treaty: "It may be proper to remark the minuteness of the present interests [in Oregon] either to Great Britain or the United States, involved in the concern; the unwillingness, for this reason, of this government to include it among the objects of serious discussion with them." (Lyman, Vol. 2, p. 121)

Certainly, visionary leaders in Congress were warning that negligence was resulting in exclusive occupation by Great Britain in Oregon. The issue was debated continually during the years of the treaty. President James Monroe even urged the establishment of a military fort at the mouth of the Columbia in 1824, but this and every attempt to save Oregon failed because "there were men in Congress who saw the unlawful character of such measure, as it was proposed….Others joined these actively on the ground that the Oregon Territory, if settled, could never become a part of the Union." (Lyman, Vol. 2, p. 121) The prevailing attitude among the circles of power was that the Oregon Territory was outside the grasp of the emerging United States of America because the Rocky Mountains and the harsh desert and rugged mountains to the west were too formidable for encroachment by westward expansion.

The Columbia Plateau Indians had virtually no understanding or appreciation of the monumental struggle for ultimate control of Oregon between the United States and Great Britain. The Oregon Territory was firmly under the control of the Union Jack and the autocratic rule of John McLoughlin. It was the Indians' quest for the white man's Book of Heaven that reversed the fulcrum of power in favor of the free men of the emerging American Republic. At this point it is illustrative to once again quote Oregon historian Horace Lyman's axiom, "every great popular movement has been accompanied by a religious awakening." (Lyman, Vol. 2, p. 131) No act of Congress or effort of free men in defense of Oregon or unscrupulous action on the part of the British caused the precipitous change in the previously unstoppable momentum in Oregon in favor of Great Britain. When the Columbia Plateau Native Americans heard word of the white man's Book of Heaven, the course of history in Oregon was forever changed.

The Columbia Plateau Indians had at best an elementary understanding of the Catholic religion of the Hudson's Bay Company, "but there is indication that they had heard from Protestant sources that the true worship and faith was not to be found in the Catholic forms, but in a book given to man directly from Heaven and that worship that pleased the great Spirit must be received from this revelation." (Lyman, Vol. I, pp. 134-35). According to William Gray, a member of the original Marcus Whitman missionary expedition, the Indians "learned from an American trapper, who had strayed into their country, that there was a Supreme Being, worthy of worship, and by going to his country they could learn all about him." (Gray, p. 106) History does not record who shared the Gospel with the Columbia Plateau Indians; however, at least one rugged mountain man of the age, Jedediah Smith, was renowned for his Bible convictions and spent many years among the Columbia Plateau Indians because of the bountiful excess of beaver. Horace Lyman reflected on the source of the Nez Perce knowledge of the Book of Heaven: "Possible it was Jedediah Smith, who was a man of piety and was frequently through their country." (Lyman, Vol. 2, p. 36)

A mountain man of piety was an odd occurrence in the golden age of free trappers in the wilderness of the Oregon Territory, as this research has documented. Why a godly man would choose to spend his life in the violently dangerous no man's land of the Pacific Northwest would be difficult to document since most of Smith's letters were destroyed by fire. Nevertheless, Dale L. Morgan, in his excellent volume on Jedediah Smith, copiously demonstrated that the mountain man "took his religion with him into the wilderness and let nothing corrode." (Morgan, *Jedediah Smith and the Opening of the West*, University of Nebraska Press, Lincoln, Nebraska, 1953, p. 8) Smith traded furs on many occasions with the Nez Perce, one of the few free trappers the Chief Factor John McLoughlin allowed to work within the dominion of the Hudson's Bay Company. Smith did not smoke, or speak profanity, or chew tobacco, and thus he was an anomaly among the white men in the Oregon Territory. "Jedediah Smith entered the West owning his rifle, his Bible, the clothes on his back and very little else." (Morgan, p. 8) The Nez Perce Indians were the dominant tribe on the Columbia Plateau in no small part because they were astute and discerning in their affairs. They were a spiritual nation as well, and the Christian witness of Jedediah Smith would have stood out like a campfire in the darkness. Just before Comanche Indians killed Smith in 1832 he wrote to his brother regarding his purpose in life: "Next my brother comes the subject for which we live, and move, and have our being, how often ought we on bended knee to offer up our grateful acknowledgments for the gift of his Dear Son: is it possible that God 'So love the world that he gave his only begotten Son that whoever should believe in him Should not perish, but have everlasting life.' Let us come forward with faith, nothing doubting and he will most unquestionably hear us." (Morgan, pp. 358-59)

The battle for religious liberty and freedom in the Oregon country began when the Columbia Plateau Indians undertook a most courageous mission of faith in search of this "Whitman's book of Heaven." (Brown, Ruby, p. 64) Four Indians, Nez Perce and Flathead, arrived in St. Louis in the fall of 1831 to meet with William Clark, the man the Indians called the "Great Father." This mission of faith compared in Indian history with the expedition of Lewis and Clark. The governor of Missouri, William Clark was the same legendary leader of the Tour of Discovery expedition of 1804-7. At the time the majority of the American public considered the Indians barbarous savages.

William Walker, a Christian who would become territorial governor of Nebraska, met three of the Nez Perce warriors in St. Louis in 1832 at the Superintendent of Indian Affairs General William Clark's residence. Walker's father had been captured by the Wyandot Indians and had adopted their culture and therein William Walker was most supportive of the Nez Perce cause. He documented the meeting in a letter that would change the Oregon Territory forever. "It appeared that some white men had penetrated into their country and had happened to be a spectator at one of their religious meetings, which they scrupulously perform at stated periods. He informed them that their mode of worshipping the Supreme Being was radically wrong, and instead of being acceptable and pleasing was displeasing to Him. He also informed them that the white people away toward the rising sun had been put in possession of the true mode of worshipping the Great Spirit. They had a book containing directions how to conduct themselves to enjoy His favor and converse with Him, and with this guide no one need go astray....Upon receiving this information they held a national council to take this subject into consideration....They accordingly deputed four of their chiefs to proceed to St. Louis to see their Great Father, General Clark, to inquire of him, having no doubt but that he would tell them the whole truth." (Lyman, Vol. 2, pp. 137-38) The Native American oral history concurred with this account, with the exception that four warriors, not chiefs, were dispatched for the epic journey.

The Columbia Plateau Indians' heroic expedition was divinely blessed even though historians have documented that all the Indian warriors perished. Dr. J. M. Cornelison, minister of the Tutuilla Presbyterian Church near Pendleton, Oregon from 1889–1942, wrote in an unpublished book, "We know that one of them did return home and his descendents are still among the Nez Perces. I knew one of that man's grandchildren. His name was Harrison Kip-Ka-pel-lil-Kan, a very large man and a very fine Christian, a Member of the First Presbyterian Indian Church of Kamish, Ida (Kamiah, Idaho)." (Cornelison, J. M., *The Seed of the Martyrs*, p. 44)

There was no other man in the Oregon Territory at that time who could have shared the word of God with the Nez Perce than Jedediah Smith. There were pious Catholic Hudson's Bay company men, especially Chief Factor John McLoughlin, but they would have been most reticent to share the word of God with the Native Americans. The Catholic faith at that time did not encourage the open expression of men seeking the word of God but required instead that man seek God through the Catholic Fathers. The impact of the Nez Perce call for the Book of Heaven rocked the status quo of the Oregon Territory. The advent of the American missionaries into the Pacific Northwest was the watershed point in the titanic, yet largely bloodless to this point, battle for the Oregon Territory. In actual fact there was no missionary movement afoot, no religious awakening, in the developing United States of America to reach the Indians of the West at this time. The story of the initiation of the missionary movement "is a tale which fitly illustrates how apparently trivial affairs will influence, and sometimes dominate, the momentous human events—how divine providence 'moves in a mysterious way his wonders to perform.'" (Parsons, William, *History of Umatilla and Morrow County*, W. H. Lever, 1902, p. 50) In historical fact it was the Columbia Plateau Indians who started the great missionary movement to the West and turned the tide for Oregon in favor of the free men of the United States.

"Though they knew that there were men of the pale-faced race on the lower waters of the Columbia, and one of these doubtless had told them of the book, they knew these uncouth trappers, hunters, and fishers were ungodly men in the main and not custodians of the precious volume for which their souls so ardently longed....They threaded their toilsome way by stealth through the dread Blackfoot country, scaled the perilous 'Stony' mountains, descending the eastern slope, followed the tributaries of the Missouri through the dreaded country of the Dakotas, and then pursued the windings of the Missouri till they struck the Father of Waters, arriving at St. Louis in the summer of 1832." (Parsons, p. 51)

The exhausted and virtually penniless Indian "wisemen" could not understand the white man's language or culture. It was a providential stroke of good fortune that these valiant warriors ever reached Governor William Clark, administrator of the Missouri Territory as well as Superintendent of Indian Affairs, the same

William Clark of the epic Lewis and Clark expedition. The Indians did not fare as successfully as the white man's expedition. They reportedly received blankets, beads and tobacco but failed in their endeavor to find the white man's Book of Heaven. An impassioned farewell speech conveyed to Governor Clark by one of the Indian warriors was recorded and somehow ended up in the hands of the local press:

"Our people sent us to get the white man's Book of Heaven. You took us where they worship the Great Spirit with candles, but the book was not there. You showed us the images of good spirits, and pictures of the good land beyond, but the Book was not among them to tell us the way. You made our feet heavy with burdens of gifts, and our moccasins will grow old with carrying them, but the Book is not among them. We are going back the long sad trail to our people. When we tell them, after one more snow, in the big council, that we did not bring the Book, no word will be spoken by our old men, nor by our young braves. One by one they will rise and go out in silence. Our people will die in darkness, and they will go on the long path to the other hunting grounds. No white man will go with them, and no Book of Heaven to make the way plain. We have no more words." (Parsins, p. 52) Whether this speech really occurred has never been verified, but the impact of that speech on the missionary organizations rising out of the Second Great Awakening in the east was monumental.

The feeble cry of the Indians would have died with the four warriors save for the intervention of George Catlin, a friend of Governor Clark and an artist of much renown. Catlin was also a gifted writer and although skeptical of the message until Governor Clark assured him of its authenticity, he was so moved by the unshakable mission of the Indians that he wrote an epic poem (portions of the speech quoted above) that was published in eastern religious journals, sparking the great missionary movement to the Oregon Territory. When news of the Indians' hunger for the white man's faith found in the Bible was illustrated in the *Christian Advocate*, a leading journal of the Methodist Church, a missionary fervor to bring God to the wilderness was ignited.

The early European frontiersmen and explorers documented that the Native American Indians, particularly on the Columbia Plateau, had a fundamental heritage of spiritual and religious faith and worship that acknowledged the "Great Spirit." The missionary movement to bring the Christian faith to the Native American Indians sparked great passion in Bible-based Protestant churches in the east. It is significant to note the Indian nations of the Columbia Plateau were equally moved with anticipation "awaiting the arrival of missionaries." (Brown, Ruby, p. 64)

One of the most pressing concerns of this study will be to answer the question posed by the Native America Indians. The Indians of the Columbia Plateau sincerely and fervently wanted to know and receive the white man's Book of Heaven so they could properly worship the Great Spirit. The white man's Book of Heaven came to Oregon in the form of Protestant missionaries. Tragically, the great schism of the Christian faith, birthed over three centuries before in Europe, also brought Jesuit "black coats" to contend with the Protestant missionaries for the souls of the Native Americans. The contention between the two Christian religions thrust great confusion and ultimately disaster upon the unsophisticated Cayuse.

For the most part the Native American Indians, particularly the Columbia Plateau Indians, had no cultural foundation to enable them to understand the schism that existed in the Christian faith between Protestant, Catholic and the multiple denominations and variant sects of Christianity including Mormonism. The Native Americans of the east coast of America confronted and eventually rejected missionaries sent to them because they could not comprehend this confusing schism dividing white man's Christianity. "Brother, you say is but one way to worship and serve the Great Spirit. If there is but one religion, why do you white people differ so much about it? Why not all agree, as you can all read the book?" (McLuhan, T. C., *Touch the Earth*, Pocket Book Publisher, New York, 1972, p. 61)

The Seneca Indians of New York faced this historic Christian dilemma decades before the same schism reached the Oregon Territory. "These men (the missionaries) know we do not understand their religion. We cannot read their book—they tell us different stories about what it contains, and we believe they make the book talk to suit themselves. If we had no money, no land and no country to be cheated out of these black coats would not trouble themselves about our good hereafter. The Great Spirit will not punish us for what we do not know. He will do justice to his red children." (McLuhan, p. 63)

The central issue of the schism the Seneca chief believed was caused by white man's religion would have a tragic and devastating impact on the Cayuse Indians that would lead to the massacre of most of the Protestant missionaries. The history of the schism of the Christian faith and the foundation of that faith found in the Bible, the white man's Book of Heaven, will be examined in detail in the next chapter.

Chapter 12

American Missionaries

The Board of Missions of the Methodist Episcopal Church, in response to the Indian's call for the white man's Book of Heaven, commissioned Jason Lee, a Canadian with a fervent zeal, to minister the Protestant Christian faith to the Indian nations west of the Rockies. Jason Lee was the youngest of fifteen children. His father died when he was five in 1808. He was supporting himself as a laborer by the age of thirteen. In his own words, he was "thrown upon the world without money, to provide for all my wants." (www.salemhistory.net/peoplejason_lee) He became a convert to Christianity at the age of 23 at a tent revival meeting. Although he had little education, he attended and graduated from Wilbraham Academy and began a career as a minister and teacher in 1830. He was chosen to lead the first Methodist missionary outreach to the Native Americans of the Pacific Northwest. He contracted Nathaniel Wyeth to accompany his party, which included naturalists J. K. Townsend and Thomas Nuttall. They reached the Oregon Territory under the protection of the 1834 fur caravan of Captain William Sublette.

In the summer of 1834, a company of Cayuse Indians heard the first sermon in the Pacific Northwest. The Cayuse could not understand what Lee was preaching; however, when Lee would rise, they would rise. When Lee kneeled down the Indians would follow, "maintaining the most strict and decorous silence." (Brown, Ruby, p. 64) Lee was so impressed with the Indians that he wrote in his journal, "Surely, the hand of Providence must be in it, for they presented them because we are missionaries, and at a time when two of our horses were nearly worn out." (Steber, p. 137)

Lee reached Fort Vancouver in late September and Dr. John McLoughlin persuaded the missionary to establish his ministry in the Willamette Valley. Certainly McLoughlin perceived the threat Lee represented to Hudson's Bay's sovereignty in the Oregon country. McLoughlin was a fair and righteous man in most every endeavor; however, he became a formidable opponent when the rule of the Crown was challenged. He perhaps had ulterior motives in persuading Lee to stay nearby where he could keep a close eye on the Protestant mission. McLoughlin must have been concerned that other missionaries would follow Lee in response to answering the Indians' call to learn the white man's Book of Heaven. The Hudson's Bay Company took council to develop a strategy to sustain sovereignty of the vast Oregon Territory from the new challenge of missionary Protestants from the expanding United States of America.

McLoughlin convinced Lee that the Flathead (Nez Perce) were too dangerous and he would be more successful ministering to the Kalapuya Indians of the Willamette Valley. The notable examples of the failed efforts of Boston's John Jacob Astor in 1810-12 and Captain Wyeth's failed effort in 1834-35 illustrated the fact that no American enterprise had successfully challenged the authority of the Hudson's Bay Company. Even the irresistible free spirit of the intrepid mountain men was ultimately neutralized by McLoughlin's shrewd policies. The Protestant missionaries would prove more formidable but only because the Protestant missionaries came with spiritual weapons against which the British had no answer. The most tangible evidence of the indomitable faith of the early Protestant missionaries was the courage and muster of the missionary women who answered the call to Oregon. These women would ultimately prove to be the one force the Hudson's Bay Company had no answer for.

The rigors and hardships of the Willamette missionary settlement caused Lee to call for reinforcements. The first party of reinforcements arrived by sea in 1837. In this party were many notable future Oregonians including Elijah White, who would lead the 1842 migration to Oregon, and W. H. Wilson and Alanson Beers, who would play prominent roles in the first Oregon government. In addition, Anna Maria Pittman came with two other women. Pittman would marry Jason Lee after a short courtship. These American women exercised a faith and courage that would birth the American Republic in the Pacific Northwest. Chief Factor McLoughlin had no weapon able to quench this threat to his empire.

In 1838 Lee returned to the nation's capital by sea to present a petition to establish an American territorial government in the Oregon country. Ten men from the mission, seventeen Americans living in Oregon at the time and nine French-Canadians who hoped to become U.S. citizens signed the petition. This petition represented the vast majority of Americans living in the Territory at that time. Lee brought a Native American convert with him. Unfortunately, while in New York, the only Native American convert from his mission died. To add to Lee's discouragement, all the other Indians attending his mission had either died as well or run away. Lee's travail was not finished. In New York he received news that his wife Maria died during childbirth in Oregon; the baby also perished. There were no doctors in Oregon at that time, with the exception of Dr. Marcus Whitman. Anna Maria Pittman Lee was an unsung hero of Oregon. She had the courage to come alone to the uncivilized American West and attempt to have her baby in a strange land with no medical help and no husband to support her.

In 1839, before he returned to Oregon, Lee would marry again to Lucy Thompson, a graduate of Newbury Seminary. She would accompany Lee to Oregon with the "Great Reinforcement" of 1839. On the ship to Oregon was a party of fifty with five ordained ministers. Despite the Great Reinforcement, the mission to the Indians was a dismal failure, simply because white man's diseases had virtually wiped out their population. Nevertheless, Lee presided over the first preliminary meeting for the territorial organization of the Oregon settlement in 1841 at Champoeg. In 1843, Lee led the movement to institute a provisional government. Perhaps Lee's greatest legacy was his promotion of education in Oregon and the formulation of the plan that resulted in the founding of the Oregon Institute, now known as Willamette University.

The Methodist mission board fired Lee in 1843 because the ministry failed to reach the Native Americans. Lee certainly was no stranger to hardship and setbacks so he was not defeated by this great affront against his character. His second wife in died 1842 shortly after childbirth. His daughter Lucy Anne Maria survived. Lee returned to the Methodist Mission Board to defend himself against charges of a "colonization scheme" and misappropriation of mission funds. He was exonerated of these charges and reappointed as missionary to Oregon, but sadly he died in 1845 before he could return to his beloved Oregon.

Some theologians and historians have argued that Jason Lee was the greatest Oregonian of all time and have questioned the accomplishments of other prominent missionaries, especially Dr. Marcus Whitman. The truth is all the early missionaries, explorers, mountain men and pioneer settlers had a significant part to play in the founding of the states of the Pacific Northwest. Their only peers would be the pioneer women who lived and died for Oregon as well. All of these men and women had a powerful and moving part in the history of Oregon and it is pointless to argue who was the greatest. Jason Lee was a great man and his testimony for Oregon will remain as long as the Republic of United States remains. Nevertheless, by divine providence the ministry of a second Protestant missionary force into the Oregon Territory would, in part because of its strategic location, exercise a monumental political and spiritual impact. The ramifications of the political repercussions of the Whitman Mission were so powerful that the central authority of Rome and the Vatican would send emmisarys to thwart the growth and influence of the Protestant missionaries.

The American Board of Commissioners of Foreign Missions, a Protestant church organization supported by Presbyterian, Congregationalist and Dutch Reformed churches, with no foreknowledge entered into the simmering confrontation between the two world powers for the great prize of the Oregon. Little did any American mission board understand the monumental stakes over the fate of Oregon caused by the Joint Occupation Treaty between Britain and the United States.

Reverend Samuel Parker of Ithaca, New York was the first minister to respond to the Nez Perce appeal for missionaries. The American board rejected Parker at first because of his age (54) and family commitments. Parker was persistent and finally the Board relented. Dr. Marcus Whitman of Rushville, New York was chosen to accompany Rev. Parker to explore the wilderness of the Oregon Territory and determine if it was feasible to bring the gospel to the indigenous Indians.

A young lady, a daughter of Judge Prentiss of Amity, New York, Narcissa Prentiss also volunteered but was rejected because the American board rarely sent unmarried women into a foreign field. Parker wrote of Narcissa, "Are young women wanted? A Miss Narcissa Prentiss of Amity is very anxious to go to the heathen. Her education is good—piety conspicuous—her influence is good." (Drury, Clifford, *Marcus and Narcissa Whitman and the Opening of Old Oregon*, Vol. I, Arthur H. Clark and Company, Glendale, CA, 1973, p. 110) Why would a young, highly educated woman volunteer to spend her life in the wilderness of the Pacific Northwest living with Native Americans who were considered heathen and uncivilized? To make the story more intriguing, Parker then suggested to Marcus Whitman "that he call on Narcissa and propose marriage." (Drury, Vol. I, p. 110)

Marcus Whitman was a young, handsome and skilled physician/surgeon of much renown and would have had his choice of future brides. Nevertheless, it appears that Whitman without hesitation followed up on Parker's suggestion. The young doctor wrote to the board in the midst of his exploratory mission: "I think I should wish to take a wife, if the service of the Board would admit." (Drury, Vol. I, p. 110) In actual fact Whitman proposed to Narcissa before he left New York and the American board approved the appointment of the now engaged Miss Prentiss on March 18, 1835. One of the great love stories of American history thus commenced. Narcissa would later record after their marriage in February of 1836: "We had to make love somewhat abruptly and must do our courtship now we are married." (Drury, Vol. I, p. 111) Narcissa's courtship and extended honeymoon was the maiden voyage of the first white woman (with Eliza Spalding) to cross the Rocky Mountains into the unknown expanse of the Oregon Territory. Thanks to the splendid research of the letters over a 49-year period of time by Dr. Clifford Drury, this heart-warming love story of Marcus and Narcissa Whitman grows in magnitude as the story progresses.

Marcus Whitman was not just a country doctor, but rather a well-trained physician-surgeon trained under eminent professors including the renowned physician Dr. John Delamater. In those days a doctor's degree and license was much easier to obtain than a ministry degree and license. When a man aspired to be a doctor he began his studies under a local physician who would take the student with him when calling upon his patients. This practice was referred to as "riding with the doctor." Whitman began riding with Dr. Ira Bryant sometime in the fall of 1823 at the age of 21. Whitman entered Fairfield College of Physicians and Surgeons in the fall of 1825 and finished the 16-week course in the spring of 1826. "At that time this school was one of the best medical colleges in the nation....The assumption is that he must have had at least two years' experience with Dr. Bryant." (Drury, Vol. I, p. 74) To obtain an M.D. degree required a second 16-week course, something fewer than half of the doctors of the land achieved. Whitman was licensed in both New York and Canada and practiced medicine in frontier communities for three years with great success. Notwithstanding his medical credentials, his passion was Christian ministry and he retired from his medical profession for a season to enter into theological studies. Ill health forced him to return to his medical practice and Whitman returned to Fairfield to obtain his M.D. degree under the eminent surgeon and teacher Dr. John Delamater in 1832. Doctor Whitman "was a well-trained physician and much better qualified than the average doctor of his day." (Drury, Vol. I, p. 78). Doctor Whitman was headed toward a distinguished career in the medical profession when Rev. Parker's zeal for the mission to the Columbia Plateau Nez Perce touched his heart.

Whitman and Parker on their maiden voyage to Oregon arrived late and were fortunate to be included in the caravan of the American Fur Company under the leadership of Lucien Fontenelle. The caravan left St. Louis in March of 1835 en route to the Green River Rendezvous. The temperate and Sabbath-observing Christians were a poor match for the rough free trappers. They were ridiculed for not traveling on Sunday. Parker wrote of the growing hostility of the free trappers who "so disliked the restraint which our presence imposed upon them that, as they afterwards confessed, they plotted our death & intended on the first convenient occasion to put this purpose into execution." (Drury, Vol. I, p. 119) Whitman also wrote about the growing animosity within the fur company, the rotten eggs they threw at him, and his ill health caused by being forced to compensate for Parker's refusal to help in cooking or packing animals. Things did not look very favorable for the forlorn missionaries or the future of the Protestant mission to old Oregon.

Once again the hand of the Almighty intervened in the affairs of men when a sinister and deadly outbreak of dreaded cholera struck the caravan. Whitman wrote on June 19, "There have been several new cases of cholera each day and one death last night. Mr. Fontenelle is sick with cholera." (Drury, Vol. I, p. 123) Parker recorded in his journal, "Three of the company died; and several others barely survived, through the blessing of God upon the assiduous attentions of Doct. Whitman, my associate, and the free use of powerful medicines. And had it not been for his successful practice, the men would have dispersed, and the caravan would have failed of going to the place of rendezvous....The medical skill of the doctor converted those (who had been hostile) into permanent friends." (Drury, Vol. I, p. 124)

Needless to say, from this point forward no more rotten eggs came the direction of the missionaries and even Parker was held in respect because of his highly esteemed associate Dr. Whitman. Marcus Whitman's name, somehow soiled in history's assessment because of the political controversy regarding the Whitman Massacre, was not held with such fickle apprehension among the now famous mountain men of the Rendezvous of 1835. The legendary Jim Bridger sought out Dr. Whitman to remove an arrow in his back he had been carrying for three years. "It was a difficult operation, because the arrow was hooked at the point by striking a large bone and a cartilaginous substance had grown around it. The Doctor pursued the operation with great self-possession and perseverance; and his patient manifest equal firmness." (Drury, Vol. I, p. 134) Dr. Drury points out the blessed benefit of anesthesia had yet to be discovered. These men understood the meaning of courage. Needless to say, Dr. Whitman's fame as a medicine man in due season knew no bounds among the mountaineers and even among the Indians. Parker writes, "His reputation becoming favorably established, calls for medical and surgical aid were almost incessant." (Drury, Vol. I, p. 134) It is interesting to note most of the glowing accounts of the exploits of Marcus Whitman on this exploratory expedition come from the journal of a fellow missionary who did not appreciate his fellow missionary's ways and manners.

Dr. Whitman and Rev. Samuel Parker shared a passion for souls but little else and they soon parted company west of the Rocky Mountains. It seems that Rev. Parker could not tolerate what he considered the slovenly manner of Dr. Whitman. (Gray, p. 108) A fellow missionary, William Henry Gray, in company on

Oil painting by David Manuel. This painting depicts Marcus Whitman being mocked and ridiculed by frontier mountain men.

the maiden expedition described Whitman as "a man of easy, don't-care habits, that could become all things to all men, and yet a sincere and earnest man, speaking his mind before he thought the second time, giving his views on all subjects without much consideration, correcting and changing them when good reasons were presented, yet when fixed in his pursuit of an object, adhering to it with unflinching tenacity….Dr. W. was a man that could accommodate himself to circumstances; such as dipping the water from the running stream with his hand, to drink; having but a hunter's knife (without a fork) to cut and eat his food; in short could rough it without qualms to the stomach." (Gray, p. 108) Whitman's temperament, predisposed to a deep spiritual commitment, unyielding courage, and medical expertise, would be sorely tested by untamed and untested principalities and spiritual dominions of the highest echelons in the pristine lands of the Pacific Northwest.

It was a daunting challenge to the most fearless and manly of missionaries to set up a mission and ministry amidst the uncivilized (in white man's eyes) indigenous Indians of the wilderness. Finding a Protestant missionary woman willing to marry such a man and accompany him to a life amidst what the white man considered savages of the unknown wilderness was another matter. On the surface this assignment appeared improbable if not impossible.

Narcissa Whitman of Steuben County, New York was a young lady of refined manners brought up in the comparative comfort of upscale New York. Narcissa was a most unlikely candidate for such an imposing call. She grew up in a strong Protestant Christian household, a member of a Presbyterian Church that zealously supported missions. It was written of Narcissa as a young lady: "No one devoted more time on personal efforts to win souls to Christ than Narcissa." (Drury, Vol. I, p. 105) Narcissa made a commitment in response to Rev. Parker's preaching to answer the call to the Nez Perce at a different church but in the same time frame as Marcus Whitman. By the standards of the hour Narcissa at age 27 was already considered an old maid, although she had rejected many proposals for marriage, including that of Rev. Henry H. Spalding, her soon-to-be fellow Oregon missionary traveling companion.

Narcissa maintained a commanding appearance, with light hair, fresh complexion and light blue eyes that radiated strength and conviction. She was considered a fine noble-looking woman, affable and free to converse with all she met. In short, the world was before her. She moved among the best of religious society and was forward to converse, especially in attention to gentlemen. One can only imagine the intimate details when the energetic young doctor came calling to seek Narcissa's hand in marriage. Marcus was proposing marriage because Narcissa had made a public commitment to go to the wilderness to reach the indigenous Indians for Christ. This was an intriguing yet most unorthodox foundation for a great love story. Unfortunately very few historical documents shed any further light on the courtship of Marcus Whitman and Narcissa Prentiss. At this point it is well left to the imagination of the reader to fill in the blanks of the intimate details of this inspiring yet tragic love story.

Only known portrait of Narcissa Whitman.

What moved Narcissa Whitman and Eliza Spalding, wife of Rev. H. H. Spalding, to take their place in history as the first American white women to journey overland across the continent? The Hudson's Bay Company had successfully withstood every challenge the upstart Americans had thrown at them. The Yankees had defeated the Crown in the Revolutionary War and the War of 1812 but had yet to mount the faintest challenge to the sovereignty of the mighty British Union Jack in the Oregon Territory. It appeared by the hour of the Protestant missionaries most of the American mountain men and fur traders had either been killed by Indians, joined the English fur company or given up and gone home. The Crown had an answer to every challenge the intrepid and fearless Americans could muster, every challenge except two harmless white missionary women willing to live in the wilderness domain of the Native American Indians. Two exceedingly courageous white American Protestant missionaries and the women who would follow them demonstrated for the entire world that families could live in the previously labeled no man's land of the Oregon Territory. These two gentle missionaries were one challenge the British had no answer for.

Once again we are moved to consider Oregon historian Horace Lyman's axiom: "Whatever the opinion of the intelligent individual as to the objective reality of religious opinion, it cannot be ignored by the historian that there is no other such universal sentiment as religious faith." (Lyman, Vol. I, p. 131) History has defined Narcissa Whitman and Eliza Spalding according to their actions in response to their religious faith. These two women gave up a life of position (high standing in the case of Narcissa) to live in a foreboding wilderness from which they would never return. Never again would they see their parents, brothers or sisters, friends, or homeland. Both sacrificed their health and both died young. Chief Factor McLoughlin and the Crown had no answer for the faith in God that these women were willing to lay down their lives for.

What moved these two women to give up everything they had for a lonely life of suffering amidst "heathen savages"? Their undaunted courage and faith shattered the British facade of an invincible boundary to westward expansion for the emerging American Republic. These courageous missionaries were not enticed by the lure of fame and fortune, the promise of brown gold, or the need to explore and conquer the unknown. These women were moved by a faith in God no power on earth could extinguish or mortal men comprehend. At the conclusion of Marcus's and Narcissa's wedding a notable missionary son illustrated the depth of Narcissa's commitment to go to the ends of the earth if need be for the cause of Jesus Christ. The custom of Narcissa's church was to conclude the wedding service with the singing of a hymn. On this particular evening a favorite missionary hymn written by Rev. Samuel F. Smith, author of "America," concluded the ceremony.

> "Yes, my native land! I love thee;
> All thy scenes I love them well;
> Friends, connections, happy country,
> Can I bid you all farewell?
> Can I leave thee, can I leave thee,
> Far in heathen lands to dwell?
>
> Home!-thy joys are passing lovely-
> Joys no stranger-heart can tell;
> Happy home!- 'tis sure I love thee!
> Can I – can I say – Farewell?
> Can I leave thee, can I leave thee,
> Far in heathen lands to dwell?

One by one, members of the choir and congregation found their throats constricted with emotion and their cheeks dampened with tears. Only a few, including Narcissa, sang the next stanza:

> Yes! I hasten gladly,
> From the scenes I love so well;
> Far away, ye billows! Bear me;
> Lovely native land! – farewell !
> Pleased I leave thee, pleased I leave thee,
> Far in heathen lands to dwell.

Muffled sobs could be heard by the time the last stanza was reached. The sentiment of the hymn was too overpowering. Narcissa in her clear soprano voice, which Reverend Joel Wakeman described as being "as sweet and musical as a chime of bells," sang the last stanza as a solo—a dramatic event which all present that evening never forgot.

In the deserts let me labor,
On the mountains let me tell,
How he died – the blessed Savior –
To redeem a world from hell!
Let me hasten, let me hasten,
Far in heathen lands to dwell." (Drury, Vol. I, pp. 161-62)

The shadow of the Almighty, through the tear-dampened singing of a small New England Protestant church, was casting a bold uncompromising silhouette over the Oregon Territory before the missionaries ever left the shores of the Atlantic.

It is an obvious understatement to bear witness that these first American Protestant missionaries were no ordinary individuals. The Spaldings and Whitmans were uniquely called and chosen for a mission of monumental importance in the history of the United States of America and the Christian faith. A young man from Utica, New York, William Henry (W. W.) Gray, who served them as lay assistant and secular agent, joined them. W. W. Gray not only accompanied and assisted the pioneer missionaries but also remained steadfast to the cause for Oregon. Gray established himself as one of the original pioneers in Oregon's government and researched and compiled the first written history of Oregon. These five individuals had made a commitment to a cause they believed to be the only cause that mattered; still, they had no historical foundation to establish a clear idea of the monumental stakes or the price of the mission they had committed their lives to achieve. Many notable frontiersmen, explorers, and fur traders had gone before them but none with a mission to live their lives amidst the (so-called) uncivilized indigenous Indians with no support save the faith found in the Book of Heaven they came to minister.

These missionaries had no possible opportunity to renew their supplies when exhausted. Certainly the Hudson's Bay Company did not wish to see them succeed. Therefore they brought with them all the materials they deemed necessary to survive in the wilderness including supplies for a blacksmith shop, a plow, seeds, clothing, mules, horses, and sixteen cows. It must be recorded for history that these missionaries followed no road, not even a trail or track at times. The Whitman wagon train demonstrated for the first time the practicality of a wagon road over the Rocky Mountains. "Ashtley, Bonneville, and Bridger had taken wagon trains into the Rocky Mountains and left them, and pronounce the experiment a failure…" (Gray, p. 118) Dr. Whitman was a visionary who understood if others were to follow he must demonstrate it was possible for a wagon train to reach the water of the mighty Columbia.

One can only imagine the intrigue and excitement the advent of the missionaries and the two white women caused to the Indians as their wagon train worked its way down the western slopes of the Rockies into the Oregon Territory. The Columbia Plateau Indians, including the Bannock, Snake, Nez Perce and Flathead, had great expectations of the missionaries' arrival promised by Rev. Parker. W. W. Gray records the excitement of the first Indians to greet the missionaries. "It was difficult to tell which was the most crazy, the horse or the rider; such hopping, hooting, running, yelling, jumping sage brush, whirling around, for they could not stop to reload their guns, but all of us as they came on gave them a salute from ours…" (Gray, pp. 118-119) When the missionaries and Indians first met they were shooting guns but not at each other. They were shooting guns in expression of unbridled joy. The missionary call of the Colombia Indians had been answered and their excitement could not be restrained.

The missionary wagon train joined a rendezvous with over a hundred American mountain men and hunters and perhaps fifty Frenchmen with the Hudson's Bay Company in an extensive valley on the Snake River near the forks of the Green River and Horse Creek. Over six hundred Columbia Plateau Indians joined the rendezvous, making the event the first major cultural event of the new age in the Oregon Territory. This rendezvous drew together the three major nations vying for the prize of the Pacific Northwest with the Protestant missionaries destined to play the crucial role. The Indians were particularly curious about the white women, passing and re-passing their tent in hopes of gaining sight of the ladies. The seasoned mountain men were equally impressed with the unprecedented advent of the two white Protestant missionaries. "No one except an eye-witness, can appreciate or fully understand the charm there was in those days in the sight of the form and white features of his mother. The rough veteran mountain hunter would touch his hat in a manner absolutely ridiculous, and often fail to express a designed compliment, which the mischief or good-humor of Mrs. Whitman sometimes enjoyed as a good joke." (Gray, p. 123)

Shortly thereafter the missionaries met a small party of Hudson's Bay men under the command of John L. McLeod and Thomas McKay along with Captain Nathaniel Wyeth. The Company had squeezed Wyeth out of business after two overland journeys to Oregon as a trader and forced him to sell Fort Hall near present-day Pocatello, Idaho. McKay was the stepson of Dr. John McLoughlin the Chief Factor of Fort Vancouver, the viceroy of British power in the Oregon Territory. McKay discerned in a moment what the missionaries could not yet comprehend. "Only two women at Rendezvous!...Their very presence proved that the Rocky Mountains were no longer a barrier to American emigration....Where two women could go on horseback other women could follow in covered wagons—wives, mothers, sisters, and daughters. The coming of families meant the establishment of homes, schools, churches, and inevitably the formation of a civil government under the jurisdiction of the United States....Hence his remark, 'There is something that Doct. McLoughlin cannot ship out of the country so easy..'" (Drury, Vol. I, p. 199)

It is difficult for the contemporary American to comprehend the commitment of these pioneer missionaries and those that followed in their tracks. Other than the Hudson's Bay forts along the way, separated by arduous weeks of travel, there were no stores along the trail. There was no shelter, provision, food, merchandise, running water, motel rest stop or welcome party awaiting them. One could imagine how Narcissa was cloyed with fresh meat. There are only so many ways one could cook meat. Narcissa provided more insight: "We have plenty of dry Buffalo meat which we purchased of the Indians & dry it is for me. I can scarcely eat it, it appears so filthy, but it will keep us alive, and we ought to be thankful for it....Do not think I regret coming. No, far from it. I would not go back for a world. I am contented and happy notwithstanding I sometimes get very hungry and weary." (Drury, Vol. I, pp. 200-201)

The standard twentieth-century history of the western expansion of the American Republic pays only passing and condescending commendation to Narcissa Whitman and Eliza Spalding. In historical truth the foundation of Oregon Territory as a vital portion of the United States of America's heritage was built upon these missionaries and the pioneer emigrants who volunteered to follow in their tracks, accepting similar privations and hardships without number.

Narcissa's wedding trip, with Marcus bringing the first wagon as far west as Fort Boise near the present Oregon border, was no honeymoon. She demonstrated the grit necessary to be his helpmate on this trip. Narcissa repeatedly mentioned in her diary the difficulties facing the men, especially as they labored to take the wagon train over terrain never before traveled by wagon wheels. Marcus must have known he was breaking trail for other American wagon trains to follow even though the rest of the company considered him stubborn and unreasonable. On July 25 Narcissa writes, "Husband has had a tedious time with the wagon today. Got set in the creek this morning while crossing, was obliged to wade considerably in getting it out. After that in going between two mountains, on the side of one so steep that it was difficult for the horses to pass, the wagon was upset twice. Did not wonder at this at all. It was a greater wonder that it was not turning a somerset continually. It is not very grateful to my feelings to see him wear out with such excessive fatigue as I am obliged to….All the most difficult part of the way he has walked in his laborious attempt to take the wagon over." (Drury, Vol. I, p. 201)

Narcissa shared her frustration that some in the company must have been feeling. "One of the axle trees of the wagon broke today. Was a little rejoiced, for we were in hopes they would leave it and have no more trouble with it. Our rejoicing was in vain, however, for they are making a cart of the hind wheels this afternoon & lashing the forward wheels to it, intending to take it through in some shape or other. They are so resolute & untiring in their efforts, they will probably succeed." (Drury, Vol. I, p. 201)

Narcissa had no historical insight to understand that the Hudson's Bay Company had convinced the American government and all the powers that would influence the western migration of the American Republic that no wagon train would ever be able to traverse the impossible terrain west of the Rockies to reach the promised land of the Oregon Territory. Marcus Whitman was a fearless Moses in the wilderness leading the American nation into the Promised Land and proving that wagons carrying families of American civilization could follow in his footsteps.

Perhaps the greatest test for the missionaries was crossing the Snake River, the seventh largest river in the United States. Once again Narcissa records the drama. "Two of the tallest horses were selected to carry Mrs. S. & myself over….The last branch we rode as much as a half-mile in crossing & against the current too, which made it hard for the horses, the water being up to their sides. I once thought that crossing streams would be the most dreadful part of the journey. I can now cross the most difficult stream without the least of fear." (Drury, Vol. I, p. 205) Today even the most experienced male rider would be challenged to attempt such a feat, but these women accomplished the feat riding sidesaddle. The greater feat was Marcus Whitman's undaunted commitment to prove a wagon train; in this case a cart pulled by mules could cross the mighty Snake as well. Narcissa describes the struggle. "Both the cart & mules were capsized in the water and the mules turned upside down in the river." (Drury, Vol. I, p. 205) Whitman would not be deterred by broken wheels, somersaulting wagons, drowning mules or mighty river torrents. Once he set his mind to the task there would be no turning back. W. W. Gray called Whitman's passion a "crazy undertaking" (Drury, Vol. I, p. 206) yet even though he finally abandoned the cart at Fort Boise near the present Oregon border his perseverance had opened the trail for the great Western migration. Whitman had proved it was possible for a wheeled wagon to cross the desert between the Blue Mountains and the Rockies.

Narcissa had no understanding of the larger drama that was unfolding with the wagon cart, nor could any of the pioneer missionary party save for the visionary Marcus Whitman. As documented previously, the British Hudson's Bay Company ruled the vast Oregon country from the western slopes of the Rocky Mountains to the Pacific Ocean, as far north as the Russian possession of Alaska and as far south as the Mexican territory of California. Even the moderate powers in American government such as Thomas Jefferson, Henry Clay and Daniel Webster demonstrated little interest in extending American sovereignty as far as the wilderness of Oregon. In 1825 Senator Thomas Hart Benton of Missouri wrote, "The natural western boundary should be the ridge of the Rocky Mountains." (Farnham, Thomas J., *History of the Oregon Territory*, p. 5) In defense of these statesmen it must be noted that the British Hudson's Bay Company had accomplished its purpose in convincing the powers that be in Washington, D.C. that large-scale overland emigration across the Rockies and through the most formidable wilderness of the Oregon Territory and especially the rugged Blue Mountains was impossible and the land was largely inhabitable. The façade of the invincibility of the natural boundaries to the Oregon Territory was forever shattered by the bravery and uncompromising faith of these Protestant missionaries.

Two of the Indians, old Takkensuitas and Ish-hol-hol-hoats-hoast (Lawyer), brought a letter from Rev. Parker communicating the kindness of the Indians at Walla Walla. The Hudson's Bay Company at Walla Walla demonstrated bitter animosity toward the American missionary but the Nez Perce took him in and treated him kindly and entreated him to bring more missionaries. The kindness of the Indians at Walla Walla was not lost on the Whitmans. Narcissa's diary, which she never intended for the public eye, presents a touching description of that momentous missionary journey to Walla Walla from the rendezvous. "We commenced our journey to Walla Walla July 18, 1836, under the protection of Mr. McLeod & his company....On the 19th did not move at all. 20th. Came twelve miles…over many steep & high mountains….I thought of Mother's bread & butter many times as any hungry child would, but did not find it on the way. I fancy pork & potatoes would relish very well. Have been living on fresh meat for two months exclusively. Am cloyed with it. I do not know how I shall endure this part of the journey." (Drury, Vol. I, p. 200)

The Treaty of Ghent between Britain and the United States in 1814 cemented the terms of peace, while the treaty of Joint Occupancy provided equal rights of trade and settlement in Oregon until a final settlement of the title to the sovereignty of the Oregon Territory could be determined. On paper the fate of Oregon was open to whichever nation could sustain a successful claim; it remained that way for nearly thirty years, with negligible enthusiasm from any American save a small remnant of fur traders, frontiersmen, romantics, legislators and missionaries. In the Oregon Territory in the midst of the political vacuum that the Treaty of Ghent established, the uncontested power of the British Hudson's Bay monopoly continued to proliferate. There was only one obstacle to complete British control. This obstacle could best be described as a Trojan horse in the form of the free men Protestant missionaries now firmly planted in the belly of the British monopoly.

Chapter 13

The Clash Between Protestants and Roman Catholics in Oregon

With the advent of the Protestant missionaries, the final bell rang for the decisive round in the three hundred year quest for the Oregon Territory. For most of the contest the yet-to-emerge United States of America had not even existed to contend for the prize. The very fact the free men of the Republic had even a chance at an opportunity to claim the great prize was a marvel in itself. The British-American joint occupation of 1818, reconvened in 1827, was in actual fact "grants of possession to Great Britain, or rather to her representative, the Hudson Bay Company, who after the merger with the Northwest Company had become sole occupant of the territory." (Parson, pp. 67, 68).

We have documented the ascent of the Hudson's Bay Company under the absolute authority of Dr. John McLoughlin in Chapter 9. It is important to reemphasize that McLoughlin had more power than most European kings and ruled an area larger than most kingdoms in the world. The Hudson's Bay Company was efficiently organized and maintained a line of communication and commerce the entire length of the Columbia River. The United States could claim title to the vast territory but in fact Great Britain occupied and possessed the commerce, trading posts, forts, and virtually all wealth that generated from the vast resources within. It was a joint occupation treaty in name only, and there was no American plan or strategy to reverse the absolute control Britain held over the Oregon Territory.

Dr. John McLoughlin, the Chief Factor of the Hudson's Bay Company, has been widely acknowledged as the "Father of Oregon." Whether the "White-Haired Eagle," as the Indians knew him, merited this lofty designation will be left to the discerning reader to determine at the conclusion of the story. At the very least there can be no dissent regarding this powerful autocrat in respect to the magnanimous impact for good Dr. McLoughlin impressed upon the Oregon Territory during the age of his reign on the Columbia from 1824 to 1846.

When McLoughlin arrived at the mouth of the Columbia River the Oregon Territory was in turmoil, primarily because of the destructive war of attrition between the two British trading monopolies. The Indian population in the Oregon Territory was in excess of 100,000 and more than 30,000 lived along the banks of the Columbia. For the most part the Native Americans were now somewhat hostile toward the European intruders and most crafty in their dealings after years of learning white man's ways. These Columbia Indians now possessed two lethal weapons, alcohol and firearms, that boded evil for the future of the Oregon Territory.

With no regiment of trained soldiers, McLoughlin seemingly miraculously restored order in the territory. He ended the selling of alcohol not only to the Indians but to the white man under his authority as well. He established forts and trading posts up and down the Columbia River and he administered law and justice equally to the white man and the Indian. McLoughlin administered the death sentence by hanging to Indians, Hudson's Bay men and Boston men equally. The result was peace in the Territory. There were no Indian wars during McLoughlin's tenure as Chief Factor. The result was that goods could move up and down the Columbia River and its tributaries without duress and commerce prospered. "Under joint-occupancy it was doubtful if either the laws of the United States or of Great Britain were in force in the Oregon country, [therefore] it was necessary for someone to assume supreme power and authority over the Indians..." (Holman, Frederick V., *Dr. John McLoughlin*, Arthur H. Clark Co., Cleveland, Ohio, 1907).

The providentially large shadow of Dr. John McLoughlin was the perfect answer to bring peace and justice to the entire Oregon Territory. He ruled as a despot, with unchallenged authority, but he ruled fairly and with equality for all three nations and peoples in every arena save one. "But woe to the American who attempted to trade with the Indian, to trap, hunt, or do anything which brought him into competition with the British corporation." (Parsons, p. 44) Many pioneer American entrepreneurs attempted to compete with the powerful monopoly. Jedediah S. Smith with the Rocky Mountain Fur Company, William Bonneville with a company of one hundred and ten men, and Captain Nathaniel J. Wyeth, who established two trading posts, all failed, essentially ending American fur trade west of the Rocky Mountains. By the time of the advent of the American missionaries, McLoughlin and the Company's representatives were seeking a new license with expanded privileges. "In enforcing its request, it pointed boastfully to its efficient services in successfully crushing out American enterprises, and in strengthening the British title to the territory....Six permanent establishments it had on the coast, and the sixteen in the interior, beside the migratory and hunting parties; to its marine of six armed vessels; to its large pasture and grain fields..." (Parsons, p. 46)

The Union Jack was firmly entrenched from the Rocky Mountains to the Pacific Ocean as far south as San Francisco and as far north as the Russian trading posts near present-day Alaska. The storied mountain men and the most hearty and enterprising American entrepreneurs could not successfully sustain their penetration into the iron grip of the British Empire under Chief Factor Dr. McLoughlin.

The most unlikely threat to her majesty's kingdom came in the most unpretentious and modest form. The two monumental figures in the history of the Oregon Territory were about to collide. Marcus Whitman, the man heralded by many as the "Savior of Oregon," and John McLoughlin, the man heralded as the Father of Oregon, actually established the most amicable relationship based on mutual respect. The very fact these two great men held each other in such high esteem was a testimony of both men's character. Both men were defined as virtuous and incorruptible. The great defining line of demarcation between the two men was that Marcus Whitman represented the Protestant principles of the American Revolution of free men under the Bible while John McLoughlin represented the monarchy of King George III of indentured servants under the Catholic Pope. McLoughlin and Whitman worked almost paradoxically together to author the emerging American state of Oregon, because the diametrically opposite spiritual and religious forces they represented had been locked in mortal conflict for men's souls since the Protestant Reformation.

The Whitman mission established at Walla Walla in 1837 near the banks of the Columbia River stood in solitary spiritual defiance of twenty thriving British Hudson's Bay forts and trading posts. Nonetheless, the impact of the positive character of these great men caused the Protestant mission and the Hudson's Bay Company to work cooperatively to bring order and civilization to the Oregon Territory. Friends or not, the political, social and religious undercurrent remained; the Protestant Reformation and the Catholic Counter Reformation were facing each other like two massive engines on one train track, and a thunderous head-on collision was inevitable. To understand why this collision was unavoidable the reader must understand the roots of both the Protestant Reformation and the Jesuit Counter Reformation.

Historically, the Protestant Reformation stood for liberty of conscience, freedom of speech, democratic institutions, social reform, religion based on the Bible and popular education. The Catholic Counter Reformation stood for absolute authority of the state and church over the individual and diametrically opposed free education and democratic institutions. The Council of Trent (1545-63) under the leadership of the Jesuits condemned the doctrines of "grace" of the Reformers. The Fourth session in April of 1546 condemned freedom of speech, freedom of conscience and freedom of the press. "Furthermore, to check unbridled spirits, it decrees that no one relying on his own judgment shall, in matters of faith and morals pertaining to the edification of Christian doctrine, distorting the Holy Spirit in accordance with his own conceptions, presume to interpret them contrary to sense which holy mother Church, to whom it belongs to judge of their true sense and interpretation…" (Fourth Session, Council of Trent, April 8, 1546)

The Protestant doctrines of "grace" threatened the very fabric of the Catholic Church.

Marcus and Narcissa Whitman stood for a religious principle that was at the heart of the Protestant Reformation and the American Revolution. That principle was liberty and freedom based upon every individual's free access to the Bible, the only and true word of God. Oregon had developed Protestant spiritual strongholds through the establishment of the Lee (Willamette), Whitman (Walla Walla), Spalding (Lapwai), Eells (Spokane) and Walker (Spokane) missions.

The reader must be reminded that the great inroads won by the Protestant reformers in Europe at the beginning of the Protestant Reformation had been over time systematically and ruthlessly crushed by the brutal force of the Jesuits, the militant wing of the Catholic Counter Reformation. Had the Catholic Church allowed the reforms to go unchallenged the Papacy would have been fatally wounded. Wherever the Protestant reformers were to go the Jesuits were sure to follow. "In France they [Jesuits] were responsible for St. Bartholomew's Massacre, Persecution of the Huguenots, revocation of the Toleration Edict of Nantes, and the French Revolution. In Spain, Netherlands, South Germany, Bohemia, Austria, Poland, and other countries, they led the massacre of untold multitudes. By these methods they stopped the Reformation in Southern Europe, and virtually saved the Papacy from ruin." (Halley, Henry H., *Halley's Bible Handbook*, Zondervan Publishing House, Grand Rapids, Mich., 1962, p. 887)

To be fair, Halley also documents that Protestants have also persecuted Catholics, although the massacres killed "at most not over a few thousand; but to Rome, untold millions." (Halley, p. 901) There are no records that indicate the extent of knowledge that Marcus or Narcissa had been taught about the history of the Jesuits and their founder Spaniard Ignatius Loyola. Nonetheless, after the successful establishment of their Protestant mission the Whitmans wrote often about their growing concern about Romanism and the Papists' "black-robed priests" that came against them. The Protestant reformers believed that Romanism was "a permanent political conspiracy against all the most sacred rights of man and the most holy laws of God." (Chiniquy, Father, *Fifty Years in the Church of Rome*, Toronto Willard Tract Depository, Toronto, Canada, 1887, p. 4) It is crucial for the discerning student of history to take an unbiased look at both the Protestant missionaries and the Jesuit movement particularly as it pertains to America and the Oregon Territory and the impact of this religious order on the Protestant missionaries. The bloody and horrific story of the Whitman massacre, for over a century and a half, has demanded answers that virtually all 20th century historians have failed to research using primary resources and the testimony of the survivors.

At this point in the drama it is once again imperative to reestablish the fundamental guiding principle of this study. The purpose of this research is to seek the truth, the whole truth and nothing but the truth. All the key players in the drama about to unfold were acting according to the principles of the organization or church they had made a commitment to serve. It would be a mistake to assume that Protestant and Catholic values that caused this tragedy have remained entrenched and unyielding. At the beginning of the twenty-first century most Catholic and Protestant Christians stand for the same principles of liberty and justice that the American nation was founded upon. Nevertheless historical integrity demands that the 19th century conflict between Protestants and Catholics/Jesuits be documented according to unbiased historical documents. The Whitman massacre was the result of this classic confrontation between the two faiths that have changed significantly in the past century and a half. Unfortunately the primary cause and impact of the Whitman massacre has never been resolved to this day leaving a cloud of confusion over the Pacific Northwest and the American nation to the present hour.

Chapter 14

The Difference Between Jesuit and Catholic Priests and Their Tragic Impact in Oregon

Most historians do not differentiate between Jesuit and Catholic priests. Dr. Clifford Drury documented that only the pioneer Romanist Peter De Smet was a Jesuit and the rest of the Papal missionaries sent to Oregon were Catholic. The work of Dr. Gilbert Garraghan, a research professor at the Institute of Jesuit History at Loyola University in Chicago, has demonstrated that Dr. Drury was in error on this issue. This research will refer to Garraghan's book, *The Jesuits of the Middle United States*, to demonstrate why all the Romanist missionaries sent into Old Oregon were Jesuits and why the differentiation was essential to understand Oregon history.

American theologian Isaac J. Lansing identified the Jesuit order as "the very core of Romanism in its purpose and its policy." (Lansing, Isaac J., *Romanism and the Republic*, Arnold Publishing Co., Boston, Mass., 1890, p. 43) Lansing stressed that the Society of Jesus (Jesuits) began under the brilliant leadership of Ignatius Loyola who, like the Protestant missionaries, forsook friends, family, and country to become the first general of the order. "Loyola's military experience and rigid military ideas appear everywhere in the modes of the society and its administration. Under the generals are provincials, who have the charge of a certain territory, and still lower grade of officers are called rectors; and a complete system of espionage is kept in all the events of the community where they dwell, a minute report of which is regularly and carefully sent to Rome. This has been their method for centuries and it is their method today." (Lansing, Isaac, p. 56)

It is difficult for the student of history to understand the absolute obedience to their superiors required by any adherent to the Jesuit order. By definition, at the time of the Whitman Massacre, a Jesuit could be an American but he could not hold allegiance to the ideals or Constitution of the United States of America. It is essential for the student of history to comprehend the consequences, especially to the American Protestant missionaries, of such absolute obedience to a foreign power, in this case to Rome and the Pope. Loyola wrote, "Obedience should be so absolutely passive that one should be like a dead body moved only by the will of another, or like the staff in the hands of an old man." (Lansing, Isaac, p. 51)

The letters of the Protestant missionaries reveal they understood the Romanists were Jesuits that operated as Papal operatives strategically placed and absolutely directed by their general at the Vatican in Rome. "This rule of absolute obedience, to go anywhere and perform any service at the command of the superior, is now fully enforced." (Lansing, Isaac, p. 51) The difference in vows between a Protestant and a Jesuit are illustrative of the extreme difference between the two opposing forces. A Protestant makes a personal vow and public confession to make Jesus Christ Lord and Savior and honor the absolute and final authority of the Word of God according to the dictates of his conscience. The vow that a Protestant takes promotes equality, liberty and freedom through submission of the will to Jesus Christ. The oath of a Jesuit is equally binding but to a different source. "Every Jesuit is bound by the constitution of the society and a solemn oath, or vow to poverty, chastity and obedience. To these is added, in the case of the so-called 'professed,' a fourth vow of absolute obedience to the Pope. Not all Jesuits take these vows, but only according to the grade to which they attain in the society." (Lansing, Isaac, p. 49)

    Eric Jon Phelps, in his excellently documented volume *Vatican Assassins*, has revealed a most chilling aspect of the Jesuit vows at the highest echelon. At this highest level the Jesuit takes a secret blood oath whereby the most ardent adherent must "promise and declare that I will, when opportunity presents, make and wage relentless war, secretly or openly, against all heretics, Protestants and Liberals, as I am directed to do, to extirpate and exterminate them from the face of the whole earth; and that I will spare neither age, sex or condition; and that I will hang, burn, waste, boil, flay, strangle and bury alive these infamous heretics, rip up the stomachs and wombs of their women and crush their infants' heads against the walls, in order to annihilate forever their execrable race." (Phelps, Eric Jon, *Vatican Assassins*, Halcyon Unified Services, 2001, p. 85) The history of post-Protestant Europe confirmed the result of the Catholic Counter Reformation led by the Jesuits. "For conspiracy, machinations and evil designing, the Jesuits have been banned necessarily from almost every state in Europe....Every nation in Europe has legislated against them." (Lansing, Isaac, p. 57)

    How have the Jesuits been able to wield this worldly power? The Jesuit priests do not carry arms nor do they occupy high positions of authority. Their vows do not even allow them to accept positions of authority in the church without special dispensations. Ex-Jesuit priest Father Chiniquy wrote copiously regarding the impact of the Jesuit order in the world in the form of Romanism. "Romanism under the mask of religion is nothing but a permanent political conspiracy against all the most sacred rights of man and the most holy laws of God." (Chiniquy, p. 4)

    Theologian Lansing's research has illustrated that the vows that the Jesuits take all fall under the principle that the end justifies the mean. "The vow of obedience to the Pope, the fourth and last of these vows, taken by the highest members of the profession, has been kept only when the Pope was obedient to the will of the Jesuits. Loyola himself, by diplomacy and evasion, contended with the Pope, and won his point too. Again and again in the history of the society the clashing of the Papal will with the will of the General of the Jesuits has resulted in the submission or ruin of the Pope. Several Popes have died, apparently by poisoning, at the hand of the order, who vowed obedience to them...Sixtus V, Urban VII, Clement VIII, and Clement XIV." (Lansing, Isaac, p. 52)

    The Jesuit order was banned in Europe but the suppression of Romanism in Europe did not end the Catholic Counter Reformation. "The unscrupulous methods of the society, which has caused prince and Pope and legislator to lay upon them their heavy hand, has never been condemned by the Jesuits nor have they ceased to practice them. But where did the banished Jesuits go?...I answer, I answer to the United States." (Lansing, Isaac, p. 58)

CHAPTER 15

THE WHITMAN MISSION

Reverend David Greene, superintendent of Indian missions of the American Board, gave these final instructions to the Whitmans in the beginning of their missionary work in the wilderness. "Let your conduct be unblameable, exemplary & free from the appearance of evil. Do not feel it necessary to be the forward reprover of everything wrong among this class of persons, remembering that your business is almost exclusively with the Indians. While you are strict & uncompromising as to yr. own principles & conduct, do not be harsh & dictatorial to others. Do them good & be kind to all as you have opportunity. Let Christian love shine brightly in all that you do….Let all yr worldly and secular concerns be as limited and compact as yr circumstances will permit….May…yr mission be a life from the dead to the benighted tribes of the remote west." (Drury, Vol. I, p. 169,70)

The historical record of the Protestant missionaries with respect to their treatment of the Pacific Northwest Indians bears the fruit of adherence of Greene's exhortation. Even the adversarial Hudson's Bay Company commended the American Calvinist missionaries, "who voluntarily came forward and pledged themselves not to trade furs." (Drury, Vol. I, p. 170) Whitman and Spalding met with Chief Factor John McLoughlin at Fort Vancouver and determined to establish two missions: the Whitmans' with the Cayuse near Fort Walla Walla and the Spaldings' with the Nez Perce in the Clearwater Valley and another later, Tshimakain near present-day Spokane with the Walkers.

W. W. Gray was critical of the missions' dependence upon the British. "To the disgrace of most of the missionaries, this state of absolute dependence and submission to the Hudson Bay Company…was submitted to and encouraged." (Drury, Vol. I, p. 220) In contrast, Whitman documented the warm reception McLoughlin accorded the missionaries; without the support of the Chief Factor in respect to keeping the Indians peaceful and providing necessary supplies, it is doubtful the American missions would have survived as long as they did.

It is interesting the three missions were so far apart: 120 miles to the Clearwater mission in Idaho and 140 miles to the Spokane mission from Walla Walla, the site of the Whitman mission. In actual fact the missionaries quarreled often despite the wide space between their stations, not just Whitman and Spalding but virtually every American missionary who arrived on the field. Certainly, doctrinal differences that have caused dissention among Protestant ministries from the beginning of the Reformation plagued the Oregon mission. The fact that Narcissa spurned Henry Spalding's marriage proposal turned out to be a wound that caused the missionary enterprise much anguish in the early years. Human frailties such as jealousy, stubbornness, unforgiveness, and misunderstandings caused turmoil and unrest among even these legendary pioneer missionaries. The stark, on the ground, reality of the Oregon Calvinist mission was a portrait of great

Painting of the Whitman Mission, 1847

suffering and loneliness and deprivation for the missionaries. They had scant support from the Christian community in the East and therefore they were forced to depend almost entirely on their own efforts and their sometimes disgruntled fellow missionaries and ultimately their faith in the Almighty. Letters home took over two years to be answered at best. The vast distance between the missions required the missionary doctor Whitman to ride days upon days to care for the medical needs of his co-laborers and Indians. He spent months of each year in the saddle.

The maiden overland honeymoon journey of the Whitmans ended abruptly with the reality of establishing a pioneer Christian mission in the midst of the wilderness. Narcissa's great comfort and strength was her Marcus. "I should like to whisper in Mother's ear many things which I cannot write. If I could only see her in her room for one half hour. This much, Dear Mother, I have one of the kindest Husbands and the very best every way." (Drury, Vol. I, p. 171) On August 27, 1836 on reaching the Grand Ronde Valley Narcissa wrote in her diary: "My husband who is of the best the world ever knew is always ready to provide a comfortable shade with one of our saddle blankets spread upon some willows or sticks placed in the ground." (Drury, Clifford, *Where Wagons Could Go*, University of Nebraska Press, Lincoln, NE, 1997, p. 90).

Indeed, Marcus was not only a skilled physician and zealous missionary to the Indians, but by necessity he became a farmer, a horticulturalist, a builder, a teacher, and a loving husband. The ardent patriotic passion of the Whitmans caused the Waiilatpu mission to become the central point between the States and the Columbia River in the great westward immigrant migration to Oregon. Soon the problem of loneliness was replaced by the larger problem of never-ending guests arriving, many desperately, at their

David Manuel painting of Marcus Whitman teaching Cayuse Indians

doorstep. The Whitman home, of necessity, became a convalescent home and hospital for weary and sick immigrants. These usually destitute frontiersmen included French Canadian trappers, Indians, Hudson's Bay men, adventurers and fellow missionaries. One can only imagine the strain of taking strangers into a cramped and primitive pioneer home. Home in this case could be termed a bit idealistic. One such visitor, Sarah Smith, described the Whitman home in her diary in 1838: "The Doctor's house would be considered in the States a very rough one. Part of it is log & part dobie or dried clay. One side of it has partly fallen down & [is] propped up with large poles. Some of the floors are nailed & some of them loose boards & all unplanned. But we are glad to find a home in so comfortable a place." (Drury, Vol. I, p. 330)

To draw a picture of the frustration the Whitmans sometimes endured, the reader needs to imagine a typical evening around the open fireplace in the kitchen where strangers and fellow missionaries would congregate to stay warm while Narcissa was preparing dinner. A typical evening in the Whitman home would include fellow missionary sister Elkanah Walker spitting chewing tobacco into the open fireplace because the Whitmans did not have a spittoon. The Whitmans had given their bedroom to a destitute immigrant couple. We can only imagine the strain on Narcissa. She had been overjoyed with the reinforcement of new missionaries, but constrained with new doctrinal burdens. "They think it wrong for females to pray in the presence of men, and do not allow it even in our small circle here. This has been a great trial to me, and I have almost sunk under it….[They] plead the necessity for wine, tobacco, etc. and now how do you think I have lived with such folks right in my kitchen for the whole winter." (Drury, Vol. I, pp. 333, 334)

David Manuel painting of the Drowning of Clarissa Whitman

Narcissa's strength and comfort was Marcus, but the duties of a frontier doctor took him away for weeks and sometimes months at a time. A wonderful blessing that made their troubles pale in comparison came when Narcissa gave birth to a child, Alice Clarissa, on March 14, 1837. The baby became the joy of the Whitman household. Narcissa wrote to her sister Jane, "Yes, Jane, you cannot know how much of a comfort our little daughter, Alice Clarissa, is to her father and mother. O, how many melancholy hours she has saved me, while living here alone so long, especially when her father is gone for so many days together." (Drury, Vol. I, p. 350)

Whitman and Spalding introduced the hoe and plow and taught the Indians how to plant vegetables, notably corn, wheat and potatoes. Whitman had plows shipped from New England to give to the Cayuse. The missionaries knew buffalo were soon to be erased from the plains and the semi-nomadic Indians would have to learn white man's ways or languish, as had the indigenous Indians of South America. They introduced cattle and helped them start small herds. Perhaps most significantly, primarily through the work of Spalding, they reduced the Nez Perce language (also used by the Cayuse) to writing and printed primers on the first press west of the Rockies. Even Dr. Drury, ever reticent to give credit to the Whitmans and fellow missionary Henry Spalding, admitted, "No missionaries did so much for the improvement of the material welfare of the Cayuse and Nez Perce Indians as Marcus Whitman and Henry Spalding." (Drury, Vol. I, p. 243) The Hudson's Bay Company had been firmly established long before the missionaries arrived, but it was never their policy to improve the welfare or position of the indigenous native people. As Drury documented, no group of individuals did more to help the Indians bridge the gap between the primitive semi-nomadic life of the Columbia Indians to a settled agricultural lifestyle required by the westward migration of Americans than the Protestant missionaries.

By 1842 the rigors and deprivations of the mission field led to divisions and fighting among missionaries to the point where the American Prudential Missionary Committee passed a resolution to reorganize the mission, moving the Whitmans and sending the Spaldings home. The Indians were becoming confrontational and in some cases demanding the missionaries to leave their country. Marcus and Narcissa had both been physically attacked and struck by their Cayuse brethren. By 1842 Marcus and Narcissa were worn out and their health was compromised. The new missionaries sent to aid the pioneer missionaries were sometimes harsh and critical of their work and efforts. Most disheartening, Marcus and Narcissa lost their precious Alice Clarissa before her third birthday in a drowning tragedy for which both blamed themselves. Narcissa wrote to her sister Jane and brother Edward two years after Alice Clarissa's death: "The Lord has taken our own dear child away so that we may care for the poor outcasts of the country and suffering children." (Whitman, Narcissa, *Letters of Narcissa Whitman*, Ye Galleon Press, Fairfield, Washington, 2002, p. 129)

A study of the extant diaries of Narcissa and letters of both Marcus and Narcissa revealed they never yielded to the grueling years of discouragement and especially Narcissa's ill health or wrote about plans to give up. Even after Narcissa was separated for over a year from Marcus because of his trip across America in the winter of '42-43 she continued to remained committed to the cause. "So long as it pleases Him to spare my life, I should like to live for my family and the poor Indians' sake. Notwithstanding I felt such a dread to return to this place of moral darkness, after enjoying so much of civilized life and Christian privileges [at Vancouver the winter of 42-43], yet now I am here, I am happy and love my work and situation and desire to live long to see the cause of Christ advanced in this dark land. Indeed, I think I never enjoyed the privilege of being a missionary, better than this winter, although I cannot do but little if any more than instruct my family and pray for and sustain the hands of my dear husband in his labors." (Whitman, Narcissa, p. 166).

The Whitmans documented numerous altercations with the Indians over ownership of land. The Protestant ministers undertook the mission to cultivate the land for their own needs and teach the Native Americans the method and science of horticulture. The Native Americans were used to allowing their horses to roam freely and eat whatever the earth produced. Obviously the rich surplus of the Whitmans' vegetable crops was more enticing to the Indians' horses than the natural grasses of the field. The local Cayuse Indians were following the Whitmans' lead, but visiting Indians knew no such restraint. Dr. Whitman was actually struck by one such Indian, Til-ka-na-ik, who became "insolent because, when his horses were eating up our corn, I sent some Indians to catch them." (Whitman, Narcissa, p. 122) Whitman later identified Til-ka-na-ik's source of agitation because, "for the year past [he had] been practicing the ceremonies of the Papists." (Whitman, Narcissa, p. 122)

In every altercation with the Cayuse over land, Whitman always referred to "the original arrangements for us to locate here and that we did not come of ourselves, but by invitation of the Indians, and that the land was fully granted to us." (Whitman, Narcissa, p. 122) This unsubstantiated accusation against the Whitmans has continued to be voiced into the 21st century.

Chapter 16

Whitman's Ride Across America

In the fall of 1842, Marcus Whitman made a monumental journey across the American continent that Whitman and his fellow missionaries believed saved the joint missions and the Oregon Territory for America. Great controversy surrounded the reasons for this most dangerous and virtually unprecedented crossing of North America in the dead of winter. Narcissa fully supported this seemingly impossible and herculean effort that would take her precious husband away for at least a year should he be fortunate enough to survive the rigors of such a trip.

Whitman's epic ride across the continent in the dead of winter required the full support of his colleagues, who would be required to endure the following year without his support or considerable medical skills. Marcus and Narcissa both knew this trip would put both of their lives in imminent danger. In actual fact, Narcissa was attacked by a Cayuse Indian chief and forced to flee Waiilatpu soon after Marcus left. Her health was failing as the winter approached even with her physician husband by her side. Whitman faced even greater obstacles, in fact virtually insurmountable challenges as he faced his Cayuse pony eastward, all the while knowing Narcissa's health and safety would be in peril during his absence. The age of protection afforded crossing the continent by American fur traders was now over and that protection never encompassed the winter. The Indian tribes beyond the Columbia Plateau were hostile to the trespass of white men, so the return trip east across the Rockies was perilous even with the favor of spring and summer weather.

The Oregon missionaries who quarreled so disruptively from the beginning had most uncharacteristically unanimously approved this most hasty and dangerous winter ride across the continent. Why? Fellow missionary Henry Spalding, who competed with, contended against and resisted Marcus Whitman through most of their early tenure as missionaries, was later to proclaim that Whitman saved Oregon by his dramatic ride across the continent. A controversy over the impact and purpose of Whitman's ride brewed and simmered for decades after his death and was so powerful that the issue of the motive of the epic journey still raged in newspapers, churches and the United States Congress until the turn of the twentieth century. In a nutshell, Whitman and the Protestant mission he served pitted the passion of the Protestant Reformation proclaiming the liberty of free men against the contending forces of the Catholic Counter Reformation proclaiming the authority of the Papacy. If Whitman received the credit for saving Oregon due to his heroic trek across the nation, then the Protestant cause would be vindicated. The best way to undermine the Protestant cause would be to malign the reputation of the messenger. This controversy has never been resolved and remains at the very center of the true heritage of the Oregon Territory to this very hour.

Dr. Whitman, Narcissa Whitman, and Asa Lovejoy—who accompanied Marcus on his historic ride—and all of their fellow Protestant missionaries have left documents regarding the motive and purpose for this. On April 1, 1847 in a letter to Secretary Greene, Whitman explained why he made the trip. "In the fall of 1842, I pointed out to our mission the arrangements of the Papists to settle in our vicinity and that it only required these measures to be completed for us to be obliged to close our Mission operations. This was urged (by me) as a reason for me to return home & try to bring those to carry on the affairs of the Mission stations and to settle in the Country who would stand on the footing of Citizens & not as missionaries." (Drury, Vol. I, p. 472)

Lovejoy wrote regarding his initial meeting with Dr. Whitman. "The Doctor was alive to the interests of this Coast, manifesting a very warm desire to have it properly represented in Washington; and after numerous conversations with the Doctor touching the future prosperity of Oregon, he asked me one day in a very anxious manner, if I thought it would be possible for him to cross the mountains at that time of year. I told him I thought he could. He next asked, 'Will you accompany me?'" (Drury, Vol. I, p. 469)

Historians of the nineteenth century have consistently documented that the government of the United States had no knowledge of the real value of the Oregon Territory. Dr. Burgess documented what all historians of hour believed. "The element of greatest importance in the settlement of the question [the Oregon question] was of course colonization within the territory and neither party had really undertaken that....It was well for the United States that the Oregon Question did not enter into these negotiations, for down to that moment the government at Washington knew almost nothing about the character of Oregon north of the Columbia. The officers of the Hudson Bay Company had continually represented it as a worthless waste of land fit only for hunting and trapping and about wore out for those purposes. It is more than probable that the government at Washington credited these statements, and it is quite possible that in 1842 it would have compromised with England on the line of the Columbia." (Burgess, John W., *The American Historical Series 1817-1853*, Charles Scribner and Sons, New York, NY, 1897, p. 314)

Narcissa wrote to Marcus shortly after he left: "I believe the Lord will preserve me....Night and day shall my prayer ascend to Him on your behalf and the cause in which you have sacrificed the endearments of home, at the risk of your life, to see advancing, more to the honor and glory of God." (Drury, Vol. II, p. 13) What was this cause that moved Marcus to leave his wife alone among the heathen, that moved a non-missionary stranger to accompany him across the vast continent in the dead of winter? It can hardly be argued, as Mowry points out, that Lovejoy had any special interest in the Protestant mission that would cause him to risk his life to cross the continent for such a motive.

Mrs. Elkanah Walker, present at the special missionary meeting in the fall of 1842, concurred that "Dr. Whitman went east in 1842 mainly to save the country from falling into the hands of the English, as he believed there was great danger of it." (Mowry, William A., *Marcus Whitman*, Silver Burditt & Co., New York, NY, 1901, pp. 134-35) Another fellow physician, Dr. William Geiger Jr., left a written record regarding the motive of Dr. Whitman's monumental ride. "I came to this country in 1839, and was at Dr. Whitman's request in charge of his station in 1842-43, while he went east, and remained there after his return about three weeks, and had many conversations with him on the object of his going, after his return....His main object in going east was to save the country for the United States, as he believed there was great danger of its falling into the hands of England." (Mowry, p. 136)

It is important to note the reason why Dr. Whitman was careful not to speak publicly about the political motive of his trip. Mrs. Elkanah Walker addressed this issue. "Much was said about that time about the Methodist missionaries coming here, and then leaving their legitimate missionary calling to make money and for other purposes, and some disgrace was brought upon the missionary cause. Mr. Walker and associates felt that Dr. Whitman, in leaving missionary work and going on this business, was likely also to bring disgrace on the cause, and were so afraid of it that for a long time they would hardly mention that object of Dr. Whitman's mission." (Mowry, p. 135)

It is clear that Dr. Whitman and his fellow missionaries believed the cause of the Protestant mission and the cause of the United States of America were one and the same. The cause of the American Republic and the American Constitution were grounded in the same Protestant biblical principles as the cause of the American Calvinist missionaries. The missionaries knew the Protestant mission would not survive outside of the protection of the Constitution of the United States of America. The cause that Narcissa spoke of that moved Marcus to "sacrifice the endearments of home at the risk of his life" was the same cause that moved free men of the Protestant Reformation to bring justice and liberty to the world. It was the same cause that moved John Wycliffe to translate the Bible at the risk of his life so all men could have access to the truth of God. It was the same cause that moved John Huss to lay down his life rather than recant his faith and allegiance to Jesus Christ as his personal Lord and Savior in defiance of allegiance to the Pope.

With this introduction it is time to examine this legendary ride of Marcus Whitman and Asa Lovejoy. The reader is challenged to ride with Whitman and Lovejoy and feel the pulse of these two unquenchably courageous patriots as they set out on one of the most incredible journeys in American history. The twenty-first century audience needs to be reminded there was no road or trail to follow west of the Mississippi with roadside rest areas save a few forts. At Fort Hall, Whitman and Lovejoy were confronted by Indians and commanded not to continue. The Columbia Plateau Indians had foreknowledge about Whitman's ride and were aware of his patriotic purposes, and those purposes had reached pro-Jesuit Indians. Hostile Pawnee and Sioux and deep snow in the passes made it impossible to cross the Rocky Mountains through the South Pass, so Whitman headed south to Fort Santa Fe along the old Spanish Trail adding a thousand miles of previously uncharted terrain. A thousand miles on horseback would be akin to five thousand miles in a motor vehicle and that only if there was a drivable road. The thousand miles Whitman traveled in the winter bore no clear trail, and he was heavily encumbered with snow to the waist in places. The travelers picked up a guide at each fort they safely reached. The reader can only imagine the biting cold and miserable conditions the stalwart sojourners encountered. The reader has to admire the persuasive talents of Whitman to convince each Indian guide to accompany the Americans. Lovejoy kept an accurate diary of some of the travails the two encountered.

"When we had been out four or five days and were passing over high tablelands we encountered a most terrific snowstorm, which forced us to seek shelter at once. A deep ravine being near by, we quickly made for it, but the snow fell so rapidly, and the wind blew with such violence, that it was almost impossible to reach it. After reaching the ravine and cutting some cottonwood trees for our animals, we attempted such arrangements for our camp as best we could under the circumstances, and remained snowed in for some three or four days, when the storm subsided, and it cleared off intensely cold. It was with much difficulty that we made our way upon the high lands; the snow was so deep and the wind so piercing and cold, that we felt compelled to return to camp and wait a few days for a change of weather. Our next effort was more successful, and after spending several days wandering round in the snow, without making much headway, and greatly fatiguing our animals, to little or no purpose, our guide informed us that the deep snows had so changed the face of the country, that he was completely lost, and could take us no farther. This was a terrible blow to the Doctor. He was determined not to give up without another effort. And at once we agreed that the Doctor should take the guide and make his way back to the fort, and procure a new guide, and that I should remain in camp with the animals until his return, which was on the seventh day, with a new guide." (Mowry, pp. 157-58)

David Manuel painting of Marcus Whitman crossing the Colorado River in the winter of 1842-43.

    Lovejoy and Whitman and their lost guide were stranded in the midst of the Rocky Mountains in the heart of winter. The winter storm cost them over a week, their guide was lost and now Whitman was proposing that Lovejoy wait alone in a cold foreboding solitary camp trusting that Whitman would somehow make it back to Fort Uncompahgre, find another guide and convince him to do the impossible. Just making it back to Lovejoy's camp in the winter wilderness would have taken a great leap of faith both to conceive and to accomplish. Lovejoy had a faithful dog to keep him company, a dog they would be required to eat in order to survive. Lovejoy's enormous faith in the missionary doctor was rewarded; miraculously, Whitman and the new guide found Lovejoy and they were on their way again. It wasn't long until they were confronted with yet another enormous obstacle, a large menacing river filled with raging ice like barges, called at that time the Grande River, now known as the Colorado River.

    "This stream was one hundred and fifty, or two hundred yards wide, and looked upon by our guide as very dangerous to cross in its present condition. But the doctor, nothing daunted, was the first to take the water. He mounted his horse and the guide and myself pushed them off the ice into the boiling, foaming stream. Away they went completely under the water, horse and all; but directly came up and after buffeting the waves and foaming current, he made his way to the ice on the other side, a long way down the stream, leaped from his horse upon the ice, and soon had his noble animal by his side. The guide and myself forced in the pack animals, followed the Doctor's example, and soon were drying our frozen clothes by a comfortable fire." (Mowry, p. 159)

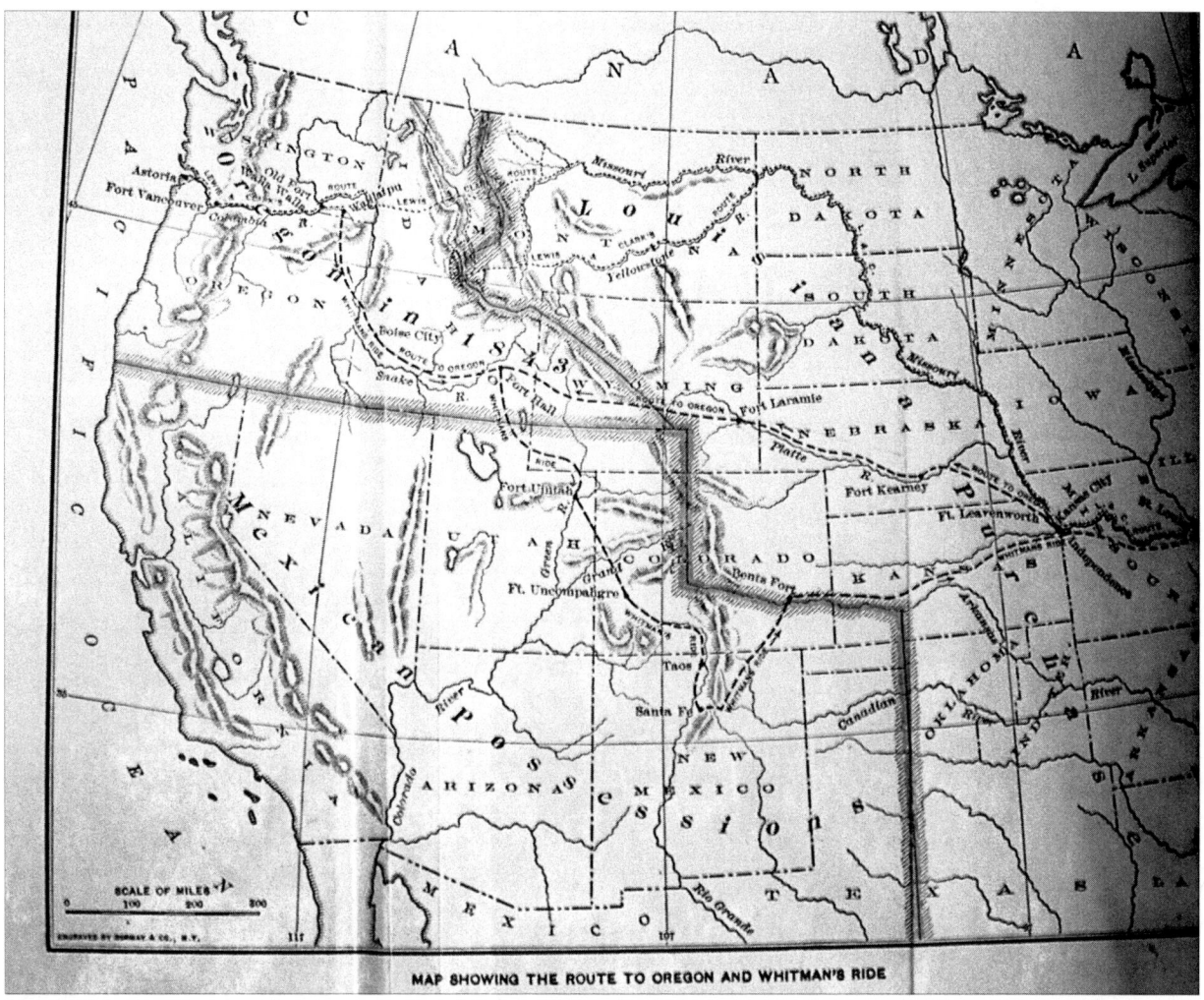

Map of Whitman's route crossing America. (Nixon, Oliver W., How Whitman Saves America, Star Publishing Co. 1895)

After over three months of constant unrelenting winter cold and peril upon peril, the uncompromising doctor faced his most severe trial. The reality of the bitter cold was reinforced by a letter Spalding wrote to A. T. Smith, demonstrating that the temperature in mid-November was the coldest the missionaries had faced in the territory, between 6 and 15 degrees below freezing. By early January Lovejoy, exhausted by the multiple afflictions of the treacherous journey, had separated from Whitman and was forced to stay at Fort Bent to recuperate while the unquenchable doctor pressed on. A most weary Whitman, against the advice of his Mexican guide in the throes of a fierce winter storm, attempted to cross the continental divide still in the midst of the Rocky Mountains of New Mexico. Marcus reluctantly finally faced the reality that he was lost and attempted to turn back and find his camp.

"But the drifting snow had totally obliterated every trace, and the air became almost as dark as night by the maddening storm; the Doctor saw that it would be impossible for any human being to find camp, and commending himself and distant wife to his covenant-keeping God, he gave himself, his faithful guide, and animals up to their snowing grave which was fast closing about them, when the guide, observing the ears of one of the mules intently bent forward, sprang upon him, giving reins, exclaiming: 'This mule will find camp if he can live to reach it.' The Doctor mounted another and followed. The faithful animals kept down the divide a short distance, and then turned square down the steep mountain. Through deep snowdrifts, over frightful precipices, down, down, he pushed, unguided and unurged, as if he knew the lives of the two men and the fate of the great expedition, depended upon his endurance and his faithfulness, and into the thick timber and stopped suddenly over bare spot, and the Doctor dismounted—the Mexican was too far gone—behold the very fireplace of their morning camp. Two brands of the fire were yet alive and smoking…the guide survived but both were badly frozen." (Mowry, pp. 159-60)

    The reader may not believe in the hand of providence, but at this point in the history of the Oregon Territory the destiny of the chosen vessel of the Almighty very nearly was extinguished on a desolate frozen mountain ridge high in the New Mexico Rocky Mountains. Would Oregon be a land of the free men of the American Republic had Whitman failed? According to the revisionist historians, whom no university or historian appears willing to challenge, Whitman's ride was largely fictitious. Fortunately, the Almighty had His hand on the doctor, and the doctor's cause would have an audience in Washington. Perhaps the man of God found comfort that chilly night in God's word: "How excellent is thy loving-kindness, O God! Therefore the children of men put their trust under the shadow of thy wings." (Psalm 36:7) The psalmist certainly understood the providential care of the Almighty, "under the shadow of thy wings."

    Marcus proved the old proverb, "where there is a will there is a way." The unquenchable doctor arrived in St. Louis in late February. Whitman had been on the trail for nearly five months. At the beginning of the sojourn the men were traveling at nearly 50 miles a day. By the time they reached the snow-covered slopes of the Rocky Mountains there were days they did not traverse beyond sight of the campfire smoke of the previous night's rest, often in snow that would cause their mules to disappear should they break through the ice. While in St. Louis Whitman stayed with Dr. Edward Hale who wrote, "I had the pleasure of entertaining Dr. Whitman at St. Louis on his late visit eastward to confer with the President & heads of departments in relation to the settlement of the N.W. boundary question with Gr. Britain by bartering away for a song the whole N.W. Pacific Territory." (Drury, Vol. II, pp. 44, 45)

    Rev. William Barrows, D.D., of St. Louis confirmed Whitman's concern to reach Washington without any further delay. Buffalo hunters, government Indian contractors and fur trappers sought Whitman for information regarding the Oregon Territory since winter crossing from the west had been heretofore without precedent. "But the doctor was in great haste, and could not delay to talk of beavers and Indian goods, and wars, and reservations, and treaties. He had questions and not answers. Was the Ashburton treaty concluded? Did it cover the Northwest? Where and what and whose did it leave Oregon? He was soon answered. Webster and Ashburton had signed that treaty on the 9th of August preceding. Then instantly he had other questions for his St. Louis visitors. Was the Oregon Question under discussion in Congress? What opinions, projects, or bills concerning it were being urged in Senate and House? Would anything important be settled before the approaching adjournment? He must leave at once and he went….Exchanging saddle for stage—for the river was closed by ice—he pressed on and arrived in Washington on March 3d." (Mowry, p. 167)

    Whitman risked his life, his ministry, his mission, and even his precious Narcissa to reach Washington. The eyewitness testimony of those who met Whitman on his historic journey across America proved his passion for his country and his God. Those historians who have claimed this now frostbitten doctor was driven with the extreme fervor of crossing the ominous snow-covered continental divide mountains in the heart of the winter with a mission to solely save his own ministry have willfully deceived the American people and robbed them of their blood-won heritage. The question of the hour as Whitman approached Washington was the fate of his beloved Oregon. Was the Oregon Territory in danger of being yielded to the British, north of the Columbia River? Did the American government (i.e., president, cabinet, Congress) have a clear understanding of the strategic and natural resource value of the Oregon Territory? Did the American government have a clear understanding of the potential reality of a significant wagon train emigration into the Oregon Territory? Were there political issues and contentions that could cause the Oregon Territory to fall into the hands of the British? What was the Webster-Ashburton Treaty and why was Whitman so concerned about it?

No historian could research this tumultuous hour of American history and not come away with the understanding that the fate of Oregon was hanging tenuously in the balance. The biblical word that the Protestant missionaries came to minister exhorts, "My people are destroyed for lack of knowledge." (Hosea 4:6) One of the reasons the Pacific Northwest has developed into one of the most un-churched areas in America is because the knowledge of the Protestant efforts to win Oregon has been destroyed through misrepresentation and deception. America's western history has been re-crafted to fit a negative picture of self-serving Protestant missionaries who largely failed in their efforts and therein sealed their own demise and deserved their own martyrdom. The major reason for the confusion of the Columbia Plateau Indians regarding the Christian faith can be traced to this deception as well.

CHAPTER 17

THE OREGON QUESTION

Revisionist historians have contended for over a century that Whitman never set foot in Washington, D.C. because he had no purpose or cause that would take him there. The foremost historian at the turn of the 20th century, Professor Edward Bourne of Yale University, wrote in January 1901: "Of Whitman's presence in Washington I have been able to find not a trace of contemporary evidence." (Mowry, p. 113) Bourne was repeating previous testimony of others such as the Hon. Elwood Even of Tacoma, Washington who wrote in 1884, "There is no evidence that he visited Washington during the spring of 1843." (Mowry, p. 112)

In actual fact, Dr. Whitman made quite an impression in the nation's capital, even though he arrived without fanfare or notice. We must remember Whitman was a missionary with no personal source of income. He wore the same clothes that carried him across the wilderness. Dr. Cushing Eells described Whitman's apparel for the eastern portion of the journey. His dress "consisted of buckskin trousers, a waistcoat, and a blue English duffle coat. This 'duffle' was firm, close-woven, and thicker than a 'Mackinaw blanket.' Over this he wore a buffalo overcoat, which was a few inches shorter than the duffle. Dr. Whitman remarked to Dr. Eells, '…it was rather fantastic for a missionary, a buffalo coat with a blue border.'" (Mowry, p. 166)

Certainly, not all of the dignitaries of Washington were impressed with the pioneer resume or clothes of the frontier doctor. Despite the claims of the revisionist "scholars," it was certain Whitman had no difficulty gaining a hearing from all the key cabinet and congressional players, including Secretary of State Daniel Webster and the President of the United States, John Tyler. Asa Lovejoy wrote that Whitman "had several interviews with President Tyler, Secretary Webster and a good many members of Congress." (Drury, Vol. II, p. 50)

Marcus Whitman had held no political position or power. He had never been to Washington before and he had no documented influential friends. He was a Presbyterian missionary doctor who had been removed from the culture of the United States for six years. How did he gain access and hearing from all the key American statesmen of the hour? There was conjecture that Whitman knew the Hon. John C. Spencer, who was Secretary of War in President Tyler's cabinet from 1841-45. The major reason Whitman received such a positive audience in Washington was without question the "Oregon question." Nothing struck a more resonant chord in the nation's capital than a living witness who alone could shed light and gravity on the Oregon question. Who better to answer the many questions that begged to be answered than this buckskin-clothed pioneer doctor who had just made an unprecedented ride across the nation in the dead of winter? The reader can only imagine the commotion that the frontier doctor made upon his arrival at the nation's capital. The Tyler administration and congressional lawmakers had questions that Whitman had risked his life to answer. It must have been quite a time in the nation's capital. The contest for Oregon, then known as the

Oregon question, had been intermittently brewing and simmering before and after the treaty of joint occupation in 1818 between the British and the Americans.

The nation had already fought two bloody wars with the Crown and only a very few in the nation's capital were pining for a third. Nonetheless, things were changing regarding Oregon and the frontier doctor was at the forefront in the campaign to win the Territory to the Union. After Whitman's Washington visit, James Polk's campaign promise in 1843 of "54 '40 or fight" appealed to the growing temper of the times for acquisition of Oregon into the Union. Polk was a dark horse Jacksonian candidate who supported the manifest destiny expansion of the nation. His successful campaign threatened war with England and led to war with Mexico over the annexation of California.

The general feeling in Washington and much of the country regarding Oregon prior to Whitman's winter visit in the spring of 1843 was that the land was intemperate and largely inhospitable. Very little factual information reached the halls of Congress, and the nation was largely ignorant of the value of the Oregon Territory. In 1842 the question of acquisition was a topic of hot debate in the top echelons of government and in newspapers around the country. The Louisville *Courier Journal* proclaimed in 1842: "Of all the counties upon the face of the earth Oregon is one of the least favored by Heaven. It is the mere riddling of creation. It is almost as barren as Sahara and quite as unhealthy as the campana of Italy. Russia has her Siberia and England her Botany Bay, and if the United States should ever need a country to which to banish her rogues and scoundrels, the utility of such a region as Oregon would be demonstrated." (Mowry, p. 247)

One could only imagine the chagrin of Dr. Whitman when he was confronted with such biased folly with respect to the "utility" of Oregon. The central issue regarding the Oregon question was the position of President John Tyler and Secretary of State Daniel Webster. Whitman risked his life to cross the continent to arrive at the most crucial hour in American history for the Oregon Territory. Despite the clear evidence of Whitman's impact on the American government for Oregon, some 20th century revisionist historians still claim Whitman never set foot in Washington.

Secretary of State Daniel Webster wrote to British esquire Edward Everett, correspondent for Lord Ashburton, on Nov. 25, 1842. "The first of these subjects is the Oregon Territory. The President quite agrees with Lord Aberdeen and Sir Robert Peel, that both governments should avail themselves to the present opportunity to settle if they can settle, all disputes respecting the territory…if a compromise be attempted….A division of this territory might be naturally suggested, and at first blush the Columbia River might seem to present itself as a convenient line of division." (Curtis, George Ticknor, *Life of Daniel Webster*, Vol. II, New York, D. Appleton and Company, 1870, p. 173)

It is clear from Webster's correspondence that the American government was ready, willing and even anxious to establish a compromise solution to the Oregon question by yielding the territory north of the Columbia River to Great Britain. Webster was feeling out the British statesmen to determine if they were willing to negotiate and he acknowledged the British government would wish to retain Vancouver and the small settlements to the north. Webster demonstrated the prevailing opinion of the negative utility of the territory by stating, "I doubt whether she (Britain) can contemplate any considerable colonization in those regions. I doubt exceedingly whether it be an inviting center for agricultural settlement." (Curtis, Vol. II, p. 173)

The British Hudson's Bay Company had been established at Fort Vancouver for nearly two decades and the comparative agricultural and natural resource riches of the Pacific Northwest were well known to the British statesmen. Henry Spalding, in his effort to give due credit to Whitman's valiant effort to win Oregon to the Union, wrote and lectured for nearly two decades after the Whitman massacre that the degradation of Oregon was a plot on the part of the British to win title to the territory. Spalding's allegedly biased anti-Catholic motive has been promoted by revisionist historians, but the facts support his advocacy and defense of Dr. Whitman. Spalding wrote of Whitman's visit with the President of the United States: "The Doctor next sought an interview with President Tyler, who at once appreciated his solicitude and his timely representations of Oregon....He said that, although the Doctor's representations of character of the country, and the possibility of reaching it by wagon route, were in direct contradiction to Governor Simpson..." (Drury, Vol. II, p. 51) Before we proceed with Whitman's interview with the President it is imperative to establish President John Tyler's position on Oregon prior to Whitman's arrival.

We know that on January 29, 1843, before Whitman arrived in Washington, Webster had once again corresponded with the British because the Linn Bill (Senator Lewis Linn) would soon be voted on in Congress, which, if successful, would ruin Webster's compromise diplomacy. Webster wrote to British Lord Ashburton, "You will have noticed that the business of the Oregon Territory is exciting and a good deal of interest in Congress. A bill was introduced into the Senate by Dr. Linn, not only for extending commercial jurisdiction over our citizens in that region (after the example of the English statute), but also making prospective regulations for granting rights to settle." (Curtis, Vol. II, p. 176)

It is illustrative to note that Webster was pressing the British because of the Linn Bill, which passed narrowly in the Senate (24-22) but failed in the House. "Your answer to this may be expected by the steamer which shall leave Liverpool on the 4th of March. On its receipt here, the President will make up his mind if not done before, as to future proceeding....The President has the strongest desire to settle the Oregon dispute, as well as every other difficulty with England....Both governments would undoubtedly like to see the object accomplished." (Curtis, Vol. II, p. 176)

Webster's correspondence demonstrated a clear picture of the direction and persuasion of the President of the United States prior to Whitman's arrival. According to Spalding, Whitman convinced the President of the United States to change his mind regarding the Oregon question. Even Dr. Drury, who considered Spalding biased because of his testimony of the Papist plot against the Protestants, supported Spalding's account of the British misrepresentation of the Oregon Territory. Spalding documented the President's response to Dr. Whitman's passion for Oregon: "His frozen limbs were sufficient proof of his sincerity, and his missionary character was sufficient guarantee for his honesty, and he would therefore, as President, rest upon these and not act according; and would detail [Lt. John] Fremont with a military force to escort the Doctor's caravan through the mountains; and no more action should be had towards trading off Oregon till he could hear the result of the expedition. If the Doctor could establish a wagon route through the mountains to the Columbia River, pronounced impossible by governor Simpson and Ashburton, he would use his influence to hold onto Oregon." (Drury, Vol. II, p. 51)

It is vital for the student of history to understand how revisionist historians change history to meet their political, religious and cultural agendas. This research has documented how Dr. Whitman interceded with the American government to protect and not compromise the Oregon Territory to the British. Furthermore, this research will document how Dr. Whitman, with the support of the president of the United States, promoted, encouraged, piloted, directed and established the first wagon train of American immigrants into the Oregon Territory. Yale Professor Edward Bourne has been heralded as the definitive source of history's revision of Whitman with scarcely a shred of historical evidence. The result has been that the Protestant church ministry and message has been compromised, the Cayuse Indians have been deceived, and truth of America's heritage and history has been robbed from succeeding generations.

In 1901 Bourne wrote, "There was in 1842 no political crisis in the fate of Oregon for Whitman to discover in Oregon, nor was there one in Washington for him to be informed of that could suggest the necessity of a journey….Under critical examination all urgent political reasons for Whitman's journey to the States disappear." (Bourne, Edward G., *Essays in Historical Criticism*, Charles Scriber's Sons, London, New York, NY, 1901, p. 68). Professor Bourne was not alive at this time in history yet dismissed each and every document, statesman, pioneer and even the President of the United States that historically supported Whitman's mission to "save Oregon." To Bourne the impact, deeds and "legend" of Marcus Whitman were "pure invention…invented by Marcus Whitman himself…or invented in common by Spalding and Eells, or Spalding invented it and Eells copied it from him." (Bourne, pp. 74,75) Twentieth century histories have continued to propagate the scholarship of Bourne and his fellow pro-Jesuit "historians."

The passion of this hour in American history and culture would soon be inflamed with the movement "westward ho," yet no man had successfully piloted a wagon train across the previously impenetrable barren desert and rugged Blue Mountains west of the Rockies. To the revisionist historians, Whitman was but a casual bystander catching a free ride on the first wave of America's manifest destiny to conquer the wilderness and win the day for the emerging American Republic. To these revisionist historians, America's manifest destiny was an inevitable force that required no divine intervention or champions of conviction, vision or faith. Let us join that first wave of pioneers across the Oregon Trail and experience for ourselves the source of the surging power of this westward movement of the free men of the emerging American Republic.

Chapter 18

Westward Ho

The Linn Bill, although it failed to pass the House, fanned the growing momentum of historical and cultural truths to excite the nation's passion to expand westward. On March 8, 1843 the Cleveland *Plain Dealer* waxed eloquent for the romanticized land of Oregon: "There is enchantment in the word. It signifies a land of pure delight in the woody solitudes of the West….That is a country of the largest liberty, the only known land of equality on the face of the earth…there is a place to build anew the Temple of Democracy." (Drury, Vol. II, p. 61) What able-bodied son of the Republic would not respond to such a "land of pure delight" and "country of largest liberty"? Indeed, the Protestant Reformation that brought liberty, equality and freedom to a world locked in the bondage of Papal oppression and servitude had opened the doors of the wilderness to these time-treasured values. The Boston *Daily Evening Transcript* on April 4, 1843 called Oregon "the pioneers' land of promise….Hundreds are already preparing to start thither in the Spring, while hundreds are anxiously awaiting the action of Congress in reference to that country as the signal for their departure….The Oregon fever has broken out, and is now raging like any other contagion." (Drury, Vol. II, p. 61)

It was no coincidence that Marcus Whitman just happened to be in Boston, meeting with his mission board, when the article appeared. Everywhere Marcus Whitman appeared on his return journey from Washington, D.C. Oregon fever broke out. The powerful implications of Dr. Whitman's passion for an American Oregon with democratic institutions on the future destiny of the nation was not lost in the editorials of the newspapers following Whitman's epic return to Oregon.

The titanic struggle between forces of liberty represented by the Protestant missionaries and the forces of oppression represented by Papal institutions had been raging for over three centuries and had been copiously documented as the source of contention for most of the major wars and insurrections since the Protestant Reformation.

On May 24, 1843 the Painesville, Ohio *Telegraph* penned the epic words "Westward Ho" that became the spirit of the great drama for the emigration into the Oregon Territory. "The tide of emigration flowing westward this season must be overwhelming. Besides the hundreds and thousands that daily throng the steamboats on the Lakes, there is a constant stream of 'moves' on the land. From ten to fifteen teams have passed through this town every day for the past few weeks, winding their way for Wisconsin and Iowa, and some, we understand, are bound for the 'far west' which in these latter days means a country somewhat between the Rocky Mountains and sundown. Those we noticed had the appearance generally of intelligence, respectability and wealth and gave indication of that enterprising and energetic character which alone takes upon itself the hardships and privations incident to the settlement of a new country." (Drury, Vol. II, p. 62)

The reader can only imagine the awe that this movement inspired among the population. Those, bound by position or disposition to stay put, wondered at the excitement of this exodus of fellow American citizens. The very fact this newspaper description of emigrants noted the intelligence and respectability of those families that were moved to give up their homes, families, position and heritage to explore and possess the unknown was indicative of the power of the movement into the West. It was not the discouraged, restless and aimless who were drawn toward the magnet of freedom, liberty and a better life. No, some of the best and most courageous the nation had to offer loaded their life treasures and cherished dreams into a small covered wagon and headed west on that first heroic wagon train. Some went as far as the heartland of the headwaters of the Mississippi and Missouri and others into the foothills of the eastern Rocky Mountains. Only the very stout of heart, fewer than a thousand men, women and children, ventured beyond into the unknown on that first wagon train into the Oregon Territory. In actual fact the first wagon train was predominantly families with many children, some born on the way. Only the persuasive presence of Dr. Whitman could have convinced that many fathers and mothers to risk the lives of their families to start anew in the land beyond the Rockies.

Dr. Whitman must have drawn a crowd everywhere he went on his return to Oregon. To the vast multitudes, Oregon was only a mirage of mystic intrigue, but to Whitman it was home. The American nation had questions and the Doctor had answers. Marcus was motivated with a passion that must have been both infectious and persuasive: to encourage his fellow Americans to let go of the present and grasp the future in a magical land called Oregon. His goal was to persuade fellow Protestant emissaries, who shared his passion for God and the Republic to join the emigration, but the fast approaching deadline for the maiden voyage curtailed his canvassing and to his great disappointment few Christ-confessing Protestants answered his call. Courage and determination, not religious affiliation or commitment, were the main criteria for the hardy stock of the first emigrants to cross the continent.

The most nation-changing reality of that first wagon train of immigrants into Oregon was the power of whole families. It was no great feat for a young man to pick up stakes and head west. All he needed was a hardy horse that matched an equally hardy spirit, seasoned with a healthy dose of common sense. In contrast, imagine for a moment the incentive for a would-be pioneer mother. To pull up stakes meant uprooting her family and leaving her home and friends and all the support groups essential for raising a family in mid-nineteenth century America. The covered wagon became her home on wheels, although the prospect of riding a shockless oxen-driven wagon across the continental divide into a domain where no wagons had previously gone must have taken some powerful convincing. The Oregon Trail was bathed in the tears of these first waves of pioneer immigrants who were forced to mark the trail with the graves of their precious children. Once the reality of the immense task of surviving the dirt, dust, disease, and contentions of life in a covered wagon had time to sink in it was too late to turn back. These pioneer women were the unsung heroes of the westward immigration. It would have taken more than the inspiration of the manifest destiny of the emerging American nation to move these women to leave their homes and heritage and put their hope in a new life in a mystical place called Oregon. Someone had to be leading them, someone these women believed in, and that someone was Dr. Marcus Whitman. Whitman understood full well that someone had to lead this exodus of pioneers into Oregon. "As I hold the settlement of this country by Americans rather than by an English colony most important, I am happy to have been the means of landing so large an emigration on to the shores of the Columbia, with their wagons, families and stock, all in safety." (Whitman, Narcissa, p. 173)

The Oregon Territory was to be populated by what evolutionist Charles Darwin called "the survival of the fittest." Over the next three decades thousands of families were willing to pick up stakes and head west primarily from the northern states of the Union. These American emigrants were the best the nation had to offer in terms of spirit, commitment and fortitude. On the maiden voyage into the Pacific Northwest only a small contingent of the pioneer emigrant families were willing to accept the ultimate challenge and venture into the unknown to reach the land known as Oregon. The reader must be reminded there was no law in Oregon. Instead there were hostile Indian lands that had to be traversed to enter into this vast wilderness. The United States House of Representatives had denied the Homestead Act so there was no guarantee that should they endure the sojourn they would win title to their new homeland. These first pioneer families were indeed the cream of the crop of the emerging free men (and more importantly women) of the Republic. Dr. Whitman was deeply disappointed not to draw any young and hearty Protestant missionary families to join him, so the Almighty substituted an alternate plan. It was the Protestant ideal of the love of freedom and liberty that moved these pioneer families to risk the lives of their precious children to start a new life in a land the Cleveland *Plain Dealer* called "the only known land of equality on the face of the earth."

Revisionist historians have deliberately denigrated the definitive role that Dr. Whitman played in this historic drama. According to them, Oregon was "a pioneer's land of promise" and the hope of a better life drew these first colonists to this Promised Land. The fact of the matter, as the reader will soon appreciate, is that most of these idealistic emigrants would never have reached the promised land without the providential direction and guidance of a missionary doctor who, according to revisionist historians, just happened to be along for the ride.

The Doctor had only a few weeks in Boston to finish up business with the American mission board. The Prudential committee had voted to send Spalding home and relocate Whitman in 1842. This was an important reason for Whitman's trip east. The Doctor easily persuaded the committee to rescind that order and support every request the missionary asked for. The respect that Whitman commanded was evidenced by the esteem generated by the committee toward the unexpected arrival of the Oregon missionary, especially when the reader considers to leave a missionary post without approval was grounds for dismissal. Whitman won the approval and support of the American Missionary Board, and the mission would continue until the hour of the tragic massacre.

The urgency of Whitman's return to the field was accentuated by his limited visits with family and friends. Time was precious and Marcus had been away from his precious Narcissa for over six months with no communication to console his heart. The Doctor must have been concerned for the welfare of his beloved wife as the hasty preparations for the sojourn east had left her in the most unsettled condition in the midst of the Cayuse Indians. Certainly, Marcus would have made a straight path back to Waiilatpu and his wife had not the pressing need to secure a hearty contingent of emigrants to Oregon been his priority.

One of the priorities of the visionary American statesmen of the hour was a line of military posts to protect and support pioneer emigration across the ominous trek to Oregon. President John Tyler in his address to Congress in December 1841 had endorsed a recommendation by Secretary of War John C. Spencer to build "a chain of military posts from Council Bluffs to some point on the Pacific Ocean within our limits." (Drury, Vol. II, p. 52) Senator Linn had included in the failed Oregon bill of 1842 a provision to build forts all the way to the mouth of the Columbia. The fact that the joint occupation agreement with Great Britain was still in effect thwarted these efforts to secure protection for the pioneer emigrants. Dr. Whitman proposed in 1843 a bill for congressional consideration that would provide a "chain of agricultural posts or farming stations" (Drury, Vol. II, p. 52) instead of forts, which he felt would better facilitate positive relations with the Indians and build democratic institutions in the Oregon Territory. Unfortunately for the pioneer emigrants to Oregon, no action was taken by Congress to build these forts or stations along the Oregon Trail.

St. Louis, Missouri was the natural port of entry for the first wagon trains west. Meetings were held in the spring of 1843 with the goal of colonizing Oregon. These meetings promoted and strengthened Whitman's vision of winning Oregon to the Union. Certainly, Whitman fanned the flames of Oregon fever everywhere he went, and his spirit must have been greatly encouraged by the growing enthusiasm across the land to somehow colonize Oregon for the Republic. There is little evidence to support the notion that the general population knew very much about the Joint Occupation Treaty with Great Britain. The emerging Republic had already fought and won two costly and bloody wars with the British Crown, so understandably King George did not intimidate this nation. Nevertheless, the Oregon Territory from the mouth of the Columbia River to the foothills of the Rocky Mountains was under control of the Union Jack, and Chief Factor John McLoughlin ruled this empire with a compassionate but iron grip.

The purpose and motive of Dr. Whitman's sojourn across America in the winter of 1842-43 and his passion to bring with him American pioneers to colonize Oregon became a raging controversy after his death, a controversy that never has been settled. The copious and painstaking research of Dr. Clifford Drury sheds great light on the passion that moved Whitman to make this historic trek.

Whitman wrote to Rev. Greene, secretary of his mission board, on May 30, 1843, the evening before he was to begin his return home with the first wagon train to Oregon. The letter illuminates the major issues facing emigrants and the future of the Protestant mission. He was forlorn that he had not prevailed upon any Protestant missionaries and commented that few of the emigrants were "pious." Whitman was most concerned with the designs of the Papists. "De Smet's business to Europe can be seen, I think, at the top of the 233 page of his Indian Sketches, etc. You will see by his book, I think, that the papal effort is designed to convey over the country to the English." (Mowry, p. 262) Whitman was deeply concerned with the designs of the Jesuits in Oregon and it was a repeated theme in his letters. On May 12 he wrote to Rev. Greene urging him to read De Smet's *Indian Sketches*. "I think a careful consideration of this book, together with these facts & movements, you will realize our feelings that we must look with much interest upon this the only spot on the Pacific [sic] coast left where Protestants have a present hope of a foot hold. It is requisite that more good, pious men & Ministers go to Oregon without delay, as Citizens, or our hope there is greatly clouded if not destroyed." (Drury, Vol. II, p.7.0)

Two personal letters to his family spoke volumes about Whitman's Protestant convictions. In a letter to his mother written on his return to Oregon in 1843 he expresses great concern for her soul. "I feel most desirous to know that my Dear Mother was determined to live the rest of her days witnessing a good profession of godliness. What keeps you from this? Is it that you are not a sinner, or if not that, is it that there is no Savior of sinners, or is it that you have too long refused & neglected to love & obey him?" (Drury, Vol. II, p. 66) To the reader who does not share Whitman's Protestant evangelical passion, this letter could appear very harsh and judgmental. There can be no question that Whitman was driven with an evangelical passion to reach the lost for Christ. If Whitman spoke so boldly and uncompromisingly to his very own mother about Jesus Christ, one could only imagine his witness to fellow emigrants along the Oregon Trail as well as the Cayuse of the Columbia Plateau.

A second letter to Narcissa's sister Mary Ann and her husband Rev. Lyman P. Judson illustrated Whitman's Christian theology. At this hour in American religious history William Miller, the founder of the Seventh Day Adventist church, had developed quite a following preaching that the world was about to end within the year. Lyman Judson and his wife Mary Ann had joined this Christian sect. The Doctor wrote to the couple and explained why he had not attempted to persuade them to join him in the ministry in Oregon. "I did conclude that inasmuch as you had adopted such sentiments, you were not prepared for any work calling for time in its execution....I was content to pass you in silence. For to my mind, all my work and plans involve time & distance & require confidence in the stability of God's government." (Drury, Vol. II, p. 68) In actual fact Whitman was very kind in his reply, as many Evangelical Christians felt Miller was a Christian fanatic and would not have been so gracious.

The American Protestant missionary board sent no more missionaries to support the fledgling Oregon mission. Dr. Whitman could well see the ominous clouds of the Catholic Counter Reformation in the form of their most aggressive order, the Jesuits, pressing down upon the Oregon mission. He knew that without help the hope of sustaining their mission would be "greatly clouded if not destroyed." Sadly, Whitman's warning turned out to be prophetic. A consistent theme in Whitman's letters was disappointment that the Prudential Mission Board consistently failed to heed his warning about the threats of Papal and Jesuit designs on the Oregon Protestant mission. Whitman reiterated his concerns about the plans of the Papists in letters to his mother and Narcissa's father in late May as well and again lamented the fact he had failed to find any Protestant families willing to re-settle in Oregon.

Another major concern troubled Whitman, which in the Doctor's mind imperiled the first wagon train and the future westward expansion of the nation. Philip L. Edwards had traversed to Oregon with Methodist minister Jason Lee in 1834 and returned in 1838. He wrote a book called "Sketch of the Oregon Territory," which was published in St. Louis in 1842. The book was a guide for Oregon emigrants that would have led to ruin on the first wagon train headed for Oregon had not Dr. Whitman interceded. Edwards wrote, "And were I to join the company of emigrants, I should always prefer horses and mules to any other mode of conveyance; and inconvenient as it may seem, I should always prefer packing the few necessaries of the journey to the encumbrance of wagons. If the latter are employed at all, let them be light but substantial, and drawn by horses and mules. Let it also be understood, that they are to be abandoned by the way." (Drury, Vol. II, p. 71)

Current history books do not validate that Whitman had a significant impact on America's westward expansion. Nevertheless, the reader can well appreciate in hindsight that few women, babies, small children or major supplies were going to successfully cross the Oregon Trail via horseback. Whitman had the foresight to understand that without women and families and adequate supplies for settlement, the American expansion into the Oregon Territory would be stalled.

Whitman vigorously countered Edward's advice as the expedition was forming in St. Louis and convinced almost all of the emigrant families "in purchasing wagons and mules." (Drury, Vol. II, p. 71) It is significant to note a meeting of the emigrants to Oregon was convened on May 18, 1843 and a committee was appointed "to return to Independence and make inquiries of Dr. Whitman, missionary, who had an establishment on the Walla Walla, respecting the practicalities of the road." (Mowry, p. 193)

A number of these pioneer emigrants have attested to the fact that it was Dr. Whitman's testimony for Oregon that tipped the scales. The reader can only imagine the incentive of having an experienced frontier doctor who ministered a Protestant mission in Oregon, guiding the first expedition into the Promised Land. It doesn't take any stretch of the imagination to comprehend how a mother would find solace and encouragement in knowing that a seasoned frontier doctor would accompany them. Nor would it take any stretch of the imagination to come to the conclusion that Dr. Whitman's presence may have been the deciding factor for most of the pioneer families that were willing to take the risk to reach this great land of liberty. Let the reader not forget that the revisionist historians have painted Dr. Whitman as a mere inconsequential passenger on this first wagon train of American citizens into Oregon.

Mr. S. M. Gilmore, one of the original emigrants, wrote, "I am sure he caused many to come that otherwise would not have come, if they had not learned that he would be with them, and that he would be of great assistance on the journey." (Mowry, p. 194) Mr. William Waldo testified, "Dr. Whitman was in some of the Eastern states in the winter of 1842 and 1843, and wrote several newspaper articles in relation to Oregon, and particularly in regard to the health of the country. These letters decided my father to move to this country…" (Mowry, p. 194) Dr. Mowry's research includes many additional letters from the first emigration to document the impact Dr. Whitman had on encouraging many of the first Oregon pioneers to join the 1843 westward migration.

A letter from John Zachrey, a 17-year-old pioneer emigrant on that historic first wagon train, reiterates the central position of Dr. Whitman in opening the Oregon Trail and bringing Oregon into the Union. Zachrey indicated that his father and several other families joined the emigration to Oregon because of an article written by Dr. Whitman exalting the climate and desirability "for American colonies, and said he had crossed the Rocky Mountains that winter, principally to take back that season a train of wagons to Oregon. We had been told that wagons could not be taken beyond Fort Hall; but in this pamphlet the Doctor assured his countrymen that wagons could be taken from Fort Hall to the Columbia River." (Mowry, p. 195)

Dr. Whitman was fully cognizant of the larger implications resting upon establishing a precedent whereby American citizens, in particular families, could successfully cross the continental divide, traverse the wilderness deserts and forge through the Blue Mountains en route to colonizing the great Oregon Territory. Whitman spoke to the issue in a letter addressed to Secretary Greene. "Two things were accomplished by my return to the United States. The establishment of the wagon-road, due to that effort alone, saved the immigration from disaster in 1843. Upon that event the present rights of the United States acquired by her citizens hung, and not less certainly upon the results of immigration to this country the existence of this mission and of Protestantism in general hung also." (Mowry, p. 198)

Dr. Whitman had become the channel of the Almighty to sustain the ministry for the cause of Jesus Christ in the Pacific Northwest because he was willing to stand against the Papal designs for Oregon and specifically against the challenge of the Jesuit priests. Whitman conveyed those convictions in his letter to the Prudential secretary in November 1843 after he successfully guided the wagon train into Oregon. "I cannot see foreign and papal influence making great efforts and we hold ourselves as expatriated. I am determined to exert myself for my country." (Mowry, p. 199) American history no longer honors Whitman's patriotism because revisionist historians under the leadership of Professor Bourne have convinced America that Whitman's leadership in our western heritage was "pure invention."

It must have gladdened Whitman's heart to join forces with that first army of nearly one thousand men, women and children and one hundred and twenty covered wagons headed for Oregon. Whitman knew if this first expedition was successful other wagon trains would follow every year. President Tyler had commissioned a regiment of thirty soldiers under the command of Lt. Fremont to accompany the train because of Whitman's intercession for Oregon. The expedition was divided into three columns; Whitman rode largely in the rear with his 13-year-old nephew Perrin, the only Christian disciple the missionary had been able to win for Oregon. The term "expedition" is rarely used for this first wagon train of pioneer emigrants; however, expedition was the correct word. These men, women and children broke new ground and successfully established the Oregon Trail that would carry the greatest immigration across the continent in the nation's history. The task this expedition was attempting had been called impossible by the statesmen of the hour because covered wagons had never proceeded west from Fort Hall in present-day Idaho.

According to the testimony of one of the first pioneers, "while with us he was clad entirely in buckskin, and rode one of those long-eared animals said to be 'without pride of ancestry or hope of posterity.' The Doctor would spend much of his time in hunting out the best route for the wagons, and would plunge into streams in search of practical fords, regardless of the depth or temperature of the water, and sometimes after the fatigue of a hard day's march, would spend much of the night in going from one party to another to minister to the sick." (Drury, p. 76) According to another emigrant there were over 3,000 and perhaps 5,000 head of cattle, mules and horses attached to the company. The cattle became an issue because they slowed the wagon train, and in time a cow column that followed the main expedition was developed.

Whitman served as guide, doctor and promoter on this maiden expedition. J. W. Nesmith, one of the party, wrote about the Doctor: "Whitman was continually exhorting the emigrants to move forward and be diligent in their ways and conservative in their supplies." Perrin wrote, "He never allowed them to stay two days nights in one place. Kept them moving every day, if it was only for a little way, as to change grass for the stock." (Drury, p. 77) Those pioneer emigrants who traveled with Whitman, such as Jesse Applegate, told a similar tale. "From the time he joined us on the Platt until he left us at Fort Hall, his great experience and indomitable energy were of priceless value to the migration column. His constant advice, which we knew was based on a knowledge of the road before us, was 'travel, travel, travel, nothing else will take you to the end of your journey, nothing is wise that does not help you along; nothing is good for you that causes a moment's delay." (Drury, p. 77)

Like any person at the beginning of any great undertaking, these emigrants were giddy with excitement and anticipation. They were entering into the great unknown, and in the beginning food and supplies were plentiful. Those who listened to the Doctor were more than grateful at the conclusion of the adventure. It is hard to imagine that pregnant mothers would be willing to climb aboard an always rocking and jolting covered wagon for the four-month sojourn across the great unknown. Fortunately for these brave women Dr. Whitman was on call. Applegate recounted the anxiety caused by a wagon forced to pull aside to allow a pioneer mother to bear her child. "There are anxious watchers for the absent wagon, for there are many matrons who may be afflicted like its inmate before the journey is over....But as the sun goes down, the absent wagon rolls into camp, the bright, speaking [sic] face and cherry look of the doctor, who rides in advance, declare without words that all is well, and both mother and child are comfortable." (Drury, p. 78)

Comfortable? The mother had just bore her child and immediately they were once again forging their way West in a rickety shockless covered wagon. Those pioneer women were more than hearty. The pioneer matron was back in the wagon as if having a baby was only a momentary inconvenience. All mothers and parents know full well there has to be more to this story. The sight and sounds of a healthy newborn babe must have been a tremendous comfort to any other expectant mother who began this expedition bearing a child. Applegate confirmed the growing respect Whitman was developing among the pioneer emigrants. "His great authority as a physician and complete success in the case referred to, saved us many prolonged and perhaps ruinous delays for similar causes, and it is no disparagement to others to say, that to no other individual are the emigrants of 1843 so much indebted for the successful conclusion of their journey as to Dr. Marcus Whitman." (Drury, p. 78) It should astound the student of history that Dr. Clifford Drury can document the incredible positive impact of Marcus Whitman and then conclude with the revisionist historians of the twentieth century that "the legend of Dr. Whitman is 90% fictitious."

Marcus Whitman was not confined to doctoring in his mission to guide and direct the expedition westward. The North Fork of the Platte River presented a huge obstacle that the lead drivers were unable to cross. The problem was quicksand that formed the base of the river, making crossing impossible. One of the emigrants gave the following account that gave strength to the growing Whitman legend. "Those who heard Dr. Whitman at the North Platte River bid the emigrants throw away their skin boats prepared for crossing, and saw him for three days crossing and re-crossing that wide stream, swimming his horse to find the best ford, and at last heard him order the teams and wagons to be chained together and driven in one long line across the ford for two miles (that river swollen by spring floods), cheering the drivers, permitting not a moment's halt, lest they should sink in the quicksand, will never forget the man and the deed." (Mowry, p. 203)

Let the reader contemplate the dilemma. Those pioneer drivers chained up their life's possessions including their wives and children. They were all locked together. They were following the directions of a frontier missionary doctor. If he was wrong they would all perish. Remember there were infant babies and pregnant mothers in those covered wagons. It could have been a disaster. They were like the children of Israel facing the Red Sea. These drivers were not even Christians, yet they were willing to follow the commands of this frontier missionary and put their lives in his hands. This history has been written in like manner so the reader "will never forget the man and the deed."

It was fortunate that the Doctor had ample opportunity in the beginning to win the respect and admiration of the vast majority of the expedition because the greatest tests remained in front of the column. A great dilemma awaited the expedition when they finally reached Fort Hall on the 27th of August. The column had been on the march for three hard months. When they reached Fort Hall the drivers were informed it was impossible to proceed further with wagons. There was no wagon trail. No wagons had ever crossed the barren deserts, and the rugged Blue Mountains were deemed impassable to the west. It would be suicide to continue, the weary emigrants were warned. Captain Burnett, the elected leader of the expedition, documented the drama of the hour.

"Fort Hall was then a trading post, belonging to the Hudson's Bay Company, and was under the charge of Mr. Grant, who was exceeding kind and hospitable....Only a few loaded wagons had ever made their way to Fort Hall, and were there abandoned. Dr. Whitman in 1836 had taken a wagon as far as Fort Boise, by making a cart on two of the wheels and placing the axle-tree and the other two wheels on his cart....We had now arrived at the most critical period of our most adventurous journey; and we had many misgivings as to our ultimate success in making our way with our wagons, teams and families. We had yet to accomplish the untried and most difficult portion of our long and exhaustive journey. We could not anticipate at what moment we might be compelled to abandon our wagons in the mountains, pack up our scant supplies upon our poor oxen, and make our way on foot through this terribly rough country, as best we could. Dr. Whitman assured us we could succeed, and encouraged and aided us with every means at his power." (Mowry, p. 206)

The expedition had been on the trail for over three months and the most difficult portion of the trek was in front of them. Fall was rapidly approaching and every emigrant knew what came after the fall. Those Oregonians who have had opportunity to drive across the rugged Blue Mountains between La Grande and Pendleton can only imagine what it must have been like to attempt to drive a wagon train through that forest with no road or trail before them. Certainly horses and mules and droves of cattle could cross the rugged Blue Mountains, but wagon trains with no trail to follow? These pioneers could only dream of the ease a chainsaw would have provided. Now the reader can understand why the visionary Whitman persevered in bringing that cart across to the foothills of the Blue Mountains. This was a promise Whitman had to deliver on. The lives of the first pioneer emigrants were dependent upon Whitman's ability to lead the expedition on the final leg of the march. The reader must bear in mind that the vast majority of the first expedition were women and children, over five hundred strong.

Certainly Mr. Grant, or Captain Grant as he was usually called, was aware of the political implications of Whitman's successful stewardship of American citizens into the Oregon Territory. This was an army of women and children. These were families that would stay and establish American institutions. Some of the members of the Hudson's Bay Company "inquired if we have come to conquer Oregon, or devour it out of hand." (Drury, p. 81) Perrin Whitman remembered Captain Grant frightening the emigrants.

"When we arrived at Fort Hall, I heard the commandant (i.e. Captain Grant) tell the immigrants that Dr. Whitman would starve them all to death in the Green (Snake) River country. He said they could never get their wagons to the Columbia Valley with their lives." (Drury, Vol. II, p. 82)

The expedition, minus those who yielded to Capt. Grant's alarms and headed to California, reached Fort Boise in 21 days, a distance of 273 miles. It turned out to be one of the easiest legs of the journey. Whitman had received a letter from Narcissa at Fort Hall urging him to "hurry home." Certainly, the mission had languished in Whitman's absence. Whitman learned the gristmill had been burned down and Narcissa had been forced to flee. Understandably, Marcus was more than anxious to return to his beloved Narcissa. They had been separated for a year and Marcus now knew that Narcissa's life had been in danger and she was forced to flee Walla Walla. Nevertheless, Marcus was constrained to stay in the rear column of the expedition to Fort Boise. Even at Fort Boise the wagon road across the Blue Mountains had yet to be forged. Once again Whitman was required to put the needs of the expedition ahead of his mission and his precious wife. When Dr. Whitman reached the beautiful Grande Ronde Valley he received word that both Henry and Eliza Spalding were desperately sick with scarlet fever. Whitman turned over the direction of the wagon trail across the Blue Mountains to his Cayuse Indian friend Stickus, a member of his church at Waiilatpu. A Cayuse Christian Indian had the honor of forging the first wagon train column over the Blue Mountains. The expedition would reach Waiilatpu before the Doctor.

When Whitman finally reached his beloved Waiilatpu the reader can only imagine the anticipation that was in his heart. He had been the across the vast continent. He had met with the president of the United States. He had secured the support of the mission board for the Oregon missionaries. He had changed the course of the United States government in favor of the American Republic for the Oregon Territory. He had assisted, motivated and piloted the first American expedition of emigrants across the continent. I believe none of these had any merit in the heart of Marcus Whitman at this climactic hour. He had not beheld his precious bride for over a year, a year in which both had suffered greatly because of the constraints of their shared passion for America and the Gospel.

What Marcus witnessed when he set his eyes upon Waiilatpu must have broken his heart. Narcissa was still at The Dalles and the mission was in disarray. The advance party of the emigration, the men on horseback, had broken into the Whitman house and "left it open to the Indians, although wheat, corn, potatoes, garden vegetables, hogs, & cattle were in abundance outside." (Drury, Vol. II, p. 84) The next day Whitman received an urgent message from Cushing Eells in Spokane, 140 miles to the north. His wife was expecting and the doctor was needed immediately. Whitman left without hesitation and waited a week for the baby to be born before he could return to Waiilatpu and then go to The Dalles to be finally reunited with his beloved wife. By this time the doctor was exhausted, but the rest that Marcus Whitman so desperately required was not going to be granted, as the winter was approaching and there was no time or opportunity to prepare. Such were the life and deeds of the missionary doctor that revisionist historians have the audacity to declare were 90 percent fictitious.

With the help of his precious friend and fellow Christian, Cayuse Indian Stickus, the wagon train had successfully accomplished what no man save Whitman had believed possible. The wagons of the first advance guard of the American Republic of free men had successfully traversed the American continent and now waves of American emigrants could follow in their tracks, initiating one of the great sagas of American history.

The truth of history of Dr. Whitman's ride at the turn of the twentieth century can be summed up by Colombia University Professor John W. Burgess: "In some way, we know not how, Dr. Whitman learned that the United States government might be induced to sacrifice Northern Oregon in ignorance of its true value, and on the later part of 1842 he set out from the mission in the Walla Walla to go to Washington and inform the government of the real character of the country which he had explored. He arrived in March of 1843 and gave President Tyler such full and truthful information concerning the great value of Oregon north of the Columbia as settled the fate of Oregon." (Burgess, p. 315)

Oregon historian William A. Mowry, one of the most prominent historians at the turn of the twentieth century, concurred with Dr. Burgess and in like manner succinctly capsulated the facts regarding Whitman's famous ride. "In the winter of 1842-43 Dr. Whitman made his famous overland journey from Oregon to the States. He went to Washington and conferred with the President, members of the Cabinet, and members of Congress; he went to Boston and interviewed the secretaries and the Prudential Committee of the American board; and he was back on the frontier early in May and helped organize and move forward a large emigration, comprising eight hundred or more men, women and children, who went to Oregon as permanent settlers. As a result of this emigration Oregon was made sure to the United States. These facts are clearly proved." (Mowry, p. 110)

Historians of the nineteenth century documented the historical facts that demonstrated why Whitman risked his life to save Oregon from succumbing to the Union Jack and Catholic dominion under the powerful grip of Jesuit priests. A significant number of historical records and books documented the reasons that caused Marcus Whitman to leave his missionary post and his wife in the wilderness and risk his life to cross the American continent in the dead of the winter of 1842-43. Some of these books and documents are Henry Spalding's Senate Documents in 1872; Rev. Myron Eells's (son of Cushing Eells) *Indian Missions*, published in 1882; Rev. William Barrows's *Oregon, The Struggle for Possession*, c. 1882; Rev. O. W. Nixon's *How Marcus Whitman Saved Oregon*, 1895; W. W. Gray's *History of Oregon*, 1872; and Rev. J. C. Craighead's *The Story of Marcus Whitman*, 1895. Each of these volumes firmly established Marcus Whitman's rightful place in American history as a man who risked his life and position to save Oregon and the great Pacific Northwest for the Union. Encyclopedias and public school history textbooks documented the heroic deeds of Marcus Whitman on behalf of his beloved Oregon into the close of the nineteenth century.

After the Whitman massacre, in large part in response to the cover-up, Whitman the man became the center of a great controversy that still rages in the American Republic regarding the heritage of the Great West. Dr. Whitman's place as an American patriot and his influence in promoting, encouraging, directing and piloting the first emigrant wagon train across America became a topic of two decades of heated debate until the turn of the twentieth century. That controversy remains at the center of this research because Whitman embodied the forward thrust of the Protestant Reformation into Oregon. Because of Marcus Whitman it was no longer possible to deceive the American people regarding the magnificent wonder of the Oregon Territory. The age-old ploy, "if you can't destroy the message destroy the messenger," became the new mantra for the revisionist re-crafting of America's western heritage.

Biblical prophet Hosea proclaimed the result: "My people are destroyed for lack of knowledge." (Hosea 4:6) Revisionist historians cunningly and methodically changed the historical facts and purpose regarding the Whitmans, particularly Whitman's ride across America, Whitman's leadership and prominence in the first American wagon train, and the powerful impact of the Protestant missionaries in winning Oregon to become a state of the American Republic.

According to Bourne, and subsequently picked up by 20th century historians, "It was an element in this extraordinary campaign of vindication that the legendary story of Whitman was developed. Nothing could more effectively catch the public ear and prepare the public mind for resentment against Catholics than to show that Whitman saved Oregon to the United States and then lost his life, a sacrifice to the malignant disappointment of the 'Jesuits' and the Hudson Bay Company." (Bourne, p. 60)

Professor Bourne correctly identified the heart of the controversy as a religious battle between the Protestant Reformers and the Catholic Counter Reformation. The so-called Whitman legend identified the Protestant missionary as a patriotic son of the American Republic. The Protestant churches of Oregon after the Whitman massacre advocated Whitman's central position as the man who was most responsible for winning statehood for Oregon. It was the conviction of these American missionaries that a Protestant American Oregon, in contrast to a Catholic British Oregon, would develop the institutions of the free men of the Republic. The institutions vital to the Protestants for Oregon were a free press, freedom of conscience, freedom of religion, freedom of speech, and associated freedoms protected by the United States Constitution. Therefore the position of Whitman as a patriot of the American Republic became hotly contested soon after his death because the controversy pitted the Protestant Reformation against the Catholic Counter Reformation authored largely by the Jesuit order.

Wherever the Protestant missionaries established ministries, historically the Catholic Counter Reformation would follow. The same world forces that caused the Protestant Reformation, i.e. liberty versus oppression and truth versus deception, caused the controversy over Dr. Whitman's place in the great wagon train migration across America. The great Catholic Counter Reformation and the onset of the Jesuit movement were established to bring the world back under Papal control. Dr. Whitman had written about his grave concerns regarding the Jesuit design to "convey over the country (i.e. Oregon) to the English." (Drury, p. 74) The great Jesuit pioneer De Smet had addressed the papal design for Oregon on page 233 of his book *Indian Sketches*.

"In my opinion, it is this spot [i.e., Old Oregon] that we must seek to establish our holy religion. It is here that we must have a college, convert & schools….Here is the field of battle where we must in the first place gain the victory." (Drury, p. 74) Whitman knew full well that the victory the Jesuit order was seeking was a physical on-the-ground victory over the Protestant missions and American democratic institutions. We have documented in chapter fifteen how the Jesuits had been sent with orders from Rome to set up a vicariate-apostolic to contend with the Protestant missionaries. Since Dr. Whitman was the focal point of the Protestant missions in the Northwest his integrity was vital to the heritage, purpose and lasting impact of the spiritual, religious and cultural destiny of the Oregon Territory.

The very fact that Marcus Whitman made his historic ride across America in the winter of 1842-43 was an incredible feat in and of itself. Those historians who have rewritten the purpose of Whitman's ride have robbed America and our heritage of one of the most exhilarating, courageous and breathtakingly spectacular epic rides of all time. In truth the great movie screen writers and directors of America should be zealously contending for the privilege of enshrining this nation-saving ride on the big screen.

The Hon. Elwood Evan of Tacoma, Washington wrote in the *Oregonian* in 1884 the essence of the historical re-crafting of Whitman's ride that in effect has robbed America of her inheritance.

"First, Dr. Whitman's winter journey in 1842-43 had no political intent or significance whatever.

Second, no feeling as to the Oregon boundary controversy, or desire or wish to defeat British claims to the territory or any part of it had any influence in actuating such a journey.

Third, his exclusive purpose was to secure the rescinding by the American Board of Foreign Missions of the order of 1841 to abandon the southern stations of Waiilatpu and Lapwai.

Fourth, there is no evidence that he visited Washington City during the spring of 1843.

Fifth, that he in any manner whatever or in the remotest degree stimulated the 'great immigration of 1843' is as untenable as the political claim we have been discussing." (Mowry, p. 112)

The controversy regarding Whitman's famous ride raged in the Pacific Northwest for half a century, and according to Mowry the friends of Whitman had the better of the debate largely waged in the *Oregonian*, the *East Oregonian* and the Walla Walla *Watchman*. Unfortunately, after the death of most of the historians who knew Whitman and/or Spalding no champion for the Protestant cause came forward to stand in the gap. Professor Edward Bourne of Yale University wrote an article in the *American Historical Review* in January 1901 essentially agreeing with Evans that turned the tide of history against Whitman and the Protestant mission. Bourne wrote, "Of Whitman's presence in Washington I have been able to find not a trace of local contemporary evidence…That Whitman influenced American diplomacy in any way is not only destitute of evidence, but is intrinsically improbable. The belief that he did so originated with Spalding….Extraordinary efforts have been made in good faith to disseminate the story of Marcus Whitman in order to raise money for a suitable memorial, and especially for Whitman College." (Mowry, pp. 113-14) The purpose of Bourne's essay was to shatter the historical position of Dr. Marcus Whitman. Bourne wrote, "It is in the highest degree improbable that either Tyler or Webster told Whitman anything about their plans." (Bourne, p. 79) Bourne used his prestigious position at Yale to undermine Whitman's place on the first major emigration wagon train to Oregon. According to Bourne, Whitman did not organize the emigration of 1843 or render any significant service to the party.

Contemporary historians or church leaders did not challenge Professor Bourne's scholarship, rejecting Whitman as a national historical figure. Bourne wielded the full weight of the prestige of Yale University and the *American Historical Review* to undermine the historical facts of Whitman's life. A second significant proponent of re-crafting the character and purpose of Dr. Whitman at the turn of the twentieth century was William Marshall of Chicago University. He joined Professor Edward G. Bourne, with the full weight of the prestige of the academic communities they represented, and both worked diligently to undermine the historical purpose and importance of Whitman and the Protestant cause the missionaries represented. Bourne's work, in the *American Historical Review*, convinced the academic world in America that Whitman's epic trip across America to save Oregon was based largely upon myth and legend and was without historical foundation. According to Dr. Drury, the work of Bourne and Marshall "demolished the Whitman legend…unfortunately the real achievements of Dr. Whitman suffered the fate of the legendary Whitman." (Drury, Vol. II, p. 385) No reputable scholar or historian during the last hundred years has refuted the position of Bourne or Marshall and the name, heritage and accomplishments of Marcus Whitman and the Protestant missionaries have been swept under the rug for over a century.

The contemporary student of history may well question how history can be rewritten after the fact to "demolish" the purpose and place of a prominent person, especially one as important as Marcus Whitman in American history. In this case the credibility of the original historians and contemporaries of Dr. Marcus Whitman, such as Rev. Henry Spalding, H. H. Gray, Rev. Cushing Eells, etc., were systematically undermined, ridiculed and demeaned to shed doubt on their character and integrity in evaluating Dr. Whitman. Those contemporaries and historians who supported the factual historical assessment of Dr. Whitman were declared to be biased by the revisionist historians of the 20th century. The revisionist historians claimed they were biased because they were pro-Protestant and anti-Catholic in their assessment. For this cause the work and documentation of Rev. Henry Spalding, William Henry Gray, O. W. Nixon, Rev. William Barrows, Rev. Myron Eells, and virtually every other historian who positively presented the impact of the Protestant missionaries, especially Dr. Whitman, in winning Oregon to the Union were systematically discredited because the new historians claimed they were biased in their research and historiography. The litmus test for these revisionist historians was based on a pro-Romanist and negative Protestant understanding of our Oregon heritage. As a result of the re-crafting of the history of Dr. Whitman and his immense impact on the Oregon Territory, an effort in 1948 to have the Washington State Legislature appropriate money for a statue of Dr. Whitman failed. Opponents circulated a petition claiming, "The Marcus Whitman legend is 90% fictitious. It is one of our historical fables…" (Drury, Vol. II, p. 386)

Dr. Clifford Drury, one of the foremost Whitman historians, has become perhaps the most unsettling of the historical revisionists because he gave support to the politically re-crafted mantra that "the Marcus Whitman legend is 90% fictitious." Drury contends Whitman's ride across America "is one of our historical fables…Today no reputable scholar claims that the primary reason for Whitman's famous ride East was to prevent the government from trading off Oregon….Spalding's Whitman-saved-Oregon story is completely discredited and rejected." (Drury, Vol. II, p. 368)

No historian has documented the heritage of the Whitmans more copiously than Drury. Dr. Drury's excellent work and documentation testifies against the very revisionist conspiracy that he has joined. Dr. Drury reluctantly admits that Whitman did visit Washington where he had interviews with high-level government officials. In Vol. II, p. 49, in a small footnote, Drury admits, "no reputable scholar makes such claims" that Whitman did not attend to business in Washington. In actual fact all the so-called scholars who publicly claimed there is no evidence Whitman ever went to Washington have all been exposed in their falsehood. None of these new wave historians actually knew Whitman or lived and experienced the times as had the original historians of the age. All of these revisionist historians claim the eyewitness accounts and primary documents of the age were biased with bigoted hatred by the Protestants against the Catholics and were therefore unreliable. In actual fact, as this research has consistently revealed, both the Protestant and Catholics were biased, as are all historians.

Dr. Drury, in his work *Marcus and Narcissa Whitman and the Opening of Old Oregon*, 1986, adhered to this revisionist historical paradigm. In his excellently documented volume, unfortunately every individual who presents a negative historical assessment regarding the impact of Catholicism, Popery, or Romanism on our Oregon heritage was considered to be biased.

Dr. Drury finds it strange, as do most Oregonians who have not studied this issue, that "a theological quarrel, which originated more than three hundred years earlier in Europe, should have been transplanted to the Indian tribes of Oregon to rend them apart." (Drury, Vol. II, p. 378) In actual fact this historical quarrel is not strange at all. Without this historical quarrel there would be no United States of America. Without this historical quarrel there would be no freedom of speech or freedom of the press to write about the Whitman massacre. Without this historical quarrel there could be no assurance the Western world would not still be under the absolute and undisputed world rule of the Roman Catholic Church as it was during the dark ages before the Protestant Reformation.

CHAPTER 19

THE CONTROVERSY OVER THE WHITMANS — ETHNOCENTRICALLY BIASED?

Revisionist historians and twentieth-century anthropologists have crafted the position that Marcus and Narcissa Whitman pressed their New England Presbyterian religious values upon the Cayuse Indians and lost their welcome and the confidence of the Columbia Plateau Indians. According to these historians this Protestant ethnocentric bias eventually led to their deaths by martyrdom. Even Dr. John Brown and Dr. Robert Ruby (*Cayuse Indians, Imperial Tribesmen of Oregon*) have contended the Cayuse were threatened by the waves of white emigrants and began to feel "as slaves" among the Protestants (see *CUJ* Jan. 05, p. 9). Were the missionaries "ethnocentric" Christians, as compared to the Jesuit priests who baptized Indian converts without any requirements for change in character or deed? According to the prevailing twentieth century historical position, the Protestant missionary efforts to "civilize" the Native Americans in effect "destroyed their culture" and led to their death. (Schwantes, Carlos Arnoldo, *The Pacific Northwest: An Interpretive History*, University of Nebraska Press, Lincoln and London, 1996). The sincere student of history must never forget the consistent and prevailing 19th century historical position of the Protestant missionaries was the Jesuit fathers incited the Indians to murder the Protestant Christians in accordance to their Jesuit mandate.

Marcus and Narcissa returned from The Dalles in late October of 1843. Narcissa was not well and would be largely bedridden for six weeks. Narcissa had paid a heavy price for being left to fend for herself in the wilderness without her beloved husband. She had been attacked by a Cayuse chief soon after Marcus left and was forced to flee Walla Walla. Fortunately, Dr. McLoughlin had received her at Fort Vancouver and she enjoyed English culture and hospitality through the winter of 1842-43. Nevertheless, by the time Marcus finally made it back to Narcissa (after he had taken care of everybody else's needs) she was languishing and it took her a long time to recover. Dr. Whitman was most discouraged with Narcissa's prognosis as evidenced by a letter to Secretary Greene in the winter of 1843-44. "Mrs. W's health does not promise to be any better. She is now about [the] house & takes considerable care but she has a throbbing tumor near the navel [umbilicus] which I fear is an aneurysm of the main artery. Consequently I have little expectation of her ever enjoying health again." (Drury, Vol. II, p. 99) Narcissa was discouraged both in body and spirit. "I have felt such a dread to return to this place of moral darkness, after enjoying so much of civilized life and Christian privileges." (Drury, Vol. II, p. 99) Narcissa had spent much of the previous year with Chief Factor John McLoughlin at Fort Vancouver.

Despite her weakened condition, Narcissa had the responsibility of two young girls, Mary Ann Bridger and Helen Mar Meek. In addition, Marcus had promised John Hobson, one of the 1843 emigrants who lost his wife during the expedition, that his young daughters could stay at the mission. Narcissa was understandably reluctant. She wrote to sister, "The girls were so urgent to stop that I could not well refuse them." (Drury, Vol. II, p. 100) Now the ailing missionary had four young girls and two teenage boys (Perrin Whitman and David Malin) to look after. When the Whitmans returned to Waiilatpu in late October they found the compound full of American emigrants. Every room was occupied except for the dining room, where the Whitmans were to spend the winter sharing their home, possessions, supplies and food resources with over twenty other emigrants (plus twenty in the house built by H. H. Gray). The reader must remember the Whitmans had no opportunity to prepare for the winter of 1843-44.

In addition to the difficult and cramped living conditions, Marcus was also enduring "a lame foot…which left me with a tumor on my instep which has given me much solicitude & may give me still much more inconvenience." (Drury, Vol. II, p. 104) The student of history may well wonder how they endured the winter of '44. Whitman's greatest concern was not Narcissa's health, which gradually improved despite the difficult living conditions, or even his foot which was so sore in the spring of '44 that he was forced to use a crutch. His greatest concern, based on his extant letters, was the increased proselyte activities of the Jesuit missionaries who continued to undermine his work with the Cayuse. Dr. Drury documented that only Father Peter De Smet was a Jesuit; however, Dr. Gilbert Garraghan, author of *The Jesuits of the Middle United States*, will be documented later in this chapter to confirm all the Roman priests that confronted the Protestant missionaries were Jesuits. Whitman also documented, "all are Jesuits who are to labor among the Indians" (Mowry, p. 285) in his last letter to Secretary Green on Oct. 18, 1847.

Before the Whitmans arrived in Oregon the Cayuse were a very small tribe, a tribe Drury documents was "a dying nation." (Drury, Vol. II, p. 208) American missionary A. B. Smith had conducted a census of the Columbia Plateau Indians in 1840 and discovered fewer than three hundred Cayuse and perhaps two thousand Nez Perce. (Drury, l Vol. II, p. 208) Whitman documented in the winter of '44 that "a congregation from two to three hundred have been in attendance on the Sab.(Sabbath)-since some time in Feb.-besides many more which come and go and have more or less opportunity of instruction." (Drury, Vol. II, p. 104) This meant that most of the Cayuse nation must have been attending the worship services at Waiilatpu along with other Columbia Plateau Indians and the emigrants and extended family of the Whitmans. The entire Cayuse nation continued to worship with the Protestant missionaries right up until the hour of the massacre.

Dr. Whitman wrote to Secretary Greene on April 8, 1844 regarding the need to educate the natives to provide a "gradual increase in knowledge" to allow the Indians to throw off "Papal forms." (Mowry, p. 268) Whitman was most concerned about the negative impact of the grievances the Cayuse were expressing that were coming from the Jesuit priests. "The Papist priests say the same thing. The Indians say they are told that we ought to expend more liberally on them and that it is peculiarly our duty to so. That we do not give goods for nothing and give large prices for all we get of them and break their lands for nothing. These are among their greatest grievances. They complain that they have been obliged to teach us their languages and we have not taught them ours in return. They have always, however, caused themselves to be paid for teaching us language and even then a teacher has been hard to obtain and keep." (Mowry, p. 268)

Whitman knew these grievances were not originating from the heart of the Cayuse but rather from the Jesuit priests. Dr. Whitman attempted to explain to the missionary board the manner in which the Roman Jesuit priests were undermining their ministry. "It seems to be a legitimate object with them to throw every possible difficulty in the way to benefit them and then to blame us for not having done for them all that was necessary to make them not only civilized, but rich and enlightened as it were without their own effort."

(Mowry, p. 269) It required up to two years to receive a reply to the urgent concerns of the Whitmans. Ministering to the Cayuse Indians in the wilderness was a difficult assignment for the very best missionary. The direct and deliberate interference of the Jesuit priests made the job nearly impossible.

The Roman Papists knew that the Columbia Plateau Indians were illiterate and superstitious and therefore vulnerable to manipulation and claims of evil intent on the part of the Whitmans. Nevertheless, the Whitmans were having great influence upon the Cayuse Indians as demonstrated by the near unanimous attendance at worship services. It would appear the Papists singled out the Whitman Protestant mission to undermine the effectiveness of that ministry instead of attempting to initiate a new ministry among another Native American tribe that knew no Christian faith. The Jesuits had the entire Pacific Northwest for a mission field. To thrust a second contending religious system upon the unsophisticated Cayuse worked only to confuse and agitate them. Whitman continued to share his Papal concerns with Greene by sharing how one of the Cayuse "told me that Mr. Blanchet (Catholic priest) told him if they would send me away he would send a mission among us. I tell them all plainly that I do not refuse to go away if they prefer the Papists to us, and urge them to decide if they wished me to do so, but that I should not except at the full expression of the people desiring me to do so." (Mowry, p. 269)

The growing contention with the Papists was not the only issue the Whitmans were challenged to handle the summer of '44. The anticipated emigration would once again draw many needy emigrants to the mission. It was no coincidence of history that the Oregon Trail would traverse through the Whitman station, since Marcus Whitman established the route of the first Oregon Trail. Revisionist historians have labeled the ministry of Marcus and Narcissa Whitman as "ethnocentric" because they encouraged and harbored the white emigrants who sought a better life out West. In this picture painted by the revisionist historians, the Whitmans were the villains because of their complicity in taking away the land and heritage of the Native Indians by encouraging and promoting the westward expansion of the nation. As a missionary, Whitman was severely criticized because he was charged with caring more for the emigrant than the Native American when he provided care, supplies and housing for many of the desperate pioneers, worn out after the long trek across the Oregon Trail.

Historian author Robert Lansing, in *Juggernaut: The Whitman Massacre*, illustrated the revisionist description of Marcus Whitman when he developed a fictional conversation with the missionary using selected quotes from a letter Marcus wrote to his parents May 16, 1844. "In the spring of 1844, when I last talked to Dr. Whitman at Waiilatpu, I asked him what he made of the rise of immigrants coming into the Oregon Country. He said, 'Our greatest work is…to aid the white settlement of this country and help…its religious institutions.' I wondered how that squared with his mission work for the Cayuse. He said that there would not be time for Indian progress because 'the white settlers will demand the soil and seek the removal of both the Indians and the mission; what Americans desire of this kind, they always effect.' I saw in that a powerful sorrow. But he said that if the Indians 'refuse or neglect to fill the designs of Providence, they ought not to complain' and Christians ought not 'to be anxious on their account.' I scratched my head and asked to know more about this Providence and how it was Christian. He said that the Indians had not 'obeyed the command to multiply and replenish the earth,' and that they could not 'stand in the way of others doing so.' That was the last I ever saw of Doctor Whitman. So for me, those were his parting words—words by which he lived and, as things turned out, words by which he died." (Lansing, Robert B., *Juggernaut: The Whitman Massacre*, Ninth Judicial Circuit Historical Society, 1993, p. 18).

Revisionist historians such as Robert Lansing have laid the blame on Marcus Whitman for his own bloody massacre. In this particular case the historian cleverly and selectively used a personal letter Marcus wrote to his parents and inserted his own ethnocentric bias into the conversation to make the reader think they were intimately communicating together. This conversation made Whitman out to be a white Christian bigot. This has become the standard stereotype for twentieth century history's portrayal of Marcus Whitman.

The actual letter in question was a letter Marcus wrote to his parents in 1844: "It gives me much pleasure to be back again and quietly at work again for the Indians. It does not concern me so much what is to become of any particular set of Indians, as to give them the offer of salvation through the gospel and the opportunity of civilization, and then I am content to do good to all men as I have opportunity. I have no doubt our greatest work is to be to aid the white settlement of this country and to help found its religious institutions. Providence has its full share in all these events. Although the Indians have made, and are making rapid advance in religious knowledge and civilization, yet it can not be hoped that time will be allowed to mature either the work of Christianization or civilization before the white settlers will demand the soil and seek the removal of both the Indians and the Mission. What Americans desire of this kind they always effect, and it is equally useless to oppose or desire it otherwise. To guide, as far as can be done, and direct these tendencies for the best, is evidently the best part of wisdom. Indeed I am fully convinced that when a people refuse or neglect to fill the designs of Providence, they ought not to complain at the results; and so it is equally useless for Christians to be anxious on their account. The Indians have in no case obeyed the command to multiply and replenish the earth, and they cannot stand in the way of others in doing so. A place will be left them to do this as fully as their ability to obey will permit, and the more we can do for them the more fully this will be realized. No exclusiveness can be asked for any portion of the human family. The exercise of his rights are all that can be desired… It is necessary that they seek to preserve their rights by peaceable means only. Any violation of this rule will be visited with only evil results to themselves." (Whitman, Narcissa, p. 174)

Dr. Whitman was not advocating or even supporting the removal of Indians from their heritage or, as Lansing suggests, that Whitman no longer was committed to his mission to the Indians. The Whitmans had come to prepare the Indians to survive and one day prosper in white man's culture. They knew their mission could one day be threatened by the onslaught of Americans especially in their thirst for land. Whitman also knew that the Cayuse tribe was not strong in number, well below 400, and in the final analysis would be no challenge to the thousands of immigrants who would answer the call for a new life in Oregon. Whitman believed mankind had a responsibility to obey God's word especially when it applied to stewardship of the earth. The particular biblical passage that Lansing shared out of context was, "Be fruitful, and multiply, and replenish the earth, and subdue it: and have dominion of the fish of the sea, and over the fowl of the air, and over every living thing that moveth on the earth." (Genesis 1:28)

Whitman was certainly a prophet, because the violent means the Cayuse resorted to in murdering the Protestant missionaries nearly destroyed the Cayuse nation. The massacre led directly to the statehood of Oregon and American laws throughout the previously controlled Native American Indian lands. The larger issue that Whitman addressed regarding the designs of Providence in relation to American treatment of Indians in the Oregon Territory will be fully addressed in the last four chapters of this research. Whitman prophesized that the Indian nations would fulfill the full design of Providence when they realized their ability to fully obey the will of God in regards to full equality and liberty in America. The full exposition of this issue must wait its turn at the conclusion of this research. Whitman was a prophet because "a place has been left for them," and at the beginning of the 21st century the Columbia Plateau nations are prospering as evidenced by the fact that the confederated tribes of the Umatilla have become the largest employer in Umatilla County.

Whitman encouraged the Cayuse to cultivate the land not only for themselves but to take advantage of the immigration of '44. The Cayuse demonstrated great enterprise in this endeavor. "Some of the Indians are hiring land broken for them by those [i.e.. immigrants] who are here still, which is done at the rate of from three to five acres for an inferior horse. Ploughs are in great demand. I have sold even my last cast plough from the States, as they are the ones preferred by the Indians." (Drury, Vol. II, p. 127) How ironic. The Cayuse, because of the Whitman mission, were now prosperous enough to hire the American immigrants to work the soil for them using ploughs that the missionary had brought from the east. It appears the Columbia Plateau Indians were well on their way to becoming prosperous entrepreneurs thanks to the foresight of the Protestant missionary.

Despite the best efforts of Marcus and Narcissa Whitman, the Papists continued to zealously undermine their ministry, and at the same time the missionary board was criticizing him for meeting the needs of the emigrants. Twentieth-century historians have routinely criticized the doctor for encouraging the destruction of the ancient nomadic Native American way of life and culture. Even the American missionary board reproved Dr. Whitman for his compassion on the pioneer emigrants. Secretary Greene wrote after the immigration of '44: "We are glad to hear of your prosperity in secular matters, and that you may be able, by means of your grain and your stock, to defray a large part of your expenses. All this is well. Still we are not quite sure that you ought to devote so much time and thought to feeding emigrants, and thus make your station a great restaurant for the weary pilgrims on their way to the promised land….We fear the effect of this on your mind and heart—that you will become too exclusively a man of business—and upon the Indians, that they will have their thoughts engrossed about improving their outward condition, while they will be led to think their spiritual interests are of little consequence." (Drury, Vol. II, p. 124)

Dr. Whitman has been criticized by the historians of the present age because he cared only for his "ethnocentric bias" of reaching the Indians for Christ while he was criticized by his missionary superiors because he cared too much for the physical and emotional well-being of the pioneer emigrants. Whitman responded to Secretary Greene, "If we are not legally, religiously nor morally bound to relieve the passing immigrants, we are necessarily; for the sick and hungry cannot be sent away however penniless." (Drury, Vol. II, p. 124)

Dr. Whitman has also been criticized that his ethnocentric bias of bringing Christianity to the Cayuse destroyed their culture. This is the mantra of 20th century historians critical of Marcus and Narcissa Whitman and the Protestant missionary effort. As early as 1836 the missionaries had noted that the white man was decimating the great buffalo herds. Henry Spalding wrote to Secretary Greene from the first Rendezvous on July 8, 1836. "What is done for the poor Indians of this western world must be done soon. The only thing that can save them from annihilation is the introduction of civilization." (Drury, Vol. I, p. 242)

Dr. Drury makes the obvious point that had no American missionaries arrived on the Columbia Plateau the Native American Indians would still have been forced to transform their lifestyle and culture or perish. Revisionist historians claim the Protestant missionaries destroyed the Indian culture by introducing religious codes of conduct and methods of cultivating the land instead of encouraging age-old practices of nomadic hunting and food gathering. According to Dr. Drury, "there is no evidence, as some have suggested, that the Indians turned reluctantly to farming." (Drury, Vol. I, p. 242) The Protestant missionaries, in particular Spalding and Whitman, were of one accord regarding their religious philosophy of ministering to the spiritual and physical needs of the American Indian. According to modern historians this dual emphasis amounted to a Protestant ethnocentric bias. "While we point to them with one hand to the Lamb of God which taketh away the sins of the world, we believe equally our duty to point with the other to the hoe, as the means of saving their famishing bodies from an untimely grave & furnishing the means of substance to future generations." (Drury, Vol. I, p. 243)

Dr. Drury also confronted one of revisionist historians' greatest criticisms of the Protestant missionaries. "A few critics have accused the missionaries of taking part in the expropriation of lands and resources of the Oregon Indians. The reverse is the case. No group of individuals did more to help the native bridge the gap from a primitive, semi-nomadic life to a civilized, settled existence than did the missionaries." (Drury, Vol. I, p. 243)

This research has previously documented the positive impact of the Protestant missionaries on the American Indians, but that research needs to be reiterated in light of the revisionist assault on the character and motive of these missionaries. It was Whitman and Spalding who "introduced the hoe and the plow and taught the natives to plant vegetables, especially potatoes, wheat and corn. They helped them obtain American cattle. They reduced the language to writing, and printed primers and other little books in the Nez Perce tongue on the first American press to be brought to the Pacific Coast. To civilize and educate the natives was a fundamental part of the endeavors to evangelize them." (Drury, Vol. I, p. 243) Dr. Clifford Drury, after 45 years of research on the missionary period of the Oregon Territory, proclaimed the historical truth virtually all historians of the nineteenth century held, "No missionaries did so much for the improvement of the material welfare of the Cayuse and Nez Perce Indians as Marcus Whitman and Henry Spalding." (Drury, Vol. I, p. 2)

A second charge against the Protestant missionaries remains a cornerstone of revisionist condemnation, i.e., the missionaries forced their ethnocentric Christian bias upon the Native Americans. Nothing could be farther from the truth. The Native American Indians of the west of the Rockies were a spiritual people that believed in a creator God long before the white man came. Dr. Ruby, in his book *The Cayuse Indians: Imperial Tribesmen of Old Oregon*, has documented the Cayuse were a spiritual nation with forms of worship long before the Protestant missionaries arrived. Whitman noted in 1837, "The present worship of the Indians was established by the Traders of the Hudson Bay Co. & it consists of the singing a form of prayer after which the Chief gives them a talk." (Drury, Vol. I, p. 241) The Columbia Plateau Indians were seeking the white man's Book of Heaven, which in actual fact initiated the Protestant missionary movement to the Native American Indians of Old Oregon. These Indian nations were seeking the ethnocentric faith of the Protestant missionaries found only in the Bible, and the historical record illustrates the Cayuse and Nez Perce nations received the faith of the Protestant missionaries gladly. The Whitmans documented that the vast majority of the Cayuse nation attended Protestant worship services right up until the Jesuit "black robes" arrived at Walla Walla to set up their rival mission weeks before the Whitman massacre.

It is true that the Protestants required the Indians to make changes in their lives and customs that the Jesuit priests did not, and this issue goes to the heart of the controversy. The Columbia Plateau Indians practiced a number of mores and customs that the Protestant missionaries preached against, causing considerable hardship between the two races. The missionaries would not allow polygamy, nor would their Protestant faith allow levirate (where the Indian widow married her husband's brother) or sororate (where a man would marry his living wife's sister). Each of these practices was prohibited in the Bible, the foundation of the Protestant faith and, according to the Founding Fathers, the foundation of American culture. In actual fact, polygamy historically has led to a number of societal maladies that have destroyed cultures by undermining the integrity of the family, the foundation of any society. The practice of sororate and levirate led to inbreeding, which caused genetic abnormalities within the Cayuse nation. The Cayuse nation was a dying race before the missionaries came, and the Protestant missionaries were teaching the Native Americans how to restore prosperity and health to their nation. In addition, the missionaries taught that age-old Indian customs such as stealing, adultery and murder, acceptable under Indian superstition and ethnicity, were sins against God and their fellow man. Whitman was particularly vulnerable because as a physician, any medicine man who lost his patient to death could be murdered by the offended family in revenge. The Cayuse custom of killing a medicine man because his patient died was also self-destructive and had to be ended if the Columbia Plateau Indians were to survive.

The Protestant missionaries documented in letter after letter the devastating impact these Native American cultural norms were having in the Indian civilization. This research has documented that the Cayuse were a dying nation before the missionaries came. They were dying because the cultural practices of polygamy, levirate, sororate, culturally justifiable murder, unhealthy medical remedies, and superstition were destroying their civilization. The Cayuse had existed for untold centuries, yet fewer than four hundred existed at the onset of the first white missionaries and settlers in their land. For any historian to state or even imply that the Protestant missionaries destroyed the culture and civilization of the Columbia Plateau Indians is pure ignorance of documented history. The very fact that revisionist historians elevate the place of the Jesuit priests because they accepted and baptized Indian converts without requiring any corresponding change in action, culture or morals according to a religious standard of living should not be held as a positive affirmation of their unbiased patronage. Revisionist historians have attacked the ministry of the Protestants as blatant ethnocentrism because these missionaries attempted to change the Indian culture in a positive manner. The same revisionist historians have commended the Jesuit priests for protecting the Indian "civilization." Historical fact, based on the historical documents of the missionary era, has clearly demonstrated that the Columbia Plateau Indians sought the white man's Book of Heaven so their civilization could know how to please the God of heaven and therein grow and prosper.

The student of history would assume that the prelude to the massacre would indicate that the relations between the Whitmans and the Cayuse would be evidenced by a growing animosity and contentiousness between the different races. Certainly all the mitigating factors that led to the massacre were increasing in intensity. More and more American emigrants were crossing the Columbia Plateau Native American land. It was only a matter of time before some would stay and claim land on the Columbia Plateau. The growing population of white emigrants at Waiilatpu certainly agitated the Indians, especially when the Jesuit missionaries became increasingly active around the missionary compound. Whitman wrote to Greene on May 20, 1845 expressing his anxiety when he discovered the Roman Catholics were actually seeking a place to locate a mission near Waiilatpu. "The Indians are all notified to meet De Smet at Walla Walla when the grass is about five or six inches long….He was seeking an invitation to locate a station among these Indians." (Drury, Vol. II, p. 133) Whitman explained to Greene that the Indians were encouraged to accept a Jesuit Catholic mission because they would provide "such supplies as the Mission is wont to furnish them." (Drury, Vol. II, p. 133)

There was no reason to doubt the integrity of Marcus Whitman regarding the promises the Jesuits were making to the Indians that put his mission in peril. In spite of these pressing concerns and other issues that are outside the parameters of this study, the Whitman and Spalding missions continued to prosper. The Cayuse and Nez Perce Indians depended on the missionaries for spiritual guidance and the multiple efforts the missionaries were making to improve their living standard. Spalding and Whitman had made it clear to the Indians that they would leave promptly should the tribal elders be in unity for them to go.

In a letter to Greene on September 6, 1846 Dr. Whitman wrote: "I think we have at no time been as much in the affections of the people as now. A much kinder disposition is manifested towards us, now more than at any former period, exhibiting the feeling that they could not do without us." (Drury, Vol. II, p. 159) The next spring Narcissa wrote, "Our prospects for usefulness among them [Indians] never have been more encouraging than at present. The field is ripe for the harvest and laborers are needed to enter in and reap."

(Whitman, Narcissa, p. 221). Narcissa, whom revisionist historians have painted as haughty toward the Cayuse, wrote to a fellow missionary wife on February 8, 1847: "As it regards this station we feel that our influence for good was never greater among them, than now." (Drury, Vol. II, p. 159)

Twentieth-century historians have consistently belittled the work and life of Narcissa Whitman. The testimony of the revisionist effort to undermine the character of Narcissa Whitman must be included in this study because the consistently unfavorable impression of Narcissa Whitman portrayed in current twentieth-century history books has become the standard and accepted image of her character. For instance, historian Patricia N. Limerick pictured her: "Descending on the Cayuse, determined to bring light to the 'benighted ones living in the thick darkness of heathenism,' Narcissa was an intolerant invader. If she was not the villain, neither was she an innocent victim." (Limerick, Patricia N., *The Legacy of Conquest: The Unbroken Past of the American West*, Norton, New York, 1987, p. 41) Limerick portrayed the modern view of Narcissa Whitman presented to the American public. "Narcissa would not have imagined that there was anything to understand, the Cayuse had religion, social networks, a thriving trade in horses, and a full culture. Whitman would have seen vacancy or worse, heathenism." (Limerick, p. 41)

Historian Carlos Arnoldo Schwantes echoed this twentieth-century critical refrain against Narcissa Whitman. "Her tendency to judge others by her own cultural standards prevented Narcissa from finding much to admire in the native peoples." (Schwantes, p. 87) Even the extraordinary compassion Narcissa extended to take into her heart and home the orphans of the Oregon Trail has been subtly questioned by these modern historians. "The increased awareness that she would not likely bear another child caused Narcissa to welcome the children of others into her 'little family.'" (Schwantes, p. 87) Unfortunately, these historians rarely documented the actual correspondence of Narcissa Whitman or extant writings of any of the original Protestant missionaries to determine why Narcissa continued to take these poor orphaned children into her "little family."

Fortunately, historical records have documented the testament of the Sager orphans, the family the Whitmans adopted, who also recorded the most accurate account of the Whitman massacre. Both Sager parents perished during the immigration of '45. Their seven children, the youngest born just before their journey west, were forced to be cared for by the Oregon emigrants on the trail. The dying father's wish was for the family to stay together. By the time the oldest six reached Waiilatpu they were exhausted and starving. The five-month-old Sager baby arrived three days later. Narcissa recounted that day: "She arrived here in the hands of an old filthy woman, sick, emaciated and but just alive." (Drury, Vol. II, p. 120) Both Marcus and Narcissa felt that the responsibility of caring for an additional seven orphaned children, plus the four they had already made a commitment to raise, was more than they should accept. Marcus and Narcissa attempted to split up the family but the dying father's wishes prevailed and the Whitmans took on the whole family including the "poor, distressed little object, not larger than a babe of three weeks old." (Drury, Vol. II, pp. 120-21) It should be noted that the Whitmans did not accept the seven Sager children because their lack of children caused them to want a "little family," as the revisionists coldly and condescendingly conjure. Catherine Sager would later write that Captain Shaw of the '45 migration "argued that as the Doctor had been sent out as a missionary that whatever came under the head was his duty, whether natives or whites, and we certainly were objects for missionary charity." (Drury, Vol. II, p. 120)

It is unfortunate that most historians of the twentieth century wrote their histories of the Whitman massacre without taking into account the actual eyewitness testimony of those present. The Jesuit priests who suspiciously established a rival mission near Waiilatpu a few days before the massacre were not even considered complicit in the brutal slayings by these twentieth-century historians. Dr. Drury, who found the "evident willingness of Bishop Blanchet to establish a Catholic mission adjacent to the Protestant station at

David Manuel painting of the Sager Children arriving at the Whitman Mission

Waiilatpu…astounding" (Drury, Vol. II, pp. 189-90) would later excuse the imminent danger these Jesuit priests were causing the Whitmans. "They were new to Oregon, it could not be expected that they would appreciate the danger to which Whitman and his family were exposed by their proposal to establish a rival mission in the vicinity of Waiilatpu." (Drury, Vol. II, pp. 191-92) The Jesuit Fathers "would not appreciate the danger" their rival mission would cause to the Whitmans? Could Dr. Drury be that ignorant of the history of the Catholic Counter Reformation? How tragic that this fine historian would undermine the credibility of 45 years of research by assuming the Jesuit priests were unaware of the impact of their rival mission on the welfare of the Protestant missionaries. The foremost Whitman historian remained steadfast for 45 years in shielding the Jesuit priests from their "astounding" (Dr. Drury's word) collusion in the horrific deaths of the Protestant missionaries.

It appeared that no matter what the Whitmans chose to do regarding the Indians or emigrants they were roundly criticized. Narcissa's "little family" was now eleven strong, and that did not include the multitudes of emigrants, Indians, half breeds, and laborers that continually resided in and about the Whitman mission home. Narcissa faced the prospect of feeding, clothing, washing, nurturing and raising eleven children in the midst of the Oregon wilderness. She labored under an ominously present shadow of a clearly documented physical threat of rival Jesuit priests enticing the Cayuse to harm her and her family. In addition, the age-old heathen customs of the Columbia Plateau Indians continued to work like yeast to potentially incite the Indians to harm or even kill her family. Marcus and Narcissa Whitman were simply Christians who had made a commitment to God to serve him, wherever God called them to serve. This was a mission they would not forsake no matter what the cost to themselves, their family or their mission.

The immigration of 1847 brought a most virulent form of measles and dysentery that would have a devastating impact on all of Old Oregon. The Columbia Plateau Indians had no immunity to these European diseases and their age-old custom of racing out of a steaming hot sweathouse into an ice cold stream would not work against this vicious epidemic. Whitman had lived in danger of being blamed for a number of Indian deaths for ten years, so the missionaries were prepared to endure this new crisis as best they could. To complicate the issue, on the twenty-third day of September Whitman met seven Roman Catholic priests at Fort Walla Walla under the newly appointed Bishop of Walla Walla, the Right Rev. A. M. A. Blanchet. Whitman learned they planned to build a number of Roman Catholic missions on the Columbia River, including two surrounding Waiilatpu. Not only was Walla Walla to be the home of two missions but also the center for the newly created diocese of Walla Walla, which included the entirety of the vast land of the Oregon Territory.

The Jesuits were planning to rule their new kingdom in the Pacific Northwest from within the heart of the Protestant mission at Walla Walla. This new Jesuit domain would include "all the territory between the Mexican province on the south, and the Russian province of Alaska on the north" and extended "from the Pacific Ocean to the Rocky Mountains." (Garraghan, Gilbert, *The Jesuits of Middle United States*, Vol. I & II, Loyola University Press, Chicago, Ill., 1984, p. 281) The Jesuit fathers also planned a mission near the Methodist mission at The Dalles that Whitman and the American missionary board had just purchased. The Jesuit General Roothaan had chosen the banks of the Columbia very near to Waiilatpu to govern the Roman Catholic empire in the Oregon Territory. Unlike the Protestant missionaries, these seven Jesuit priests were fully funded and absolutely accountable to a foreign power in Rome. The Roman papacy knew from three hundred years of experience in Europe and America precisely how much confusion among the Indians and contention toward the Protestant missionaries their competing Catholic missions would cause. The Catholic Counter Reformation had been following and contending with the Protestant Reformation for three hundred years with a powerful record of bloodshed-purchased success.

The Jesuit General Roothaan was moving decisively because the American Republic under the vanguard of the Protestant missionaries was winning the west. The first great expedition of American emigrants into the Oregon Territory essentially settled the Oregon question in favor of the United States. That first wave was fewer than one thousand, but nearly fifteen hundred followed in 1844, and the immigration of 1845 swelled Oregon settlers with over three thousand new pioneer families. Over fifty thousand American pioneer immigrants would follow on that Whitman Trail to Oregon until the railroad supplanted transcontinental wagon train transportation in the late 1860s.

Great Britain realized the contest for Oregon was lost and yielded to an international boundary on the 49th parallel on June 15, 1846. When the news reached Whitman of the boundary settlement he wrote to Secretary Greene reiterating his conviction that his trip to Washington and effort to sustain the first immigration of 1843 settled the Oregon question in favor of the United States. "By means of the establishment of the wagon road, which is due to that effort alone, the immigration was secured and saved from disaster in the fall of forty-three. Upon that event the present acquired rights of the U. States by her citizens hung. And not less certain is it that upon the result of immigration to this country the present existence of the mission and of Protestantism in general hung also." (Mowry, p. 285)

Marcus and Narcissa Whitman's central place in the development of Old Oregon toward statehood ultimately cost both their lives and fifteen members of their Protestant mission. It was the Whitman massacre that directly caused the Oregon Territory to become part of the United States, a necessary step toward statehood in 1859. The events that led up to the brutal massacre are central to the unadulterated history of the Oregon Territory. Controversy has surrounded the Whitman massacre for over one hundred and fifty years. Cayuse historian Dr. Robert Ruby has written that the Cayuse Indians were unfairly convicted of the murder of the Protestant missionaries. (See *CUJ*, "1847 Whitman Massacre," Jan. 05) Virtually all the Protestant missionaries, eyewitness accounts and early historians believed and documented that the Jesuit Romanist priests were the primary motivating factor for the bloodshed. Most twentieth-century historians, such as the pro-Catholic Dr. Drury, have written the Catholic priests were not responsible for the massacre. These historians contend the tragedy was caused by a combination of factors—primarily a measles epidemic and the relentless onslaught of western immigration into the Oregon Territory, of which the Cayuse held the Whitmans primarily responsible.

With the addition of Jesuit priests the stage was set for the final act of the Oregon Territory. All the key players in the drama for Oregon were now on the front stage at Walla Walla, deep in the wilderness of Old Oregon. The discerning reader who enjoys the drama of a murder mystery thriller should not be hard pressed to put the clues together to separate the villains from the innocent in the violent drama about to commence. Nonetheless, historians, theologians and citizens alike have debated and argued the causes of the Whitman massacre for over one hundred and fifty years and still the pieces of the puzzle remain in disarray. All the main players of this historical drama have been cast as villains. The Cayuse were the villains because they heinously murdered the missionaries who courageously came to minister to them. The Protestants were the villains because they destroyed the Indians' culture and encouraged American immigration that brought devastating epidemics. The Jesuits were the villains because they incited the Indians to kill the missionaries by falsely claiming the Protestants were poisoning them. Conversely, all the central players have been cast as innocent. The Cayuse were innocent because they were coaxed, deceived and driven to kill the missionaries. The Protestants were innocent because they were martyred when they refused to desert their post and leave their beloved Cayuse. The Jesuits were innocent because they did their best to support and protect the surviving Protestants from additional abuse from the Indians. The heritage of the citizens of the Pacific Northwest will not revealed until the mystery of the Whitman Massacre has been solved.

The author stated at the beginning a bias for the Protestant principles of freedom of conscience and liberty and justice as found in the Bible and the Constitution of the United States. That does not necessary mean this history is pro Protestant and anti-Catholic. At this point it is necessary to present two essential points to the reader. Not all Protestants in America and the Pacific Northwest believe in the Protestant principles of liberty and freedom of conscience as represented in the Bible. In contrast, many American Catholics do believe in the Protestant principles of freedom of liberty and conscience and reject the Romanist principles of the Catholic Counter Reformation in their absolute allegiance to the Pope and Rome instead of to the Constitution of the United States of America and the Bible.

The second point is that Whitman's prophecy for the Cayuse and Columbia Plateau Indians has been partially fulfilled. The Confederated Tribes of the Umatilla Indian reservation (Walla Walla, Umatilla, and Cayuse) in the twenty-first century are thriving because they have seized the initiative to protect their sovereignty under the treaty of 1855 and exercise their rights as free men under the protection of the Constitution of the United States of America, one of the crowning principles of the Protestant Reformation.

Nevertheless, the controversy and confusion of the Whitman massacre and the contention of the Jesuit Priests against the Protestant faith has largely separated many of these Indian tribes from the faith of the Protestant missionaries who came to minister to them. Still, Whitman's vision for the civilization of the Confederated Tribes of the Umatilla to one day prosper has been fulfilled by a Native American Indian renaissance in Umatilla County at the beginning of the twenty-first century. (See *East Oregonian*, Feb. 7,

2005) One of the purposes of this work is to document the truth of the Whitman massacre so the faith in the Book of Heaven these Columbia Plateau Indians received in the beginning can be restored to them. The Protestant faith in the Almighty is consistent with the Indian historical faith in the Great Spirit Chief. This research will revisit this monumental issue at the conclusion of this work.

The Native American Indians of the Columbia River and its tributaries were spiritually predisposed to the same values as the American sons of the Republic. The current Umatilla Confederated Indian renaissance is indicative of the great enterprising initiatives the Indians have seized upon that were also a direct result of the Protestant Reformation that brought freedom and liberty to the whole world. Marcus Whitman predicted this would happen. Tragically, revisionist historians have rewritten history denying these American Indians the historical documented source of their freedom and liberty found in the Protestant message and ministry of the missionaries. The Native Americans of the Oregon Territory will never be free until the truth of God, found in the Book of Heaven, ministered to them by the Protestant missionaries, has been restored to their heritage. The central place of the Native American Indian along with the Protestant missionaries in establishing American sovereignty in the Pacific Northwest has never been honestly presented by historians of the twentieth century, in stark contrast to historians of the nineteenth century who have been quoted copiously in this research. If this work accomplishes nothing save the restoration of unity and goodwill between the Protestants, Catholics and Indians that stand for liberty, freedom, America, and God, this author will be satisfied. Now let us return to our narrative as the hour of the climactic collision between the Protestant Reformation and Jesuit-led Counter Reformation was about to explode. Let us examine the advent of the Jesuit priests into the Oregon Territory and Walla Walla to set the train tracks leading to this monumental collision.

Chapter 20

The Advent of the Jesuit/Catholic Priests

To identify the participants essentially conducting this impending train wreck we must research the history of the Jesuits who followed the Protestants into Oregon. This research has documented the historical spiritual battle for liberty and freedom versus papal world authority between the Protestant Reformation and the Catholic Counter Reformation, destined to battle for the Oregon Territory.

Pope Gregory XVI on August 15, 1832 articulated the fundamental teaching of the Church of Rome against liberty of conscience, the foundational principle of the Protestant Reformation. "From the polluted foundation of indifference flows that absurd and erroneous doctrine, or rather raving, in favor and in defense of 'liberty of conscience' for which most pestilential error the course is open by the entire and wild liberty of opinion which is everywhere attempting the overthrow of civil and religious institution; and which the unblushing imprudence of some has held forth as an advantage of religion." (Dowling, John, *History of Romanism*, New York, Edward Walker, 1845, p. 631)

The Protestant missionaries wrote often regarding their concern with the growing presence of Romanism in the Oregon Territory in their extant diaries and letters of correspondence. It is essential for the astute student of history to understand the temper of the times regarding these concerns. These Protestant missionaries knew full well that Romanism stood in direct opposition to the spiritual and religious freedoms they were promoting, enshrined in the Constitution of the United States of America and their Protestant faith.

The Whitmans and Spaldings noted ever-growing concerns in their correspondence with respect to the work and advent of the Jesuit fathers near Walla Walla. The Columbia Plateau Indians understood the difference between the two contending religions according to Catherine Sager, one of the survivors of the massacre. "The feelings of the Indians were that both missionaries could not occupy the same field....The principle chief, Ellis, said: It will do for the French and English to have two religions, as they have laws; but for the Indians, who have no laws it will not do. We have one religion, with which we are satisfied. If the Catholics come into the country, there will be fighting immediately." (Sager, Catherine, *The Whitman Massacre*, Ye Galleon Press, Fairfield, Wash., 1986, p. 44)

The historical fact of the Oregon Territory, as noted earlier, was that there was never a murder, killing, or uprising between the Americans and the Indians for the entire eleven years of the Protestant missionary era until the advent of the Jesuit mission of St. Anne at Umatilla just two days before the Whitman massacre. That fact alone should be enough evidence to force an honest evaluation of the real cause of the Whitman massacre.

The research in chapter six has already documented that the Catholic Counter Reformation at the Council of Trent in the sixteenth century had issued edicts that denied freedom of conscience and freedom of religion. These were historical issues that went to the very heart of the passion and conviction of the Protestant mission in Old Oregon. The Protestant missionaries were teaching the indigenous Indian nations the word of God as written in the Bible and they were using a printing press to put the message of the Bible in the language of the native Indians. The constitutional protected freedoms of the United States east of the Rocky Mountains did not extend to the American Indians in the hotly contested territory of Old Oregon. Again we must digress to reiterate that the Council of Trent had demanded, "The right of private reading of the scriptures prohibited, and its exercise punished. The liberty of the press authoritatively forbidden." (Dowling, p. 488) The impact of the powerful work of the Protestant missionaries in the Oregon Territory had reached the very citadel of the Roman Catholic Church in Rome.

The advent of the Jesuit fathers into the Oregon Territory changed the playing field. These early Jesuit fathers did not operate according to the shared values of the Methodist (Jason Lee) or Calvinist (Whitman, Spalding) missions or even the Catholic values of Hudson's Bay Chief Factor Dr. McLoughlin. According to Oregon historian Horace Lyman, "The spirit of these [Jesuit] missions was strongly sectarian, and that the intention was to win the Indians entirely from the Protestant faith, to which many had been already, more or less, attached, is not at all concealed in the picturesque accounts given by the priest, and it was the most aggressive order of the Catholic Church—the Jesuits—that began these missions." (Lyman, Vol. 3, p. 421)

The Jesuit missionaries came with the express purpose of contending with the Protestant missionaries over Indian converts. The journals of the Jesuits will be documented in this chapter to demonstrate that political control of the Oregon Territory was their ultimate goal. The initial reason for sending the Jesuits was to contend against American interests in Oregon. In contrast, the Protestant missionaries were never sent to contend against the Jesuits for political control of the Oregon Territory or win allegiance of the Indian nations in order to gain political control of the land.

Father Roothaan, the Jesuit General, directed the activities of the Jesuits in Oregon from Rome. (Garraghan, Vol. II, p. 331) Unfortunately, the primary biographer of the Whitmans, Dr. Drury, does not differentiate between Catholic and Jesuit and as previously documented inaccurately identifies many Jesuit priests as Catholic. The distinction is very important. The Jesuit order is by definition a military order whereby all soldiers obey the commands of their commander, otherwise known to the Jesuits as their General. Catholic priests serve under appointment from the Pope with much greater freedom. For the purposes of this research we will call this Catholic Pope the White Pope. The conflict and conspiracy between the two orders has been well documented in many books, especially in relation to the position and power of the Jesuit General known as the Black Pope. (See Cysack, M. F., *The Black Pope*, London: Marshal, Russell & Co., 1896); Griesinger, Theodor, *The Jesuits; Their Complete History*, London: W. H. Allen & Company, 1903); Nicolini, G. B., *History of the Jesuits; Their Origin, Progress, Doctrines, and Designs*, London: Henry G. Bohn, 1854)

The first Jesuit priest in the Territory, Father Blanchet, arrived in Oregon in 1838. His ministry centered in the Willamette Valley in the Mount Angel area. The pioneer of the Columbia Plateau Indians was Jesuit Father Pierre-Jean De Smet. The Jesuit General John Roothaan sent De Smet from St. Louis in 1841 to establish a mission in the Oregon Territory among the Flathead. For the first two years the Protestant mission at Walla Walla worked with no interference from Romanism. With the arrival of Father Blanchet and his associate Father Demers things began to change. Dr. Whitman wrote in May of 1839 to Secretary Greene: "The prospects of (doing) good to the Indians are as favorable as ever if we are permitted to labor without molestation from the Catholics." (Drury, Vol. I, p. 385)

In the summer of 1839 Father Demers spent two weeks at Fort Walla Walla teaching and baptizing the Cayuse Indians. Rev. Spalding recorded the missionaries' concerns in his diary on September 19, 1839: "Doct. speaks of some difficulty with the Catholic priest. He is now at Walla Walla calling the Indians & telling the Indians that we are false teachers because we do not feed & clothe the people, that we have wives as other men, & wear pantaloons as common men & not frocks as he does. The people are told not to come near the Doct. as he is a bad man, & has made no Christians as yet but he [i.e., the priest] will fix them all for heaven soon." (Drury, Vol. I, p. 385)

Marcus Whitman had already put his life on the line as a man of medicine to the indigenous Columbia Indians. It was the custom of these Indians for the right of relatives of a deceased person to kill a te-wat (medicine man) if he was unable to cure the patient. Now the Catholic fathers were spreading deception among the Indians who had no understanding of the age-old conflict between Protestants and Catholics. It was a most troubling time for the Whitmans. Narcissa shared her concerns in a letter to her family in the fall of 1839. She knew the impact of the Jesuit advent into their mission could be ominous. "A Catholic priest has already been at Walla Walla and held meetings with the Indians and used their influence to draw all the people away from us. Some they have forbidden to visit us again, and fill all their minds with distractions about truths we teach, and their own doctrines, say we have been talking to them about their bad hearts long enough, and too long; say we ought to have baptized them long ago, etc, etc. The conflict has begun; what trials await us we know not." (Drury, Vol. I, p. 385)

The Jesuit Father Demers was taking advantage of the Protestant biblical position that to earn eternal life believers must repent of their personal sins, i.e. bad hearts, and commit their hearts to Jesus Christ as personal Lord and Savior. The Protestant missionaries were willing to baptize only those Indian converts who had repented and demonstrated by their changed life Christian fruit. The Jesuits fathers baptized all Indians regardless of action or deed and promised eternal life based on the act of baptism. Indeed, the spiritual conflict that had torn Europe asunder had begun in earnest on the western front.

According to revisionist historians, "The Indians did not take kindly to the Protestant missionaries' theory that he should work and support his family, neither did they find much comfort in the Presbyterian idea of hell, nor the incessant talk about the Indians' manifold sins. While they were naturally very devout, a characteristic that had been noted by many travelers, yet they had grown more or less indifferent to the Protestant forms of worship, and many of the natives looked with favor upon the advent of the priest. These missionaries did not attempt an immediate transformation of character on the part of the Indian…" (Cannon, Miles, WAIILATPU, Capital News Pub. Boise, Idaho 1915, p. 90) No original sources are cited by Miles Cannon to sustain this purported Indian belief system.

Research of the original Protestant letters revealed that the advent of the Jesuit "black robes" grieved the Protestant missionaries. Narcissa Whitman wrote in October of 1841, "The company of Jesuits, twelve in number, consisting of three priests….It is not known where they will settle, but it is reported that they expect to locate themselves somewhere in this region and in the same language that part of our missionaries are occupying. Now we have Catholics on both sides…we feel no disposition to retreat from our work." (Garraghan, Vol. II, p. 266)

On August 23, 1842 Narcissa demonstrated her alarm at the suspicious motives and the growth of the Jesuit mission that was gaining in strength and numbers. "Romanism stalks abroad on our right hand and on our left and with daring effrontery boast that she is to prevail and possess the land. I ask, must it be so? The zeal and energy of her priests are without a parallel and many, both white and Indians, wonder after the beasts. Two are in the country below us and two far above in the mountains." (Garraghan, Vol. II, p. 267)

Narcissa wrote in the same letter, "One of the latter is to return this fall to Canada, the States and the eastern world for a large re-enforcement." (Drury, Vol. I, p. 471) Whitman personally knew that Jesuit Father De Smet was returning to Rome to gather reinforcements for the Catholic Church's design on Oregon. A Bible exists in the possession of George H. Hinds dated 1839, which reads, "Presented to Dr. M Whitman by P. J. De Smet." (Drury, Vol. I, p. 471) While De Smet was in Rome the Jesuit General Father Roothaan established Oregon as a vicariate-apostolic with Jesuit Father Blanchet as bishop. "They believed it best to ask the Holy See to confide the new vicariate to a Jesuit…because they considered that this mission, in order to succeed, should be entrusted principally to Jesuits…" (Garraghan, Vol. I, p. 280)

We have previously documented in chapter six that the Jesuits were the militant wing of the Catholic Church. The Jesuits were a military order under secret direction from the Jesuit General known as the Black Pope. The Jesuit fathers do not submit to the Catholic Pope but rather to the Black Pope. The new vicariate embraced "all the territory between the Mexican province of California on the South, and the Russian province of Alaska on the north and extended from the Pacific Ocean to the Rocky Mountains."(Garraghan, Vol. I. p. 281)

Indeed, the great impact of the Protestant missionaries was not lost upon the Church in Rome. The emerging American Republic was earnestly debating the value or lack of value of Oregon at the very hour the agents of Romanism were attempting to establish papal (Jesuit) authority over the vast Territory. This research has documented that the highest levels of the Tyler administration and the U.S. Congress, swayed by the powerful presence of Secretary of State Daniel Webster, were prepared to yield the Oregon Territory above the Columbia River to the British.

Let us never forget it was the bravery and commitment of these valiant missionaries, particularly Narcissa Whitman and Eliza Spalding, that tipped the scales in the favor of the tiny, self-supporting and often criticized Protestant contingent in the wilderness in the Pacific Northwest. The only obstacle for the new vicariate-apostolic stronghold for the Roman Catholic Church was these isolated Protestant missionaries who represented the ideals of the Republic and refused to relinquish their post. They refused to yield their missionary posts in spite of the imminent danger the designs of Rome placed on them. In 1846 Marcus Whitman wrote to his brother-in-law J. P. Judson who was caught in the Seventh Day Adventist belief that the Lord would return in 1843. "Had I have been of your mind I should have slept, and know the Jesuit Papists would have been in quiet possession of this the only spot in the western horizon of America not before their own. They were fast fixing themselves here, and we missionaries had no American population to come in to hold on and give stability, it would have been a small work for them and the friends of English interests, which they had fully avowed, to have routed us, and then the country might have slept in their hands forever. Time is not so short yet but it is quite important that such country as Oregon should not on one hand fall into the exclusive hands of the Jesuits, not on the other under the English government." (Whitman, Narcissa, p. 216)

Whitman was grieved that no Christian missionaries or families were willing to come to Oregon and support him at Walla Walla. The very missionary heroes who spilled their blood for the prized possession of Oregon would be equally grieved to see into the future the contemporary historical rendition of their missionary purpose, achievements and character.

CHAPTER 21

THE WHITMAN MASSACRE: THE FINAL ACT OF THE OREGON TERRITORY

This research has established the position of the Jesuit priests and the Protestant missionaries. Let us consider next the position of the Cayuse Indians. They had lived in peace with the Protestant missionaries for eleven years. The Indian way of life had changed more in that short period of time than ever before in multiple centuries of history in the Oregon Territory. The buffalo were nearly gone, and Indians' way of life was changing before their eyes. The emigration of white civilization was coming in large waves with each passing year. The Cayuse were reaping material benefits, although the large numbers of emigrants concerned them. The fall of 1847 brought a terrible epidemic of measles and dysentery that killed nearly half of their tribe. W. H. Geiger Jr., the faithful pioneer who managed the Whitman mission the year Marcus and Narcissa were separated, was in a unique place to offer a forthright testimony regarding the relationship between the Cayuse and the Protestant missionaries.

"I was in charge of the station among the Cayuse Indians, who informed me on many occasions that the priests and half-breeds were urgent that they should drive Mr. Spalding and Dr. Whitman out of the country, so that they [the priests] could occupy the country and places of Whitman and Spalding. I asked them on many different occasions if they wanted Messrs. Spalding and Whitman to leave their country after they had been there so long and taught them so much, both in religion and in civilization, and cultivating the soil....They answered, 'Oh, no; it is the priests that are continually desiring us to drive them away.' And again, in 1846 the priests became very urgent and the Catholic Indians became so noisy about the matter that the tribe held a great council about the matter. Doctor Whitman made them a speech. He told them his locks were getting gray. He had spent his best days in trying to do them good, but if they wished him to leave he would be ready to leave in two weeks. After three hours of conference they made their reply as follows: 'When you first came to our country we knew nothing about cultivating the land and making a living that way. We had no cattle, hogs, plows, or hoes. Now we have all these that you have assisted us to procure and taught us to use. Before you came we were always hungry in the winter; now we have plenty to eat and to spare. Formerly we knew but little about God; now we worship him every day in our families. After receiving so much we do not wish you to leave us but stay with us as long as you live, and occupy the place that you now occupy.' I say most emphatically that the Jesuit priests then in this country were the true instigators of the murder of doctor Whitman and those with him, and the Roman Catholic Indians the principle actors.'" (Letter from the Secretary of the Interior, Ye Galleon Press, Fairfield, Wash., 1903, p. 47)

It would be difficult for any modern historian to challenge the testimony of W. H. Geiger, a pioneer Oregon emigrant who witnessed firsthand most of the Protestant missionary era. The Cayuse Indians were indeed prospering under the ministry of the Whitmans, both materially and spiritually. Certainly there were issues of contention between the Protestant missionaries and the Indians over the eleven years, particularly the rising numbers of American emigrants, but nothing to cause the violence and madness that was about to be unleashed against these Presbyterian missionaries.

On August 23, just three months before the massacre, Narcissa wrote a letter to her parents expressing the growing concern the Cayuse were feeling regarding the number of American emigrants who came every summer and fall. "The poor Indians are amazed at the overwhelming numbers of Americans coming into their country. They seem not to know what to make of it. Very many of the principal ones are dying, and some have been killed by other Indians, in going south into the region of California. The remaining ones seem attached to us, and cling to us the closer; cultivate their farms quite extensively, and do not wish to see any Sniapus (Americans) settle among them here; they are willing to have them spend the winter here, but in the spring they all must go. They will be willing to have more missionaries stop and those devoted to their good. They expect that eventually this country will be settled by them, but they wish to see the Willamette filled up first." (Whitman, Narcissa, p. 224).

In Dr. Whitman's last correspondence to Secretary Greene he pointed out his great concern that the Romanists had established two new missions near Waiilatpu. This is the crisis that Whitman had been warning the board about for six years. "A bishop is set over this part of the work, whose seat as the name indicates will be at Walla Walla. It will be well for you to know that from what we can learn, their object will be to colonize around them. I cannot blame myself that the plan I laid down when I was in Boston was not carried out. If we could have had good families, say two or three together, to have placed in select spots among the Indians, the present crisis which I feared would not have come." (Mowry, p. 285)

For six years Marcus and Narcissa had been urging and encouraging and nearly begging other Christians to come and help them. Nobody answered the call. Marcus and Narcissa had accomplished all the legwork to ease the transition for additional Protestant families to come to support the work. In stark contrast Brigham Young was able to lead a small flock of believers into the comparative desert of Utah, with the support of Jesuit priest De Smet, but Whitman was not able to convince one family to join ranks with his Protestant vision for America and Oregon. Marcus wrote, "Can a mind be found so narrow as not to be willing to part with a pastor, or a pastor not to part with a church member, simply because they are good men and useful where they are?" (Mowry, p. 286)

The Cayuse Indians were caught and completely confused in a crossfire between the great spiritual combatants of the modern age. In actual fact most Christians did not understand the dark mysteries of the spiritual battle between Romanism versus Protestantism that continues unabated in the present age. With that truth in mind how could the mostly illiterate, unsophisticated Native American Indians understand the spiritual battle raging between the Protestants and the Romanists? The Columbia Plateau Indians held both the Jesuit "black gowns" and the Doctor and his fellow Protestant missionaries in high esteem. How were the Native Americans to correctly discern the truth regarding the source of agitation about to turn their civilization upside down?

It must have been heartrending for these Cayuse Indians who had faithfully attended the Whitman worship services for a decade to hear accusations that their faithful minister was actually gaining their confidence in order to poison them and take their land as the Romanists claimed. As the hour of the massacre was approaching the Cayuse children and wives were dying daily from the ravages of the measles and dysentery epidemic, yet the white children and women seemed to be protected from horrors of the dreaded

David Manuel painting of Cayuse Indians dying of white man's diseases

epidemic. The shocking brutality and rage perpetrated upon the doctor and his wife and their American co-laborers cannot be understood unless the discerning reader factors in the coaxing and deliberate deception that the black-robed Jesuit fathers were feeding the grief-stricken Indians. Some of the most heinous crimes against the Protestant missionaries were committed by some of their most faithful followers. Some of the closest Cayuse friends of the Whitmans were moved to turn viciously and cold-bloodily against their benefactors.

Let us examine afresh those terrible days and hours before the impending massacre and allow the living witnesses to tell the story. To fully appreciate the terror that was soon to challenge and confront the commitment and courage of those valiant missionaries, this research will examine the diary of twelve-year-old Catherine Sager. By now all the Christians of age at the mission and probably even the little children sensed something was very wrong. This was one crisis that wasn't going to go away. The Jesuits were now on the ground directly confronting the Protestants. The Jesuits most ingeniously used a colorful drawing of a ladder that actually pictured the Protestants poisoning the Indians and leading them to hell to drive their message home. Catherine Sager fully understood that as a Protestant Christian she was one of the enemy the Jesuits were picturing to incite the confused Indians. She knew full well it wasn't just the Doctor who was now in mortal danger from the now highly excited and agitated Indians. The diaries and testimonies of many of the living witnesses who refused (or had no choice) to abandon their posts and survived the horrors of that vicious massacre tell the true story of what really happened. Let us begin with Catherine's diary to set the stage for the horrific slaughter soon to commence.

Old Oregon Under the Shadow of the Almighty 116

"24th (Nov. 1847, five days before the massacre). Today a child of Mr. Osborne's died. We hoped that this afflicting Providence would show the Indians that the whites, in common with themselves, were exposed to the ravages of disease. But from the grave, Timtimmisi, a chief, followed us to the house, and repeated to us the old declaration. 'The Samk Sismussimi (Black gowns) everywhere tell that you are causing us to die. I do not believe it myself, but some of the people do.'"

"25th. Today with Mr. Jackson, Mr. Rogers and myself...encamped with Walla Walla Chief, Piyu, Piyu, Maks-Maks. He said that they had frequently told him that we were poisoning the Indians; that the Bishop told them that the Americans brought the measles into the country....It was on the mouth of every Indian, old and young. The great chief of the Black Gown (the bishops) tells us that the Americans brought the measles into the country; that God sent this disease among the heretics to show the Indians how he hates the Americans. The excitement was intense, and we felt our situation to be most critical. Now that the blood transaction has taken place, circumstances seem to point so plainly to this as the source whence originated the indirect cause of the Massacre, that many are ready to exclaim, 'Why did you not leave your field before?' But so entirely hidden from the eye of the Christian were those influences we feared, that had we left three days before the Massacre the Papists would have settled quietly throughout the country...(and) who would have believed us? The world, the church, and the board would have condemned us as cowards leaving our work before there was danger."

"26th...On returning to the Fort, I entered into a familiar conversation with Rev. Mr. Brisnette, one of the priests who spoke very good English, on the subject of the 'Catholic Ladder,' which for several years has been distributing among our Indians....This ladder and the instructions that usually follow it, generally in the hands of half-breeds previously instructed, declare the Roman Catholic Church to be the only true church, that the Heretic has left the true church when Luther laid aside his black gown and cross and went after a maid; that all were going to Hell; that while we Protestants were by our poisons causing them to die, by our instructions we were sending them to Hell. The excitement produced by these means was most intense, and it is impossible for anyone who was not a constant witness to conceive of the agitated state of the natives when this alarm was fastened upon their superstitious minds, and consequently of our dangerous and critical situation." (Sager, Catherine, Sager, Elizabeth & Sager, Matilda, *The Whitman Massacre of 1847*, Ye Galleon Press, Fairfield, Wash., 1986, pp. 48, 49, 50)

In spite of the almost certain horror that awaited Catherine Sager, this twelve-year-old girl refused to leave or forsake the Protestant ministry. Would you or I have stayed at this post? The fear and dread that the deception was winning in the minds and hearts of the understandably agitated Indians must have been a devastating realization to the virtually defenseless missionaries and their families. There could hardly be one Indian tepee that was not grieving as the epidemic took nearly half their camp. The Sager children had already experienced the loss of both parents on the Oregon Trail. Could they endure being orphaned again? Was Catherine Sager saying she would rather die a vicious horrendous death than compromise the Protestant ministry she was now committed to defend because of the faith of her adopted parents?

Catherine was the oldest of the Sager girls. She was nine when she arrived at the Whitman mission in 1844. She was twelve at the hour of the massacre. The history of the Sager family has been fictionalized throughout most of the twentieth century just like the Whitman massacre. Willsie Morrow wrote a novel called *On to Oregon* in 1926 that sensationalized the Sager children and their courageous journey across the western frontier. This great, but fictionalized, story led to a movie nearly fifty years later called "Seven Alone" which claimed to be a "true story." The problem with *On to Oregon* and "Seven Alone" was the same problem with the twentieth-century rendition of the Whitman massacre. Ms. Morrow, paraphrasing Napoleon in her disingenuous book, said it best: "What is history but a lie agreed upon." (Morrow, p. 7)

This research will document the rest of Catherine Sager's testimony about what really happened at the Whitman massacre. In Catherine's own words, her testimony was given because "it would seem as though truth and justice demand that a true and accurate account should be given by some one who was an eye witness of the melancholy tragedy." (Catherine Sager, p. 9) This testimony will begin with the days leading up to the massacre and with Catherine's explanation why the Whitmans and the Protestant missionaries and teachers did not flee Waiilatpu even though they had been warned their lives were in danger. "Besides, the Board has ever enjoined with us, as also the Captain of our Salvation, to content earnestly for the pure principles of Christianity against error and subverting principles of Romanism, and not to flee before them." (Catherine Sager, p. 49)

Why was Catherine Sager, a child of twelve at the time and married at sixteen, so passionate about her Christian convictions particularly as they related to the Jesuit priests? Perhaps a question that Catherine posed in her memoirs will provide insight into that question. "Let it be distinctly noticed that the Bishop was appointed 'Bishop of Walla of Walla,' and sent into this field with his priests, while there was as yet not a Catholic church or station or priest (stationary) in the whole district, but the field was entirely occupied by Protestant missionaries, most of whom had been quietly laboring in their places for eleven years." (Catherine Sager, p. 50)

Catherine Sager pointed out what every historian has confirmed. There was no war, no warfare, and no killings between the Protestant missionaries and the American emigrants as they molded and rubbed shoulders with the Indians of the Oregon Territory the entire era of the Protestant missionary movement until the Jesuit priests set up a vicariate-apostolate two days before the Whitman massacre. The Columbia Plateau Indians and the American emigrants were similar in spirit and culture. Both races loved independence and freedom. Both races had developed an innate heart to worship their creator without creed or ritualistic form. Both races had a genuine love for the land and wonders of the Oregon Territory. Because of the positive impact of the Americans in the Oregon Territory, from Lewis and Clark to the mountain men and the Protestant missionaries, the two races had merged very favorably with few of the violent confrontations so prevalent throughout history when two divergent races met for the first time.

The advent of the Jesuit priests changed things for the Americans and the Indians in the Pacific Northwest. No evidence of the negative impact of the Jesuits on the American Protestants could be more pronounced than the witness of the Catholic ladder. The living witness of the Catholic ladder and subsequent Protestant ladder constructed by Eliza Spalding are still on display at Tamastslikt museum near Pendleton. The confusion in the hearts and minds of the Cayuse Indians over the dueling ladders remains to this day.

One of the greatest spiritual confrontations of all time, let alone in the history of the Oregon Territory, came from the pen of the twelve-year-old Catherine Sager as she stood uncompromisingly against the power and might of the Jesuit priests. That the Almighty would choose to use a twelve-year-old girl to confront the Romanist designs of the Vatican for Oregon was extraordinary. "My attention had been suddenly arrested by the outcries and wailing of the whole camp, occasioned by the arrival of someone with an additional explanation of the Catholic ladder, always accompanied with the declaration, 'The American missions are causing you to die.'" (Catherine Sager, p. 50) The Cayuse Indians would lose half their tribe to this virulent measles and dysentery epidemic. The whole Cayuse village was wailing because of the additional grief they were enduring because they were being led to believe with the added illustration of the Catholic ladder that the Americans were in fact poisoning them to destroy their nation and culture. Not only were the Americans poisoning them but also they were teaching them lies that would cause them to go to hell. It was the Christian Protestant doctrine of Catherine Sager that was being challenged and in fact putting her life in jeopardy.

Most twentieth-century historians blame both Protestants and Catholics for confusing the Columbia Indians with the so-called dueling ladders. In actual fact, as documented by Catherine Sager, the Protestants developed similar ladders in a defensive attempt to contend with the incendiary and inflammable accusations of the Catholic ladder against the Protestants. The unsophisticated and unworldly Cayuse Indians were caught in the crossfire of the spiritual battle of the age between the Protestant Reformation and the Catholic Counter Reformation. "I told the priest that in self defense and in order to counteract these false ideas, I had prepared a chart on which was exhibited the rise of the Papal Church as predicted by Paul, 1st Timothy IV, 3; 2nd Thess. II, 3." (Catherine Sager, p. 50) One of the scriptures that Catherine referred to was First Timothy chapter four where Paul warned, "In the latter times some shall depart from the faith, giving heed to seducing spirits, and doctrines of devils; speaking lies in hypocrisy; having their conscience seared with a hot iron; Forbidding to marry…" (I Tim. 4:1-3)

In the chart that the twelve-year-old Protestant orphan developed she pictured the Romanists as those who came in the name of God but in truth having departed from the true faith, "speaking lies in hypocrisy; having their conscience seared with a hot iron; Forbidding to marry." The Jesuit and Catholic priests forbid marrying, fulfilling the scripture Paul exhorted eighteen centuries earlier. The Jesuit oath of absolute subservient obedience to the superior General of the Order instead of Jesus Christ fulfilled the scripture "having their conscience seared with a hot iron." This twelve-year-old orphan was better versed in Christian doctrine than many Protestant ministers in the twenty-first century. How many Protestant ministers of the present age would be willing or have the courage and conviction to stand and confront toe to toe the Vicar General of the Jesuit Order?

"Not to do anything like working behind their back, the 'Chart' was brought out and spread before the Bishop and his priest, and briefly explained: The equality of the Apostles as declared by their great Head is exhibited on this chart; the rise of the man of Sin as foretold by Paul, and which history and observation compel us to believe to be the Church of Rome by one marked sign, 'Forbidding to marry'; and the abominable sin of idolatry in the worship of images and bowing to the cross, is represented in the chart sitting in the temple of God, proclaiming himself God by the act of forgiving sin for fixed sums of money….The exhibition of this chart called forth a close but friendly discussion."

"I told him we understood where each other stood, he and his church looked upon us as vile heretics, and worthy to be persecuted and expelled from the country, and reminded him of the means, the Catholic Ladder, which would soon effect this object if not counteracted. On the other hand we Protestants regarded the Papal church as the 'Man of Sin'; and while I would as a neighbor afford them every facility my limited means would allow to aid them in beginning, in the way of provisions, seeds, native books, etc., as I presumed they would do the same for us in like circumstances, as a minister of the gospel of Christ set for its defense in this part of the world, and especially as having been first and longest in the field, we should exert ourselves to the utmost to enlighten and instruct the people and to disabuse them of the errors and highly inflammatory doctrines spreading through the country by this Catholic Ladder and its teachers, greatly to our prejudice and danger." (Catherine Sager, p. 51)

Catherine wrote this testimony a few years after the massacre. She was no longer a twelve-year-old girl but was nonetheless still a teenager. She presented the greatest defense of the Protestant ministry against the Jesuit ministry of the Catholic ladder on record during the confrontation between the great spiritual rivals. She was not intimidated by her adversaries and by her account the Jesuit fathers were most respectful and apparently enjoyed the spiritual sparring. Catherine fearlessly confronted the Jesuit bishop and his priests. The scripture she referred to was the second book of Thessalonians chapter two, verse three, "Let no man deceive you by any means: for that day shall not come, except there come a falling away first, that the man of sin be revealed, the son of perdition." The "day" the scripture was referring to was the coming of the Lord Jesus Christ. Not only did she confront them by boldly presenting her own "ladder," she also fearlessly challenged them that Paul actually was speaking about the Roman Church and the Pope as the "Man of Sin." Catherine Sager's theology and understanding of scripture would challenge many seminary theologians of the 21st century America.

The purpose of this history is not to criticize the Catholic Church. At the turn of the 21st century the Catholic Church in America has been at the forefront of the cause of justice in the land in defense of the unborn against the genocidal practice of abortion. In like manner the Catholic faith has been at the forefront in the spiritual battle to uphold the word of God regarding the sin of homosexuality. The purpose of this research is not to champion any faith or religion but rather uplift the timeless values of truth, liberty and the authority of the inerrant word of God.

The exchange between Catherine and the bishop just days before the massacre, incited largely by the Catholic ladder, was a classic confrontation illustrating the root source of the contest for the Oregon Territory. The Cayuse Indians probably would never have properly understood the actual chart that Catherine had developed; however, the impact on the Papists was most fascinating for the student of history. We are documenting a twelve-year-old orphan girl confronting multiple Jesuit priests representing General Roothaan, the Black Pope of Rome. Catherine was in fact calling the Pope, their superior, the very one Paul had prophesized to be the terrible "man of sin" warned about through much of the New Testament, especially in the book of Revelation.

The next exchange between the soon-to-be-twice-orphaned twelve-year-old and the Jesuit priests was illustrative of the much larger battle that was taking place between the Protestant Reformation and the Catholic Counter Reformation. "I asked them, 'is it true, as claimed by one of your authors, that the priests have the power to reproduce the body of Christ?' Mr. Brisnette replied distinctly that he and every priest had power given to them to recreate the person of Jesus Christ entire, flesh, blood, and bones, head, hands, and feet, just as he was here on earth; and further have the power to communicate the Holy Ghost, and to give the Father himself. My blood ran cold! I was shocked at the blasphemy of my friend, who otherwise treated me like a gentleman." (Catherine Sager, p. 51)

The central issue that brought on the Whitman massacre was the same issue that brought on the Protestant Reformation. Martin Luther, a former priest of the Church of Rome, described the Catholic Mass as "an unspeakable abomination, quite contrary to the principal article of justification by faith alone." (Semlyen, p. 37) According to the Church of Rome, when Christ said "It is finished" he did not mean he had once and for all time died for the sins of all mankind but rather "that he had finished his earthly life and was now ready to offer himself as the perpetual victim or host." (Semlyen, p. 36)

The Jesuit priest attempted to calm Catherine's dismay and disgust at the Catholic ceremony of Mass whereby the real body of Christ was cut into pieces and fed to the believers. "'It was the glorified body of the Lord that they reproduced and sacrificed; therefore it was incapable of suffering when cut up.' I replied, 'Your Mass then answers no purpose. The law of God requires as the condition of salvation, 'without the shedding of blood, i.e., without suffering there is no remission of sins. The glorified body of Christ cannot shed blood nor suffer.' He then shifted back again and said, 'We continue the sacrifice that was commenced on the cross.' I rejoined, 'You admit the awful fact: the natural real person of our blessed Savior was nailed to the cross and murdered by wicked Jews. You claim to continue that wicked murder. Therefore by your own position you are murderers and cannibals, and it unavoidably follows that the system of Catholicism is downright cannibalism or base deception.'" (Catherine Sager, p. 52)

It is amazing that historians for over a century have missed one of the most remarkable theological debates of all time. The profound theological doctrinal differences between the Protestant and Catholic positions regarding Jesus Christ and the eternal salvation through his death on the Cross have never been so dramatically addressed in such an intense environment with so much at stake. To the Jesuit priests the Protestant missionaries were the heretics, the enemies of the mother church to be purged by whatever means necessary to restore Papal authority. To the Protestant Reformers the Catholic mass and worship of the Pope were blasphemy. The two religions could never coexist. The Cayuse Indians had no cultural or heritage foundation to comprehend these profound theological differences. They would soon be caught in the crossfire of a massacre with their own hands red with the blood of their blessed benefactor and his wife and fellow Americans. The Cayuse Indians have never properly recovered from this tragedy.

Catherine Sager wrote only days before the massacre "…the Indians appeared friendly, were constantly coming for medicine, gruels, and other food,

Photo of Catherine Sager Pringle

and were warm in expressing their gratitude to the Doctor for his unwearied attention to them. Before the epidemic the Cayuse were in a more promising condition than ever before. They were enlarging their farms, fencing them better, employing the Doctor to build granaries, breaking up the land, building fences, etc., who kept from time to time several teams employed for this purpose. Their attention to religious instruction was not abated, and they were giving him no trouble as formerly about the mill, the land, the timber, etc. In fact, aside from the alarming movements of the Catholics crowding upon him, he was more encouraged than at any other time." (Sager, Catherine & Sager, Matilda, p. 53)

We have considered the position of Catherine Sager, the orphaned pioneer emigrant. Let us consider the plight of Dr. Whitman. He had not only petitioned the American missionary board to send some Christian reinforcements, but more significantly Whitman had petitioned the United States government to establish a series of forts or stations to bring order, communication and protection to the American citizens living in the Territory. Whitman had sent the synopsis of the bill he was proposing to the Secretary of War on his return from Washington in 1843. Even after the successful resolution of the Joint Occupation Accord with England, Congress and the Polk administration had not responded to the great need for the American institutions of law and order in the Territory. Just six weeks before Whitman and his Protestant missionaries were murdered he again petitioned the Secretary of War to establish a line of posts and American troops to enforce protection and regulation of the Indian Territory.

The day before the massacre the Jesuit Bishop Blanchet, Vicar General Father Brouillet and LeClair were to open their mission at Young Chief's house on the Umatilla River. A messenger from the Indian village had been sent to seek Dr. Whitman's aid for the sick at the camp in Umatilla. Many were sick at the Whitman station and Helen Mar Meek and Louise Sager were gravely ill. It is surprising Whitman made the twenty-five mile journey. Henry Spalding was with Whitman that morning and recalled the journey. "The Doctor requested me to accompany him to the Umatilla, leaving dear Sister Whitman…greatly exhausted with her long and incessant watching with the sick, with three of her own and one of Mrs. Osborne's [children] dangerously ill, to require her constant attention, Mrs. Osborne not yet able to leave her bed…" (Drury, Vol. II, pp. 218-19) When the reader considers that this trip would put them in the camp of the Jesuit priests on Sunday morning, the Christian Sabbath, the rationale for the trip takes on a greater urgency. Dr. Whitman rarely traveled on the Christian Sabbath and only the greatest emergency would cause him to vacate his post at Walla Walla on the Sabbath.

Certainly it was highly probable that the Doctor's call was more than a sick call. For the first time in the missionary era in Oregon the Jesuits had a mission planted within the midst of the Presbyterian mission. Spalding recalled their thoughts that evening. "But the principle topic of conversation that dark night was the danger that threatened from another source….We felt that the present sickness among the Indians afforded the Catholics a favorable opportunity to excite them to drive us from the country….[Whitman said] unless the Indians requested us to leave, his days were few….If I am to fall, through the machinations of Papists, my death may do as much good to Oregon, as my life can." (Drury, Vol. II, p. 219)

The Whitmans had made a life commitment to serve God and honor his call to the Cayuse Indians. They must have known their days were not to be long on the earth, but where could they find relief from the perilous agitation all around him? If they were to flee, where would they go? How could they move the entire missionary compound? Chief Factor McLoughlin had been replaced at Vancouver and another pro-Jesuit Catholic half-breed, William McBean, now commanded Fort Walla Walla. The reader may wonder why Whitman didn't arm his men and protect his mission and his family. Throughout Whitman's eleven-year ministry in Old Oregon he had adhered to a policy of non-violence. To take up arms against the Indians he had committed his life to minister to was unthinkable. There was no alternative for the Whitmans except trust the Lord and stay the course.

The two men spent the night with Stickus, the Cayuse Indian who led the first wagon train across the Blue Mountains. Stickus conducted Sunday morning worship and provided a hearty breakfast, which encouraged the missionaries. Spalding was moved to compare "their present abundance of comfortable living (with) their wretchedness and starvation when we came among them, eleven years before." (Drury, Vol. II, p. 220) Stickus warned Whitman that the half-breed Joe Lewis was inciting the Indians and Tamuscky was going to kill him.

Whitman visited the new Saint Anne Jesuit Mission at Young Chief's house. Father Brouillet recorded the visit: "…We were visited by Dr. Whitman, who remained but a few minutes at the house, and appeared to be much agitated. Being invited to dine he refused, saying that he feared it would be too late, as he had twenty five miles to go, and wished to reach home before night. On parting he entreated me not to fail to visit him when I would pass by his mission, which I very cordially promised to do." (Drury, Vol. II, p. 221)

This was the reason Whitman made the visit to the Jesuit mission at Saint Anne. He knew the two rival missions would destroy the Christian witness to the Cayuse Indians. The Protestant ministry was not compatible with the Jesuit Catholic ministry. Whitman knew full well that at the very best the only result would be confusion and dissension in the ranks of the Cayuse. One mission would have to go. Spalding recorded Whitman's thoughts: "About four, the Doctor returned, much fatigued, but said the sickness in his family made it necessary to return. Said he had taken tea with the Bishop and two of his priests….Said he invited them to come and see him, which they had promised to do in a short time. The Doctor was much pleased with the idea, hoping that we might come to some understanding and bring it before the Indians to say who should be their missionaries." (Drury, Vol. II, p. 221) Whitman rode to Umatilla to press the Jesuits to meet with him and the Cayuse with the purpose of determining which ministry would stay and which would leave. Whitman knew two rival Christian ministries would be disastrous for the Cayuse.

Whitman rode home alone that winter night. Spalding had injured his knee and could not travel for a few days. Whitman was exhausted and even during his renowned ride across America in the winter of '42-43 he had only traveled on Sunday once. The ominous situation at Waiilatpu bade him ride on Sunday. Whitman was ready to yield his mission if the Cayuse so affirmed. If not, then it would be the responsibility of the Jesuits to leave their station and end the contention they had initiated. Surely he must have reasoned they were reasonable men and would respect such a plan that could only work to the benefit of the Christian witness to the Cayuse nation.

When Marcus arrived at Waiilatpu late in the evening he relieved John and Francis Sager who were up caring for the sick children. Catherine Sager recorded the last night of the missionary. "I could see Father was much troubled about something and I supposed it was about the sick children. After making the rounds, Marcus called Narcissa. She arose and the two sat by the stove in the living room, where they talked in low tones. He related to her what Stickus had told him that day; also that he had learned that the Indians were holding councils every night….His manner and portions of their conversation, which I had heard, kept me awake. Father observed my wakefulness and seemed to understand the reason. He soothed me with kind words until I finally fell asleep and slept until morning." (Drury, Vol. II, p. 222)

Marcus and Narcissa and even twelve-year-old Catherine must have known full well that they would not survive the councils that were being held to take their lives. It was to be the final night of their ministry at Waiilatpu, the final night of their Protestant mission in Oregon and the final night of the Whitmans' lives. Thirteen other Protestant missionaries were to be slain alongside the martyred Christians. The two sick children would die of attrition in the coming months. The horror of the massacre would be very painful to document. The frenzied Cayuse driven to destroy and molest their Christian benefactors would brutalize the surviving girls.

The sheer madness of the events that transpired in the now famous Whitman massacre have been re-crafted and revised to make them politically, culturally and religiously acceptable. Fortunately, the eyewitness testimony of the living witnesses has been recorded for posterity. It would be an understatement to record that the testimony of the living witnesses does not match up to the re-crafted and sanitized rationale now rendered in modern history books for this bloody massacre.

Based on the research of this book it most certainly was the plan of the Almighty for Protestant Christians to answer the call of Marcus and Narcissa Whitman to support this mission with the future of the Oregon Territory in the balance. But precious few answered the call. It was the will of the Almighty for the United States government to answer Whitman's call and send troops and build stations to protect the fragile American investment secured by a tiny Protestant contingent. But no troops were sent and no stations were built. There was only one other way for the Almighty to keep the Oregon Territory under his protective shadow. Marcus and Narcissa and their fellow Christians had to be sacrificed to pay the price for freedom and liberty the government and the Protestant Christians in the East were unwilling to pay.

The light of freedom and liberty gifted to the world by our Protestant Reformation heritage was about to be snuffed out throughout the Oregon Territory by the forces of darkness sent from a foreign power in Europe. It would appear that the free men of the Christian Church in the East who had heard Whitman's call and were blessed with liberty and freedom from birth were not willing to respond to God's call for help. Will the Christians of the present hour be willing to respond to the truth of history of what really happened at the

Whitman massacre and sustain the ministry and message the Whitmans and their fellow missionaries laid down their lives for?

CHAPTER 22

EYEWITNESS ACCOUNTS OF THE WHITMAN MASSACRE

If the significant historical events in the land of the Pacific Northwest were the progressive movements of a symphony, then the Whitman massacre would be the climax of over three centuries of progressive movements toward ultimate control of Oregon. The titanic clash of Protestant values versus Roman Catholic values was about to collide head on. There would be no coexistence, peace accord, joint occupation treaty, or mediated settlement.

The seven Roman Catholic missionaries Dr. Drury documents who met Dr. Whitman on September 23, 1847 just over two months before the brutal slaying of the Protestants were actually seven Jesuit Romanists under direct order from the Jesuit General Father Roothaan, the Black Pope. Roothaan wrote in February of 1847 "that under no circumstances was the mission to be abandoned." (Garraghan, p. 331) These soldiers of the Jesuit order were not American. Their origin and heritage was European and their allegiance was to Rome, not the American Constitution or the ideals of the American Republic. They came under a "special charge of obedience" (Garraghan, p. 280) established in 1843 because it was most unusual for Jesuits to accept ecclesiastical dignities. The proposed vicariate-apostolic for the entire Oregon Territory to be established at Walla Walla was to be confided to the Jesuit fathers "because in order to succeed [the vicariate-apostolic] should be entrusted principally to the Jesuits." (Garraghan, p. 280)

This mission was so vital to Rome that the seven Jesuit priests were fully funded and commissioned with orders to establish seven Catholic mission stations to compete with the Protestant missionaries for religious sovereignty in the Oregon Territory and the allegiance of the Indian nations. Ex-Catholic priest Rev. Charles Chiniquy warned, "Romanism and liberty can not live on the same ground....Romanism, under the mask of religion, is nothing but the permanent political conspiracy against all the most sacred rights of man and the most Holy laws of God." (Chiniquy, p. 4) Romanism worked clandestinely behind the scenes to destroy the Protestant ministry of the Whitmans. While the Jesuit General was the power and the priests were the commanders in the battle, they never picked up arms or bloodied their own hands. That was always left to terrorist agents trained for such warfare. In this instance subterfuge was the tool of choice to enrage the ignorant to commit acts of violence. In that manner the Jesuit priests could always appear innocent and above such dastardly deeds.

Joe Lewis was the secret agent hit man of the Jesuits. The Christian Church of Oregon in 1870 tied Joe Lewis directly to the Jesuit priests. "This vicar-general (Brouillet) was on the ground at Waiilatpu during the horrible butchery, which lasted eight days, with his bishop and thirteen priests, direct from Europe, camped at helping distance around, and with one of his overland party—an educated half breed from Canada, by the name of Joe Lewis—at the window outside, by Dr. Whitman's head, to give the signal for the tomahawks to commence, who shot Mrs. Whitman through the breast, and with his own hands butchered Hoffman and two other Americans; who told the Cayuse and Oregon Indians he had seen, before he left the States, the letters of Spalding and Mrs. Whitman calling for poison to come by the emigrants to kill the Cayuse and the Nez Perce." (Spalding, 41st Congress, p. 54)

It was common knowledge in the Protestant Church of the 19th century after the Whitman massacre that Joe Lewis came with the Jesuit party from Europe for the express purpose of directing and taking part in the murder of the Whitmans and most of the male Protestant Christians at Walla Walla. Joe Lewis was a well-educated, outwardly devout Catholic of mixed Canadian Indian blood who accompanied the emigration of '47. Upon his arrival he immediately began stirring up trouble for the Protestants. Whitman clothed him and sent him away with an emigrant heading for the valley but Lewis mysteriously returned three days later.

David Manuel painting of Joe Lewis

Three other non-Cayuse individuals, two somewhat employed at the mission, figured heavily in the massacre. Joseph Stanfield was a Canadian Frenchman and Nicholas Finlay was a French half-breed formerly employed by the Hudson's Bay Company. Lewis, Stanfield, and Finlay orchestrated the slaughter and all were Catholic and/or Jesuit. The fourth non-Cayuse who figured prominently in the massacre was Jesuit priest Rev. J. B. A. Brouillet, Vicar General of Walla Walla. His testimony of the massacre was recorded in a document called "Protestantism in Oregon" which will be examined closely in the next chapter for answers to these brutal murders that have eluded historians since the turn of the twentieth century.

Joe Lewis was the ringleader in this diabolical plot conceived in the citadels of Rome. "He told the writer (Henry Spalding) he was born in Canada and educated in Maine. He was a good scholar and good mechanic and had the appearance of an eastern half-bred, spoke the English and his native tongue and was a devoted Catholic, wearing his cross and counting his beads often. The emigrants of that year saw him first at Fort Hall, and Mrs. Lee testifies that he was

David Manuel painting of the murder of Dr. Marcus Whitman

several times heard to say, 'There will be a change in that country (Walla Walla) when the Fathers get down.'" (Spalding, 41st Congress, p. 28)

Lewis showed up mysteriously at Fort Hall. Dr. Ruby has documented that Lewis was protected and found refuge at the Mormon camp in Utah after the massacre. Fort Hall was not far from the Mormon enclave in the Utah Territory. Spalding documented that Lewis told the Cayuse Indians "they would receive plenty of ammunition from below." (Spalding, 41st Congress, p. 28) J. Ross Browne previously documented that the Mormons sent ammunition, muskets, and gunpowder to the Cayuse Indians after the Whitman massacre. Joe Lewis joined forces with American emigrants of 1847 at Fort Hall. All historical documentation proved that his sole purpose was to go the Protestant mission at Waiilatpu to incite the Cayuse Indians through lies and deceptions to kill Whitman and the Protestant missionaries and fellow American emigrants at the station.

Henry Spalding in his report to Congress established that "Lewis was evidently engaged in Canada to do this work, as he came over with the party from Europe" (Spalding, 41st Congress, p. 28). Lewis had been trained in Europe, probably Rome, under the military covenants of the Jesuits. Dr. Ruby has documented that Lewis found sanctuary in the Mormon camp in Utah after he murdered, in their sleep, three Cayuse Indians who fled with him.

In the previous chapter we left the Whitmans on the eve of the horrific events to commence the following day. About one-thirty in the afternoon, Nov. 29, 1847, the Cayuse began to gather in large numbers. The Americans were butchering a beef and the Whitmans were attending to the sick, Lorinda

Bewley and Catherine and Elizabeth Sager, who were recovering from the measles. A group of Cayuse came to the house and Chief Teloukaite engaged Marcus in a conversation while Tamayhas worked behind him with a hidden tomahawk. Two blows to the head mortally wounded Whitman. "John Sager, sitting in the room, drew his pistol but was shot by Indians who had their Hudson Bay muskets concealed under their blankets." (Helm, Myra Sager, *Lorinda Bewley and the Whitman Massacre*, Metropolitan Press, Portland, Oregon, 1951, p. 37)

The slaughter had begun and would continue off and on for two weeks. Joe Lewis and perhaps a dozen young braves along with Chief Teloukaite, Tamayhas and Tamuscky took part in the massacre. Narcissa and Mrs. Hayes dragged Marcus into the living room. She "placed his head upon a pillow, doing all she could to stop the bleeding and revive him but to no purpose; the dreadful work was done. She begged him to speak to her, questioning him, but at all her questions he replied 'no,' in a low voice." (Helm, p. 38)

Frank Sager helped his sisters to hide in the attic but Joe Lewis was on to them and ordered them down. "Frank did not come down with the others, no doubt could have escaped, but he understood the Indian language, and hearing them say they were going to kill them all he came down and going to his beloved little sister Matilda he put his arms around her and said, 'The Indians will kill me, but if you are spared, be a good girl, and meet me in heaven." (Helm, p. 39) Lewis shot and killed Frank Sager; however, the Indian chief Teloukaite did not have the heart to kill the children and they were spared. Fortunately, Lewis did not make that decision or probably all the children would have been killed.

Sager sisters

Narcissa Whitman was shot in the breast as she looked out the window. "She sank on her knees, praying fervently to God to protect her adopted children; again to be left orphaned, and her aged Mother and Father, that they might be sustained under this terrible shock. She prayed also for the savages, for they knew not what they did. Some of them, it is said, hearing her pray for them, turned away in shame and took no further part in the massacre." (Helm, p. 39) Narcissa was taken out of the house on a settee with Mr. Rogers carrying one end and Joe Lewis the other. Lewis had promised her there would be no more killing but he lied, and the Indian shot both Rogers and Whitman when Lewis dropped the settee. Both were left to die on that cold November night.

Josiah Osbourne, who along with his family witnessed the initial killings at Waiilatpu, miraculously escaped with his family. "As the guns fired and yells commenced, I leaned my head upon the bed and committed myself and family to my maker. My wife removed the loose floor. I dropped under the floor with my sick family in their nightclothes, taking only two woolen sheets, a piece of bread and some cold mush, and pulled the floor over us. In five minutes the room was full of Indians, but they did not discover us. The roar of guns, the yells of the savages, and the crash of the clubs, and the knives, and the groans of the dying continued till dark. We distinctly heard the dying groans of Mrs. Whitman, Mr. Rodgers, and Francis till they died away, one after the other. We heard Mr. Rogers's last, in slow voice, 'come Lord Jesus, come quickly,' and heard no more. Soon after this I removed the floor, and went out. We saw the white face of Francis by the door. It was warm as we laid our hand upon it, but he was dead. I carried my two youngest children who

David Manuel painting of the murder of Narcissa Whitman

were sick, and my wife held on to her clothes in her great weakness. We had all been sick with the measles. Two infants had died. She had not left her bed for six weeks till that day, when she stood up a few minutes. The naked, painted Indians were dancing the scalp-dance around a large fire at a little distance. There seemed no hope for us, and we knew not which way to go, but we bent our steps toward Fort Walla Walla. A dense, cold fog shut out every star and the darkness was complete." (Spalding, Henry, "Letter for the Secretary of the Interior," (41st Congress, Ex. Doc 37. pp. 31, 32)

    The chances for survival for the Osbourne family were slim at best. Osbourne's wife was very sick with measles and his children were not much stronger. It was a cold winter's night and Fort Walla Walla was nearly twenty miles away. There were rivers to cross and frantic Indians to evade. They would need some providential help to make the Fort and even that would not guarantee their survival. "My wife almost fainted but staggered along. Mill Creek which we had to wade, was high from the late rains, and came up to my waist. My wife in her great weakness came near washing down but held on to my clothes. I braced myself with a stick, holding a child in each arm. I had to cross five times for the children. The water was icy cold and the air freezing some. Staggering alone about two miles, Mrs. Osborne fainted and could go no farther, and we hid ourselves in the brush of the Walla Walla River, not far below Tom Stuckey's (a chief) lodges, who was very active at the commencement of the butchery. We were thoroughly wet and the cold fog, like snow, was about us." (41st Congress, Ex. Doc. 37, p. 32)

    There can be no question that the Osbornes were prepared to protect their lives as the hour of the massacre drew near. They had prepared a hiding place under the floorboards of the roughly finished cabin. It must have been terrifying to listen to the frenzied, bloodthirsty cries of the Cayuse Indians and the

David Manuel painting of the Osbourne family escaping the Whitman Massacre

agonizing groans of their dear compatriots as they took their dying breaths. It was a miracle that the Osbornes escaped, particularly considering the impact of the ravages of measles and the infirmity of the bedridden mother now lying in the frozen mud. It would take a greater miracle for a measles-ravaged family to make the twenty-mile journey to Fort Walla Walla in the bitter cold of winter.

"I spread one sheet down on the frozen ground; wife and children crouched upon it. I covered the other over them. I thought they must soon perish, as they were shaking and their teeth rattling terribly with the cold. I kneeled down and commended us to my maker." (41st Congress, Ex. Doc. 37, p. 32) The Osbornes could not travel by day as the Indians furiously worked the trail toward Fort Walla Walla. They hid by day and traveled by night toward Fort Walla Walla. "That day seemed like a week. Expected every moment my wife would breathe her last. Tuesday night felt our way to the trail, and staggered along to Suctucks Nima (dry creek), which we waded as we did the other creek and kept on about two miles, when my wife fainted, and could go no farther. Crawled into the brush and frozen mud, to shake and suffer on from hunger and cold without sleep." (41st Congress, Ex. Doc. 37, p. 32)

Osborne was also suffering from measles as well as exposure, but nevertheless he knew his only hope was to set out with his strongest son for Fort Walla Walla and safety. He did hear one passing horseman in the dead of night and later learned it was Henry Spalding also traveling by the cover of darkness. Miraculously Osbourne safely reached the fort without being discovered. "Reached Fort Walla Walla after daylight; begged Mr. McBean for horses to get my family, for food, blankets and clothing, to take to them, and to take care of my child till I could bring my family to his fort. Mr. Hall (another Protestant missionary

Old Oregon Under the Shadow of the Almighty   130

who escaped the massacre) had come in on Monday night, but he could not have an American at his fort, and he had put him over the Columbia River; that he could not let me have horses, or anything for my wife and children, and I must go to Umatilla. Insisted on bringing my family to the fort, but he refused, said he would not let us in. I next begged the priests to show pity, as my wife and children must perish, and the Indians would undoubtedly kill me, but with no better success. I then begged to leave my child, who was now safe at the fort, but they refused." (41st Congress, Ex. Doc. 37, p. 32)

Professor Bourne and fellow revisionist historians have ridiculed evidence of Hudson's Bay complicity against the Protestant missionaries as anti-Catholic bigotry. William McBean and the Jesuit priests had refused sanctuary to another Whitman mission refugee, Peter B. Hall, sentencing him to his death. Only his clothes were found near Fort Walla Walla. When Henry Spalding publicly challenged McBean in 1866 to supply an explanation why he did not provide sanctuary for Peter Hall, McBean replied: "He (Hall) finally resolved to leave and make to The Dalles. I remarked to him that it was rash and imprudent....The fort being enclosed, doors locked day and night, and fortified with two bastions, he would be safer in it than he would be in the open plain. My argument had no force. I then asked him if he left a wife and children at the Mission. He replied that he had, but supposed them all killed. I observed that it was only a supposition; they might still be living, and it was wrong to leave them without ascertaining their fate. With tears in his eyes, he begged and entreated me to let him go, being sure to reach The Dalles. Finding he was determined, I provided him with a coat, provisions, and other necessaries for his voyage, and advised him to take the route less frequented by the Indians (across the Columbia River), and to travel only during the night, he would then have a better chance of evading any camp by noticing their fire. I saw him safely across and the last tidings I had of him was that he had safely reached within a few miles of the Deschutes, but unfortunately having taken a canoe from the Indians and being near a rapid he run down and was drowned." (Drury, Vol. II, pp. 242-43)

When William McBean sent his personal interpreter to Fort Vancouver to provide word of the massacre he "gave Bushman strict orders not to say anything to Perrin Whitman or others at The Dalles regarding what had taken place at Waiilatpu." (Drury, Vol. II, p. 267) According to revisionist historians, McBean was fearful that if the Cayuse should discover that he had written to Fort Vancouver they would become angry and attack his fort. The Cayuse feared the Hudson's Bay Company. Their numbers were decimated by the measles epidemic. Only a few leaders took part in the Whitman massacre. No honest historian of Oregon history would swallow the lies of McBean.

Dr. Henry Saffrons was at The Dalles when Bushman arrived. "A Frenchman, as expressed from Walla-Walla to Vancouver, had arrived in haste, and desired Mr. Hinman (early merchant pioneer) to assist him on as all the men at Fort Walla-Walla had died of measles, and Mr. Hinman had left for Vancouver. Scarcely had they gone when the Indians came in and told us that Dr. Whitman and his wife and all the Americans at his station had been killed by the Cayuse. We could not believe it, as no letter had arrived from Walla-Walla, and the French man had told us that he did not believe that Dr. Whitman was dead. Some days after an Indian came and said the Cayuse had collected at Des Chutes; that they had said the Catholic priests had made known to them that the doctor was a dangerous medicine-man to have among them; that Mr. McBean, in charge of Fort Walla-Walla, had said that Dr. Whitman determined to have all their spotted horses." (41st Congress, Ex. Doc. 38, p. 38)

The contorted logic historians have developed to cover the actions of William McBean has defied explanation for a century. McBean claimed he provided sanctuary, provisions, clothing, etc. for Hall and he provided only the assistance of an Indian (with a stern command not to return to the fort) for Osbourne who he knew was going back to save his wife and children. McBean thereafter attached a coward label upon Hall for refusing to help his wife and children, when in fact McBean was the coward for refusing to help Osbourne or Hall save their families. Furthermore, McBean claimed he advised Hall to seek refuge at The Dalles, but gave strict orders to Bushman to keep the news of the massacre from the Protestant missionaries at The Dalles. No historian has ever established evidence that the Hudson's Bay Company or any foreigners (non-Protestant) in the Oregon Territory were ever in danger from the Indian uprising at this time. William McBean actually claimed on March 12, 1866 in the Walla Walla *Statesman* that he sent his spokesman Bushman on the second day of the uprising "who was able to prevent the massacre of the women and children" (Drury, Vol. II, p. 272). Jesuit Father Brouillet, who was intimately involved in the Cayuse uprising, declared: "If Americans only have been killed, it is because the war had been declared by the Indians against the Americans only, and not against the foreigners..." (Brouillet, Rev. J. B. A., *Protestantism in Oregon*, 35th Congress, Ex. Doc. 38, p.48)

While there has been no documented evidence that the Hudson's Bay Company and the Jesuit priests were ever in danger from the Columbia Plateau Indians, historians in the twentieth century have turned a blind eye to irrefutable evidence of the complicity of both in the war on the Americans. If Brouillet knew firsthand the Cayuse had only declared war on the Americans how can he excuse his failure to help the Americans based on fear for his own safety?

It will be difficult for the reader to comprehend how the Jesuit priests could reject the desperate begging of a fellow Christian at Fort Walla Walla. Most twentieth-century historians, such as Dr. Clifford Drury, have justified the actions of the priests. According to these historians the priests had to be careful not to do anything that would endanger their own lives. There is not one single solitary shred of evidence from any source to verify the Jesuit excuse that their lives would have been in danger should they have attempted to help the desperate Americans. This was the excuse that Jesuit Vicar General Brouillet used to justify why he could not help the Protestants being slaughtered in the midst of his presence during the Whitman massacre. These Jesuit priests were safe and secure at Fort Walla Walla, as verified by the testimony of McBean in 1866. What possible excuse could they offer for their heartless refusal to help Hall or Osbourne and his family? How could any man, let alone a fellow man of God, justify not protecting an innocent man and his helpless family from certain death at the hands of Indians incited to murder, torture and rape without mercy?

Once again the hand of providence intervened in the affairs of men. Osbourne and his family would live to tell their testimony to the world. An artist of much renown happened to be sojourning at the fort. He intervened for the Americans. "Providentially, Mr. Stanley, an artist, came in from Colville, narrowly escaped the Cayuse Indians by telling them he was 'alian,' H. B. He let me have his two horses, some food he had left from Rev. Eells and Walker's Mission; also a cap, a pair of socks, a shirt and handkerchief, and Mr. McBean furnished an Indian, who proved most faithful; and Thursday night we started back, taking my child but with a sad heart, that I could not find mercy at the hands of the priests of God." (41st Congress, p. 32)

Osbourne, his son and the faithful Indian discovered their family miraculously still alive. They made haste to seek refuge at the Jesuit mission of St. Anne under the protection of Vicar General Brouillet, but a Cayuse Indian warrior discovered them. "He told my Indian he had come to kill us all. My Indian replied, 'Yes, you had better kill them, you have no scalps now, but then you will have five - The sick man's, this woman's and the three children's. You will then be big brave." (Spalding, 41st Congress, p. 32) This Indian knew Cayuse culture. He knew his witness of the innocent slaughter of these defenseless Americans would bring shame once the insanity of the Whitman massacre finally passed over. Why did this Indian stand firm for the Americans? Did he risk his life, as the Jesuit priests have argued, by contending for the lives of the innocent Americans? "By this he shamed the Cayuse, who said 'I will not kill them, but they will be killed at Umatilla, and that will do.' He left, and we crossed the Walla-Walla River, and the guide said, 'Go to the fort.' My wife said, 'If I am to die, I will die at the door of a white man." (41st Congress, p. 32)

The Cayuse Indian, the Indian guide and the Osbornes all knew after this encounter with a Cayuse brave they would die under the "care" of the Jesuit priests at Umatilla. They had no choice but to return to Fort Walla Walla. Once again Captain McBean refused the Osbornes entry and threatened to send them to their death as he had Mr. Hall. This time it was the voices of a sick and shivering mother and her three children laying at his door more dead than alive that McBean had to refuse. This time he would be forced to watch and listen to the brutal slaughter at the gatepost of his fort. "He finally opened and took us into a secret room, and set an allowance of food for us every day. Next day I urged him for blankets for my sick wife to lie on. He had nothing. Next day I urged him again. He had nothing to give, but would sell a blanket out of the store. I told him I had lost everything and had nothing to pay, but if I should live to get to the Willamette, I would pay. He consented. But the hipbones of my dear wife wore through the skin on the hard floor. Stickus, the chief, came in one day and took the cap from his head and gave it to me, and a handkerchief to my child." (41st Congress, pp. 32, 33) Once again Stickus proved to be a great friend of the Americans.

The Osbornes lived to give their testimony to the world, a testimony that twentieth-century historians have rejected because it does not fit their re-crafting of American history. Let us proceed to another testimony twentieth-century historians have not documented or only document selectively to cover the actions of Father Brouillet. Lorinda Bewley was a devout Christian of twenty-three years and a missionary teacher at Waiilatpu. No history of the Whitman massacre could be complete without her full testimony. This young teacher, sick with fever, was forced to watch and listen to the murder of her father and eight days later the brutal murder of her brother Crocket by the Cayuse Indians. She had cared for her sick brother and Mr. Sails for eight days until, unexpectedly, both were savagely beaten to death with the wooden legs of their beds by the Cayuse Indians. "He (her brother) had seen me (Lorinda) dragged out by the savages and had become almost frantic, and declared he would try to deliver me if he died in the attempt. I had noticed Jo. Stanfield and Jo. Lewis listening to us, and think they overheard us, as word came from the Umatilla to kill my brother and Mr. Sails, and I have always felt the Catholics were the cause." (41st Congress, Ex. Doc. 37, p. 35) Lorinda Bewley later testified that Edward Tilokaikt (Teloukaite) (the chief's son) killed her brother because "the great chief had told them their disease would spread…(the great chief is the principal white man at a given place according to the dispositions of A. Hinman and J. B. Whitman)." (41st Congress, p. 38)

The disposition of Daniel Young confirmed Ms. Bewley's assertion that the "great chief" Brouillet had ordered the Bewleys' and Sails's deaths. Daniel's younger brother was killed by the Cayuse, and his own life was spared only by circumstance and the fact his family was operating the saw mill in the Blue Mountains east of Waiilatpu at the time of the massacre. "…Edward, Tilokaikt's son, had gone to Umatilla to the 'great chief' (Brouillet), to see what to do with the young men who were sick. This, Stanfield told me, was the business which Edward Tilokaikt had gone for….I learned from Mrs. Canfield and her daughter, that the same Edward Tilokaikt, after he had returned from the Umatilla, gave the first blow with his whip, and broke and run out of doors, when the other Indians finished the slaughter of the sick men." (Gray, W. H., *A History of Oregon*, H. H. Bancroft and Co., Portland, Oregon, 1870, p. 477)

Mr. McLane, secretary to Colonel Gilliam, substantiated Lorinda Bewley's suspicions in a report of the Oregon Volunteers first meeting with a delegation from the Cayuse camp after the massacre. They met the Cayuse Chief Stickus, a Christian convert of Dr. Whitman, who led the first wagon train across the Blue Mountains. McLane documented Chief Stickus's testimony at that time. "When we had but one religion, we had peace; but when another religion come, there was trouble. We were told the doctor was poisoning us; most of us didn't believe. But the Indians killed Dr. Whitman, and after he was dead another chief who told us where these things came, and we told him to show us the poison. He went to the doctor's room, took up several little bottles, then selecting one and holding it said, 'This is the poison with which the doctor was killing you. Bury this in a box, or you will all be dead." (41st Congress, p. 35)

Father Brouillet testified in "Protestantism in Oregon": "The war had been declared by the Indians against the Americans only, and not against foreigners…" (41st Congress, p. 4) If Father Brouillet knew the Cayuse would only war against Americans why by "his own testimony (did he do) nothing to save the victims, but (immediately commenced) baptizing the children of the murdering Indians and otherwise stimulating them in their work of death"? (Spalding, 41st Congress, p. 79). Rev. Spalding for twenty years testified that the ministerial act of baptizing the children of the murdering Indians by Jesuit Father Brouillet could only have sanctified the killings and encouraged the murderers to continue their actions. Could any reasonable person view the actions of this Jesuit priest in any other light? For Spalding's tireless efforts to expose the crime of Father Brouillet he has been labeled an "anti-Catholic bigot," a "lunatic," and worse by twentieth-century historians. The campaign incited by the Jesuits to destroy Spalding's reputation was so pervasive and insidious that this research will devote the next chapter to the issue.

Two other survivors of the massacre, Eliza Spalding and Catherine Sager, both supported Lorinda Bewley in her testimony that Vicar General Father Brouillet spent the evening at the mission and the following day the Cayuse asked for proof that Whitman was poisoning them. The Jesuit priest led the contingent of Cayuse Indians and Joe Stanfield to the doctor's house. "We trembled lest something should be found and made a pretense for killing us all. The Indian women were gathering around us with their dull tomahawks, and we expected every moment they would split our heads open. Joe Stanfield came out, the Indians following him, and said, "'The Father has found the poison; here it is;' holding up a phial which he put into a box with earth, nailed it up and took it away to bury it." (41st Congress, p. 34)

Lorinda Bewley later testified, "The priests said it was poison. Stanfield and Nichols were their interpreters to us….The Indians said the priests had found it among the Doctor's medicine, and showed it to them, and told them if it broke it would poison the whole nation." (Spalding, 41st Congress, p. 38) No wonder Lorinda Bewley believed the Jesuit priests had ordered the brutal killing of her defenseless brother and Mr. Sails. She had watched the Jesuit Vicar General lead the Cayuse Indians into the Whitman house seeking evidence of the Protestant poison that was killing the Indians. The Cayuse had lost half of their nation to the virulent measles and dysentery epidemic. The Indians had every reason to believe the Jesuit man of God was telling them the truth. After all, Vicar General Brouillet, arrayed in his priestly black robes, represented God. How could many of these superstitious, mostly illiterate Cayuse Indians know any better?

Lorinda Bewley must have been grieved when the Cayuse riders came seeking her and her alone. Suddenly without explanation she was summoned to the Jesuit priest's mission at Umatilla. "After shaking with a chill of ague, and while the fever was yet raging and my head and bones in great pain, the Indians started with me for the Umatilla in the afternoon. I rode Eliza Spalding's horse, which the Indians had brought for me. This led us to suppose that the Indians had killed Mr. Spalding, somewhere. I had no choice, but had to submit to whatever the Indians directed." (Spalding, 41st Congress, p. 34) "The Indian led away my horse, and as I rode away I thought my heart would burst with anguish. The thought of leaving my dear brother unburied; the idea of turning my back forever upon white people; to see my mother no more; to be doomed to suffer and live with the savages! Oh, how I begged God to send down help or send death." (Spalding, 41st Congress, p. 35)

The horse that Lorinda rode was one of the horses that Henry Spalding had given to Father Brouillet to look after for him when they met on the trail between Waiilatpu and Fort Walla Walla. Lorinda knew full well that Vicar General Brouillet had to be behind her extraction from Waiilatpu because she was riding the mount that only the priest could have provided. The knowledge that Lorinda was going to Umatilla to the Jesuit mission of St. Anne and the Jesuit priests did not provide comfort for the distraught missionary teacher. When she arrived at St. Anne she met the seven Jesuit emissaries: Vicar General Brouillet, Bishop Blanchet, two priests and three Frenchmen. Surely all unbiased historians would expect these fellow white Christians to protect this innocent maiden from the savage lusts of the now uncontrolled Cayuse Indians. Soon chief Five Crows came to the Jesuit mission to seek Ms. Bewley, which she passionately refused.

Bishop Blanchet wrote to Governor George Abernathy on December during the time that Lorinda Bewley was staying at St. Anne Mission under his and Brouillet's care. Blanchet assured Gov. Abernathy that "he had sent word to the chiefs whose lodges are near my house. After having made known to them without delay how much I was grieved in consequence of the commission of such an atrocious act, I told them I hoped the women and children would be spared till they could be sent to the Willamette. They answered, 'We pity them; they shall not be harmed; they shall be taken care of before.' I have since had the satisfaction to learn they have been true to their word, and they have taken care of these poor people." (Spalding, 41st Congress, p. 39)

From the testimony of Lorinda Bewley we shall discover what really happened under the care of the Jesuit priests. "As soon as Five Crows left the door, Bishop Blanchet spoke first and said; 'you had better go and be his wife.' I refused; I had rather die. Then Brouillet, who could speak better English, said, 'You must go, or he will come back and do us all an injury.' I arose, terrified at his words and looks, and commenced crying, begging him not to send me, and to have pity on a poor, helpless girl. He said I must go and called to Joe, his servant, to take me over. And the servant came in. I fell on my knees before the priest. 'Oh do pity me; save me, save me, don't give me to the Indians, but shoot me.' He rose up and brushed away my hands, and said to the servant to take me over. I then sprang up toward the two young priests, holding my hands appealingly, but they said nothing and moved not a hand, and the servant, half dragging me, half carrying me, hurried me away. I can never describe the feelings of my soul as I cast a last look upon these white men." (Spalding, 41st Congress, p. 35)

This research has documented previously how the Jesuit order required absolute obedience to the superior. The Jesuit order was the militant army of the Catholic Counter Reformation. It was pointless for Ms. Bewley to seek help from any of the subordinates. Revisionist historians who had the integrity to examine the testimony of the living witnesses of the Whitman massacre bring shame upon themselves to accept the excuse given by the Jesuit priests for refusing to help the Protestants against the brutality and carnage of the Cayuse Indians. In this particular case Jesuit General Brouillet, serving directly under the Black Pope the Jesuit General Roothaan, contended that to protect this fellow Christian maiden from the lust of the Indian chief would have caused him injury. There was one Indian and seven priests. Were the priests cowards or was something more sinister motivating them?

There has never been a shred of evidence introduced by any historian that the newly arrived Jesuit priests were ever in any threat of danger from the Cayuse, even during the most vicious hours of bloodshed. According to Cayuse historian Dr. Robert Ruby, (previously documented) the Catholics have finally admitted to complicity in causing the massacre. If the Jesuit priests had nothing to fear from the Cayuse, why would Father Brouillet send for Lorinda Bewley to be taken against her will to the abode of an Indian chief? Had Father Brouillet made a deal with the Indian chief? "As I was pushed into the lodge, the chief told me to sit down on a buffalo robe. A good fire was burning, and no one was in the lodge but the Indian. He was silent for sometime, and then turned and said kindly to me, 'If you do not wish to be my wife, go back to the white man's house. I will not trouble you. Take your bundle of clothes.'" (Spalding, 41st Congress, p. 36)

Lorinda Bewley returned to the mission at St. Anne. She was fed and clothed and she begged to be sent to Fort Walla Walla. On the third day Chief Five Crows returned and this time his countenance had changed toward her. This time he was violent in imposing his will upon her. Before, the Cayuse chief had accepted the refusal of the American teacher to be his "wife." What had caused him to change his mind and his spirit toward her? "I was forced out of the room and the Indian took me by the arm and led or dragged me away. And from that time on I was subject to the Indian. I would return to the bishop every morning. One morning as I was wringing my hands and crying, one of the young priests spoke kindly to me, telling me to pray to the virgin. On another morning when I came in, the other young priest laughingly asked me 'how I liked my new husband.'" (Spalding, 41st Congress, p. 36)

In time Jesuit Father Brouillet grew tired of having to put up with the crying and suffering of Ms. Bewley. He finally demanded she not return to St. Anne's mission. "I told one of the young priests what Brouillet had ordered, and begged him to protect me. He said the bishop did not like to have young women around his house, but if the Indian came for me I would have to go." (Spalding, 41st Congress, p. 36)

Did Cayuse chief Five Crows send for Lorinda Bewley or did Jesuit Father Brouillet? Let us remember she arrived on Brouillet's mount that he had received from Henry Spalding. What caused Chief Five Crows to change his mind and force himself on Ms. Bewley? Rev. Henry Spalding warned Americans in Oregon and Washington for two decades after the massacre to beware of the sinister designs of Father Brouillet in recruiting young women for new and flourishing Jesuit schools. For his efforts to warn his compatriots Rev. Spalding has been labeled an anti-Catholic bigot and hatemonger by revisionist twentieth-century historians.

The lies and deception over the Whitman Massacre and the Protestant missionaries have grown to the point that Spalding is now considered a modern-day cult leader. For instance, the *Idaho Statesman* ran an insert called "Nimiipuu" in September 2005 where Vera Sonneck, the Nez Perce tribe's cultural director, wrote that Spalding was "a very strict follower of the Old Testament book of Proverbs, in which the people were punished by whipping and stoning." (Woodward, Tim, "Nimiipuu," *Idaho Statesman*, Sept. 2005, p. 11) According to present-day historians Spalding was a vicious man who intimidated the Nez Perce. "He'd have people whipped if they didn't cut their hair or get rid of traditional garb....You weren't even allowed to speak your language in his presence." (Woodward, p. 11) The whippings according to present-day lore were administered to women and children. "A woman who hadn't embraced her new religion was whipped for leaving her abusive husband. Hungry children were whipped for stealing food." (Woodward, p. 12)

Is there any documented history to confirm that Spalding mistreated the Nez Perce Indians? All historical accounts confirm that Spalding not only encouraged the Nez Perce tongue, he spoke it fluently and was the first man to develop a written language of the Nez Perce dialect. Spalding was greatly loved by the Nez Perce nation and there is not one single firsthand document, letter, diary or written testimony to verify these lies. The main reason for this very successful smear campaign was that Rev. Spalding also warned his fellow Americans that Jesuit Vicar General Brouillet was the mastermind of the plot to incite the Indians to kill the Americans and thwart the Protestant revival in the west. The plot, as the evidence of this research has clearly demonstrated, was in reality hatched in the Vatican in Rome.

How did the Oregon American emigrants respond when they heard the charge of a Jesuit conspiracy and complicity in the Whitman massacre? In actual fact the Americans living in Oregon at that hour were incensed. A bill was introduced in the Oregon senate to expel all Catholic priests from the territory in 1849. Our Oregonian forefathers were so incensed with the conspiracy of the Jesuits that the issue simmered and at times boiled over for a generation after generation until the close of the 19th century. Even with all the controversy most Americans could not believe that the Jesuit priests of God could possibly conceive of or in any way be culpable for such an evil deed. Those Americans who continued to expose the truth of the Jesuit conspiracy to destroy the ministry of the Protestants and incite the Indians to war against the Americans were branded as anti-Catholic bigots and hatemongers by Romanist defenders. In the twentieth century, historians and writers have continued to endorse the Jesuit conspiracy, and the smoldering deception of the Whitman massacre remains buried and the lies first coined by Father Brouillet continue to be spread. In the *Idaho Statesman* 2005 history of the Nez Perce, the Whitmans and the Spaldings were portrayed as charlatan ministers. According to the *Idaho Statesman* Spalding's and Whitman's "un-Christian practices in the name of Christianity were their undoing." (Woodward, p. 12)

Fortunately the records, documents, testimonies and resolutions of the nineteenth century remain for the seeking of truth. P. S. Ogden of the Hudson's Bay Company purchased the redemption of all the Protestant family members in late December 1847. They were first taken to Fort Walla Walla where Mr. McBean had a "miraculous" change of heart and received the massacre survivors, all women and children. The Oregon government closed all Protestant and Catholic missionary activity in the Oregon Territory and the title of occupied mission lands was confirmed to those respective boards on August 14, 1848. The Protestant missionaries did not leave voluntarily but according to government decree. The Jesuit missionaries defied the authority of the Oregon Territorial Legislature since their authority was issued from Rome and continued to send more priests into the now vacant field, greatly agitating the Indian nations. War plagued the Oregon Territory for the next decade and the Jesuits were at the core of the conflict.

Throughout the entire era of Protestant missions in the Oregon Territory from 1835 to 1847 there had been no wars, and no Indians or whites had been killed by the advent of American immigration. In addition, no white emigrant had settled in Cayuse land or for that matter any of the lands of the Columbia Plateau Indians. Once the Protestant missionaries left the Oregon Territory and the Jesuit missions, in violation of territorial legislation, moved in, war between the two races began in earnest.

The unresolved issues and questions are as vital today at the dawn of the twenty-first century as they were in the middle of the nineteenth century. Dr. Robert Ruby has passionately called for congressional investigation into the Whitman massacre. Dr. Ruby believes the five Cayuse chiefs should "be absolved of murder because they were not murderers." (Ruby, Robert, "The 1847 Whitman Massacre," *Confederated Umatilla Journal*, Vol. IX, Issue 1, Jan. 2005, p. 30) Dr. Ruby believes the case "belongs in a special category in which the perpetrators of various killings are found innocent of murder by reason of certain criteria, as insanity or self-defense such as soldiers in war confronted by insurgents….In this instance the major terrorists were the knowledgeable mixed-blood bullies who knowingly falsified stories, bringing the illiterate Cayuse into believing they were being terrorized by the white." (Ruby, p. 30)

Dr. Ruby, author of many books on northwest Indians and documented often in this work because of his excellent scholarship of the Cayuse, has called on the United States Congress (January 2005) to revisit the Whitman massacre and hanging of five Cayuse Indians. Ruby contends, "The five should be absolved of murder because they were not murderers; because descendants of the Five suffer the injustice; because the stigma is unfair to the families; because the portrayal of the Five is incorrect; because the public should be privy to the facts leading to the Massacre and to set the history straight." (Ruby, p. 39) According to Ruby the illiterate Cayuse Indians were coerced and incited by Jesuit priests and Jesuit mixed breed bullies to murder the Protestant missionaries. "The Cayuse were deceived and coaxed to believe he (Whitman) was (a terrorist)." (Ruby, p. 30)

The indisputable evidence from the Protestant missionaries and the survivors of the Whitman massacre support Ruby's contentions, however the savage brutality of the perpetuators of the massacre continued for over two weeks. The Cayuse murderers must take some responsibility for their crimes against the innocent missionaries. Nevertheless Dr. Robert Ruby has once again exposed the great lie of the Whitman massacre. This research has documented the facts that support Ruby's call that the Cayuse Indians were incited to murder the Protestants by the lies of the Jesuit insurgents. The Jesuit assassins were no different than the fanatic Islamic terrorists who are willing to kill and maim the innocent, including women and children, to reach their goals. The documentation of this research fully agrees with and supports the call of Dr. Ruby for justice, but it is the legacy and heritage of the Protestant missionaries that has been smeared and defiled. The lies and coverup of the Jesuit priests has resulted in a spiritual and cultural separation and distrust between the Cayuse Indians and the Protestant missionaries who came to minister to them that continues to the present hour. The Cayuse Indians and all of the Columbia Plateau tribes share a common heritage with the Protestant missionaries who came to minister to them. The Protestant missionaries and the Cayuse Indians were the victims of the wicked plot conceived in Rome and authored by the Jesuit "black gowns," in particular Father Brouillet. The heart of the cover-up can be found in a booklet Brouillet presented to the United States Congress in 1857 called "Protestantism in Oregon."

When Henry Spalding learned of Brouillet's spurious defense he was so impassioned with the Jesuit accusations against himself, Whitman and his fellow Protestants that he was moved to cross the continent as an aged man to bring evidence of the Romanist deceptions before the United States Congress in 1871. This research will examine in depth Jesuit father Brouillet's "Protestantism in Oregon" and Spalding's rebuttal received in the congressional record in 1871.

The Jesuit father Brouillet would be the first to write the "truth of history" of what happened at Waiilatpu. The Romanist disparaging version of the Protestant missionary heritage in Oregon would spur five decades of controversy and contention. By the turn of the twentieth century Napoleon's version of history, "what is history but a lie agreed upon," would ultimately rule the day. Let us examine Father Brouillet's version of the Whitman mission.

CHAPTER 23

PROTESTANTISM ACCORDING TO FATHER BROUILLET

The thesis of this work, that the Oregon Territory has been kept under the shadow of the Almighty since the creation of the world, has been documented with multiple foreign nations attempting to gain control of the great prize of Oregon. The primary testimony of the living witnesses of the actual Whitman massacre and its aftermath has illustrated the Jesuit missions represented yet another foreign power attempting to win control of the Oregon Territory. In particular this research has documented the Jesuit priests encouraged, aided and authored the massacre. Brouillet's version of Protestantism in Oregon, written to defend against the Jesuit conspiracy that caused the Whitman massacre, must be documented in detail because Brouillet's account has become the accepted historical view of the events of the Whitman Massacre, the watershed event of the American west. The website of the Umatilla Confederated tribes contains the Brouillet history of the Protestant missionaries.

"In 1847 Dr. Whitman and his followers were killed by a band of Cayuse, along with some Umatilla and Nez Perce allies. The reasons are many and varied but include:

- non-payment for property taken
- increasing immigration
- Whitman's encroachment on Indian trade
- fear of Whitman himself, who the Indians believed had poisoned them
- the constant outbreak of diseases introduced by Whitman and other non-Indians

Whitman claimed to be a doctor and preacher as well as being a missionary, merchant and trader." (www.umatilla.nsa.su/hst2.html) The spurious coverup of the instigator of the Whitman Massacre, published ten years after the event in the nations capital on the other side of the nation, has become the accepted history of the viscious bloodbath of innocent American missionaries. How could this happen in America, a nation that champions a free and unbiased press?

The *Idaho Statesman* ran a story of the Nez Perce by Tim Woodward in September 2005 that perpetuated the deception of Father Brouillet. "At Walla Walla, Whitman openly belittled the spirituality that had sustained the tribes for generations, and fueled a land rush by recruiting emigrants who appropriated land Indians had held for centuries." (Woodward, p. 12) At the Whitman mission in Walla Walla school children and tour groups are taught that the missionaries conduct and behavior toward the Nastive Americans caused their own deaths. Brouillet's version of Protestantism in Oregon has become the accepted history of the Columbia Plateau Native Americans as well. The Jesuit history of Oregon, first penned by Father Brouilett, has led most Native Americans to believe that Whitman and Spalding were charlatans and their phony Christianity and aggressive behavior caused their own demise.

Vera Sonneck, the Nez Perce cultural resources director, was quoted in Woodward's article labeling Spalding as "a very strict follower of the Old Testament book of Proverbs, in which the people were punished by whipping or stoning." (Woodward, p. 11) This research has found no documentation from any original source to substantiate Vera Sonneck's description of Henry Spalding. Where did the charge that Spalding whipped or stoned the Nez Perce Indians come from? Nez Perce historian and former tribal chairman Allen Pinkham claimed the Nez Perce warriors who sought the white man's Book of Heaven "didn't go there for the Bible. They went to learn how to communicate with written words. They wanted the technology of writing that they had first seen with Lewis and Clark, not the Christian faith. We already knew about the Creator. We had our own faith." (Woodward, p. 11) According to Woodward's article Nez Perce oral tradition taught that Spalding gave "potatoes without eyes to those that offended him. When the potatoes failed to sprout, he told the would-be farmers it was their fault because they were devils. Oral history holds that he put sheep due in melons to poison those who failed to please him." (Woodward, p. 12)

The research of this book has found no documentation from any reputable source that the Whitmans owed the Cayuse Indians any money for their mission. The consistent witness of all original documents in every instance indicates that the Whitmans came to the Cayuse by invitation and would leave at any time the tribe asked them to go. It is historically correct that Whitman encouraged American immigration to Oregon; however, there is no documentation that the Cayuse Indians could have been moved to murder the Protestant missionaries because of American immigration before the hour of the massacre. In 1847 not one American immigrant had established a homestead on the Columbia Plateau. For the most part at this hour the Indian tribes along the Columbia River plateau were not threatened and in fact looked down on the ragged immigrants, exhausted by the time they reached the Columbia River. There is documentation that the Native Americans believed in time that the Americans would settle on their lands in the Columbia River basin east of the Cascades.

The argument that Whitman somehow encroached on Indian trade was ludicrous. The consistent witness of every firsthand observer was that the Whitmans sacrificed their lives to help the Columbia Plateau Indians to one day prosper in the white man's civilization. Whitman taught the Indians to cultivate crops and trade their crops, horses and cattle to the white immigrants right up to the massacre. The argument that the Cayuse Indians somehow feared Whitman is equally ludicrous. Weeks before the massacre and before the Jesuit priests arrived all the Cayuse Indians were documented to be present on Sunday morning worship services with the Whitmans. The historical record is without refutation that the Whitmans abhorred violence and refused to retaliate even when struck or attacked.

This research has painstakingly documented the values, heritage and purpose of the Protestant missionaries, and none of the charges still believed by the Confederated tribes of the Umatilla Indians have any historical foundation or validity. Nevertheless, this has become the accepted version of the Protestant missionaries and their ministry to the Columbia Plateau Native Americans. Where did these lies, deceptions and outright falsehoods come from? The perpetrator of the Whitman massacre wrote an elaborate cover-up called "Protestantism in Oregon: Account of the Murder of Dr. Whitman, and the ungrateful calumnies of H. H. Spalding, Protestant Missionary." This cover-up will be the subject of this chapter.

The Whitman massacre was the watershed historical event in the history of the Oregon Territory. The causes of the massacre, i.e. the culpability and complicity of the Jesuit priests in causing the horrific slayings of the Protestant missionaries, were debated for nearly three generations in dueling Congressional documents, newspapers, history books, church conferences, and historical societies until the turn of the 20th century. This debate that dominated Pacific Northwest history, politics and religion for nearly 60 years may be a tedious process to document; nevertheless, the falsehoods still believed about the Protestant missionaries will never go away until the truth comes to the surface. The issue of responsibility has never been resolved, lending greater urgency to the task.

The same fundamental opposing forces that brought the "Second Awakening" of the Protestant Reformation to Oregon and the Jesuit Counter Reformation that followed were drawn into mortal combat and have continued to battle for supremacy in the land of the Oregon Territory to this very day. The battle line was drawn from the beginning of creation: light vs. darkness, good vs. evil, God vs. Satan, liberty vs. oppression, freedom vs. slavery, truth vs. falsehood, freedom of conscience vs. subservience to authority. Both sides claim to be on the side of God and truth. There could be no common ground of unity between the two historical positions. Paradoxically these two great religions of the Christian faith have developed a significant level of unity in the Pacific Northwest and in America at the dawn of the 21st century. This unity has transpired because the Catholic Church in the Pacific Northwest has in large part answered the call to biblical truth, especially in the areas of marriage and the sanctity of life. This research will examine this exciting unity developing between the Catholic Church and the conservative Protestant Church at the end of the book.

Father Brouillet's "Protestantism in Oregon" was an elaborate defense of sixteen accusations against the Jesuit priests that were issues of public debate. It is important to list these accusations against the Romanist priests because the case was only tried in the court of public opinion, never in a court of law. The accusations against the Romanist priests have never been resolved. For the purposes of this research the ramifications of the unresolved issues of the Whitman massacre have remained as a heavy spiritual cloud over the Pacific Northwest. This black cloud has remained to this day, thwarting the cause of the Christian Church in the Pacific Northwest birthed by the early Protestant ministers. These unresolved issues have continued to cause division, confusion and contention in two significant arenas in the Pacific Northwest. First, a negative shadow has continued to rest over the Columbia Plateau Indians regarding their spiritual heritage. The trial and hanging of five Cayuse chiefs for the murder of the Protestant missionaries and associated Americans at the mission remains a controversy to the present hour. Second, the Pacific Northwest has remained the most un-churched area in the United States. Why? The unresolved issues of the Whitman massacre, which have pitted the Protestant Reformation against the Catholic Counter Reformation, have caused a spiritual cloud of confusion that in effect has thwarted the cause of Christian ministries throughout the twentieth century in the Pacific Northwest and in America.

In the case of the Whitman massacre both sides issued strong arguments that were enshrined as Senate documents. This research will examine these documents to determine the truth and accuracy of the statements of both Senate documents. The very fact that these documents have rarely been examined for historical integrity and authenticity, especially in comparison, by any twentieth-century historian or university remains a mystery. For this reason the history of the American west must now proceed through two unlikely individuals, Jesuit father Vicar General J. B. A. Brouillet and Protestant missionary Henry Spalding. Father Brouillet, also known as Rev. Brouillet, represented the Romanist Counter Reformation while Rev. Henry Spalding represented the Protestant Reformation. The two frontier missionaries were drawn together shortly after the massacre. Vicar General Brouillet presented a brave testimony of saving Rev.

Spalding's life near the massacre, whereas Spalding presented a contradictory testimony of Brouillet's complicity and connivance in an attempt upon his life by the Cayuse Indians.

This chapter will document Vicar General Brouillet's testimony regarding the causes and facts of the Whitman massacre. Revisionist historians have all, most accommodatingly, accepted Jesuit Father Brouillet's testimony without question and the Columbia Plateau Native Americans have followed suit. In stark contrast, historians have relentlessly criticized the Christianity, integrity and mental balance of the Protestant missionaries, particularly Henry Spalding, for over a hundred years. This criticism can be found in Native American histories as well as documented at the beginning of this chapter. Jesuit Father Brouillet has been defended by virtually all 20th century historians as an innocent and venerable Catholic priest.

This research will pose the following question. Why has the alleged mastermind of the Whitman massacre, Vicar General Rev. J. B. A. Brouillet, been given a free pass by historians of the twentieth century? Virtually every firsthand testimony of the living witnesses of the massacre and the Protestant missionaries on the field at that hour accuse this Jesuit priest of complicity and culpability in these slayings. Why wasn't Brouillet brought to trial? Rev. Henry Spalding presented the charges and testimonies that incriminated Father Brouillet in 1848-49 in a series of articles in the *Oregon American*, edited by the Hon. P. H. Burnett. Burnett would later figure prominently in the controversy. The first public acknowledgment of the true cause of the Whitman massacre was brought to the light of day when Rev. J. S. Griffin published eight booklets between 1848 and 1849 under the title of "Oregon American and Evangelical Unionist" wherein Henry Spalding revealed the Jesuit/Catholic Priests were behind the Whitman massacre. "The Catholics took part in the murders and in the distribution of the plundered goods…that they actually placed the seal of their bloody approbation upon the bloody dead, by baptizing the children of the murderers." (Drury, Vol. II, p. 377) In response, Jesuit Father Brouillet wrote "Protestantism in Oregon," published in 1853. Spalding's articles were published in the *Oregon American* in 1848-49 in the Pacific Northwest and Brouillet's articles were published in the *New York Freeman's Journal* on the east coast in 1853 where nobody knew anything about the Whitman Massacre.

Before this tragic event the Territory had known peace between the Indian and White races that was unprecedented in American history, especially during the age of Protestant missionaries. The Cayuse wars that lasted until 1857 began as a result of the Whitman massacre. There were no Indian Wars in the Oregon Territory before the Whitman massacre. J. Ross Browne was sent by the American government to investigate the causes of the Indian Wars that plagued the Oregon country. In his report he referred to Spalding's claim that the massacre "was done with the knowledge and connivance of the Catholic missionaries." (Drury, Vol. II, p. 378) According to Dr. Robert H. Ruby, "The Catholic Priests in the area during the epidemic were complicit in the massacre by not reassuring the Indians with the truth about the disease and Whitman's intent to cure them. The Catholics have since admitted to this complicity." (Ruby, *CUJ*, Jan. 2005, p. 30) Dr. Ruby had the courage to document what no other twentieth-century author had admitted regarding the complicity of the Catholics (really Jesuits) in the massacre. The definition of complicity is "partnership in crime."

Browne's report to Congress in 1857 has reinforced the central theme of this book. The Whitman massacre was a direct result of the historical battle between the Protestant Reformation and the Catholic Counter Reformation. "A perusal of the pamphlet," wrote Browne, "will abundantly show the bitterness of feelings existing between the different sects, and its evil effects upon the Indians. It will be readily seen that, as little dependence can be placed upon the statements by one side as by the other, thereby showing a very bad example to the races with whom they chose to reside." (Drury, Vol. II, p. 378)

The confusion of the contending religious forces upon the Columbia Indian nations has continued to this very hour. The Cayuse Tamastslikt Cultural Center near Pendleton, Oregon reveals an exhibit of the conflicting Protestant and Catholic "ladders" to heaven to illustrate the unresolved controversy over the Whitman massacre. At the center of the controversy is the question regarding whether both sides were equally responsible for the confusion and rending of the Indian nations or whether one side was complicit, as Dr. Ruby contends.

The controversy made it all the way to the floor of the United States Congress, not once but twice. Brouillet's "Protestantism in Oregon" pamphlet was published as "Executive Document No. 38, House of Representatives, 35th Congress, 1st Session," in 1858. Rev. Spalding was understandably upset when he heard nearly a decade after the fact that Brouillet's derogatory exposition on the Protestant mission in Oregon was included in the Congressional record. The elderly missionary rode the newly constructed transcontinental railroad across the United States in 1870, armed with documentation to defend against Brouillet's attacks on the Protestant missionaries. Spalding had prophesied this transcontinental crossing thirty years earlier. His collection of documents successfully appeared as an 81-page pamphlet under the title "Executive Document No. 37, U.S. Senate, 41st Congress, 3d Session." These two documents are the prime sources for the Protestant and Catholic version of the Whitman massacre.

This research has previously documented that the United States Congress commissioned J. Ross Browne to go to Oregon in 1857 and develop a report on the causes of the "late Indian war in Oregon and Washington Territories." Browne submitted his report to the House of Representative on January 25, 1858. In Browne's report he documented Rev. Henry Spalding's charge that the murder of the Protestant missionaries "was done with the knowledge and connivance of the Catholic missionaries." (J. Ross Browne, 35th Congress, Ex. Doc. No. 38, p. 3) Curiously, Browne does not document the evidence of Spalding's charges against Vicar General Brouillet that would have gone to the heart of the causes of the "late Indian War." Instead, Browne introduced the rebuttal of Father Brouillet called "Protestantism in Oregon: Account of the Murder of Dr. Whitman, and the Ungrateful Calumnies of H. H. Spalding, Protestant Missionary." (35th Congress, Ex. Doc. No. 38, p. 13) The effect of Browne's introduction of Brouillet's version of Protestantism in Oregon established Congressional approval of a document most critical toward the Presbyterian missionaries. As the reader most certainly would ascertain, Brouillet's testimony completely absolved the Jesuits of any complicity, knowledge or connivance with the Whitman massacre.

The passion, thrust and conviction of the Protestant Reformation was birthed and planted in the Pacific Northwest by the early Protestant missionaries led by Marcus and Narcissa Whitman and Henry and Eliza Spalding. The Whitman mission was destroyed, the perpetrators of the brutal slayings were never tried and convicted, and the causes of the massacre were covered up by Jesuit Father Brouillet to protect the guilty, in this case the Jesuits. The result: The Protestant message, ministry and heritage, boldly, courageously and uncompromisingly birthed in the Pacific Northwest, has been blunted, confused and distorted. The Protestant message of freedom in Christ through an uncompromised preaching of the word of God has not been able to impact the peoples of the Pacific Northwest, where it was birthed, because the truth of the message and heritage of the early Presbyterian missionaries has been compromised through a spurious cover-up. The purpose of this history of Oregon is to challenge and refute this historic cover-up that has undermined the integrity of the first Protestant missionaries and protected and covered over the treachery of the Jesuit priests.

The sixteen accusations, and more that were leveled by the survivors of the massacre, were so divisive and contentious they were publicly debated for half a century! The open democratic institutions of free press and free speech, birthed by the Protestant Reformation, maintained a strong and vibrant church in the Pacific Northwest throughout the age of spirited debate over the true causes of the Whitman massacre. With the passing of the nineteenth-century historians and Protestant leaders, revisionist historians and theologians unfavorable to the Protestant mission perpetuated the sophistry of Brouillet's "Protestantism in

Oregon" regarding the causes of the massacre and the Christian convictions of early Protestant missionaries. No Protestant historians or theologians rose with any vigor or conviction in the twentieth century to rebut this re-crafting of the true purpose and impact of the Protestant ministry, which has caused a cloud of confusion to hang over the Pacific Northwest. That cloud remains to this very hour. The unresolved issues of the Whitman massacre, unaddressed by or conflicting with accounts from Jesuit Father Brouillet as presented in "Protestantism in Oregon," are listed below.

> The massacre at Waiilatpu was committed only against Protestant Americans; all Catholics were spared, and the slaughter was instigated by the Jesuit priests.
>
> Bishop Brouillet baptized the children of the Cayuse directly after they murdered the American Protestants and thereby sanctioning the murders.
>
> The Jesuit bishop and the priests freely operated and went to and fro amidst the murdering and raping of the Americans, demonstrating their authority and support of the massacre.
>
> The Jesuit priests began preparation to take over the Whitman station directly after the massacre.
>
> The Jesuit priests made no effort to help, support or free the Whitman captives after they came upon the massacre.
>
> The Romanist bishop had offered a great price to purchase Whitman's mission, but Whitman refused causing the Catholic priests to pursue other means to gain the mission.
>
> The priests at Fort Walla Walla refused to help the Osbornes when they fled to the Fort from the Whitman massacre.
>
> The Jesuits aggressed upon the Protestant mission, which had operated peacefully for eleven years, causing the Indians to rebel against the Protestants.
>
> Joseph Lewis, Joseph Stanfield, and Nicholas Finlay, who were co-conspirators against the Protestant missionaries, were all Catholic.
>
> Bishop Brouillet neglected to have the bodies of the slain missionaries properly buried.
>
> Bishop Brouillet purposely neglected to give Rev. Spalding critical information he needed regarding his daughter and other captives.
>
> One particular young man was murdered during the massacre as the priest arrived, thereby insinuating Bishop Brouillet was complicit in his death.
>
> The Jesuit priests and Mr. McBean of the Hudson's Bay Company attempted to deceive the public regarding the true cause of the massacre based on a letter sent to Fort Vancouver after the massacre.

The Catholic missionaries despised the authority of the Oregon governor and the Indian agent who commanded them to leave the Oregon country after the massacre.

Bishop Brouillet actually conspired to murder Rev. Spalding instead of warn him of the Whitman massacre when they met as Spalding was in route to Waiilatpu.

The Jesuit priests actually told the Cayuse and Nez Perce Indians that the Protestant missionaries were poisoning them to gain their land and possessions.

One of the purposes of Brouillet's "Protestantism in Oregon" was to provide a defense against these grievous charges. In actual fact these were not the only charges the American citizens and survivors of the massacre leveled against the Jesuit priests. The circumstances of Father Brouillet's defense were most peculiar. The charges were leveled directly after the massacre and the public debate continued unabated for the rest of the century in Oregon and Washington. Brouillet did not offer his defense until 1857 and even then his defense "Protestantism in Oregon" did not appear in Oregon or Washington but rather at the nation's capital in the United States House of Representatives where it was attached to J. Ross Browne's report on the causes of the Cayuse War. Had Brouillet's "Protestantism in Oregon" appeared in print in Oregon directly after the Whitman massacre the response would have been inflammatory against the Jesuit/Catholics. Brouillet was very shrewd to have the attack against Protestantism attached to a report published over three thousand miles from Oregon in the nation's capital.

    Brouillet's testimony in "Protestantism in Oregon" was virtually unchallenged until Henry Spalding initiated a rebuttal campaign that also won unanimous affirmation as a Senate resolution in 1871. Spalding was not aware of Brouillet's Congressional testimony for a number of years. Curiously, twentieth-century historians have been largely silent in response to these two documents. A thorough study of these dueling Senate documents will be illustrative in the century-old battle for Oregon between the Protestant Reformation and the Romanist counter strategy. Brouillet's testimony will be central to understanding the Romanist strategy to defeat Protestantism in Old Oregon, which now has assumed center stage at the heart of this research.

    As far as special agent J. Ross Browne was concerned, the conflict between the Catholics and the Protestants was purely a sectarian issue, an issue of "bitterness of feeling existing between the different sects, and its evil effects upon the Indians. It will be readily seen that, as little dependence can be placed upon the statements by one side as by the other, and that, instead of christianizing the Indians, these different sects were engaging in quarrels among each other, thereby showing a very bad example to the races with whom they chose to reside." (Brouillet, Browne, 35th Congress, p. 3) Browne may have stated the massacre was caused by bitterness between two contending sects of Christianity but he demonstrated his personal bias by presenting only Brouillet's Romanist version to the American Congress.

    According to Browne, the cause of the war was the universal cause of all the Indian wars in America, "encroachment of a superior upon an inferior race….It was a war of destiny, bound to take place whenever the causes reached their culminating point." (Brouillet, Browne, 35th Congress, pp. 2, 3) Browne also documented Mormon complicity in the Oregon Indian wars. "In the Simcoe, at a council of the tribes in 1854, a chief from the Mormon country urged them to war. The talk of this chief, as detailed by a friendly Indian who was at the council, was to this effect: That far in the desert there lived the greatest people on earth, who controlled the sun. He had been among them and talked with them, and they had sent him here to say what they were. They could strike dead anybody at any distance; they could make the sun stand still; they could make powder and muskets, and they were the friends of the Indians. The Americans were the enemies of the Indians. They wanted the Indians to kill them all. They would send them powder and muskets, &c. That the Mormons did furnish several of the tribes with ammunitions is proved by the narrative of Captain Shaw, of the Walla-Walla volunteers. At the last battle up there, he found powder, muskets, balls, &c., among the Indians bearing the Mormon brand." (Brouillet, Browne, 35th Congress, p. 11)

Dr. Ruby has documented that the chief instigator of the Whitman massacre, Joe Lewis, fled to sanctuary at the Mormon camps (Ruby, *CUJ*, p. 30) in the present state of Utah. The complicity in the Jesuit/Mormon connection through Jesuit Father De Smet and Brigham Young and Joe Lewis's flight to the Mormon camp will be examined in detail later in this research. Father Brouillet's testimony in "Protestantism in Oregon" will be central in the purposes of unraveling the causes of the Whitman massacre. It should come as no surprise that Rev. Spalding and fellow Protestants were energized to present a spirited defense when they discovered the inflammatory Jesuit version of their missionary efforts and purposes nearly a decade later. The very fact that J. Ross Browne had attached Brouillet's most critical history of the Protestant missionary work to a Congressional document approved by the United States legislature without giving opportunity for rebuttal should have raised red flags in the halls of Congress. Unfortunately, communication between the East and the West had not improved much from the days of Whitman's famous ride in 1842-43. The knowledge of the Oregon Territory in Washington was mostly uncharted terrain for the lawmakers of the hour. All these legislators knew was what Browne and Brouillet provided for them.

The portrait of American Protestantism painted by the Romanist Papist, serving directly under Jesuit General Roothaan in Rome, was not a very pretty picture. "Protestantism in Oregon" framed the American mind regarding the Whitman massacre for a decade and a half until the Protestants finally provided a rebuttal in 1871. No twentieth-century historians have questioned the integrity of Brouillet's "Protestantism in Oregon" even though Father Brouillet was accused by eyewitnesses of connivance and complicity in the murder of the Whitman missionaries. In stark contrast, the Protestant defense of their ministry and heritage under the leadership of Henry Spalding has been severely questioned by revisionist historians as anti-Catholic bigotry.

Brouillet in his critique of Protestantism takes credit together with his bishops and the clerk at Fort Walla Walla for saving the lives of the survivors of the massacre through their "influence, their advice, their repeated solicitations, (calming) the fury of the Indians." (Brouillet, 35th Congress, p. 13) According to Brouillet the Jesuit clergy and the Hudson's Bay Company "also had the good effect of preventing for a time the Indians from carrying their hostilities any further." (Brouillet, 35th Congress, p. 13) Brouillet wrote that Rev. Spalding, "moved by religious fanaticism, and ashamed of owing his life and that of his family and friends to some priest, began to insinuate false suspicions about the true causes of the disaster, proceeded, by degrees, to make more open accusations, and finally declared publicly that the Bishop of Walla-Walla and his clergy were the first cause and the great movers of all the evil." (Brouillet, 35th Congress, p. 14)

In chapter one of Brouillet's defense he presented the remote causes of the massacre. Brouillet noted that many friends and associates of Dr. Whitman warned him to leave Waiilatpu because the Cayuse would kill him if he stayed. Brouillet wrote, "Dr. Whitman had declared many times during the last years that he wished to leave; that he knew the Indians were ill-disposed towards him, and that it was dangerous for him to remain among them; that for a couple of years he had done nothing for the teaching of the Indians because they would not listen to him." (Brouillet, 35th Congress, p. 16)

In chapter two Brouillet turned to his assessment of the true causes of the massacre, relying on a number of testimonies from those who knew the Protestant missionaries. According to Brouillet in a statement written by a Mr. John Toupin, an interpreter with the Hudson's Bay Company, Presbyterian Rev.

Parker promised the Cayuse in 1835: "After the doctor is come there will come every year a big ship loaded with goods to be divided among the Indians. These goods will not be sold, but given to you. The missionaries will bring you ploughs and hoes to learn you how to cultivate the land, and they will not sell but give them to you." (Brouillet, 35th Congress, p. 17) Toupin claimed Rev. Parker promised to the Nez Perce, "Next Spring there will come a missionary to establish himself here, and take a piece of land; but he will not take it for nothing: you shall be paid every year; this is the American fashion." (Brouillet, 35th Congress, p. 17)

Toupin asserted he was at the house of Splitted Lip (Yomptipi) in the winter of 1838 when the Indian chief warned Dr. Whitman, "Doctor, you have come here to give us bad medicines; you come to kill us, and you steal our lands. You had promised to pay me every year, and you have been here already two years, and have, as yet, given me nothing. You had better go away; if my wife dies, you shall die also." (Brouillet, 35th Congress, p. 18) Brouillet next related how Toupin often heard the Indians speaking critically about the Whitmans. "The Indians often complained that the doctor and his wife were very severe and hard on them and often ill-treated them, which occasioned frequent quarrels between them and the doctor." (Brouillet, 35th Congress, p. 18) Father Brouillet quoted Toupin's assertion that the Indians were most grieved by Whitman's ride across America in the winter of '43. "A short time afterwards he started for the United States, telling the Indians that he was going to see the great chief of the Americans, and when he would return he would bring with himself many people to chastise them; and the Indians had been looking for his return with a great anxiety and fear." (Brouillet, 35th Congress, p. 18)

Father Brouillet then turned his attention to the teaching of the Protestants that caused the Indians to turn against the Presbyterian missionaries. Rev. Spalding had condemned Indian chief Blue Coat to a severe punishment of fifty lashes for causing great damage to the whole nation. According to John Toupin, Nez Perce Chief Tonwitakis tied up Blue Coat and said to Spalding, "Now whip him. Mr. Spalding answered him: 'No, I do not whip; I stand in the place of God; I command. God does not whip; he commands.' 'You are a liar,' said the Indian chief; 'look at the image' (pointing to an image hanging on the wall which Spalding had made for the instruction of Indians); 'you have painted two men on it, and God behind them with a bundle of rods to whip them. Whip him, or if not, we will put you in his place, and whip you.' Mr. Spalding obeyed, whipped the Indian, and received from him the horse that he had exacted." (Brouillet, 35th Congress, p. 19).

This accusation that Spalding whipped an Indian to protect himself has become the standard teaching regarding Spalding's character among Native Americans to this day. There is no recorded documentation from any source, Hudson Bay, Native American, Oregon pioneer, or disgruntled Protestant workers that support the allegations of Father Brouillet that Henry Spalding mistreated and whipped the Nez Perce Indians.

Father Brouillet next offered the testimony of John Young who worked for Whitman during the winter of 1846. Dr. Whitman had given Young some arsenic to poison some wolves that were active near the mission. Some Indians had inadvertently been poisoned by the arsenic. "Some days afterward the doctor told me, laughing, that he would certainly have died if they had not drunk a great quantity of warm water to excite vomiting." (Brouillet, 35th Congress, p. 21)

Father Brouillet then introduced a statement by William Craig, a French Canadian who lived with his Nez Perce wife ten miles from the Spalding Presbyterian mission. Craig met with the Nez Perce Indians at the Spalding mission for the purpose of receiving a messenger who arrived with the news of the massacre. According to Craig, the "cause of the murder was, that Dr. Whitman and Spalding were poisoning the Indians. They asked him, 'Are you sure that they were poisoning the Indians?' He said, 'Yes. How do you know it? Joseph Lewis said so. What did he say? Joseph Lewis said that Dr. Whitman and Mr. Spalding had been writing for two years to their friends in the east, where Joseph Lewis lived, to send poison to kill off the Cayuse and Nez Perce; that they had sent them some that was not good, and they wrote for more that would kill them off quick, and that the medicine had come this summer. Joseph Lewis said he was lying on the settee in Dr. Whitman's room, and he heard a conversation between Dr. Whitman, Mrs. Whitman and Mr. Spalding in which Mr. Spalding asked the doctor why he did not kill off the Indians faster. 'Oh,' said the doctor, 'they are dying fast enough; the young ones will die off this winter and the old ones next spring.' Mrs. Whitman said that our new friends will be on, and want to settle in this country....Joseph Lewis, the messenger said, told the Cayuse in the counsel that unless they (the Indians) killed Dr. Whitman and Mr. Spalding quick they would all die. The messenger went on to say himself that one hundred and ninety seven Indians had died since the immigration commenced passing that summer." (Brouillet, 35th Congress, p. 25)

At this point in Brouillet's version of "Protestantism in Oregon" he made a summation of the testimony he had collected against the Protestant missionaries, in particular Dr. and Narcissa Whitman and Henry Spalding. Father Brouillet personally defined the case against the Whitmans that caused their own disaster that ended in their violent deaths. "Lacking sincerity and faithfulness to their word and promise, violence of character and imprudent expressions, together with an excessive seeking for temporal welfare in some of the missionaries. We have seen that they promised to pay the Indians for their lands and to give them a great many things which they never gave." (Brouillet, 35th Congress, p. 28)

The Cayuse Indians to this present hour believe that one of the reasons that Whitman died was for non-payment of land taken from the Native Americans. Unfortunately, there was no one in the United States Congress to question the allegations of Father Brouillet against the character of the Protestant missionaries. Father Brouillet particularly attacked the "violence of character and imprudent expressions" (Brouillet, 35th Congress, p. 29) of Marcus Whitman. The Jesuit Father testified he heard Whitman scold the Indians at Fort Walla Walla in the fall of 1847: "Since you are so wicked—such robbers—we shall call for troops to chastise you; and next fall we will see here five hundred dragoons who will take care of you." (Brouillet, 35th Congress, p. 29)

To support Brouillet's assertion that the Protestant missionaries were seeking material gain at the expense of the Indians he quoted a remark he attributed to the Indian agent Joel Palmer: "…In his opinion the application of the missionaries to get excessive riches had been a great obstacle to the prosperity of the missions; that it absorbed too much of their attention and excited against them the jealousy of the Indians; that his opinion was, the government ought to prohibit them from getting more than a certain amount of revenue as considered necessary for their habitual subsistence." (Brouillet, 35th Congress, p. 29)

According to Father Brouillet the great part of the volunteer soldiers of 1848 "came to the general conclusion that the missions were prejudicial to the Indians, made them worse, and had better be abandoned. When they came to that conclusion, however, they could speak of the Protestant missions only, because they had had as yet no opportunity of knowing what the Catholic missions are, and what effects they produce among the Indians…" (Brouillet, 35th Congress, p. 29) Under testimony, Joel Palmer, commanding general of the Oregon volunteers, denied these statements and that testimony will be examined later in this chapter.

In Chapter II, Father Brouillet shared in the first person his testimony of the events that led up the Whitman massacre. Brouillet recounted his very first meeting with Dr. Whitman on September 23, 1847, a most divergent version from the testimony of Dr. Whitman based on his extant letters. This account presented the clearest picture of the Romanist Jesuit priest's testimony regarding his view of Dr. Whitman.

"On the 23rd of September Dr. Whitman, on his way from The Dalles, stopped at Fort Walla-Walla. His countenance bore sufficient testimony to the agitation of his heart. He soon showed by his words that he was deeply wounded by the arrival of the bishop. 'I know very well,' he said, ' for what purpose you have come.' 'All is known,' replied the bishop. 'I have come to labor for the conversion of the Indians, and even the Americans, if they are willing to listen to me.' The Doctor then continued in the same tone to speak of many things. He attributed the coming of the bishop to the Young Chief's influence! Made a furious charge against the Catholics, accusing them of having persecuted Protestants, and even of having shed blood wherever they have prevailed. He said he did not like Catholics; that he should oppose the missionaries to the extent of his power. He spoke against the 'Catholic ladder!' and said he would cover it with blood, to show the persecution of Protestants by Catholics. He refused to sell provisions to the bishop, and protested that he would not assist the missionaries unless he saw them in starvation." (Brouillet, 35th Congress, p. 31)

The Jesuit priest's account was not consistent with Dr. Whitman's recollection of Vicar General Brouillet in chapter nineteen. The next charge against Dr. Whitman by Father Brouillet was contrary to every known testimony of Marcus Whitman. The bishop was not astonished in hearing…"Dr. Whitman, on leaving the fort, went to the lodge of Pipipmoxmox (or Yellow Serpent): that he had spoken a great deal against the priests; that he had wished to prevail upon this chief to co-operate with him, in order that, by the aid of his influence with the Cayuse, Des Chutes, and The Dalles Indians, he might be enabled to excite these nations against them, &c., &c." (Brouillet, 35th Congress, p. 31) For the student of history to accept Father Brouillet's assertion that Dr. Whitman intended to excite the Indians to take up arms against the priests, the reader would have to reject the known fact that Whitman was a pacifist who would not even take up arms to save his own life or the life of his wife or the lives of his adopted children or the lives of his American friends and co-missionaries.

The research has previously documented that Vicar General Brouillet and the Jesuit priests were sent directly from Rome and the Pope to establish an apostolic-vicariate at Walla Walla to govern the entire Oregon Territory. Father Brouillet affirmed that he was under a direct commission from Rome to the Cayuse Indians and the whole Oregon Territory. The Indian chiefs put many questions to the bishop: "…Asking him whether it was the Pope who had sent him to ask for land for the mission; how the priests lived in the country; who maintained them; whether the priests would make presents to the Indians; whether they would cause their land to be ploughed…&c, &c. The bishop replied that it was the Pope who had sent him; that he had not sent him to take their land, but only for the purpose of saving their souls; that, however, having to live, and possessing no wealth, he had asked for a piece of land that he could cultivate for his support…" (Brouillet, 35th Congress, p. 32) The Jesuit priests were fully financed by Rome, the richest state in the world. The Jesuits had accused the Protestants of taking the Indians' land without retribution; however, these priests were not willing to pay for the Indian lands themselves.

On March 2, 1848 Father Brouillet wrote a letter to Colonel Cornelius Gilliam explaining the circumstances of the Jesuit priests with respect to the Whitman massacre. In this letter Brouillet gave an impassioned defense of his innocence in the massacre and his concern for the Protestant missionaries with assurances he would never consider any actions that would endanger their welfare. "…We dined with Mr. Spalding and Mr. Rogers (two days before the massacre) and I assure you that it was a satisfaction to me to have the acquaintance of those gentlemen. I then indulged the hope more strongly than ever of living in peace with them all, which was in perfect accordance with my natural feeling; for those who are acquainted with me know that I have nothing more at heart than to live at peace with all men, and that, exempt from prejudices, I am disposed to look with an equal eye upon the members of all religious denominations—to do all I can for the good of all, without regard to the name by which they may be called." (Brouillet, 35th Congress, p. 33)

Father Brouillet next explained the circumstances of his reasons for going to Waiilatpu. He arrived at the Whitman mission "between seven and eight o'clock in the evening. It was impossible to conceive my surprise and consternation, when, upon my arrival, I learned that the Indians the day before had massacred the Doctor and his wife, with the greater part of the Americans at the mission. I passed the night without scarcely closing my eyes." (Brouillet, 35th Congress, p. 34)

The savage slaughter, rape, torture, and pillage continued for eight days. The last American was brutally murdered over a week after Whitman was slain. The rape of the women and girls continued unabated, often in the presence of the Jesuit priests, until the survivors were finally rescued nearly a month later. Father Brouillet recounted his benevolent aid and support of the American victims. "Early the next morning I baptized three sick children, two of whom died soon after, and then hastened to the scene of death to offer to the widows and orphans all the assistance of my power. I found five or six women and over thirty children in a situation deplorable beyond description. Some had just lost their husbands, and others their fathers, who had been massacred before their eyes, and were expecting every moment to share the same fate. The sight of those persons caused me to shed tears, which however I was obliged to conceal, for I was in the greater part of the day in the presence of the murderers, and closely watched by them, and if I had shown too marked an interest on behalf of the sufferers, it would have only endangered their lives and mine; these therefore entreated me to be upon my guard." (Brouillet, 35th Congress, p. 34)

Father Brouillet documented that the grief-stricken wives and children "entreated" him to be upon his "guard" against the murderous Indians. Father Brouillet documented he was free to minister, baptizing children of the Indians who murdered the Protestants. According to Brouillet the terror-stricken women did not entreat the priest to save them. The brutality and murder raged on for two weeks during and after Father Brouillet's visit. According to Brouillet the grief- and terror-stricken women and children were concerned for his welfare, not there own, as he ministered and walked freely amid the brutality with no constraints.

Father Brouillet proceeded to assist Joseph Stanfield, a French conspirator in the massacre, in the burial of the slain missionaries. "What a sight did I behold! Ten dead bodies lying here and there, covered with blood, and bearing the marks of the most atrocious cruelty; some pierced with balls, others more or less gashed by the hatchet. Dr. Whitman had received three gashes on the face. Three others had their skulls crushed so that their brains were oozing out." (Brouillet, 35th Congress, p. 35)

Brouillet defended his actions at Waiilatpu to Col. Gilliam. "I assure you, sir, that during the time I was occupied in burying the victims of this disaster, I was far from feeling safe, being obliged to go here and there gathering up the dead bodies, in the midst of the assassins, whose hands were still stained with blood, and who by their manners, their countenances, and their arms which they still carried, sufficiently announced that their thirst for blood was yet un-satiated. Assuming as composed a manner as possible, I cast more than one glance aside and behind at the knives, pistols, and guns, in order to assure myself whether there were not some of them pointed towards me." (Brouillet, 35th Congress, p. 35)

There is no documented evidence from any source that Father Brouillet was at any time in danger from the Cayuse or any other Indian tribe. Father Brouillet's professed bravery amidst the "treacherous Cayuse," courageously hiding his real feelings of compassion for the desperate survivors while he, with heroic tenacity, buried the dead, convinced the floor of the United States Congress and a hundred years of twentieth-century historians of his innocence in this massacre. His "Protestantism in Oregon" has hardly been challenged or even examined, save for the Protestant missionaries of that hour and a number of nineteenth-century historians who were labeled "anti-Catholic zealots" and therefore biased in their scholarship.

In actual fact the testimony of the living survivors has been readily available for all historians for over one hundred and fifty years. It would have been easy for any historian, government official, army officer or concerned citizen to validate or repudiate Father Brouillet's plea of innocence for his part in this massacre with the testimony of the survivors. This research will examine those testimonies to determine if Brouillet was indeed telling the truth, but first let us continue with his defense.

Brouillet next related his version of the causes of these horrific murders. "The ravages which the sickness had made in their midst, together with the conviction which a half-breed, named Joe Lewis, had succeeded in fixing upon their minds, that Doctor Whitman had poisoned them, were the only motives I could discover which could have prompted them to this act of murder. This half-breed had imagined a conversation between Doctor Whitman, his wife, and Mr. Spalding, in which he made them say that it was necessary to hasten the death of the Indians in order to get possession of their horses and lands. 'If you do not kill the Doctor,' said he, 'you will all be dead in the spring.'" (Brouillet, 35th Congress, p. 35)

Rev. Henry Spalding had evidence introduced in the United States Congress that Joe Lewis was "engaged in Canada to do this work." Spalding believed that Lewis had been engaged to incite and participate in the murder of Christian missionaries and American citizens. Spalding believed Lewis was engaged for the mission of inciting the Whitman massacre because "he came over with the party from Europe." The Jesuit priests knew Joe Lewis intimately because he traveled from Europe with them. According to Spalding's testimony Joe Lewis was trained and commissioned in Europe with the assignment to incite the Cayuse Indians against the Protestants. The party of Jesuit priests came from Europe, to be precise France and Rome, in the summer of 1847 with the charge from the Pope to establish a Jesuit vicariate-apostolic in the Oregon Territory.

Bishop Blanchet, shortly after arriving at his Episcopal see at Walla Walla, set out for openings among the Indians. "I have very much in my mind to establish a mission among the Sakaptiens (Nez Perce). They have with them a Presbyterian minister whom for the most part they do not like. The presence of a black-robe in this place would force him to retire. Father Joset knows some of the chiefs and is going to speak to them." (Garraghan, p. 343)

Next Brouillet approached a subject of great controversy between the Americans and the Jesuit priest. "Having buried the dead, I hastened to prepared for my return to my mission, in order to acquaint Mr. Spalding of the danger which threatened him....I wished to meet him in time to give him a chance to escape. This I repeated several times to the unfortunate widows of the slain, and expressed to them my desire of being able to save Mr. Spalding....On leaving the Doctor's house I perceived that the son of Tilokaikt followed, in company of my interpreter, who himself was an Indian, his friend and his relative by his wife. I did not think that he had the intention of coming far with us…but when after having crossed the river, he continued on with us, I began strongly to fear for Mr. Spalding….What could I do in such a circumstance? I saw no remedy; I could not tell the Indian to go back, because he would have suspected something….I resolved, then, to leave all in the hands of Providence." (Brouillet, 35th Congress, p. 36)

We have documented how the Jesuits wanted to get rid of Spalding, i.e. "make him retire,'" from their own quoted sources. Why was Father Brouillet so worried about the welfare of Rev. Spalding? How would the son of Tilokaikt (Teloukaite) know that Father Brouillet was on a mission to save Spalding's life? According to Brouillet he was afraid for his own life and that was the reason he failed to end the bloodshed at the Whitman mission. The incredulous story of Father Brouillet's courageous and life-threatening effort to save Spalding's life continued.

"Fortunately, a few minutes after crossing the river, the interpreter asked Tilokaikt's son for a smoke. They prepared the calumet, but when the moment came for lighting it there was nothing to make fire. 'You have a pistol,' said the interpreter, 'fire it, and we will light.' Accordingly, without stopping, he fired his pistol, reloaded it, and fired it again. He then commenced smoking with the interpreter, without thinking of reloading his pistol. A few minutes later, while they were thus engaged in smoking, I saw Mr. Spalding come galloping toward me. In a moment he was by my side, taking me by the hand, and asking for news." (Brouillet, 35th Congress, p. 36)

According to Father Brouillet, Spalding was so grateful to see his dear friend that he took him "by the hand." Put yourself in Henry Spalding's place. He had just heard two gunshots. The situation was most tense even if Spalding had yet to receive word of the slaughter of his friends. It is well documented that Spalding had good reason not to trust the Jesuit "black coats." There were two Cayuse Indians with Brouillet, whom Spalding knew well after living in Oregon for eleven years, especially considering there were fewer than two hundred Cayuse natives left in Oregon. Spalding no doubt was studying the Jesuit "black coat" and the two Indians especially after hearing two shots. Let us continue with the dubious Jesuit version of this momentous meeting in the early evening between the Jesuit spokesperson for the Catholic Counter Reformation and the Protestant spokesperson for the spiritual battle that has raged through the twentieth century.

"'Have you been to the Doctor's?' he inquired. 'Yes,' I replied. 'What news? Sad news. Is any person dead? Yes sir. Who is dead? Is it one of the doctor's children?' (He had left two very sick.) 'No,' I replied. 'Who then is dead?' I hesitated to tell him. 'Wait a moment,' said I, 'I can not tell you now.' While Mr. Spalding was asking me those different questions, I had spoken to my interpreter, telling him to entreat the Indian, in my name not to kill Mr. Spalding; which I begged of him as a special favor, and hoped he would not refuse it to me. I was waiting for his answer, and did not wish to relate the disaster to Mr. Spalding before getting it, for fear that he might by his manner discover to the Indian what I had told him; for the least motion like flight would have cost him his life, and probably exposed mine also. The son of Tilokaikt, after hesitating some moments, replied that he could not take it upon himself to save Mr. Spalding, but that he would go back and consult the other Indians; and so he started back immediately to his camp." (Brouillet, 35th Congress, p. 36)

The reader is left with the impression these bosom missionary friends are still hand in hand as the Jesuit priest wrestled with words to find a way to save his ministry colleague's life. In actual fact, Spalding was proficient in the language of the Cayuse and he did not require an interpreter, as did the Jesuit priest. Spalding would have known exactly what the two Cayuse Indians were saying. As a matter of fact, the Indians knew Spalding spoke their language. The ridiculous story of Brouillet's heroic effort to save Spalding's life, a story that was received by the United States Congress and twentieth-century historians, never happened according to Spalding. But since Spalding, according to revisionist historians, was mentally unbalanced and bigoted in his anti-Catholic prejudice, the spurious story has established the standard of historical truth between Spalding and Brouillet.

The next question begged to be asked. Why didn't Father Brouillet entreat the Indians at Waiilatpu to save the lives of the Americans who were yet to be slaughtered after he left if he was so concerned for the Protestant missionaries' lives? Brouillet had no trouble entreating, even begging the son of Tilokaikt for Spalding's life. The other question that begged to be asked was why didn't Father Brouillet go directly to Fort Walla Walla and obtain help from the Hudson's Bay Company to stop this massacre and free the hostages if he was, by his own estimate, a minister of peace and good will? The Hudson's Bay Company had exercised law and order under Chief Factor John McLoughlin for two decades. McLoughlin was gone but the authority of the British was something the Indians respected and feared. The Jesuits and the Hudson's Bay Company worked hand in hand and the Cayuse had never challenged their authority nor has there ever been any evidence that any Columbia Plateau Indian tribe had any intention of challenging the authority of the Hudson's Bay Company even after murdering the missionaries.

Father Brouillet took full credit for Spalding's perilous escape. According to Brouillet, the son of Tilokaikt and fellow Cayuse were angry he was responsible for Spalding's escape. "The priest ought to have attended to his own business, and not to have interfered with ours, they said, in an angry tone, and started immediately in pursuit of him." (Brouillet, 35th Congress, p. 37)

Father Brouillet finished his letter to Col. Gilliam contending since his life was in danger for "saving the life of a fellow-creature at the peril of my own" (Brouillet, 35th Congress, p. 38) he could not return to the Whitman mission "fulfilling the promise I had made to the widows and orphans of returning to see them." (Brouillet, 35th Congress, p. 38) Brouillet concluded the letter thanking Col. Gilliam for the opportunity "you have given me of presenting to you a full and candid exposition of my conduct and intentions in the circumstances so dangerous and so delicate in which I accidentally found myself involved." (Brouillet, 35th Congress, p. 38) The next chapter will examine Father Brouillet's "Protestantism in Oregon" according to the testimony of the survivors of the Whitman Massacre and governmental records, church documents and newspaper accounts of the hour.

Chapter 24

The Testimony of the Protestant Church and the Oregon Government Concerning Romanism in Oregon

The Protestant church conferences corporately developed resolutions that reflected the voice of Oregonians in response to Jesuit Father Brouillet's "Protestantism in Oregon" and vociferously stood against the Jesuit ministries that refused to yield their missions among the Indians in obedience to the governmental edict. The Oregon Presbytery of the Old School, Cumberland and United Presbyterian Churches, the Oregon Conference Methodist Episcopal Church, the Oregon Congregational Association, the Oregon Christian Church and the Pleasant Butte Baptist Church issued a document called "The Oregon Mission and the United States Government" that detailed the evidence of the Jesuit conspiracy against the Protestant missionaries. This document represented a third of the citizens of the Oregon, "full 30,000 of the best inhabitants of the state." (41st Congress, Ex. Doc. 37, p. 80) The purpose of the document was to record in the United States Congress the truth of what happened at the Whitman massacre: "to that every watchful care over the truth of history, and to that sacred regard for unselfish patriotism which animates the bosom of every American....We have thus allowed the leading citizens of the State of Oregon and the Territory, and nearly all the Federal officers of the country, to speak for themselves..." (41st Congress, p. 80)

    The Book of Heaven, the foundation of the Protestant Reformation, proclaimed, "My people are destroyed for lack of knowledge." (Hosea 4:6) The knowledge of the "truth of history" preserved by the Protestant forefathers of the nineteenth century has been hidden from the American people of the Pacific Northwest. The "truth of history" that this research has documented was well known during the latter portion of the nineteenth century in Oregon as evidenced by the following statement affirmed by the previously documented six combined Protestant churches of Oregon:

    "It is, therefore, not surprising that the British officials in that region were greatly incensed against Dr. Whitman and his associates. It is now a matter of authentic history that extreme measures were soon resorted to by the agents of the Hudson's Bay Company to check the growth of American influence. Special agents from Europe appeared on the ground, and, by the aid of certain Roman Catholic priests, the Indians were themselves incited to violence by false reports concerning the missionaries, as i.e., that they had come to poison the Indians and possess their lands…. Throughout the eight days of slaughter, Americans only were the victims. The priests and others who were there in the interests of the Hudson's Bay Company were unharmed, and there is every reason to believe that they only encouraged and assisted the savages in their bloody work." (41st Congress, p. 79)

It is difficult to comprehend how any American historian, enjoining the liberty of expression won by our American patriot forefathers, could re-craft the "truth of history" to protect the treachery of foreign agents of Romanism that purportedly came to kill and drive out all Americans from the Oregon Territory. There is only one plausible answer to this dilemma: "My people are destroyed for lack of knowledge." (Hosea 4:6)

In a resolution adopted by the Pleasant Butte Baptist Church of Linn County, Oregon in 1869, this Protestant church corporately held that Jesuit Father Brouillet, the vicar-general of the Pacific coast, the head of a Roman foreign contingent in Oregon, was the ringleader behind the Whitman massacre. "This Brouillet, to remove all doubt from the minds of the Oregon Indians as to his abhorrence of Americans, and as pay down for the butchering the heretics, actually proceeded to baptize the blood-stained children of the butchering savages, while the butchery was going on and the unburied dead and gasping bodies lay about his feet, hogs and dogs running about with parts in their mouths, the screams of the ever-to-be-pitied young women writhing in the hands of unrestrained brutality…" (41st Congress, p. 72) The reader is not left with any doubt regarding the convictions of this Baptist church about Jesuit Father Brouillet and Romanism in 1869 in Oregon.

This church resolution, affirming the research of this study, also demonstrated that Brouillet's "Protestantism in Oregon" was an outreach of the Jesuit Counter Reformation in the Pacific Northwest. Brouillet's scathing rebuke of Protestantism was published in *"Freeman's Journal*, New York, a paper that has always proclaimed its hatred of Protestantism and our free schools and free press." (41st Congress, p. 72)

The early Protestant church leaders minced no words in declaring to the world the deeds of Romanism in Oregon. These Christian leaders were not intimidated by the "anti-Catholic bigot" label certain to be lofted against them in defense of the Papist designs for Oregon. The passion of the hour over the true cause of the Whitman massacre of 1847 and the complicity of Romanist operatives continued unabated for over five decades. This research has documented the passion of this debate continued into the twentieth century. There is an old saying in the ministry that is relevant to the Protestant/Romanist relationship of the second half of the nineteenth century in Old Oregon. To paraphrase this equation in regard to earning or inheriting something very valuable, "the first generation earns it, the second generation abuses it, and the third generation loses it." In the case of the Protestant defense of the early missionary Christian achievements in the Oregon Territory, by the time the third generation of Christians took their place on the battlefield at the beginning of the 20th century, the cause was no longer worth the battle and the faith of their fathers was compromised.

The leading statesmen of Oregon, such as Governor George Abernathy (1845-49), General Joel Palmer, commissary general in the Cayuse War, J. S. Griffin, editor of the *Oregon American*, Hon. S. R. Thurston of the Oregon Congress, and Commander Wilkes of the United States Navy all passionately supported defending the integrity of the Protestant missions and their cause. They denounced Jesuit Father Brouillet's "Protestantism in Oregon," particularly in defense of Rev. Henry Spalding.

Perhaps the defense of these statesmen was passionate because Brouillet had made Rev. Spalding the center point of his criticism of Protestantism: "But a certain gentleman, moved on by religious fanaticism, and ashamed of owing his life and that of his family and friends to some priests, began to insinuate false suspicions about the true causes of the disaster, proceeded, by degrees, to make more open accusations, and finally declared publicly that the bishop of Walla Walla and his clergy were the first cause and great movers of all the evil. This gentleman is the Rev. H. H. Spalding, whose life had been saved from the Indians by a priest, at the peril of his own." (Drury, Vol. II, p. 377)

Brouillet claimed to have saved Spalding's life. Spalding found it hard to believe that Brouillet could claim to have saved his life when he was "traveling with an Indian who had the avowed intention of killing him." (Cannon, p. 146) Brouillet admitted he knew Edward Tiloukaikt was accompanying him with the intent to kill Rev. Spalding. "I knew that the Indians were angry with all Americans and more enraged against Mr. Spalding than any other. But what could I do in such a circumstance? I saw no remedy." (Drury, Vol. II, p. 256) Brouillet claimed when they met that fateful evening Spalding "was at my side, taking me by the hand and asking for news." (Drury, Vol. II, p. 256) Next Brouillet claimed he entreated his Indian interpreter to go to Edward, who had removed himself to load his gun, "in my name, not to kill Mr. Spalding." (Drury, Vol. II, p. 256)

Dr. Drury, in an attempt to make Brouillet's story plausible, offered that perhaps he spoke in French to the Indian because Spalding was unaware of this exchange. Providential intervention and an unloaded revolver saved Henry Spalding, not Father Brouillet, yet virtually all twentieth-century writers such as Miles Cannon side with Brouillet in this controversy. For an example of the standard demeaning picture of the Protestant missionary he wrote, "Mr. Spalding's name, whose delight over sectarian controversy and power of imagination have led many authorities to discredit his writings to a great extent." (Cannon, p. 146) Henry Spalding became the object of Jesuit ridicule because he became the messenger to expose their crime.

How did the leading statesmen, newspapers and historians of the hour characterize this Protestant missionary who was to become the standard bearer for the Christian faith after the Whitmans perished? Commander Wilkes, in his *Exploratory Expedition Around the World, 1840-43, Vol. IV*, wrote about the character of Henry Spalding: "Among the other duties of Mr. Spalding, he has taught them [the Native American Indians] the art of cultivation, and many of them have plantations; these are kept in good order....The women are represented as coming miles to learn to knit, spin, and weave, and to assist Mrs. Spalding in her large school and domestic avocations....The great endeavor of Mr. Spalding is to induce the Indians to give up their roving mode of life, and to settle down, and cultivate the soil....In the winter the school at the station numbers about five hundred scholars, but in the summer not one-tenth of that number attend." (41st Congress, p. 6)

In response to Brouillet's "Protestantism in Oregon," Alex Smith, Judge First Judicial District, Territory of Idaho defended Spalding in an article in the *Pacific*, San Francisco, California, Feb. 6, 1864. "On Sunday last I had the pleasure of attending church in this place (Lewiston). The Rev. H. H. Spalding, who came to this people with his heroic wife in 1836, conducted the services in the Nez Perce language. The governor of the Territory was present, and all the federal officers and nearly all the country officers, with most of the citizens of Lewiston. The large courtroom was crowded to its capacity. The scene was deeply solemn and interesting; the breathless silence, the earnest, devout attention of that great Indian congregation (even the small child) to the words of their much-loved pastor; the spirit, the sweet melody of their singing, the readiness with which they turned to hymns and chapters, and read with Mr. Spalding and the Sabbath lessons form their Testaments, which Mr. Spalding had translated and printed twenty years before." (41st Congress, p. 7)

Father Brouillet had accused the Protestant missionaries of abandoning their posts after the massacre. The combined Protestant resolution, written by the Presbytery of Steuben, and affirmed by eight Church conferences, in 1869 challenged the Romanist assertion that the Protestant missions were voluntarily abandoned. "First driven away by the murdering savages of the Whitman Massacre, the missionaries were afterward taken out of the country, and the country was closed against all missionaries by the Government until 1858....It is well known and proved that so soon as it was thought safe Mr. Spalding attempted to return, but was forbidden; and when he did and opened his schools among his old people, who were rejoiced to see him, and at once filled up church and school-room—as testified by Agent Anderson, these schools were broken up and himself forced from his old home, his orchards and buildings, his people and native (Indian) church, by the United States Government; nor has he since been permitted to return." (41st Congress, p. 37) Why would the government of the United States of America resist the very missionary who helped cause the Nez Perce nation to loyally stand with the Americans and the Oregon volunteers during the Indian Wars? Why would the U.S. government stand against one of the pioneer missionaries who opened up the Oregon country to become a vital part of the emerging republic? Had the work of the foreign Romanist operatives, first penned by Jesuit Father Brouillet, created a poisoned environment in the nation's capital for the Protestants as well as the Nez Perce Indians? This research will examine these questions in the next chapter.

    The turmoil of the controversy over the Whitman massacre extended well beyond Old Oregon. The *Sacramento Union* in July 1869 warned of the danger of Romanism and the impact of Brouillet's "Protestantism in Oregon." "Given the sophistry of the Jesuit mind, which directly attempted to show that the missionaries were horse thieves and poisoners laboring only to make money out of the Indians, giving them no instruction, and continually breaking plighted faith with them." (41st Congress, p. 51)

    Once again the quotation attributed to Napoleon aptly defined what happened to Old Oregon because of Brouillet's dissertation: "What is history but a lie agreed upon." (Catherine Sager, p. 7) The Protestant missionaries were not allowed back into their Indian fields because the United States government had swallowed the lie of Romanist sophistry. That Romanist lie has continued to the present hour as demonstrated by the documented histories of the Nez Perce and Confederated Tribes of the Umatilla that are critical of the Protestant missionaries and positive toward the Jesuit priests.

    The *Pacific* of San Francisco on July 22, 1869 expanded upon the reason the United States government swallowed the Jesuit deception: "...this false narrative ("Protestantism in Oregon") was, by Congress, published to the world, with no reply to its enormous statements. It is one of the strongest, shrewdest measures of the Jesuits of which we have read in American history, to get Congress to publish this narrative of over fifty pages, filled with the most erroneous charges against the Protestant missionaries, trying to throw off from themselves the well-founded public belief that they were the real cause of this horrible massacre, and place the blame on Americans." (41st Congress, p. 51)

    Governor Abernathy and General Palmer both testified that Romanism and the British influence caused the bloody massacre of the Protestant missionaries and the American emigrants. (41st Congress p. 53) J. S. Griffin, editor of the *Oregon American*, wrote, "an overwhelming majority of the Americans held it as proved, that the Jesuit missionaries were the procuring cause of the Whitman Massacre and the other Americans who fell with him, and of the Indian wars that followed. So fully were the Jesuits convicted that no one has ever attempted a reply in Oregon in their behalf." (41st Congress, p. 53). This research has documented that Prof. Bourne and William Marshall both re-crafted Oregon Territory history without ever considering the testimony of the leading statesmen, governors or volunteer commanders of Oregon's heritage. These two historians essentially expanded on the sophistry of the Romanist agents in Oregon. The documented history of Oregon, as evidenced by J. S. Griffin, proved that Americans of that age corporately believed Roman agents and Hudson's Bay operatives were behind the Whitman massacre and the subsequent Indian Wars.

    The Hon. S. R. Thurston declared in the Oregon Congress, "Mr. Speaker, could you read in the records of heaven the deeds of this power, (Hudson's Bay Company) in Oregon, your whole moral nature would be shocked by the baseness of the designs and the means for their accomplishment....Of the murder of Dr. Whitman and that great number of American emigrants, which murder I have no more doubt was instigated by the Hudson's Bay Company than I doubt my existence." (41st Congress, p. 48) This research has documented how the Hudson's Bay Company supported the Jesuit missionaries and provided many of their supplies and transportation needs. The Jesuit-Hudson's Bay Company conspiracy was strongly exposed by the complicity of William McBean of Fort Walla Walla in the massacre.

Governor Abernathy and General Palmer both testified that all missionaries were ordered to leave the Oregon Territory by the order of the Oregon territorial legislature in mid-summer of 1848 because of the hostilities of the Cayuse Indians after the Whitman massacre. Gov. Abernathy testified the Jesuit priests did not honor the order of the United States government to leave the Indian lands. "It is true as to arms and powder being taken up by the priests, and seized at The Dalles. I ordered the muskets and ammunition sent back, and detained them at Oregon City until Governor Lane arrived." (41st Congress, p. 55) According to the evidence provided by General Joel Palmer, the weapons and arms captured by Lt. Rodgers were meant "to furnish the upper savages, who were assembled at Des Chutes in great numbers, waiting, as they declared openly and defiantly, to receive it from the priests, and then fall upon the little garrison, and then come down upon the infant settlements and cut them off, and take their women and cattle as booty, and return and cut off the on-coming emigration of that fall." (41st Congress, p. 55) The student of history needs to appreciate the predicament of the Oregon volunteers. "The whole of the Oregon Army had been able to obtain no more than five hundred pounds of powder." (Victor, Francis, *Early Indian Wars of Oregon*, Frank Baker State Printer, Salem, Oregon, 1894, p. 219).

Not only did the Jesuits defy the Oregon territorial legislation edict to leave the Columbia mission fields, they also actively encouraged the Indians to war with America and the early pioneers of Oregon. They provided arms and promises of support to encourage the hostilities between the Indians and the Americans initiated at the Whitman massacre. The Jesuits were working in concert with the British Hudson's Bay Company to reclaim Oregon for the Crown and for the designs of Rome.

Other than the few Cayuse Indians incited to murder the Protestants at the Whitman mission there were no Indian nations ready to war with the American pioneers prior to the massacre. Once the Protestants obeyed the Oregon provisional government's edict to leave their mission field, the Jesuit missionaries quickly expanded their operation in defiance of American law. Once again the Jesuits used their most powerful tool of deception to advance their cause, the guise of Protestant anti-Catholic bigotry. Not only did the Jesuits refuse to honor American law, they also skillfully used subterfuge to continue their campaign to turn the Oregon Territory Indians against the Americans.

Jesuit historian Gilbert Garraghan presented the Romanist argument for disobeying the order of the Oregon territorial legislature and the rationale for the priests to bring a large quantity of arms up the Columbia River into the contested areas of hostility. According to Lt. Rodgers, four thousand pounds of powder and balls and three boxes of guns were seized at Fort Wascopum, only fifteen miles from the great camp of the combined hostile tribes of the Columbia Plateau. Once again the common Romanist argument of anti-Catholic bigotry, so conveniently seized upon by revisionist historians, was used to excuse Jesuit treachery against Americans by Jesuit historian Garraghan.

"The excitement caused by the Whitman Massacre had simmered down when an incident occurring in the mid summer of 1848 kindled anew the flames of bigotry. As a measure incident to the Cayuse war a law had been passed by the Oregon territorial legislature forbidding the delivery of all firearms and ammunition to the Indians. Father Joset on hearing of this measure came down to Oregon City, where the legislature was sitting, to enter a protest against it on the ground of the hardship it would entail on the

Catholic Indians, who were peaceably disposed and loyal to the provisional government. These Indians got their livelihood from hunting; moreover, the Flatheads absolutely needed arms to defend themselves against the Blackfeet. One of the legislators in particular was much impressed by Joset's representations and pledged himself to make efforts to have the law repealed. It happened at this juncture that a considerable supply of arms and ammunition for the Jesuit missions had arrived at Fort Vancouver. It was in fact the entire annual shipment for all the mission posts of the Upper Columbia country, consisting of one thousand and eighty pounds of powder, fifteen hundred pounds of balls, three hundred pounds of buckshot and thirty-six guns. Joset, expecting that the law would soon be repealed, directed Accolti to forward the consignment to its designation. The latter did, and without any attempt, it would seem, to conceal the character of the consignment. At The Dalles, Lieutenant Rodgers intercepted the material, seized it, and reported the affair to Gov. Abernathy, who directed him to explain to Father Accolti what had been done. The latter in a communication to Major Lee, commanding the American forces against the Cayuse, pointed out that the law did not prohibit the shipment of munitions, but only their distribution among the Indians; and he asked that, in case the munitions were not to be confiscated, they would be returned to Fort Vancouver." (Garraghan, Vol. II, pp. 345-46).

The Jesuits worked within the Oregon Territorial legislature to win support for their covert operations in Oregon. The Jesuits had carefully curried favor with many pioneer Oregon statesmen, drawing heavily upon their well-funded European purse strings. It was hard for most Oregon pioneers to believe these "black-robed men of God" would conspire against America. Governor Abernathy was one such Oregon pioneer who was courted and deceived by the Jesuits. We have documented ample testimony that he changed his mind as the overwhelming evidence of Jesuit culpability came to the surface. Unfortunately in 1849 he helped defeat the petition to ban the Jesuits from Oregon by publicly offering an alibi for the Indian confession to Captain Rodgers that the Jesuit arms were intended for the hostilities against Americans. "I am well acquainted with the Indian character and know their disposition to carry false reports from one to another, sometimes merely to see what effect a report unfavorable to the person they are speaking of will have. I am, therefore, satisfied that the Indians, in making the statement they did to Mr. Rodgers, did it to mislead him. For I cannot believe the priests would be so remiss as to say anything of the kind to the Indians while there was so much excitement in the community." (Victor, p. 221) Once again the covert operations of the Jesuits were sanctioned by Gov. Abernathy who was deceived to believe the venerable Jesuit priests represented God. The Jesuit campaign to incite the Indians to make war on the Americans proceeded without governmental opposition.

The greatest ally the Jesuits have depended upon through the ages has been the perception the gentle and venerable "black-robed" priests could not be capable of the very wicked deeds they were in fact orchestrating. Had Governor Abernathy not been deceived in 1849 the Jesuits would have been expelled from Oregon by the territorial legislature like they had been from every state in Europe and South America. Had the Jesuits been expelled from the Oregon Territory the Indian Wars of the 1850s would never have commenced. Unfortunately, Jesuit Bishop Accolti successfully and adroitly challenged Governor Abernathy's integrity. "Yet sir, I presume that you who hold authority…and are not biased by prejudice—I presume that you and all sensible citizens know that it is not through any fault of the Catholics, if this fact exists, that the Catholics have done nothing to cause excitement or bitter feelings against them, and that the fact is based only (on) unfounded suspicions, growing out of unjust prejudices and a groveling jealously." (Victor, p. 220)

The truth of the matter is almost all American Catholics on the field of Old Oregon would never condone or support the secret designs and actions of the Jesuits. According to the Jesuit agents, still operating in the Oregon Territory in clear violation of territorial legislation, the American interception of arms intended for the Indians "kindled anew the flames of bigotry" "based only (on) unfounded suspicions, growing out of unjust prejudices and a groveling jealousy." Where in Oregon history was any unjust prejudice pressed against Catholics in Oregon? The Jesuit priests were bringing weapons of war up the Columbia River into areas of great hostilities between the Americans and the Columbia Plateau Indians. Not only were they unlawfully maintaining their mission to the Columbia Plateau Indians, they were also transporting a large quantity of gunpowder, rifles, and buckshot and bullets (balls) to supply Indians during the period of Cayuse Wars. The quantity of gunpowder was over three times the amount of gunpowder of the entire Oregon volunteer army. By their own admission the Jesuit priests supplied these weapons of war annually.

Why would these supposedly "venerable" and "harmless" Jesuit priests be central in transporting arms of war in an arena that knew only peace during the hour of Protestant missionaries? The Jesuits claimed the weapons were for hunting and defense against hostile tribes. The historical fact of the Cayuse Wars was that all the Indian tribes of the Pacific Northwest, save the Nez Perce, combined to war against the Americans. These tribes had been historically peaceful to the advent of white men for over half a century! The Jesuit priests were most insistent that the confiscated weapons would be returned to the British at Fort Vancouver. The Hudson's Bay Company continued to emphatically deny they were arming the Columbia Indians. In actual fact the war arms were returned to the Jesuits at Fort Vancouver.

The Jesuits had skillfully worked their way into positions of authority in the provisional Oregon government based on their professed innocence and skillful deception as professed men of God. "In February, 1849, the legislative assembly having inquired of the governor what disposition had been made of the arms and ammunition of the priests…replied that he had felt himself justified in retaining possession of them until then; but application had been made to him to return the property to Vancouver to be placed to the credit of the Catholic missions on the companies' books, accompanied by an assurance that no powder should be sent to the upper country without the sanction of the Oregon government, and that he had done so." (Victor, p. 222)

Governor Abernathy was to learn later that the Jesuits did not operate under the sanction of the Oregon government but rather the sanction and complete obedience of the Jesuit General in Rome. Jesuit historian Gilbert Garraghan complained about the charges of Jesuit treachery against Americans after the Whitman massacre. "What disposition was finally made of them (the confiscated Jesuit weapons) is not known; but the incident itself was at once seized upon by prejudiced minds as evidence to smuggle arms into the interior to be put into the hands of the Catholic Indians for the extermination of the Protestants. The preposterous charge met with widespread credence and anti-Catholic hostility was soon fanned to a white heat. In December, 1848, a petition for the expulsion of the Catholic clergy from Oregon was introduced into the territorial legislature but failed of passage." (Garraghan, Vol. II, p. 346)

An example of this straw man, an anti-Catholic scapegoat, consistently used to explain away Jesuit treachery, can be found in most twentieth-century history books covering the Cayuse wars. For example, in George L. Converse's volume *A Military History of the Columbia Valley 1848-1865*, during the Yakima War Major Rain's troops discovered a keg of powder buried at a Catholic (Jesuit) mission. "Under the mistaken impression that the Catholics had been supporting the Indians with ammunition, the mission was burned by some of the volunteers. Parenthetically, it should be remembered that some of the fanatical anti-Catholic Protestant clergy in the Willamette Valley were blaming the Catholics and the Hudson Bay Co. for all the sins they could invent." (Converse, George L., *A Military History of the Columbia Valley*, Pioneer Press Books, Walla Walla, Washington, 1988, p. 21) As a matter of documented historical fact, affirmed both by

Jesuit and Protestant sources, the Jesuits were arming the Columbia Indians and that explained why the American troops found a keg of powder buried at a Jesuit mission.

The overriding reality of the Cayuse wars that every student of Oregon and American history must soberly consider was every Indian tribe, people or nation wherein the Jesuits established a mission work in the Oregon Territory turned against the Americans during the so-called Cayuse Wars. Governor Abernathy testified that Colonel Nesmith, as superintendent of Indians affairs, confirmed that the Americans fought against all the Indian tribes that Romanism had impacted. Col. Cornelius affirmed Col. Nesmith's assessment. "I was in command of the Oregon volunteers in 1855-'56 when there was a concert of actions with all the tribes on the Northwest coast against the Americans, except the Nez Perce alone, who have always been friendly. In 1856, they furnished several hundred horses to remount my command." (41st Congress, p. 56) It was no coincidence that Henry Spalding, the man scorned by Father Brouillet and historians to this hour, was the missionary to the Nez Perce, the great friends of the American nation.

J. Ross Browne documented that the Nez Perce were strongly encouraged to join forces with all the Indians of the Oregon Territory against the Americans. Governor Abernathy testified if the Nez Perce had joined forces with the combined Indian nations the "Americans would have been destroyed." (41st Congress, p. 56) Gov. Abernathy also testified that Romanism defied the legislative dictates of the Oregon Congress and sustained their Jesuit missions among the tribes that declared war on America. (41st Congress, p. 56)

The Christian Church of Brownsville, Oregon on Oct. 29, 1869 documented that while Rev. Spalding was forced to leave his mission at Lapwai because of the Cayuse insurrection and again in 1863 by the United States government, Jesuit priests were allowed to remain and agitate among the Nez Perce contrary to the Oregon Territorial Legislature proclamation of 1848. "…our brother Spalding the last Protestant missionary in five territories, while some fifteen Jesuit mission stations, most of them taken in defiance of the Government, and some twenty three Jesuit missionaries, remained unmolested in the same field, and some of them known to be the identical instigators of the horrible massacre of American missionaries and American citizens." (41st Congress, p. 57)

The order to remove the Protestant missionaries from the field after the Whitman massacre was upheld by the United States Congress, which had been heavily influenced by the false proclamations of Brouillet's "Protestantism in Oregon." After the United States government ordered Spalding to once again leave his beloved Nez Perce he learned of the Jesuit sophistry and began his final mission to bring the light of truth to what really happened between the Protestant and Jesuit missionaries. When Spalding made his triumphant trip to the nation's capital in 1871 his documentation was received unanimously. The deception of the Jesuits was revealed and the Protestant missionary cause was exonerated. Whitman's place in history as the true father of Oregon was secure, sealed by the unanimous vote of Congress. Spalding could die in peace believing the historical heritage of the Protestant missionaries would be taught to succeeding generations of Oregonians.

It was not so much the so-called legend of Marcus Whitman that was on the line but rather the cause that he and his fellow pioneer missionaries stood for. Spalding's mission to the United States Congress restored the truth of the fundamental standards of the Protestant Reformation, i.e. the liberty of free men found in faith in Jesus Christ and the Constitution that the Founding Fathers of the American Revolution fought to establish. These missionaries established the Protestant principals of the right of all men to come to God through faith based on the word of God, the Bible, not through a priest or a church. Now it would be up to the Protestant ministers and historians who followed to defend the ground their forefathers had won with their blood and uncompromising faith.

Whitman's position as a great American statesman and patriot was so highly esteemed at the turn of the 20th century that he was included in a vote of America's greatest men by New York University's Hall of Fame. Dr. Drury and his fellow revisionist historians have questioned the authenticity of Whitman's position, complaining the doctor scored higher than John Charles Freemont and George Rogers Clark. Prof. Bourne ridiculed Dr. Whitman's esteem among Americans at that hour by stating, "History will be sought in vain for a more extraordinary growth of fame after death." (Drury, Vol. II, p. 385)

This author will leave it to history and the reader to determine if the life and works of John Freemont and George Clark equal the large shadow still being cast over America and the Oregon Territory by Dr. Marcus Whitman. It is apparent to this writer that the past century's efforts by revisionist historians to re-craft the heritage and impact of Marcus Whitman and Henry Spalding based on the spurious work of Father Brouillet have cast another type of shadow over the Oregon Territory. Could this revisionist history of the early Protestant missionaries have anything to do with the Pacific Northwest being the most un-churched area in America? This research will examine this question as the drama over the Whitman massacre boiled over for half a century after the tragedy.

CHAPTER 25

THE NEZ PERCE INDIANS:
GREAT PATRIOTS FOR AMERICA AND OREGON

The Nez Perce Indians foiled the designs of the Jesuits and the British after they incited the Columbia Plateau Indians to join forces to defeat the Americans. This historical truth was affirmed by the combined voice of the Protestant church of Oregon. "It was under God, Protestantism in Oregon which…did succeed, in the teeth of the most unrelenting and bloody opposition of Romanism and British influence, to establish the first successful and permanent settlement on these vast shores…By the steadfast devotion of the Protestant Nez Perce, the most powerful tribe west of the mountains, to the Americans and the American Government. Through that long and severe struggle to prevent or destroy the American settlements and annihilate Protestantism in Oregon; during the Whitman Massacre, and the long wars that followed, till 1857, the Nez Perce, true to the teachings of their Protestant Missionaries, remained constantly the firm allies and friends of the Americans…" (41st Congress, pp. 74, 76)

General Bert Alvord of the United States Army on December 28, 1858 documented the positive impact of the Nez Perce on the successful completion of the Cayuse War. "He (Colonel Steptoe) often descanted on the manly traits and Christian perseverance and fortitude of Timothy (a Nez Perce chief) and many of the Nez Perce. Accounts concur as to the remarkable preservation by the Nez Perce of the habits derived from the missionaries a dozen years ago. Such docility deserves encouragement. Their devotion to our people, our arms, and our Government, has also endeared them to all who have been watching the history of their position." (41st Congress, p. 16)

The Oregon country was closed to missionary work until after the Indian wars and the peace accord of 1855. In 1858 missionaries were allowed to return to their fields, but the Rev. Spalding after a joyous reunion with his beloved Nez Perce was once again forced to flee, this time by the United States government in the early 1860s. Why would the United States government force Rev. Spalding to leave the Nez Perce Indians who had saved the day for Oregon because of their loyalty to America instilled by this Protestant missionary? The policy of the United States government shamefully upheld the Romanist values which undermined the Nez Perce nation so loyal to the Americans because of the ministry of Henry and Eliza Spalding. This ill-conceived policy, based on a combination of Jesuit sophistry and pure greed on the part of many American immigrants seeking gold and land, was a dark hour for America, especially for the great friends of America, the Nez Perce Indians.

The Nez Perce were vital to the cause of freedom and liberty in America. Had the Nez Perce Indians, the most powerful tribe west of the rocky Mountains, not come to the aid of the Americans, the Romanists would have prevailed in Oregon during the Indian Wars and the Protestant cause could have been lost. What motivated the Nez Perce to stand against their blood brethren, the associated Columbia Indian tribes, whom they had been at peace with for centuries, to protect and support the Americans? The Nez Perce could well have supported the Hudson's Bay Company who opposed the emigration of American settlers at every opportunity. Did not the Nez Perce understand the white Americans would contend with the Indians for their land and resources? Virtually every Columbia Plateau Indian tribe, save the Nez Perce, combined to battle the Americans after the Whitman massacre. The American nation and especially the emigrant pioneers of the developing states of the Oregon Territory owed their newfound freedom and liberty to the loyalty of the Nez Perce Indians. No Indian nation did more for America, as documented from the earliest exposure with white men beginning with the expedition of Lewis and Clark, than the Nez Perce.

The Pleasant Butte Baptist Church developed a resolution that documented the conviction of the Protestant Church in Oregon in 1870. "During the long and expensive war following the massacre, this tribe alone among the Indians was friendly to the Americans. And there is no doubt, as many have testified, that this was owing in a great measure to the teachings of Mr. Spalding; and, according to Mr. Anderson, several years agent of the Nez Perce, 'Mr. Spalding by his own personal labors has accomplished more good to this tribe than all the money expended by the government has been able to effect.'" (41st Congress, p. 79)

Many accolades have been addressed to the ministry of Henry and Eliza Spalding on behalf of the Nez Perce Indians, but did the Spaldings and the Protestant message actually cause the Nez Perce to remain loyal to the Americans? After all, Spalding, like all the Protestant missionaries, was forced out of the Columbia Plateau, the scene of future hostilities between the Americans and the Indians. Spalding sent a final letter to his beloved Nez Perce brethren as he was leaving the mission under the protection of the Hudson's Bay Company. He addressed each of the twenty-one Nez Perce chiefs by name and exhorted them to stand with the Americans in the war he feared the Jesuits were agitating to initiate. "My friends…from us the Americans…from the great chief…Keep quiet, ye young men! Do not go over to the Cayuse. Wait till the commissioners speak clearly to you. The good are not to be punished. Only the bad are to be punished. The Nez Perce and the Americans are one; therefore do not depart from us." (Victor, p. 171)

There is no plausible historical explanation other than the Nez Perce stayed loyal to the Americans because they trusted the man of God who came to minister to them. They heeded his call to stand with the Americans. Had Spalding not interceded on behalf of the Americans to the Nez Perce there could have been a terrible bloodbath of American pioneers in Oregon. The combined Indian tribes were better armed than the American volunteers, thanks in part to the Jesuits, and they knew the terrain of Oregon intimately. It was their ancient homeland. The Nez Perce saved the day for the so-called Manifest Destiny of America in the Pacific Northwest, and twentieth-century historians give Spalding zero credit and only belated credit to the Nez Perce Indians for the American victory in the Indian war of 1847-57.

The benevolent and faithful loyalty of the Nez Perce Indians virtually saved the lives of the Protestant Americans after the Whitman massacre. The Nez Perce Indians came to the defense of Henry and Eliza Spalding and stood against the rebellion of the Cayuse Indians. The Nez Perce protected Eliza Spalding from a band of forty Cayuse sent to kill the Spaldings. The Nez Perce were instrumental in inducing the Cayuse to give up the fifty women and children hostages of the Whitman massacre. In addition, the Nez Perce Indians stood against the Cayuse after they had received the ransom payment for the hostages, "urged on by the Jesuit Lewis…made an attempt to retake Mr. Spalding and the Americans." (41st Congress, p. 77)

The resolution adopted by the Pleasant Butte Baptist Church previously cited, developed in 1869, documented the Oregon Protestant position of appreciation of the "steadfast devotion of the Protestant Nez Perce, the most powerful tribe west of the mountains, to the Americans and the American Government." (41st Congress, Ex. Doc. 37, p. 76) These Protestant leaders documented the consistent service of the Nez Perce nation to America in the face of consistent opposition, as well as enticements to join ranks, from the British Hudson's Bay Company, the Jesuits and all the previously kindred Indian tribes of the Pacific Northwest.

Had it not been for the Nez Perce the combined forces of the Columbia Plateau Indians under the covert leadership of the Jesuits would have routed American forces. "In 1848, when all the tribes of the Northwest, under Jesuits, had assembled at Des Chutes, waiting for ammunition to be brought to them from the English post by the priests, with which to cut off the Willamette settlements and take their women and herds…they (Nez Perce) sent word to the combined camp if they attempted to fall upon the American settlements they would fall upon their rear, sweep the country of their herds of horses, and retire east of the mountains." (41st Congress, p. 77)

In historical hindsight this was an incredibly difficult position for the Nez Perce nation to take in defense of the Americans in Oregon. Most of the young and vigorous American men in Oregon at this time would soon be drawn to California by the intoxicating magnet of the gold rush of 1849, leaving their families vulnerable. Had the Jesuit war armaments reached the combined Columbia tribes even the Nez Perce could have been in serious trouble.

In 1850 it was the Nez Perce, at the request of the American government, who overtook the warring Cayuse on the Upper John Day River. They engaged the Cayuse in vicious combat, killing some braves and capturing the five principle leaders of the Whitman massacre. They delivered these Cayuse chiefs to the Oregon provincial government where they were tried and executed at Oregon City.

In 1855 Colonel Cornelius testified that the combined Columbia tribes under the Jesuit priests attempted to induce the Nez Perce to join them with a large feast where thirty-seven oxen were sacrificed. Fortunately the Nez Perce refused to join the Jesuit-led alliance of Indian nations and continued to supply essential provisions, intelligence and cattle to the American troops. "They (Nez Perce) flew to the rescue of Governor Stevens and party when their retreat was cut off, and when Colonel Steptoe was defeated in a two days' fight, one-fourth of his company killed or wounded, his retreat and water cut off and ammunition gone, which disaster was brought about by a treacherous Jesuit priest, acting the friend of the American camp, but really a spy for the savages, learning the Colonel's small amount of ammunition, sent the savages word, and joined them as soon as the fight commenced with his packs of so-called groceries and nails, but really balls and powder. Then, it was Timothy, the Protestant Nez Perce preacher, and his two brothers, fighting with the Americans, discoursing an unguarded opening in the rocks, taking advantage of the darkness and the uproar of the surrounding savages at their dance fires awaiting the dawn to scalp the last American, led out the Colonel and his remnant, and, with the stillness of death, on through the night, to his country thus saved them and furnished them food." (41st Congress, p. 77)

In light of the unwavering and undaunted loyalty of the Nez Perce to the American emigrants, how did the Oregon beneficiaries respond? The answer has become one of the great tragedies of American culture. The Nez Perce nation had been a blessing to virtually every American exploration and subsequent encroachment upon Native American land from the hour of the Lewis and Clark expedition to the advent of the Indian wars after the Whitman massacre. The Nez Perce nation had the skill, horses, manpower, and military intelligence to defeat the Americans and drive the emigrant pioneers from Oregon had they chosen. Their Native American brethren, particularly the Cayuse, Umatilla, Walla Walla, Shoshone, and Bannock wooed the Nez Perce to join forces to save their common heritage and way of life. In every instance the Nez

Perce tribal council refused the temptation to join forces with the warring tribes. Twentieth-century historians disdain any credit the Protestant missionaries Henry and Eliza Spalding have received for counseling the Nez Perce to remain faithful to the Americans. The impact of the Protestant ministry to the Nez Perce speaks louder than the twentieth-century revisionist effort to demean the reputation of Henry Spalding and distort the impact of the Protestant biblical message to these Native Americans.

Let us consider for a moment the impact of the Jesuit defiance on the delicate balance of power that existed in the Oregon Territory after the Whitman massacre. Before the massacre, virtually all the Native American Indians of the Columbia Plateau were willing to live with the growing number of American emigrants. Before the massacre a spirit of diplomacy, communication, good will and reciprocal consideration predominantly ruled between the two races. Nonetheless, the growing number of emigrants did bring pressure on the land and resources the two nations were now sharing. Although no American emigrants settled on Columbia Plateau lands, still the growing number of American emigrants began to enforce their laws, dictated from American traditions and standards, as they began to establish homes, farms and communities west of the Cascade Mountains. The Indian nations heard rumors that the American government was planning to systematically give all the land of the Oregon Territory to the emigrants without honoring Indian claims to the land. The Donation Land Act of 1850, without Native American tribal consent, encouraged even more emigrants to move to the promised land of Oregon. Consideration from the American capital of Washington, D.C. for the rights and lands of the indigenous Indians was never formally established. In light of these historical facts it is amazing the Nez Perce did not at least use their position to leverage concessions from the American government for their unflinching support of the pioneer emigrants.

The Protestant missionaries had come to prepare the way for the Native Americans of the Columbia Plateau to develop the skills, values and lifestyle to compete one day evenly with American emigrants and therein join ranks as free men with equality under the Constitution of the United States of America. The Cayuse Indians at the Whitman mission were already proving themselves to be skillful entrepreneurs, cultivating their land and selling their produce to the nearly destitute wagon train emigrants. Tragically, the Whitman massacre removed the Protestant American missionaries, who came to prepare the Indians for white man's culture and civilization, from the Native Americans to whom they came to minister. As more and more emigrants, in the form of settlers, gold miners, farmers and cattlemen, arrived on the Columbia Plateau the hostilities initiated by the Whitman massacre multiplied. Both the American emigrants and Native Americans suffered atrocities at the hands of vengeful militants.

In 1853 the Columbia Indian nations under the leadership of the Yakimas under Kamiakin joined forces for the first time with associated Columbia Indian tribes in an effort to protect their ancient lands. Governor Joel Palmer of the Oregon Territory and Governor Isaac Stevens of the newly formed Washington Territory represented the Americans in an effort to negotiate and sign treaties to avoid further bloodshed. In 1855 the American Congress authorized the negotiation of these treaties to purchase Indian lands and establish reservations for the Indians to own and live on. The Native Americans knew the Americans wanted peace from the hostilities and the growing numbers of emigrants wanted the Indians removed from their ancestral lands. The American government provided multiple incentives for the Indians to cede their land. In addition to money, ancestral rights for fishing and hunting on ceded land, the American government also offered large reservations the Indians would own and govern and additional promises to build and strengthen their culture, some of which were honored and some of which were not.

The chief of the Nez Perce, Joseph, refused to sign these peace accords. Chief Joseph was so grieved by these treaties, which called for his nation to relinquish the lands of their fathers, that he renounced his Christian faith. Chief Joseph equated the Christian faith of the Protestant missionaries to be consistent with the Christian faith of the American government. Chief Joseph and the Nez Perce had been betrayed. Instead of being rewarded for their loyalty to the American Republic they were treated like the rest of the Indian tribes, like a conquered and defeated foe. The peace accord of 1855 actually divided the Nez Perce nation between those tribes that signed the accord and those that stood with Chief Joseph. Chief Joseph opposed the treaty not only because the Nez Perce had been betrayed but also because of principle. He believed that no man could claim ownership of the land because man did not create the land nor could man reproduce the land. The idea of land ownership to Native Americans like Chief Joseph was unnatural and inconceivable.

Gold was discovered on the land ceded to the Nez Perce in Idaho and the Wallowa valley in the early 1860s and overnight American mining settlements appeared on the reservation land in direct violation to the treaty of 1855. To enable the American emigrants to mine the Nez Perce lands, another treaty was negotiated with the Nez Perce tribal elders in 1863 further dividing the nation into two factions and forcing them to cede 90% of their reservation, including the land occupied by Chief Joseph on the Wallowa River, to the American people. Once again Chief Joseph refused to sign this treaty.

Chief Joseph's son assumed leadership of the Nez Perce as settlers began pouring into the beautiful Wallowa valley in the 1860s. Chief Joseph the younger was immediately confronted with an untenable situation. He had promised his father that he would never yield his father's ancestral heritage. At the same time Chief Joseph held no ill will toward most of the American settlers who came innocently and in good faith to attempt to start a new life in the Wallowa valley. The situation became so tense that Chief Joseph finally held a council with the white settlers and informed them they must leave because he could no longer guarantee them safety on his land. A United States governmental decree supported his position, but within a year the local commissioner of Indian affairs reversed the decree without informing Chief Joseph.

The injustice generated toward Chief Joseph and his nation by the American government and the American people remains one of the darkest moments in American history. Was this American treachery grounded in Jesuit sophistry? Perhaps that argument could be established in the beginning of the Nez Perce betrayal, but the mistreatment of the Nez Perce by the American people could not be laid at the feet of the Jesuits this time. This research has documented the conspiracy of the Jesuit priests to undermine the heritage of both the pioneer Americans and the Native Americans. The complicity of the Jesuit priests pales in comparison to the ungrateful injustice meted out to the Nez Perce by the American government. The Nez Perce nation had proven to be one of the greatest friends of the early pioneers, particularly in terms of uncompromising loyalty and forbearance toward their fellow Americans. The Nez Perce aided and supported American discovery, exploration, missionary outreach and immigration from their first contact with the white men. The grievous actions of an ungrateful nation would continue to escalate, to the great shame of the mighty Republic. There can be no question that the lies of "Protestantism in Oregon" had negatively impacted the American government in Washington against both the Protestants and the Nez Perce, whom the Jesuits resented for thwarting their effort to wrestle the Oregon Territory from the Americans. Nevertheless, the shame for America's treatment of the Nez Perce cannot be laid at the feet of the Jesuits.

In light of this historical travesty this research will document the tragic plight of the Nez Perce nation ending with the historic speech of Chief Joseph in Lincoln Hall in Washington, D.C. on January 14, 1879. The ignorant and unjust policy of the American government placed Chief Joseph the younger in an untenable position. This great ally of the American people, the greatest Native American nation west of the Rocky Mountains, was forced to attempt to flee to Canada to sustain their liberty and freedom. The speech of Chief Joseph, one of the greatest speeches in American history, documented one of the darkest hours of American culture. The greatest congressmen, diplomats and dignitaries of the American Republic heard this chief, the great patriot of the Nez Perce nation, open his heart to the American people and eloquently plead for justice for his people. Chief Joseph passionately exhorted the American government to hear the cry of the Nez Perce, the great friend of the American people. To these honored statesmen of America Chief Joseph was the object of great wonder in Washington, D.C. in 1879. His people's 1700 mile flight to the border of Canada to achieve freedom and liberty from white man's broken promises and oppression had become a major media event in America.

The problem of the hour was that the American people had virtually no idea that Chief Joseph and his people were the great friends of the American Republic. The American people had no idea of the injustice meted out to the Nez Perce at the hands of their own government. Even the prominent American statesmen whom Chief Joseph addressed in 1879 had little to no knowledge or understanding of the broken treaties and promises to the Nez Perce or their unwavering loyalty to America in the midst of great pressure to join the hostilities during the Indian Wars of the Pacific Northwest. Had these statesmen known the truth of the betrayal of the Nez Perce nation by the American government they would have repented on that day in Washington, D.C. Once again the words of the prophet Hosea ring true, "My people are destroyed for lack of knowledge." (Hosea 4:6)

Chief Joseph surrendered forty miles from his objective, freedom in Canada, to save what was left of his women and children. The promises made to him that convinced him to surrender were broken (a promise to return with his people to Lapwai, Idaho) and at the time of his speech his people were being ravaged by a malaria epidemic in a foreign prison reservation in Kansas. It was against this backdrop that Chief Joseph opened his heart to the American people to seek justice for his people. This research has found no evidence of support from the press or Protestant leaders at that hour. The American people had the opportunity to hear the truth about the extraordinary faithfulness of the Nez Perce, the real reasons for his flight and the real reasons why he surrendered. His speech was published in the *North American Review*. The published version may not have been verbatim; however, this speech remains to this very hour one of the "greatest portraits of the Indian experience that has ever been voiced by any American." (Nerburn, Kent, ed., *The Wisdom of the Great Chiefs*, New Classic Wisdom Collection, San Rafael, Ca., 1994, p. 18) One of the purposes of this study is to present the truth of the rightful place of the Nez Perce nation as great American patriots. It is never too late to repent and bring justice so that the heritage of the Nez Perce can be exalted to their rightful place in history. The place of the Nez Perce, as the great American patriots of the Oregon Territory, must be restored to them if America is to sustain the high calling as the great land of liberty and freedom envisioned by our founding fathers.

CHAPTER 26

CHIEF JOSEPH'S HISTORIC SPEECH TO AMERICA

This research will examine and attempt to shed historical light on Chief Joseph's speech to America. The entire speech will be documented at this time because the message of the Nez Perce is central to the heritage of America. The Nez Perce were God's instruments to establish the divine purpose and framework for the Oregon Territory to become a state under the government of the United States of America. Unfortunately, the greater purposes of the Almighty for Oregon have been delayed, and freedom and liberty for all Oregonians (including Native Americans) has been, in varying degrees, hindered to the present hour. Since the Americans assumed sovereignty in the lands of the Oregon Territory, material wealth has prospered at the expense of the magnificent natural resources. The magnificent forests of the Pacific Northwest have been greatly diminished. The mighty rivers of the old Oregon Territory are in many places sick and dying. The Columbia River has gone from the purest coldest river in the West to one of the most polluted rivers in the world. The powerful Bible church started by the Protestant missionaries in the Pacific Northwest has digressed to a minor church attracting less than five per cent of the

Chief Joseph

population. The West Coast of America has become the most godless, humanist society in all of America. The answers to the decline of American culture and civilization can be found in Chief Joseph's speech.

"My friends, I have been asked to show you my heart. I am glad to have a chance to do so. I want the white people to understand my people. Some of you think an Indian is like a wild animal. This is a great mistake. I will tell you about my people, then you can judge whether an Indian is a man or not. I believe much trouble would be saved if we opened our hearts more. I will tell you in my way how the Indian sees things. The white man has more words to tell you how they look to him, but it does not require many words

Old Oregon Under the Shadow of the Almighty 169

to tell the truth. What I have to say will come straight from my heart, and I will speak with a straight tongue. The Great Spirit is looking at me, and will hear me.

My name is In-nut-too-yah-lat-lat (Thunder Traveling over Mountains). I am Chief of the Wal-lam-wat-kin band of the Chute-pa-lu, or Nez Perce. I was born in Eastern Oregon, thirty-eight winters ago. My father was Chief before me. When a young man he was called Joseph by Mr. Spaulding, a missionary. He died a few years ago. He left a good name on earth. He advised me well for my people.

Our fathers gave us many laws, which they had learned from their fathers. These laws were good. They told us to treat all men as they treated us, that we should never be the first to break a bargain, that it was a disgrace to tell a lie, that we should speak only the truth, that it was a shame for one man to take from another his wife or his property without paying for it. We were taught to believe that the Great Spirit sees and hears everything, and that He never forgets; that hereafter He will give every man a spirit home according to his desserts: If he has been a good man, he will have a good home; if he has been a bad man, he will have a bad home. This I believe, and all my people believe the same." (Nerburn, pp. 19, 20)

The foundations of Nez Perce culture that Chief Joseph was exhorting mirrored the Christian biblical convictions and teachings of the Protestant missionaries who worked with the Nez Perce and Chief Joseph's father beginning in 1837. The consistent thesis of this research has been the unity of the spiritual faith of the Protestant missionaries and the Columbia Plateau Indians. It was the Nez Perce nation that sent envoys to the "great white fathers" seeking the white man's Book of Heaven before any missionaries were sent to the Oregon Territory. This research will document that the values that Chief Joseph and the Nez Perce exhibited were largely Christian values taught by the Protestant missionaries, in this case Henry and Eliza Spalding. The golden rule of Christianity exhorted by Jesus Christ, "Do unto others as you would have them do unto you," had been received by the Nez Perce. The Nez Perce in like manner received the Christian concept of "thou shalt not bear false witness against thy neighbor." The Christian concept of a monotheistic Creator God that was omnipresent and omniscient and rewards those who obey Him with heaven and judges those who reject Him with hell according to a man's works was also exhorted in Chief Joseph's speech.

The discerning student of history may surmise that these laudable Nez Perce values were central to their culture before the advent of Protestant missionaries. In some cases these virtuous values were present before the advent of white men. The Christian values that Chief Joseph espoused in his speech were common only in part among the Nez Perce before the missionaries arrived. "Nez Perce Albert Moore indicated that his people did indeed have standards quite different from those espoused by the missionaries. Men in the old days might have many wives, and 'there was no law against a man running away from his family.'" (Coleman, Michael C., *Presbyterian Missionary Attitudes towards American Indians, 1837-1893*, University Press of Mississippi, Jackson and London, 1985, p. 86)

The early missionaries were grieved at some of the moral values of the Columbia Indians as documented in the writings of the Whitmans and Spaldings. Presbyterian missionary Kate McBeth, who continued the ministry of the Spaldings, spending over thirty five years with the Nez Perce, lamented the fact "that Nez Perce women who would not steal a piece of bread when hungry would think it nothing more than fun to steal a man, husband, from another woman (primarily because) they had no fixed standards of right (before the advent of the Protestant missionaries)." (Coleman, p. 85) Presbyterian missionary George Deffenbaugh concurred with McBeth's assessment, "noting the infidelity seemed to have been part of religion, or at least a thing of constant occurrence and regarded as alright. As a result of such indulgence in sensuality, syphilis was widespread." (Coleman, p. 85)

The speech of Chief Joseph demonstrated that the band of Nez Perce people had accepted the universal moral truth of the teachings of the Bible as ministered by the Protestant missionaries and turned from many of their old ways. This speech reveals the true heart and understanding of the Nez Perce Indians after the advent of Protestant missionaries. Let us continue with the speech.

"We did not know there were other people besides the Indian until about one hundred winters ago, when some men with white faces came to our country. They brought many things with them to trade for furs and skins. They brought tobacco, which was new to us. They brought guns with flint stones on them, which frightened our women and children. Our people could not talk to these white-faced men, but they used signs that all people understand. These men were called Frenchmen, and they called our people 'Nez Perce,' because they wore rings in their noses or ornaments. Although very few of our people wear them now, we are still called by the same name. These French trappers said a great many things to our fathers, which have been planted in our hearts. Some were good to us, but some were bad. Our people were divided in opinion about these men. An Indian respects a brave man, but despises a coward. He loves a straight tongue, but hates a forked tongue. The French trappers told us some truths and some lies. The first white men of your people who came to our country were named Lewis and Clark. They also brought many things that our people had never seen. They talked straight, and our people gave them a great feast as a proof that their hearts were friendly. These men were very kind. They made presents to our chiefs and our people made presents to them. We had a great many horses, of which we gave them what they needed, and they gave us guns and tobacco in return. All the Nez Perce made friends with Lewis and Clark, and agreed to let them pass through their country, and never to make war on white men. This promise the Nez Perce has never broken. No white man can accuse them of bad faith and speak with a straight tongue. It has always been the pride of the Nez Perce that they were friends of the white men." (Nerburn, pp. 21-22)

This research has documented the Protestant missionaries' exhortation to the Nez Perce to remain faithful to the Americans after the Whitman massacre. Chief Joseph represented the portion of the now divided tribe that rejected the treaty, the reservation, and the ministry of the Protestant missionaries after the peace accord of 1855. Chief Joseph's speech will further document that no nation in the nineteenth century exercised greater grace and loyalty toward the United States of America than the Nez Perce nation. At the time of Chief Joseph's speech this faithful nation was dying of white man's diseases, in a prison reservation in Kansas, at the hands of the nation it faithfully supported. This research has given credit to the work and impact of Henry and Eliza Spalding for the loyalty of the Nez Perce to America. Chief Joseph and his son Chief Joseph the younger had rejected the Christianity of the Spaldings when the American government attempted to force them on to reservations. The younger Chief Joseph gives credit to Lewis and Clark for the Nez Perce loyalty.

"When my father was a young man there came to our country a white man (Rev. Henry Spalding) who talked spirit law. He won the affections of our people because he spoke good things to them. At first he did not say anything about white men wanting to settle on our lands. Nothing was said about that until about twenty winters ago, when a number of white people came into our country and built houses and made farms. At first our people made no complaint. They thought there was room enough for all to live in peace, and they were learning many things from the white men that seemed good. But we soon found that the white men were growing rich very fast, and were greedy to possess everything the Indian had. My father was the first to see through the schemes of the white men, and he warned the tribe to be careful about trading with them. He had suspicions of men who seemed anxious to make money. I was a boy then, but I remember well my father's caution. He had sharper eyes than the rest of our people."(Nerburn, pp. 22-23)

Chief Joseph reflected on the foundation of the "spirit law" that he used as a foundation to guide his nation. The foundation of the spirit law came from the Bible taught by Protestant missionary Henry Spalding. The younger Joseph had been baptized by Henry Spalding and grew up under the Christian teachings of the

Protestant missionaries. Long before the missionaries came to the Nez Perce, most of the indigenous Indians of North America were a spiritual people who believed in a Creator God they called the "Great Spirit." The Protestant missionaries discovered "the distinction between natural and supernatural was never simply drawn by Indians, who tended to blend the two into one harmonious whole. Such activities as the vision quest, success in hunting and war, and general performances in life were all inextricably tied together. For the Nez Perce, wrote Kate McBeth, "civil and religious is one." (Coleman, p. 82)

"Next there came a white officer (Governor Isaac Stevens of the Washington Territory), who invited all the Nez Perce to a treaty council. After the council was opened he made known his heart. He said there were a great many white people in our country, and many more would come; that he wanted the land marked out so that the Indians and the white men could be separated. If they were to live in peace it was necessary, he said, that the Indians should have a country set apart for them, and in that country they must stay. My father who represented his band refused to have anything to do with the council, because he wished to be a free man. He claimed that no man owned any part of the earth, and a man could not sell what he did not own." (Nerburn, pp. 23-24)

How ironic was the powerful logic of the elder Chief Joseph. The very heart of the Protestant Reformation was the teaching that every man was born with an innate freedom to serve (or not to serve) God as he chose. Freedom and liberty were the very foundation of the American Revolution. The elder and the younger Chief Joseph could well have spoken Patrick Henry's famous words, "Give me liberty or give me death."

"Mr. Spaulding took hold of my father's arm and said, 'Come and sign the treaty.' My father pushed him away, and said, 'Why do you ask me to sign away my country? It is your business to talk to us about spirit matters and not to talk to us about parting with our land.' Governor Stevens urged my father to sign the treaty, but he refused. 'I will not sign your paper,' he said. 'You go where you please, so do I. You are not a child. I am no child. I can think for myself. No man can think for me. I have no home other than this. I will not give up to any man. My people would have no home. Take away your paper. I will not touch it with my hand.' My father left the council. Some of the chiefs of the other bands of the Nez Perce signed the treaty, and then Governor Stevens gave them presents of blankets. My father cautioned his people to take no presents, for 'after a while,' he said, 'they will claim that you have accepted pay for your country.' Since that time four bands of the Nez Perce have received annuities from the United States. My father was invited to many councils, and they tried hard to make him sign the treaty, but he was firm as a rock, and would not sign away his home. His refusal caused a difference among the Nez Perce." (Nerburn, pp. 24, 25)

The Nez Perce, the great friends of the Americans, were now divided among themselves between those who signed the treaty and those who refused to cede their homeland to the Americans. The heart of the issue for Chief Joseph was freedom and liberty. This wise old chief knew that once they signed away their homeland and received gifts and compensation in return they would lose forever their freedom and liberty. Chief Joseph and the Nez Perce had always supported the Americans in their time of need. They expected to be treated in the same manner they had treated the free men of the Republic.

"Eight years later (1863) was the next treaty council. A chief called Lawyer, because he was a great talker, took the lead in the council, and sold nearly all the Nez Perce country. My father was not there. He said to me: 'When you go into council with the white man, always remember your country. Do not give it away. The white man will cheat you out of your home. I have taken no pay form the United States. I have never sold our land.' In this treaty Lawyer acted without authority from our band. He had no right to sell the Wallowa country. That has always belonged to my father's own people, and the other bands had never disputed our right to it. No other Indians ever claimed Wallowa." (Nerburn, p. 25)

The Wallowa country referred to the beautiful valley in northeastern Oregon the Nez Perce called the "land of winding water." The Nez Perce under Chief Joseph claimed the Wallowa valley as their ancestral homeland. Historically no foreign Indian tribe could intrude upon their domain without the approval of the tribal chiefs. For the historical record it is important to note the Nez Perce did not claim to own any portion of the land of the "winding water" until they were forced to adopt American principles of land possession forced by the encroachment of the white man on their land.

"In order to have all people understand how much land we owned, my father planted poles around it and said, 'Inside is the home of my people. The white man may take the land outside. Inside this boundary all our people were born. It circles around the graves of our fathers, and we will never give up these graves to any man.' The United States claimed they had bought all the Nez Perce country outside the Lapwai Reservation from Lawyer and other chiefs. But we continued to live on this land in peace until eight years ago, when white men began to come inside the boundaries my father had set. We warned them against this great wrong, but they would not leave our land, and some bad blood was raised. The white men represented that we were going upon the warpath. They reported many things that were false." (Nerburn, p. 26)

Chief Joseph attempted to set boundaries to protect his people. The Nez Perce attempted to compromise with the American homesteaders. Unfortunately the standard that Chief Joseph established for joint occupation was never clearly related to the white homesteaders. The Nez Perce were slowly but irresistibly squeezed by the growing number of Americans discovering the beautiful Wallowa valley.

"The United States government again asked for a treaty council. My father had become blind and feeble. He could no longer speak for his people. It was then that I took my father's place as chief. In this council I made my first speech to white men. I said to the agent who held the council: 'I did not want to come to this council, but I came hoping that we could save blood. The white man has no right to come here and take our country. We have never accepted any presents from the government. Neither Lawyer nor any other chief had authority to sell this land. It has always belonged to my people. It came unclouded to them from our fathers, and we will defend this land as long as a drop of Indian blood warms the heart of our men.' The agent said he had orders from the Great White chief at Washington for us to go upon the Lapwai reservation, and that if we obeyed, he would help us in many ways. 'You must move to the agency,' he said. I answered him, 'I will not. I do not need your help. We have plenty, and we are contented and happy if the white man will leave us alone. The reservation is too small for so many people with all their stock. You can keep your presents. We can go to your towns and pay for all we need. We have plenty of horses and cattle to sell, and we won't need any help form you. We are free now; we can go where we please. Our fathers were born here. Here they lived, here they died, here they have their graves. We will never leave them.' The agent went away and we had peace for awhile." (Nerburn, pp. 26, 27)

Unlike all the associated Columbia Plateau tribes of the Pacific Northwest, the Nez Perce under Chief Joseph never ceded their ancestral homeland to the American government, nor did this tribe of indigenous Indians ever accept compensation for their land. The Nez Perce had been loyal to the American frontiersmen and immigrants and peaceful and a good neighbor to the first American homesteaders on their ancestral lands. Unfortunately, the American government and the early homesteaders staking claims on their land considered all Indians the same. There was no American advocate for the Nez Perce who could put the rights and patriotic loyalty of the nation in historical perspective. Perhaps there were American Nez Perce advocates who stood up for the Nez Perce, but nevertheless the government had already established its Indian policy irrespective of past loyalty.

The research of this book has documented the historical fact that the Nez Perce and like-minded Columbia Indians demonstrated mercy and grace to the first Americans who reached the Oregon Territory.

Without the help of these Indians many of the original explorers, fur trappers and missionaries would have perished. The hand of the Almighty had strategically placed this dominant Indian nation of the Oregon Territory directly in the line of American immigration. This research has documented the Indian nations of the Pacific Northwest that combined forces to drive out the American settlers and how the Nez Perce stayed faithful to the United States. Once again the prophetic refrain was tragically fulfilled, "My people are destroyed for lack of knowledge." (Hosea 4:6) The Nez Perce people were about to be destroyed because there was no influential advocate among the Americans to defend their rightful heritage in the Wallowa valley of Northeastern Oregon.

"Soon after this my father sent for me. I saw he was dying. I took his hand in mine. He said, 'My son, my body is returning to my mother earth, and my spirit is going very soon to see the Great Spirit Chief. When I am gone, think of your country. You are the chief of these people. They look to you to guide them. Always remember that your father never sold this country. You must stop your ears whenever you are asked to sign a treaty selling your home. A few years more, and white men will be all around you. They have their eyes on this land. My son, never forget my dying words. This country holds your father's body. Never sell the bones of your father and mother.' I pressed my father's hand and told him I would protect his grave with my life. My father smiled and passed away to the spirit land. I buried him in that beautiful valley of winding waters. I love that land more than all the rest of the world. A man who would not love his father's grave is worse than a wild animal.

For a short time we lived quietly. But this could not last. White man had found gold in the mountains around the land of the winding river. They stole many horses from us, and we could not get them back because we were Indians. The white men told many lies for each other. They drove off a great many of our cattle. Some white men branded our young cattle so they could claim them. We had no friends who would plead our cause before the law councils. It seemed to me that some of the white men in Wallowa were doing things on purpose to get up a war. They knew that we were not strong enough to fight them." (Nerburn, pp. 28, 29)

Perhaps the most poignant words that Chief Joseph spoke were, "we had no friends who would plead our cause before the law councils." The great cause of the American Revolution was the unjust and unfair treatment afforded the colonists by King George. For over half a century the Nez Perce were the great Native American patriots championing the cause of the free men of the republic of the United States. In their hour of need there was not one man who would stand in their defense in the white man's court to plead their cause. What a tragedy! The Nez Perce were not treated with justice and equality because they were Indians. These same Indians, time after time, rescued the virtually helpless Americans, and those in authority of this generation of American pioneers honored only the god of greed, possession and power. The Americans were squeezing Chief Joseph and his people on every side and they had little room to maneuver. The exodus of free emigrants to the Promised Land that the Protestant missionaries had championed were systematically stealing the Indians' land and driving the Native Americans onto reservations, and even some of these reservation lands were methodically being whittled down to the dregs. The Protestant missionaries had been forced out of the Pacific Northwest by the American government and there was no advocate to stand in the gap for Chief Joseph and his people.

"I labored hard to avoid trouble and bloodshed. We gave up some of our country to the white men, thinking that then we could have peace. We were mistaken. The white man would not let us alone. We could have avenged our wrongs many times, but we did not. Whenever the government has asked us to help them against other Indians we have never refused. When the white men were few and we were strong, we could have killed them all off, but the Nez Perce wished to live in peace. If we have not done so, we have not been to blame. I believe that the old treaty has never been correctly reported. If we ever owned the land, we own it still, for we never sold it. In the treaty councils the commissioners have claimed that our country had been sold to the government. Suppose a white man should come to me and say, 'Joseph, I like your horses, and I want to buy them.' I say to him, 'No, my horses suit me. I will not sell them.' Then he goes to my neighbor and says to him, 'Joseph has some good horses. I want to buy them, but he refuses to sell.' My neighbor answers, 'Pay me the money, and I will sell you Joseph's horses.' The white man returns to me and says, 'Joseph, I have bought your horses, and you must let me have them.' If we sold our lands to the government, this is the way they were bought." (Nerburn, p. 29)

The grievances that Chief Joseph addressed over one hundred years ago have never been honestly redressed. The Nez Perce nation represented the finest and most noble character the Native Americans of the Pacific Northwest had to offer. Even when the American settlers were trespassing on their ancestral homeland, desecrating the burial grounds of their fathers, the Nez Perce responded with grace and forbearance. The stage was set for the beginning of a chapter of shame upon the "manifest destiny" of the American Republic. The question must be asked. Where was the Protestant support and defense for the noble Nez Perce? It is true that Chief Joseph the elder publicly denounced Christianity and Chief Joseph his son outwardly rejected the Protestant faith. Nevertheless, could any objective historical witness blame either Chief Joseph or his son for their distrust of Christianity? Despite the outward rejection of white man's Christianity, the Nez Perce nation exemplified a people of truth, justice, grace, forbearance, and righteousness that would put most Protestant Christian nations to shame. The standard bearer of the righteousness of God had received a crown of thorns instead of an elegant headdress.

"On account of the treaty made by the other bands of the Nez Perce, the white men claimed my lands. We were troubled greatly by white men crowding over the line. Some of these were good men, and we lived on peaceful terms with them. But they were not all good. Nearly every year the agent came over from Lapwai and ordered us on to the reservation. We always replied that we were satisfied to live in Wallowa. We were careful to refuse presents or annuities that he offered. Through all the years since the white men came to Wallowa, we have been threatened and taunted by them and the treaty Nez Perce. They have given us no rest. We have a few good friends among white men, and they have always advised my people to bear taunts without fighting. Our young men were quick-tempered, and I have had great trouble in keeping them from doing rash things. I have carried a heavy load on my back ever since I was a boy. I learned then that we were but few, while the white men were many, and that we could not hold our own with them. We were like deer. They were like grizzly bears. We had a small country. Their country was large. We were content to let things remain as the Great Spirit made them. They were not, and would change the rivers and mountains if they did not suit them." (Nerburn, pp. 31, 32)

The dichotomy separating the red man and the white man was manifest from the very beginning in the contest for the Wallowa valley. The Indian wanted to sustain the valley as it was. The American homesteader wanted to harvest the bounty that the lush Wallowa valley had to offer in timber, gold, pasture and fisheries. The American settlers mined the streams and mountains, harvested the timber and parceled out and fenced the magnificent valley for cattle and sheep. They was no room or safe haven left for the rightful heirs to the valley, the last vestige of free indigenous American Indians in the Pacific Northwest. Just as the Protestant missionaries Marcus and Narcissa Whitman were burdened to bear the taunts of the Jesuit priests and the Cayuse Indians under their control, so were the Nez Perce under Chief Joseph. Just like for the Whitmans, ominous storm clouds were beginning to form on every horizon.

"Year after year we were threatened, but no war was made upon my people until General Howard came to our country two years ago and told us he was the white war-chief of all that country. He said, 'I have a great many soldiers at my back. I am going to bring them up here, and then I will talk to you again. I will not let white men laugh at me the next time I come. The country belongs to the government, and I intend to make you go upon the reservation.'" (Nerburn, p. 32)

The government of the United States could not entice or persuade the Nez Perce under Chief Joseph to cede their beloved Wallowa valley to the Americans. What they could not gain by persuasion and inducements, they would now take by force. The issue had become an issue of precedent, power and pride to the commanders of the nation's armed forces of the West. "America's divine plan had been downgraded and its future threatened by greed, pride, and self-righteousness." (Marshall, Manuel, back page)

General Oliver Otis Howard

"I remonstrated with him against bringing more soldiers to the Nez Perce country. He had one house full of troops all the time at Fort Lapwai. The next spring the agent at Umatilla agency sent an Indian runner to tell me to meet General Howard at Walla Walla. I could not go myself, but I sent my brother and five other head men to meet him, and they had a long talk. General Howard said, 'you have talked straight, and it is all right. You can stay in Wallowa.' He insisted that my brother should go with him to Fort Lapwai. When the party arrived there General Howard sent out runners and called all the Indians in to a grand council. I was in that council. I said to General Howard, 'We are ready to listen.' He answered that he would not talk then, but would hold a council the next day, when he would talk plainly. I said to General Howard, 'I am ready to talk today. I have been in a great many councils, but I am no wiser. We all sprung from a woman, although we are unlike in many things. We cannot be made over again. You are as you were made, and as you were made you can remain. We are just as we were made by the Great Spirit, and you cannot change us. Then why should children of one mother and one father quarrel? Why should one try to cheat the other? I do not believe that the Great Spirit Chief gave one kind of men the right to tell another kind of men what they must do.'" (Nerburn, pp. 33, 34)

General Oliver Howard was a distinguished Civil War veteran. He had commanded troops at the bloodiest battles of the war including Antietam, Fredericksburg, Chancellorsville, and Gettysburg. He lost his right arm at the battle of Far Oaks in 1862. Howard was a strong Christian and early opponent of slavery. After the Civil War President Andrew Johnson appointed him Commissioner of the Freedom Bureau established to support freed slaves and grant them complete equality with white citizens. Perhaps no American general was better suited to have empathy for the plight of the Nez Perce than this general. Howard would later commit the rest of his life to bringing equality to the American Negro. The Nez Perce Indians were claiming the same liberty that the American blacks had won through the Civil War. Strangely, General Howard did not see the Nez Perce in the same light that he beheld the black slaves. Once again the refrain of the prophet Hosea rings true. "My people are destroyed for lack of knowledge." (Hosea 4:6)

"General Howard replied, 'You deny my authority, do you? You want to dictate to me, do you?' Then one of my chiefs – Too-hool-hool-suit – rose in the council and said to General Howard, 'The Great Spirit Chief made the world as it is, and as He wanted it, and He made a part of it for us to live upon. I do not see where you get authority to say that we shall not live where He placed us.' General Howard lost his temper and said, 'Shut up! I don't want to hear any more such talk. The law says you shall go upon the reservation to live, and I want you to do so. But you persist in disobeying the law. If you do not move, I will take the matter into my own hand and make you suffer for your disobedience.' Too-hool-hool-suit answered, 'Who are you, that you should ask us to talk, and then tell me I shan't talk? Are you the Great Spirit? Did you make the world? Did you make the sun? Did you make the rivers for us to drink? Did you make the grass to grow? Did you make all these things, that you talk to us as though we were boys? If you did, then you have the right to talk as you do.'" (Nerburn, pp. 34, 35)

    The treaty of 1855 and the second treaty of 1863 both granted the Wallowa valley to the Nez Perce. In 1877 the United States reversed the conditions of the signed treaty in order to remove Chief Joseph and the Nez Perce from the Wallowa valley. In actual fact it was the United States government and General Howard that were in violation of the law and the Indian treaties. "General Howard replied, 'You are an impudent fellow, and I will put you in the guard house,' and then ordered a soldier to arrest him. Too-hool-hool-suit made no resistance. He asked General Howard, 'Is that your order? I have nothing to take back. I have spoken for my country. You can arrest me, but you can not change me or make me take back what I have said.'" (Nerburn, p. 35)

    Too-hool-hool-suit asked a number of profound questions that have never been answered by the American government. These questions proposed to the American general are at the heart of this document. The Nez Perce chief wanted to know if the general spoke for the Great Spirit Chief. He wanted to know by what authority was the American government taking the land and heritage of the Nez Perce nation. If the Americans did not create the land, or the sun, or the rivers, or the grass, then by what authority did they claim to own the land that belonged by ancestral heritage and treaty to the Nez Perce? The Nez Perce believed the Great Spirit Chief made the world as it was and they were responsible to the Great Chief for their stewardship of their ancestral heritage. The Nez Perce nation under Chief Joseph had honored every request and need presented to them by the American explorers and settlers until the hour they were told to leave their land.

    "The soldiers came forward and seized my friend and took him to the guard house. My men whispered among themselves whether they should let this thing be done. I counseled them to submit. I knew if we resisted that all the white men present including General Howard would be killed in a moment, and we would be blamed. If I had said nothing, General Howard would never have given another unjust order against my men. I saw the danger, and while they dragged Too-hool-hool-suit to prison, I arose and said, 'I am going to talk now. I don't care whether you arrest me or not.' I turned to my people and said, 'The arrest of Too-hool-hool-suit was wrong, but we will not resent the insult. We were invited to this council to express our hearts, and we have done so.' Too-hool-hool-suit was prisoner for five days before he was released." (Nerburn, pp. 35, 36)

    General Oliver Howard was a man of Christian faith. He also represented the government of the United States of America. This research has documented this great American historical controversy according to the perspective of the Nez Perce Indians and Chief Joseph. In fairness to General Howard, he was an officer of the United States government under direct orders from the Department of War and the Nez Perce did not honor or accept his authority over them. Nevertheless, it was significant to document the Christian qualities exhibited by Chief Joseph and his war chiefs. When the Nez Perce were insulted they turned their cheeks and did not seek revenge. The Nez Perce did not claim a Christian faith; however, they truly demonstrated a Christian witness not common to their Indian heritage before the Protestant missionaries. These Nez Perce chiefs were taught as young men Christian principles by Henry and Eliza

Spalding. They may have rejected white man's Christianity because of their ill treatment by the Americans but they continued to exhibit Christian grace and forbearance.

"The council broke up for the day. On the next morning General Howard came to my lodge and invited me to go with him and White Bird and Looking Glass to look for land for my people. As we rode along we came to some good land that was already occupied by Indians and white people. General Howard pointing to this land, said, 'If you will come on to the reservation, I will give you these lands and move these people off.' I replied, 'No, It would be wrong to disturb these people. I have no right to their homes. I have never taken what did not belong to me. I will not now.' We rode all day upon the reservation and found no good land unoccupied. I have been informed by men who do not lie that General Howard sent a letter that night telling the soldiers at Walla Walla to go to the Wallowa valley and drive us out upon our return home.

In the council the next day, General Howard informed me, in a haughty spirit, that he would give my people thirty days to go back home, collect all their stock, and move onto the reservation, saying, 'If you are not here in that time, I shall consider that you want to fight, and will send my soldiers to drive you on.' I said, 'War can be avoided, and it ought to be avoided. My people have always been friends of the white man. Why are you in such a hurry? I cannot get ready to move in thirty days. Our stock is scattered, and the Snake River is very high. Let us wait until fall. Then the river will be low. We want time to hunt up our stock and gather supplies for winter.' General Howard replied, 'If you let the time run over one day, the soldiers will be there to drive you onto the reservation, and all your cattle and horses outside of the reservation at that time will fall into the hands of the white men." (Nerburn, pp. 36, 37)

The dye was set. The white man's mode of civilizing the continent was to put the indigenous Indians in reservations where they would be separated from the free men of the Republic. The moral concept of setting the black slave free did not apply to the indigenous red man of the Oregon Territory. It would set a very bad precedent to allow the Nez Perce to defy the American government, especially when rebellious Indian tribes under the charismatic leadership of chiefs like Sitting Bull, Crazy Horse and Geronimo were causing great anxiety in the West at the same time. The Nez Perce had to be confined under the sovereignty of the United States government at the Lapwai reservation at all costs. Once again Chief Joseph reminded General Howard of the great loyalty of the Nez Perce nation to the American Republic. Unfortunately, General Howard was a trained soldier of war. This general apparently knew little about the great debt America owed the Nez Perce, nor did he exhibit much compassion toward these Native Americans he considered insubordinate. According to the words of Chief Joseph, the Nez Perce would have peacefully moved on to the reservation in the fall if the General exercised Christian restraint.

"I knew I had never sold my country and that I had no land in Lapwai. But I did not want bloodshed. I did not want my people killed. I did not want anybody killed. Some of my people had been murdered by the white men, and the white murderers were never punished for it. I told General Howard about this, and again I said I wanted no war. I wanted the people who lived upon the lands I was to occupy at Lapwai to have time to gather their harvest. I said in my heart that rather than have war, I would give up my country. I would give up my father's grave. I would give up everything rather than have the blood of white men upon the hands of my people. General Howard refused to allow me more than thirty days to move my people and their stock. I am sure that he began to prepare for war at once. When I returned to Wallowa I found my people very much excited in the Wallowa valley. We held a council and decided to move immediately, to avoid bloodshed." (Nerburn, p. 38)

It is in times of great duress that a man's, or in this case a nation's, true character rises to the surface. The Nez Perce were willing to yield their ancestral heritage to avoid bloodshed. Chief Joseph was willing to give up his father's grave and the promise he made to him on his deathbed to avoid bloodshed. The Nez

Perce were willing to give up their homeland and be squeezed onto the Lapwai Reservation in a final humiliation to avoid the bloodshed of both their own nation and the American nation. This Nez Perce nation was not historically a pacifist nation. The Nez Perce were renowned among the American Indians as both fierce warriors and brilliant military strategists. This research has documented the testimony of pioneer Oregon statesmen that unanimously confirmed the historical fact that had the Nez Perce joined the combined Columbia Indian tribes after the Whitman massacre the American volunteers would have been routed. This Nez Perce nation under Chief Joseph had made a spiritual commitment to avoid bloodshed consistent with teachings of Jesus Christ taught in the white man's Book of Heaven. The Protestant missionaries had exhorted the Columbia Plateau Indians to accept the Christian spiritual teachings and western ways of civilization in order to survive the advent of white men into the Oregon Territory. The Nez Perce under Chief Joseph may have outwardly rejected the white man's Christianity, but by their actions they demonstrated they had accepted the spiritual teachings of Christ found in the New Testament. General Howard, as a Christian man of faith, was bound by the same teachings but in this situation he put pride and his position ahead of his Christian convictions and the result was disastrous for both nations.

"Too-hool-hool-suit, who felt outraged by his imprisonment, talked for war, and made many of my young men willing to fight rather than be driven like dogs from the land where they were born. He declared that blood alone would wash out the disgrace General Howard had put upon him. It required a strong heart to stand up against such talk, but I urged my people to be against such talk. I urged my people to be quiet, and not to begin a war. We gathered all the stock we could find, and made an attempt to move. We left many of our horses and cattle in Wallowa, and we lost several hundred in crossing the river. All of my people succeeded in getting across in safety. Many of the Nez Perce came together in Rocky Canyon to hold a grand council. This council lasted ten days. There was a great deal of war talk, and a great deal of excitement. There was one young brave present whose father had been killed by a white man five years before. This man's blood was bad against white men, and he left the council calling for revenge. Again I counseled peace, and I thought the danger was past." (Nerburn, p. 40)

Unfortunately, the hour of a peaceful resolution for the desperate plight of the Nez Perce had passed. Chief Joseph was no longer able to control the passions of his people, especially those young braves who had experienced injustice at the hands of the white settlers. Hostilities would soon commence, and the responsibility for the bloodshed rested entirely upon General Howard because had failed to exercise restraint, forbearance, wisdom or compassion toward the Nez Perce nation.

"We had not complied with General Howard's order because we could not, but we intended to do so as soon as possible. I was leaving the country to kill beef for my family when news came that the young man whose father had been killed had gone out with several other hot-blooded young braves and killed four white men. He rode up to the council and shouted, 'Why do you sit here like women? The war has begun already.' I was deeply grieved. All the lodges were moved except my brother's and my own. I saw clearly that the war was upon us when I learned that my young men had been secretly buying ammunition. I heard that Too-hool-hool-suit, who had been imprisoned by General Howard, had succeeded in organizing a war party. I knew their acts would involve all my people. I saw that the war could not be prevented. The time had passed. I counseled peace from the beginning. I knew that we were too weak to fight the United States. We had many grievances, but I knew that war would bring more. We had great white friends, who advised us against taking the warpath. My friend and brother, Mr. Chapman, who had been with us since the surrender, told us how the war would end. Mr. Chapman took sides against us, and helped General Howard. I do not blame him for doing so. He tried hard to prevent bloodshed. We had hoped the white settlers would not join the soldiers. Before the war commenced we had discussed this matter all over, and many of my people were in favor of warning them that if they took no part against us they should not be molested in the event of war being begun by General Howard. The plan was voted down in war council." (Nerburn, pp. 40, 41)

The reader may well believe that Chief Joseph was naïve to believe any white settlers would support the Nez Perce, but it was the Nez Perce who supported the white settlers against the persuasion of the combined Columbia Indian tribes after the Whitman massacre. The Nez Perce had treated the white settlers with grace and loyalty and they hoped (at least Chief Joseph did) the golden rule of Christianity would be returned to them. Unfortunately, the Protestant missionaries were largely unsuccessful in their attempts to settle the Oregon Territory with Christian men and families of faith. The brand of freedom and liberty that ruled in the Columbia Plateau for the white settler was primarily an independent spirit to start a new life with few constraints, especially from government. Nevertheless, Protestant support for the Nez Perce was strong in the Willamette Valley. Unfortunately, the true cause of the Nez Perce arising never reached the light of day in the press of the hour in Oregon or Washington. To most white settlers in the Oregon Territory the Nez Perce were insubordinate troublemakers unwilling to live according to the treaties they had signed. The sooner they were rounded up and pacified the better.

"There were bad men among my people who had quarreled with white men, and they talked of their wrongs until they roused all the bad hearts in the council. Still I could not believe they would begin the war. I know my young men did a great wrong, but I ask, 'Who is the first to blame?' They had been insulted a thousand times. Their fathers and brothers had been killed. Their mothers and wives had been disgraced. They had been driven to madness by whisky sold to them by white men. They had been told by General Howard that all their horses and cattle which they had been unable to drive out of Wallowa were to fall into the hands of white men. And, added to all this, they were homeless and desperate. I would have given my own life if I could have undone the killing of white men by my own people. I blame my young men and I blame the white men. I blame General Howard for not giving my people time to get their stock away from Wallowa. I do not acknowledge that he had the right to order me to leave Wallowa at any time. I deny that either my father or myself ever sold that land. It is still our land. It may never be our home, but my father sleeps there, and I love it as my mother. I left there hoping to avoid bloodshed. If General Howard had given me plenty of time to gather up my stock, and treated Too-hool-hool-suit as a man should be treated, there would have been no war." (Nerburn, pp. 41, 42)

After four decades of peace with American explorers, frontiersmen, missionaries, fur trappers, emigrants and soldiers the Nez Perce were so grieved and mistreated they were forced to seek justice by fleeing their beloved Wallowa valley in the hopes of finding liberty elsewhere. Chief Joseph's cry for justice against the oppression of the American government has never been redressed. The land of the "winding river" still belongs to the Nez Perce nation just as Chief Joseph claimed. The Nez Perce have never sold their ancestral heritage to the American government and General Howard did not have the right to order Chief Joseph off his land.

"My friends among the white men have blamed me for the war. I am not to blame. When my young men began the killing, my heart was hurt. Although I did not justify them, I remembered all the insults I had endured, and my blood was on fire. Still, I would have taken my people to the buffalo country without fighting if possible. I could see no other way to avoid a war. We moved over to White Bird Camp, sixteen miles away, and there encamped, intending to collect our stock before leaving. But the soldiers attacked us, and the first battle was fought. We numbered in that battle sixty men, and the soldiers a hundred. The fight lasted but a few minutes, when the soldiers retreated before us for twelve miles. They lost thirty-three killed, and had seven wounded. When an Indian fights, he only shoots to kill. But soldiers shoot at random. None of the soldiers were scalped. We do not believe in scalping, nor in killing wounded men. Soldiers do not kill many Indians unless they are wounded and left upon the battlefield. Then they kill Indians." (Nerburn, pp. 42, 43)

The Nez Perce had attempted to avoid bloodshed with a white flag in order to seek a truce. Captain David L. Perry impulsively rejected the offer and was ill prepared for the results. None of the other Columbia Plateau indigenous tribes were as skillfully organized or as militarily proficient when they faced the American soldiers in the earlier Indian wars in the Pacific Northwest. Some of the Columbia plateau Indian tribes had adopted the brutal ritual of scalping their fallen adversaries; a prize the British had historically been willing to pay a bounty for. The Nez Perce had always maintained a Protestant Christian ethic of warfare where wounded adversaries were not killed and slain soldiers were not scalped and captured women were not insulted. According to Chief Joseph, the American soldiers did not reciprocate Christian grace on the battlefield and killed wounded Indians.

"Seven days after the first battle, General Howard arrived in the Nez Perce country, bringing seven hundred more soldiers. It was now war in earnest. We crossed the Salmon River, hoping General Howard would follow. We were not disappointed. He did follow us, and we got back between him and his supplies, and cut him off for three days. He sent out two companies to open the way. We attacked them, killing one officer, two guides, and ten men." (Nerburn, pp. 43, 44)

No doubt General Howard and the Americans believed the unsophisticated Nez Perce who had been living in peace with both the white and fellow red men for four decades would provide only marginal opposition to the well-trained and highly disciplined United States cavalry, many of whom were Civil War veterans. Some of these Americans had watched the pacifist Nez Perce accept ridicule and humiliating taunts from the white men. They hardly expected more than a few weeks at best to bring these rebellious heathens under control. Chief Joseph was not a man of war, but many of his war braves were. Looking Glass was a seasoned warrior and brilliant military strategist. He would never have joined with Chief Joseph had not General Howard unwisely attacked his village and attempted to arrest him. It was Looking Glass who convinced Joseph to attempt to gain freedom by fleeing to Canada. Joseph's brother Ollokot, Rainbow, Five Wounds, White Bird and Too-hool-hool-suit were also courageous chiefs and seasoned warriors.

Major Lee Moorehouse photograph of Nez Perce Chief Looking Glass

"We withdrew, hoping the soldiers would follow. But they had got enough fighting for that day. They entrenched themselves, and the next day we attacked them again. The battle lasted all day, and was renewed next morning. We killed four and wounded seven or eight. About this time General Howard found out we were in his rear. Five days later he attacked us with three hundred and fifty soldiers and settlers.

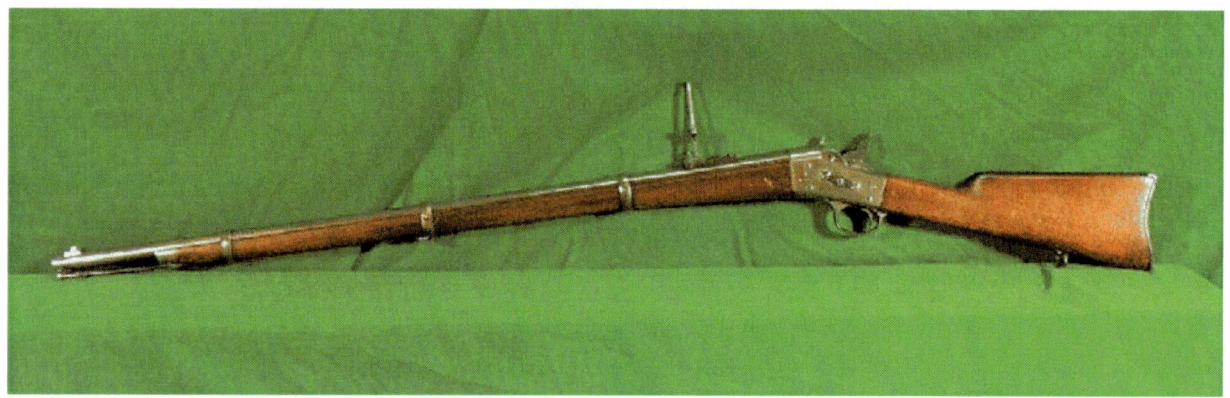
Springfield rifle

We had two hundred and fifty warriors. The fight lasted twenty-seven hours. We lost four killed and several wounded. General Howard's loss was twenty-nine men killed and sixty wounded. The following day the soldiers charged upon us, and we retreated with our families and stock a few miles, leaving eighty lodges to fall into General Howard's hands." (Nerburn, p. 44)

Hotchkiss Mt. Cannon

General Howard was a highly decorated and seasoned Civil War veteran. His cavalry was made up of equally seasoned professional soldiers who had fought in many wars. Men assigned to the cavalry enlisted for five years, and those who joined the infantry enlisted for three years. They had the model 1873 Springfield rifles, Hotchkiss Mountain cannons, seasoned horses and supplies necessary for the task. They had no women or children to protect or make allowance for. They had vastly superior numbers, provisions, arms, and supplies. The Nez Perce had been forced to leave most of their cattle and horses in the Wallowa valley. They could only travel as fast as their old men and women and little children would allow. They could only fight when they had secured their women and children. They had no hospitals to take their wounded or doctors to treat their wounds. They had limited arms and weapons because they had not been preparing for war.

"Finding that we were outnumbered, we retreated to the Bitterroot valley. Here another body of soldiers came upon us and demanded our surrender. We refused. They said, 'You cannot get by us.' We answered, 'We are going by you without fighting if you will let us. But we are going by you anyhow.' We then made a treaty with these soldiers. We agreed not to molest anyone, and they agreed that we might pass through the Bitterroot country in peace." (Nerburn, p. 45)

Captain Charles C. Rawl, the commander of Fort Missoula, was widely criticized for allowing the Nez Perce safe passage; however, volunteer settler W. B. Harlan wrote, "We were not silly enough to uselessly incite the Indians to devastate our valley and I do not think our critics would have done otherwise had they and their families and homes been situated as ours were. If they want Indians for breakfast, they are still within reach and have been ever since the fiasco of Fort Fizzle on the Lo Lo Trail." (Thackeray, Lorna,

"Campaign Casts a Shadow on Career," *Billings Gazette*, July 28, 2002) Fort Fizzle was the evaporated stand of Captain Rawl on the Lo Lo Trail.

"We bought provisions and traded stock with the white men there. We understood there was to be no more war. We intended to go peaceably to the buffalo country, and leave the question of returning to our country afterward. With this understanding, we traveled on for four days. And thinking the trouble was all over, we stopped and prepared tent poles to take with us." (Nerburn, p. 45)

The passage through the Bitterroot valley was so uneventful the Nez Perce actually shopped in a town called Stevensville. One of the volunteers in the Battle of the Big Hole, Amos Buck, owned a store there. "They camped just over the river from town and came over to trade. They found all the stores closed. Chief Looking Glass represented that they had money to pay for what they bought and would do so. Looking Glass represented that his people needed provisions, and if refused sale, would take all they wanted anyway. Whereupon the stores opened their doors and sales commenced." (Gransbery, Jim, "Nez Perce War of 1877, Valley Pause," *Billings Gazette*, August 5, 2002)

"We started again, and at the end of two days saw three white men passing our camp. Thinking that peace had been made we did not molest them. We could have killed them or taken them prisoners, but we did not suspect them for being spies, which they were." (Nerburn, p. 45, 46)

Chief Joseph's naïve assumption that a single treaty with the American soldiers at Bitterroot meant permanent peace with America would prove disastrous for the Nez Perce. Chief Joseph did not understand the threat his nation was to the United States Indian pacification policy. If the rebellion of the Nez Perce was to prove victorious, then other indigenous tribes might be encouraged to join ranks. Lakota chief Sitting Bull had routed Colonel Custer at the Little Big Horn the year before and had found sanctuary across the border in Canada. Apache warrior Geronimo would evade American troops for over two decades until his capture in 1886. A Bannock and Piute uprising in southern Idaho was already smoldering. General Howard was being lambasted in the nation's press because the Nez Perce were making a laughing stock of the United States cavalry already in disarray because of Colonel Custer's foolhardy demise at Little Big Horn. The Nez Perce called General Howard "Day After Tomorrow" because they were able to stay one step ahead of him even with over five hundred women, children and old men.

The battle of Big Hole was to change everything for the Nez Perce. Some of the Nez Perce warriors sensed danger, but Looking Glass and Chief Joseph were strangely unconcerned. Five Wounds warned Looking Glass that he felt danger lurking around them. Wahlitits (Rainbow) lamented, "My brothers, my sisters, I am telling you! In a dream last night I saw myself killed. I will be killed soon." (Gransbery, *Billings Gazette*, August 12, 2002) Lone Bird concurred, "My shaking heart tells me trouble and death will overtake us if we make no hurry through this land. I cannot smother. I cannot hide what I speak what is revealed to me." (Gransbery, *Billings Gazette*, August 12, 2002) Looking Glass remained so confident that the war was over that he refused to post sentries or back-scout the trail.

"That night the soldiers surrounded our camp. About daybreak one of my men went out to look after his horses. The soldiers saw him and shot him down like a coyote. I have since learned these soldiers were not those we had left behind. They had come upon us from another direction." (Nerburn, p. 46)

One of the American settler volunteers in the Battle of Big Hole, Major John Catlin, later lamented that "the citizens went into that battle without just cause." (Gransbery, *Billing Gazette*, August 12, 2002) Another volunteer, James Chaffin, agreed. "When we got to the Sleeping Child Creek, I told Scott Sherrill that I thought we were doing wrong. The Indians had gone through the valley and had done just as they agreed to. I do not think we had any right to follow them up and pick a fight." (Gransbery, *Billings Gazette*, August 12, 2002)

"The new white war chief's name was Gibbon. He charged upon us while some of my people were still asleep. We had a hard fight. Some of my men crept around and attacked the soldiers from the rear. In this battle we lost nearly all our lodges, but we finally drove General Gibbon back." (Nerburn, p. 46)

Colonel John Gibbon was the commander of the Military Department of Montana. He walked his army of 146 enlisted men and 34 volunteers in the dead of night to fewer than 200 yards from the 89 tepees. Colonel Gibbon was a seasoned Civil War veteran, seriously wounded at both the battles of Fredericksburg and Gettysburg. He had been hardened by the anguish of war, being forced to battle against two of his own brothers fighting for the South. Many of his men questioned attacking a sleeping camp and some refused to kill women and children, but once the battle began the carnage was unstoppable. Amazingly the Nez Perce warriors, numbering around 125, withstood the early surprise assault and Gibbon and his men were forced to retreat. As the new battle lines were drawn the Nez Perce returned to camp to help their wounded and find their dead. Gibbon later wrote, "Few of us will soon forget the wail of mingled grief, rage, and horror which came from the camp four or five hundred yards away when the Indians returned to it and recognized their slaughtered warriors, women and children. Above this wail of horror we could hear the appeal of the leaders urging their followers to fight, and the war whoops in answer boded us no good." (Gransbery, *Billings Gazette*, August 12, 2002)

"Finding that he was not able to capture us, he sent his camp a few miles away for his big guns (cannons). But my men had captured them and all the ammunition. We damaged the big guns all we could, and carried away the powder and the lead. In the fight with General Gibbon we lost fifty women and children and thirty fighting men. We remained long enough to bury our dead. The Nez Perce never make war on women and children. We could have killed a great many women and children while the war lasted, but we would feel ashamed to do so cowardly an act. We never scalp our enemies. But when General Howard came up and joined General Gibbon, their Indian scouts dug up our dead and scalped them. I have been told that General Howard did not order this great shame to be done." (Nerburn, pp. 46, 47)

One of the great tragedies for Chief Joseph and his people was the lack of cultural understanding on the part of the Americans for the Nez Perce. In the beginning General Howard had great compassion for the non-treaty Nez Perce. One of the premier historians of the West, Jerome Green, called General Howard "one of the humanitarian Generals of the time." (Lorna Thackeray, July 28, 2002) In a report to the War Department at the beginning of the conflict Howard wrote, "I think it is a great mistake to take from Joseph and his band of Nez Perce that valley." (Thackeray, July 28, 2002) Unfortunately for the Nez Perce, General Howard was not a student of history and the consequence of what he did not know would prove disastrous. Historian Green provided the missing pieces of why General Howard failed to accomplish the purposes of the Almighty whom as a Christian he came to serve. "Howard had little understanding of the native peoples under his charge. He made no distinction between the cultures of one tribe or another and considered the non-treaty Nez Perce heathen children stubbornly refusing to see what was best for them." (Thackeray, July 28, 2002)

The so-called heathen children exemplified the noblest characteristics of mankind in the midst of the most vicious and unprovoked attacks and carnage against their people, in particular their women and children. As evidenced by the documentation of this research, these Nez Perce Indians could not be defined as heathen. This culture of Native Americans according to all reports represented many of the finest and most righteous attributes of any civilization ever to walk the face of the earth.

"We retreated as rapidly as we could toward the buffalo country. After six days General Howard came close to us, and we went out and attacked him, and captured nearly all his horses and mules. We then marched on to the Yellowstone Basin." (Nerburn, p. 47) The Nez Perce had no choice but to attack the

Americans. They could not afford to allow the soldiers to gain access to the main column of retreat featuring their wounded and their women and children. At this time they knew their only hope for sanctuary was Canada, and that hope was growing slim.

"On the way we captured one white man and two white women. We released them at the end of three days. They were treated kindly. The women were not insulted. Can the white soldiers tell me one time when Indian women were taken prisoners and held for three days, and then released without being insulted? Were the Nez Perce women who fell into the hands of General Howard's soldiers treated with as much respect? I deny that a Nez Perce was ever guilty of such a crime. A few days later we captured two more white men. One of them stole a horse and escaped. We gave the other a poor horse and told him he was free. Nine days' march brought us to the mouth of Clark's Fork on the Yellowstone. We did not know what had become of General Howard, but we supposed that he had sent for more horses and mules." (Nerburn, pp. 47, 48)

The Nez Perce inspired terror and excitement on the part of white settlers and tourists on the next leg of their flight. They exited the rigorous and breathtaking wonders of Yellowstone National Park to cross the wide expanse of Montana. The fact that the Nez Perce could continue to elude not one but three of the finest fully seasoned armies of the United States western command was a wonder to behold. The nearly faultless strategy of the Nez Perce, their ability to endure hardships and their uncanny perseverance in the face of nearly impossible situations was incredible. The will in the heart of the Nez Perce for liberty and freedom was unquenchable. Nevertheless, the grief they must have felt leaving their sick and wounded behind must have been excruciating. The Bannock Indian scouts of General Howard's army would kill every Nez Perce straggler and scalp the male warriors, even those in the grave, despite the orders of Howard for safety. The Nez Perce were guilty of a few murders of white settlers and tourists at the park as well. Chief Joseph could not control all his of warriors, especially after the battle of Big Hole. Looking Glass, White Bird, Poker Joe (Lean Elk), Too-hool-hool-suit and especially his brother Ollokot exercised greater power over war council decisions than did Joseph.

"He did not come up, but another new war chief (General Sturgis) attacked us. We held him in check while we moved all our women and children and stock out of danger, leaving a few men to cover our retreat. Several days passed, and we heard nothing of General Howard, or Gibbon, or Sturgis. We had repulsed each in turn, and began to feel secure when another army, under General Miles, struck us. This was the fourth army, each of which outnumbered our fighting force, that we had encountered within sixty days." (Nerburn, p. 48)

Chief Joseph and the Nez Perce were within forty miles of sanctuary in Canada. Hunkpapa Sioux Chief Sitting Bull was encamped with perhaps as many as two thousand braves across the border. The Nez Perce were exhausted and ravaged by the hardships of the retreat. They had repelled and eluded every attack of three mounted American cavalries in a trek of 1,700 miles for over four months. They were out of provisions and supplies. The few remaining Indian tepees would not shield the Nez Perce from the freezing winter winds of Bear Paw Mountain. Most of their lodges had been destroyed at Big Hole. The surviving Nez Perce could not build fires to warm their bodies from nearly five inches of snow for fear the Crow warriors would see their fires. They could not believe the Crow had turned against them. Yellow Wolf lamented, "Many snows the Crows have been our friends. But now like the Bitterroot Salish, turned enemies. My heart was like fire." (Thackeray, *Billings Gazette*, Sept. 16, 02) Looking Glass could not believe the soldiers could be close. The Nez Perce warriors had separated the horses and provisions of each of the three American armies. None could be close. Looking Glass had no understanding that a fourth American army under the command of Colonel Miles was now rapidly approaching from the southeast and would be upon them within the hour.

"We had no knowledge of General (Colonel) Miles' army until a short time before he made a charge upon us, cutting off our camp in two and capturing nearly all our horses. About seventy men, myself among them, were cut off. My little daughter, twelve years old, was with me. I gave her a rope and told her to catch a horse and join the others who were cut off from the camp. I have not seen her since, but I have learned that she is alive and well." (Nerburn, p. 48)

Chief Joseph would never see his daughter or one of his wives again. Both were able to find sanctuary in Canada with Nez Perce chief White Bird and nearly a third (233) of the tribe. The Nez Perce and Colonel Miles' army fought the bloodiest confrontation of the war on that cold snowy morning. When the last shot was fired most of the Nez Perce chiefs had been slain including Joseph's brother Ollokot, Too-hool-hool-suit, Poker Joe, and later Looking Glass, killed by a sniper. Colonel Miles' army did not fare any better. One half of the three companies involved in the charge were either dead or wounded including most of the officers. Lt. J. W. Biddle and Captain Owen Hale were killed along with all three first sergeants and four other sergeants. Captains Miles Moylan and Edward Godfrey were wounded. Colonel Miles dared not attempt to attack the weakened Nez Perce again even with vastly superior forces because the Indian warriors skillfully directed their defense to kill every officer, leaving the soldiers without direction. Chief Joseph gave voice to his undaunted faith. "I thought of my wife and children, who were now surrounded by soldiers, and I resolved to go to them or die. With a prayer in my mouth to the Great Spirit Chief who rules above, I dashed unarmed through the line of soldiers. It seemed to me that there were guns on every side, before and behind me." (Nerburn, p. 49)

Chief Joseph and his father may have renounced the Christianity of the white people but they continued to pray to the Great Spirit Chief who rules above. One of the great teachings of the Bible is that God (the Great Spirit Chief) seeks those who "shall worship the Father in spirit and in truth." (John, 4:23) The Nez Perce under the leadership of Chief Joseph demonstrated a much greater Christian witness in grace, forbearance, mercy, meekness and forgiveness than any of the Christian Americans who came to pacify them. Christianity as a religion believes in a supreme God that can be accessed only through obedience, prayer and faith. It is also a religion that teaches faith must be manifest by deed and action, not solely by profession of the mouth. Chief Joseph and his people demonstrated great faith in deed and action throughout the whole so-called War of the Nez Perce. The fault of the Christians of the hour, in particular the Christian military commanders, was demonstrated in their failure to study, understand and appreciate Nez Perce culture. They wrongly assumed they were the superior culture and the uncivilized heathen needed to be either Americanized or locked away on reservations. In reality the opposite was the truth. God had placed his mantle upon the Nez Perce because they were willing to live their lives according to the standard of righteousness and stewardship the Almighty required for the ultimate destiny of Oregon.

"My clothes were cut to pieces and my horse was wounded, but I was unharmed. As I reached the door of my lodge, my wife handed me my rifle, saying 'Here's your gun. Fight!' Six of my men were killed in one spot near me. Ten or twelve soldiers charged into our camp and got possession of two lodges, killing three Nez Perce and losing three of their men, who fell inside our lines. I called my men to drive them back. We fought at close range, not more than twenty steps apart, and drove the soldiers back upon their main line, leaving the dead in our hands. We secured their arms and ammunition. We lost, the first day and night, eighteen men and three women. General Miles lost twenty-six killed and forty wounded." (Nerburn, p. 50)

Chief Joseph was not a war strategist for his people. The other chiefs were all warriors. Chief Joseph was a man of peace and fought only when he was forced to fight, usually to protect his wife and family. In actual fact he had more than one wife, as did most of the tribal chiefs, perhaps one of the reasons he rejected the white man's Christianity. In this particular case it was the white man's form of Christianity that Chief Joseph rejected.

"The following day General Miles sent a messenger into my camp under protection of a white flag. I sent Yellow Bull to meet him. Yellow Bull understood the messenger to say that General Miles wished me to consider the situation, that he did not want to kill my people unnecessarily. Yellow Bull understood this to be a demand for me to surrender and save blood. Upon reporting this message to me, Yellow Bull said he wondered whether General Miles was in earnest. I sent him back with my answer, that I had made up my mind, but would think about it and send word soon. A little later he sent some Cheyenne scouts with another message, I went out to meet them. They said they believed General Miles was sincere and really wanted peace. I walked to General Miles' tent. He met me and we shook hands. He said, 'Come, let us sit down by the fire and talk this matter over. I remained with him all night. Next morning Yellow Bull came over to see if I was alive, and why I did not return. General Miles would not let me leave the tent to see my friend alone. Yellow Bull said to me, 'They have got you in their power, and I'm afraid they will never let you go again. I have an officer in our camp, and I will hold him until they let you go free.' I said, 'I do not know what they mean to do with me, but if they kill me you must not kill the officer. It will do no good to avenge my death by killing him.' Yellow Bull returned to my camp. I did not make any agreement that day with General Miles. The battle was renewed while I was with him. I was very anxious about my people. I knew we were near Sitting Bull's camp in King George's land, and I thought maybe the Nez Perce who had escaped would return with assistance. No great damage was done to either party during the night." (Nerburn, pp. 50, 51)

The escaping Nez Perce under the leadership of White Bird did in fact reach the camp of Sioux Chief Sitting Bull. There is no evidence to indicate whether Sitting Bull would have come to the aid of the Nez Perce. He had been warned by Canadian authorities that should he cross the border he would not be welcomed back. There is also conjecture that he did not want to take on Colonel Nelson Miles again. The Sioux eventually surrendered their Canadian refuge, primarily because the winters were too harsh, and accepted confinement to a reservation where Sitting Bull was killed.

"On the following morning I returned to my camp by agreement, meeting the officer who had been held a prisoner in my camp at the flag of truce. My people were divided about surrendering. We could have escaped from Bear Paw Mountain if we had left our wounded, old men, and children behind. We were unwilling to do this. We had never heard of a wounded Indian recovering while in the hands of white men.

On the evening of the fourth day, General Howard came in with a small escort, together with my friend Chapman. We could now talk understandingly. General Miles said in plain words, 'If you will come out and give up your arms, I will spare your lives and send you to your reservation.' I do not know what passed between General Miles and General Howard. I could not bear to see my wounded men and women suffer any longer. We had lost enough already." (Nerburn, p. 52)

Nez Perce warrior Yellow Bull remembered the Bear Paw camp. "A young warrior, wounded, lay on a buffalo robe dying without complaint. Children crying with cold. No fire, there could be no light. Everywhere there was crying, the death wail." (Thackeray, *Billings Gazette*, Sept. 30, 2002)

"General Miles had promised that we might return to our own country with what stock we had left. I thought we could start over again. I believed General Miles, or I would never have surrendered. I have heard that he has been censured for making the promise to return us to Lapwai. He could not have made any other terms with me at that time. I would have held him in check until my friends came to my assistance, and then neither of the generals nor their soldiers would have ever left Bear Paw Mountain alive." (Nerburn, pp. 52, 53)

Colonel Miles did not have the authority to offer Chief Joseph and the Nez Perce the opportunity to return to Lapwai. This was another example of white man's forked tongue in regard to the Indians. Certainly, the U.S. army was not prepared to attack these Nez Perce warriors again. Colonel Miles and General Howard knew full well that Sitting Bull could be on his way to aid the Nez Perce. The Nez Perce had already proved to be superior warriors and the addition of Sitting Bull would spell doom for the combined forces of the western command of the United States army. The American commanders had no choice but to induce Chief Joseph to surrender. The fact that they were offering concessions they could not honor was an issue they would deal with after these Nez Perce were pacified. "On the fifth day I went to General Miles and gave up my gun, and said, 'From where the sun now stands I will fight no more.'" (Nerburn, p. 53)

The actual words of Chief Joseph's surrender were directed toward the Nez Perce, not Colonel Miles. All of the Nez Perce war chiefs were dead, with the exception of White Bird who escaped to Canada. Had any of the war chiefs been still alive it is doubtful the Nez Perce would have surrendered. This speech became one of the great speeches in American history, capturing for all time the plight of the Nez Perce as their flight had impacted the entire Pacific Northwest.

"Tell General Howard I know his heart. What he told me before I have in my heart. I am tired of fighting. Our chiefs are killed. Looking Glass is dead. Toolhoolhoolzote is dead. It is the young men who say yes or no. He who led on the young men is dead. It is cold and we have no blankets. My people, some of them have run away to the hills and have no blankets, no food. No one knows where they are, perhaps frozen to death. I want to have time to look for my children and see how many of them I can find. Maybe I shall see them among the dead. Hear me my chiefs. I am tired; my heart is sick and sad. From where the sun now stands, I will fight no more." (Oct. 5, 1877) (Thackeray, *Billings Gazette*, Sept. 30, 2002)

Chief Joseph surrendered to the American army. He gave up over eleven hundred Appaloosa horses and saddles. These horses had run circles around the best steeds the United States cavalry could muster. Once the Nez Perce masters were captured and removed, the army riflemen indiscriminately slaughtered these magnificent animals. Perhaps these riflemen and their superiors believed the Appaloosa were joined in spirit with their masters and must be destroyed like their riders. The four hundred thirty exhausted Nez Perce Indians did not fare much better than their slaughtered horses. Instead of going to Lapwai as promised they were sent to Tongue River where the entire tribe including their sick and wounded were placed on flatboats and wagons and sent four hundred miles in the dead of winter to Bismarck, Nebraska. Shortly thereafter they were moved to Fort Leavenworth, Kansas.

Chief Joseph lamented his decision to surrender. "We were ordered to get into railroad cars. Three of my people died on the way to Baxter Springs (Kansas). It was worse to die there than to die fighting in the mountains." (Nerburn p. 55) "At Leavenworth we were placed on a low river bottom, with no water except river water to drink and cook with. We had always lived in a healthy country where mountains were high and the water was cool and clear. Many of our people sickened and died and we buried them in this strange land. I cannot tell how much my heart suffered for my people while at Leavenworth. The Great Spirit Chief who rules above seemed to be looking some other way and did not see what was being done to my people." (Thackeray, *Billings Gazette*, Oct. 7, 2002)

Chief Joseph lost as many of his people to sickness as he did to the relentless heavily armed armies chasing him on his flight to freedom. They were moved again to Oklahoma to their permanent reservation home and things got worse. Nez Perce Yellow Wolf lamented, "all the babies died; and many of the old people too. It was the climate. Everything so different from our old home. No mountains, no springs, no clear running waters." (Thackeray, Oct. 7, 2002)

Chief Joseph lamented that the Great Spirit Chief who rules above did not see what was being done to his people. In the introduction of this research the author referred to the renowned evangelist of the Second Great Awakening Lyman Beecher, who cautioned that God not only sees but also will require recompense. "If this nation is, in the providence of God, destined to lead the way in the moral and political emancipation of the world, it is time she understood her high calling, and were harnessed for the work. For mighty causes, like floods and distant mountains, are rushing with accumulating power to their consummation of good or evil, and soon our character and destiny will be stereotyped forever." (Marshall, Manuel, p. 371)

The government of the young emerging union of states had established a military policy of force to settle the question of emancipation for the Native American Indians. Would this policy of military might stamp forever its character upon the destiny of the United States? Would America when facing duress in the future resort to military force instead of reasoned restraint?

Fortunately, the plight of the Nez Perce did not go unnoticed by the statesmen of the hour. Three of Chief Joseph's greatest supporters were Generals Howard, Miles and Gibbons. In 1880, Miles was promoted to commander of the Department of Columbia, which just happened to include the Nez Perce homeland, and he used his position to press for justice for the Nez Perce. The United States Congress came under growing pressure in the press and from political circles to redress the injustice done by the American military and government to the Nez Perce Indians. The free press of America was doing its job, a job essential for a democracy to survive. Chief Joseph had the opportunity to plead his case for his beloved nation personally before three American presidents, Rutherford B. Hayes, William McKinley and Theodore Roosevelt. By 1883 the first Nez Perce were finally allowed to go home. By 1885 all the Nez Perce had returned to their beloved Pacific Northwest. One hundred fifteen returned to Lapwai and one hundred fifty, including Chief Joseph, settled at the Colville reservation in Washington. Unfortunately the non-treaty Nez Perce were now a divided tribe, only a shadow of the mighty tribe that once ruled the Columbia Plateau.

The challenge of Andrew Jackson to the Senate and House of Representatives in 1837 at the introduction of this document bears repetition at this time. The ultimate responsibility for the injustice meted to the Nez Perce was on the shoulders of these elected officials of the United States of America. Andrew Jackson said, "You have the highest of human trusts committed to your care. Providence has showered on this favored land blessing without number, and has chosen you as the guardians of freedom, to preserve it for the benefit of the human race. May He who holds in his hands the destinies of nations make you worthy of the favors He has bestowed, and enable you, with pure hearts and hands and sleepless vigilance, to guard and defend to the end of time the great charge He has committed to your keeping." (Marshall, Manuel, p. 372)

The Almighty, who holds in his hands the destinies of nations, had blessed America beyond all nations save perhaps the nation of Israel under King David and King Solomon. The Nez Perce from their earliest encounter with white men were the great friends of America and Americans. The Nez Perce illustrated by deed and action the most noble characteristics of the emerging American Republic. The question of the hour remained: Would the young nation repent from its evil dealings toward the Nez Perce and set a course to "guard and defend the great charge He has committed to your keeping"?

Chief Joseph asked the same question. "I cannot understand how the government sends a man to fight us, as it did General Miles, and breaks his word. Such a government has something wrong with it. I cannot understand why so many chiefs are allowed to talk so many different things. I have seen the Great Father Chief (President), the next Great Chief (Secretary of the Interior), the Commissioner Chief (Hayt), the Law Chief (General Butler), and many other law chiefs (congressmen), and they all say they are my friends, and that I shall have justice. But while their mouths all talk right I do not understand why nothing has been done for my people. I have heard talk and talk, but nothing is done. Good words do not last long unless they amount to something. Words do not pay for my dead people. They do not pay for my people, now over run by white people. They do not protect my father's grave. They do not pay for all my horses and cattle. Good words will not give me back my children. Good words will not make good the promises of your War Chief General Miles. Good words will not give my people good health and stop them from dying. Good words will not get my people a home where they can live in peace and take care of themselves." (Nerburn, pp. 57, 58)

It was astonishing that Chief Joseph's words fell on deaf ears. Had the American powers forgotten their own roots? Had these men forgotten that they had been blessed by the Almighty (in Lyman Beecher's words) "to lead in the moral and political emancipation of the world"? Had they forgotten or had President Andrew Jackson's exhortation never been instilled in their hearts and souls that they were chosen "as guardians of freedom to preserve it for the benefit of the human race"? What had become of the virtue that had fueled the manifest destiny of the triumphantly emerging Republic of the United States of America? Samuel Adams, one of the founding fathers of the American Republic, warned exactly one hundred years earlier: "A general dissolution of principles and manners will more surely overthrow the liberties of America than the whole force of the common enemy. While the people are virtuous they cannot be subdued; but when they lose their virtue they will be ready to surrender their liberties to the first external or internal invader….If virtue and knowledge are diffused among the people, they will never be enslaved. This will be their great security." (Federer, p. 23)

The American government did not give justice and liberty to these Native American Indians because that generation of leaders had compromised their virtue and they lacked understanding and knowledge of the great debt America owed to the Nez Perce nation. Once again the biblical refrain "my people are destroyed for lack of knowledge" (Hosea 4:6) was played like a funeral dirge over the Nez Perce. Chief Joseph spoke of the suffering and oppression caused when knowledge and virtue are not diffused among the people.

"I am tired of talk that comes to nothing. It makes my heart sick when I remember all the good words and broken promises. If the white man wants to live in peace with the Indian he can live in peace. There need be no trouble. Treat all men alike. Give them the same law. Give them all an even chance to live and grow. All men were made by the same Great Spirit Chief. They are all brothers. The earth is the mother of all people, and all people should have equal rights upon it. You might as well expect the rivers to run backwards as that any man who was born a free man should be contented when penned up and denied liberty to go where he pleases. If you tie a horse to a stake, do you expect he will grow fat? If you put an Indian up on a small part of earth and compel him to stay there, he will not be contented, nor will he grow and prosper." (Nerburn, pp. 58, 59)

The very essence of the founding ideal of the American Republic was enshrined in the words of the Declaration of Independence: "We hold these truths to be self-evident, that all men are created equal. That they are endowed by their Creator with certain inalienable Rights, that among these are Life, Liberty and the Pursuit of Happiness…" (Federer, p. 200) Why did the Declaration of Independence not apply to the indigenous American Indians who occupied America before the white men came? This question will be examined in the next chapter. The Nez Perce Indians and American free men were inspired and accountable to the same Creator whether He was named God or the Great Spirit Chief. The American free men came to the Promised Land to seek and secure liberty and freedom. Once they had gained their liberty and freedom would they extend it to others?

"I have asked some of the great white chiefs where they get their authority to say to the Indians that he shall stay in one place, while he sees white men going where they please. They cannot tell me. I only ask the government to be treated as all other men are treated. If I cannot go to my own home, let me have a home in some country where my people will not die so fast. I would like to go to the Bitterroot valley. There my people would be healthy; where they are now, they are dying. Three have died since I left my camp to come to Washington. When I think of our condition my heart is heavy. I see men of my race treated as outlaws and driven from country to country, or shot down like animals. I know my race must change. We cannot hold our own with the white men as we are. We only ask an even chance to live as other men live." (Nerburn, pp. 59, 60)

The first Protestant missionaries recognized the realities that Chief Joseph expressed regarding the future of the indigenous Americans. The Whitmans and the Spaldings labored to minister the Christian gospel as well as teach the Indians American ways, including cultivating the land and learning the necessary skills to hold their own economically. The Protestant missionaries knew if the American Indians were to survive they must learn to survive in white man's culture. Chief Joseph recognized this reality and concluded his message to America with one final plea.

"We ask to be recognized as men. We ask that the same law shall work alike on all men. If the Indian breaks the law, punish him by the law. If the white man breaks the law, punish him also. Let me be a free man – free to travel, free to stop, free to work, free to trade where I choose, free to choose my own teachers, free to follow the religion of my fathers, free to think and talk and act for myself – and I will obey all laws or submit to the penalty. When the white man treats an Indian as they treat each other, then we will have no more wars. We shall all be alike – brothers of one father and one mother, with one sky above us and one government for all. Then the Great Spirit Chief who rules above will smile upon the land, and send rain to wash out the bloody spots made by brothers' hands from the face of the earth. For this time the Indian race are waiting and praying. I hope that no more groans of wounded men and women will ever go to the ear of the Great Spirit Chief above, and that all people may be one people. In-mut-too-yah-lat-lat has spoken for his people." (Nerburn, pp. 60, 61)

The shadow of the Almighty was now upon the Nez Perce Indians as Chief Joseph spoke on behalf of the Creator that America would become "one Nation under God, indivisible, with liberty and justice to all." The Indian race was waiting and praying for the age when they could live in liberty and equality in the new white man's America. The dawn of the twentieth century was approaching. Would the American dream of liberty and freedom include the American Indians?

Chapter 27

Manifest Destiny and the Native American Indians

In the previous chapter this research posed the question: Would the Native American Indians be included in the "manifest destiny" of the Republic? The treatment of the Nez Perce Indians, great friends of the emerging American Republic in the Pacific Northwest, gave cause to question the virtue and integrity of the American government's policy toward the Native American Indians. Was the treatment of the Nez Perce an isolated regrettable blemish on the cherished ideals of the Republic or was the treatment of the Nez Perce consistent with America's treatment of all indigenous Indian tribes? How did the ideals of liberty, freedom and justice for all American citizens square with the emerging Republic's Indian policy?

The first major confrontation between the emerging American Republic (after the Declaration of Independence) and the indigenous American Indians occurred in the lower South at the turn of the eighteenth century where white settlers considered the Indians an obstacle to "progress." These white settlers pressured the government to purchase lands belonging to the Cherokee, Creek, Choctaw, Chickasaw and Seminole nations. Andrew Jackson commanded U.S. military forces that forcefully acquired 22 million acres of Creek Native American hereditary lands. From 1814 to 1824 Jackson negotiated nine treaties where these five southern indigenous tribes exchanged their native lands for new lands in the west. The Indians yielded their native lands for strategic reasons in hopes of retaining a portion and in an attempt to live in peace with the white settlers.

In 1823 the Supreme Court was called upon to settle the issue of Indian rights on native lands the white settlers coveted. The Court determined the Native American Indians could occupy their native lands but could not hold title to these lands. The Court determined the Indians' right of occupancy was subordinate to the United States' "right of discovery." Chief Joseph asked the question by what authority did the white man claim the Indian land. The authority for removing the Native American Indians from their land came from this Supreme Court decision.

The indigenous American Indians were consequently faced with some very difficult decisions. The Creek, Cherokee and Chickasaw nations responded by initiating a policy of restricting land sales to the government. These three nations in consort with the Choctaw and Seminole nations copied the white civilization agricultural policies of large-scale plantations, western education and slave holding in an attempt to coexist with the white settlers. These same tribes also ceded portions of their property in an attempt to save the remainder. Only when these methods failed did the Indian tribes resort to armed force to protect their heritage and only the Seminole nation took up arms to defend their homeland. The Seminoles encouraged fugitive Negro slaves to join their resistance, inciting the white slave holders to seek government assistance to crush the rebellion. Jackson's army defeated the Indians in the First Seminole War of 1817.

The Cherokee nation attempted to use legal means to save their tribal lands. In 1827 they developed a written constitution declaring them a sovereign nation within the United States. This tribe shrewdly based their sovereignty on U.S. policy that declared them sovereign so the Indian nations would be legally capable of ceding their lands. The state of Georgia did not recognize the Native American sovereignty but rather saw them as tenants living on state land. In other words, the state did not recognize the Indians as free men, equal to white Americans. The state of Georgia expected the Indians to obey state laws, yet their law maintained, "No Indian or descendant of any Indians shall be deemed a competent witness in any court in the State to which a white person may be a party." (Marshall, Manuel, p. 348). The Cherokee took their grievance to the Supreme Court, which once again ruled against them.

When white settlers claimed land granted by treaty to the Cherokee they once again appealed to the Supreme Court. The Georgia legislature had written a law to remove from Cherokee lands the white missionaries who were supporting the Native American right to their native heritage. The Protestant missionaries had been sending articulate reports to their churches in the north exposing southern injustice. Two Protestant missionaries were arrested and appealed to the Supreme Court. In a unanimous opinion delivered by Chief Justice Marshall the Supreme Court declared: "From the commencement of our Government, Congress has passed acts to regulate trade and intercourse with the Indians, which treat them as nations, respect their rights, and manifest a firm purpose to afford that protection which treaties stipulate." (Marshall, Manuel, p. 349) This time the Supreme Court supported the right of self-government for the Cherokee nation and declared Georgia's extension of state law "repugnant to the Constitution, laws, and treaties of the United States." (Marshall, Manuel, p. 349). The state of Georgia refused to abide by the Supreme Court decision and then President Andrew Jackson refused to enforce the law protecting the Cherokee nation. Jackson's attitude was: "John Marshall has made his opinion; now let him enforce it." (Marshall, Manuel, p. 349)

The dye was established for the place of indigenous American Indians in the "manifest destiny" of the emerging Republic. The impact of the manifest destiny for the American Indians was that white Americans were empowered by military might to expand the national dominion by whatever force was expedient. In 1830, the great Indian fighter Andrew Jackson, as president of the United States, rammed the Indian Removal Act through congress. This legislation gave Jackson power to negotiate treaties throughout the United States to open up America to its manifest destiny. Under this Act the indigenous Indians were required to cede their lands east of the Mississippi for new lands to the west. The removal was by statute voluntary and peaceful, but those Indian nations that refused to move were forcibly removed. The Indian tribes that refused to cede their homeland and sign Jackson's treaties were systematically robbed or coerced by deception to sell their land by unscrupulous whites. So dreadful was the treatment of these indigenous Indians that even the white newspaper in the capital of Alabama finally spoke out. "(The red men's property) has been taken from them—their stock killed, their farms pillaged—and by whom? By white men….Such villains may go unpunished in this world, but the day of retribution will certainly arrive." (Marshall, Manuel, p. 351) Some Christian historians have gone so far as to surmise that indeed retribution did arrive in the form of the Civil War thirty years later. (Marshall, Manuel, p. 349)

Andrew Jackson, like most Americans, did not expect America to ever extend west beyond the Mississippi. According to the rationale of those Americans who believed in America's manifest destiny, the most humane policy America could "manifest" toward the Indians was removal "before all semblance of civilized behavior toward them collapsed." (Marshall, Manuel, p. 351) By 1837 Jackson had removed 46,000 Native American Indians from their homelands, opening up 25 million acres of land to white settlement and to white slavery of the Negro race. The Indian nations that Jackson removed from their homeland, the Cherokee and Choctaw, were the same Indian nations that fought as allies to Jackson in the War of 1812 and the Battle of Horseshoe Bend. The Cherokee and Choctaw supported the American Republic against the British in the same manner the Nez Perce supported the American Republic in the Oregon Territory four decade later.

May 1838 was established as the final month for the Cherokee nation to remove themselves from their homeland to make room for white civilization. Cherokee Chief William Cooley documented the stark reality of this holocaust of their nation: "Multitudes were allowed no time to take anything with them, except the clothes they had on. Well-furnished homes were left a prey to plunderers….The property of many has been taken and sold before their eyes for almost nothing, the sellers and buyers in most cases having combined to cheat the poor Indians…unoffending, unarmed, and unresisting Cherokees." (Marshall, Manuel, p. 351)

Fifteen thousand Cherokee began a forced march west, "driven by brutal power from all they loved and cherished in the land of their fathers, to gratify the cravings of avarice." (Marshall, Manuel, p. 351) These Indians, like Chief Joseph and the Nez Perce, had been driven from their homeland by greed and ignorance. These Indians were friends of the Americans. They had adopted American customs, traditions and civilization, yet they were treated as sub-human vassals to the superior American white race. "These Indians, martyrs to the color of their skin, had assimilated the ways of the white man so completely that their ministers requested the march be halted on the Lord's Day and for alters to be erected and services conducted….Some whites present affirm it to have been the most solemn and impressive service they have ever witnessed." (Marshall, Manuel, p. 352)

The forced march of the Cherokee became known as the Trail of Tears. Four thousand Cherokee died on that march to Oklahoma. Were it not for the mercy of wilderness Christian churches along the way the toll would have been greater. The Cherokee were promised all of Oklahoma save the panhandle "as long as the grass shall grow and the rivers run."

The indigenous American Indians of the south attempted to live according to white man's traditions and rules. With the exception of the Seminole tribe they did not resist with force of arms the oppression and injustice of the white race. These Indians accepted the Christian teachings of the Protestant missionaries who came to assist them, and the standard of their faith in God was an indictment against the so-called virtue and integrity of the nation that claimed in Andrew Jackson's words to be the "guardians of freedom, to preserve it for the benefit of the human race." (Marshall, Manuel, p. 372)

This chapter began with the question whether the treatment of the Nez Perce Indians was an isolated regrettable blemish on the cherished ideals of the emerging American Republic or whether it was U. S. government policy. The Supreme Court of the United States of America established the precedent in 1823 that the indigenous American Indians' right of "occupancy" was subordinate to the United States right of "discovery." In other words, the white settlers could discover and claim Native American ancestral lands at will throughout the United States. Even when the Supreme Court ruled in favor of the American Indians the President could claim executive power and refuse to enforce justice on behalf of the Indians. The government of the United States legislated this policy under the Indian Removal Act of 1830 whereby the president and those appointed to represent the United States could forcibly remove Indian nations from their land by requiring them to sign treaties. These treaties gave the Indians lands to the west that no white settlers desired, at least not yet. The only reason the indigenous American Indians were deemed sovereign nations was to allow them to legally sell their land to the whites. The fact that the Native American Indians were sovereign also meant they were foreigners and not equal before the law in American courts. According to the American statesmen, congressmen, Supreme Court judges, and presidents of the emerging American Republic in the first half of the nineteenth century, the indigenous American Indians stood in the way of progress. America's manifest destiny required the indigenous American Indians be removed by whatever means necessary from lands required by the emerging American civilization.

It is not fair to write that all Americans agreed with the United States' Indian policy. Indeed, there was an outcry that arose from white newspapers in the deep South. The legendary Davy Crockett protested so vigorously against the injustice to the Native American Indians that he lost his seat in Congress. Ralph Waldo Emerson protested to President Martin Van Buren warning, "the name of this nation, hitherto the sweet omen of religion and liberty, will stink to the rest of the world." The Protestant missionary movement in New England labored valiantly to expose the injustice and end the prejudicial treatments of the original Americans. It was this same Protestant evangelical movement that sent the first missionaries to the Pacific Northwest. In the end it was greed and avarice that ruled the day in the South and the dye was set for the same treatment of the Nez Perce and the Native American Indians of the Pacific Northwest long before Chief Joseph was born. The lust for land overpowered the cherished ideals of the founders of the Republic: liberty and equality for all. If the southern landowners were to enslave the Black man, the Red race would fare no better.

Protestant missionaries were sent to the indigenous Indians in the South and the West to resurrect their culture, to educate, and to instill the knowledge and understanding of white man's civilization and the hope of eternal life through Jesus Christ. In most instances the American Indians received the gospel and walked and lived according to the dictates of Christian standards. Unfortunately some missionary societies pressed their cultural values on the indigenous Native Americans. More tragically the Protestant values that brought freedom and liberty to America did not bring freedom and liberty to the Native Americans. Chief Joseph became the spokesman of the Great Spirit Chief who rules from above. "When the white man treats an Indian as they treat each other, then we will have no more wars. We shall all be alike, brothers of one father and one mother, with one sky above us and one government for all. Then the Great Spirit Chief who rules above will smile upon this land, and send rain to wash out the bloody spots made by brothers' hands from the face of the earth. For this time the Indian race are waiting and praying." (Nerburn, p. 61)

Would Chief Joseph's cry and prayer be heard in the emerging states of the Pacific Northwest? Would the Great Spirit Chief who rules from above smile upon the land and send rain to wash out the bloody spots?

CHAPTER 28

INDIAN RESERVATIONS

This research has documented the social, political and spiritual reasons why the Whitman massacre was the watershed event in the Oregon Territory. Immediately after the massacre in December 1847 a Provisional Legislature drafted a memorial to present to the American Congress to establish Oregon under the sovereignty of the United States. Joseph Meek and a party of nine delegates took their petition to Washington, D.C. On August 14, 1848 President James Polk signed the Organic Act creating the Oregon Territory. The following year the government created the Oregon Donation Land Act establishing a system of land distribution and survey. By mid-century the Oregon Territory had nearly twelve thousand American citizens living within its confines. Unfortunately, the Whitman massacre had forced all the Protestant missionaries out of the Columbia Plateau. The Jesuit missionaries refused to obey the edict to leave their Indian missions and continued to exercise their influence and hegemony among the Columbia Plateau Native Americans.

Whitman had advocated a system of military garrisons along the Oregon Trail in an attempt to ensure an orderly and fair merging of the white and red nations. In 1846 Congress had allocated $76,500 for these garrisons but the advent of the Mexican War diverted the funds. Without military garrisons and with no Protestant missionaries to act as intermediaries on behalf of the Columbia Plateau Indians now under the influence of the Jesuit priests, trouble began to ferment in every arena. The American pioneers came to Oregon for the promise of a new life and the opportunity to claim some of the most prime and pristine real estate left in the world. These emigrants had paid a heavy price to reach Oregon and their reward was real estate. There was one problem: the indigenous American Indians of the Pacific Northwest already occupied a significant portion of this prime real estate. Fortunately, for the immigrants, the Supreme Court had already ruled the Indians' right of occupancy was subordinate to the Americans' right of discovery.

For half a century the two races had developed an exemplary relationship in the land of the Oregon Territory. That relationship was about to be severely tested. In the beginning of the white American immigration into the West the two races melded together under the positive covering of Chief Factor John McLoughlin and the Protestant missionaries. There was plenty of land for all.

Everything changed after the Whitman massacre. The Indian Wars in Oregon led to the peace accord of 1855. Even after the Native Americans of the Pacific Northwest moved onto the reservations major problems continued to develop between the races. The American pioneers began to log the forests, mine the rivers and fence the valleys. The rivers began to choke with mud, killing the freshwater mussels, crayfish, eels and trout that the Indians depended on for sustenance. Soon the salmon and steelhead runs began to diminish, further compromising the Indian way of life. The pioneer homesteads required fencing, necessary for cultivation and domestic animals, which greatly undermined Native American field burning which in turn ended harvest of blackberries and tarweed seeds. The Indians protested and threatened to retaliate. The American settlers in southern Oregon formed vigilante groups called "exterminators" which began indiscriminate killing of Indian tribes that stood against the Americans. There were Indian massacres in the south against the Chetos, Lower Coquille and Takelma between 1853-1855. Indian sub agent Frederick Smith wrote: "Bold, Brave, Courageous men! To attack a friendly and defenseless tribe of Indians: to burn, roast, and shoot sixteen of their number all on suspicion they were about to rise and drive from their country three hundred men." (Oregon Blue Book, http://bluebook.state.or.us/cultural/history/history14.htm Indian Wars)

It appeared the majority of Americans of the Oregon Territory were no different than many other whites that came upon the indigenous American Indians on the North American continent. The Indian Wars of the Oregon Territory were not a proud testimony for the early Oregon pioneers. In truth there were atrocities on both sides; however, the burden of responsibility rested upon the early American pioneers. The indigenous Indians occupied the Oregon Territory first. They had welcomed and allowed American encroachment on their domain for over half a century. Some of the tribes, such as the Nez Perce, were the best friends the American nation would ever have in the new land of opportunity. There truly was land for everybody should visionary and righteous men have ruled in that hour.

Unfortunately, the great benefactors for the Indian race, the Protestant missionaries, had been driven out of the Columbia Plateau. President Andrew Jackson had already established the precedent of removing Indians from their land and placing them on reservations. In this new scenario the Jesuit priests went from villain to Native American protectorate. The Jesuit priests armed the Indians and supported their cause. The research of this document has fully exposed the treachery of the Jesuit priests; however, their culpability pales in comparison to the injustice meted to the American Indians by the United States government. In 1853 Superintendent Joel Palmer of Oregon and Governor Isaac Stevens of the newly formed Washington Territory initiated the treaty process whereby the Native American Indians were to abdicate their position and their ancestral homeland to make room for progress, the so-called manifest destiny of the American Republic in Oregon.

The Indian nations of the Pacific Northwest were not ignorant of the American treaty policy of land displacement. By the hour the Native American Indians had been removed to reservations, their numbers, especially west of the Cascades, had been decimated by white man's disease. Over a thousand Suquamish and Duwamish Indians met American President Pierce's designated Governor, Isaac Stevens, when he arrived by ship at Puget Sound. The Chief of the allied tribes of the Whulge was a Duwamish, well known to both races as a man of peace named Seattle. Chief Seattle had accepted the white settlers and attempted to accommodate the conflicting lifestyles of the white people who lived as families, not bands or tribes like the Indians.

Seattle addressed Governor Stevens on the fateful day he arrived on the Pacific coast in December 1853. Dr. Henry A. Smith, who witnessed the event, recorded this address. The fact he did not publish his account of the speech until October 1887 in the Seattle *Sunday Star* has led some to claim he embellished Seattle's speech. The Indian chief spoke in the Salish language and Dr. Smith was a linguist and could have translated the speech for posterity. In addition, Chief Seattle spoke English and could have given the speech, or a portion of the speech, in English. This speech has been widely quoted and honored to represent the wisdom of the indigenous Indians of the Pacific Northwest and for that reason this research will document Smith's research.

"The White Chief (Governor Stevens) says that the Big Chief in Washington sends us greetings of friendship and goodwill. This is kind of him, for we know he has little need of our friendship in return. His people are many. They are like the grass that covers the prairies. My people are few. They are like the scattered trees of a storm-swept plain. The Great Chief sends us word that he wishes to buy our lands, but is willing to allow us enough to live comfortably. This indeed appears just, even generous, for the red man no longer has rights that he needs respected. And the offer may be wise also, as we are no longer in need of an extensive country. There was a time when our people covered the land as the waves of a wind-ruffled sea cover its shell-paved floor. But that time long since passed away with the greatness of tribes that are now but a mournful memory. I will not dwell upon, nor mourn over, our untimely decay, nor reproach my white brothers with hastening it, as we too may have been somewhat to blame." (Nerburn, pp. 69, 70)

In retrospect, with the advantage of one hundred fifty years of insight, the concept of uncivilized savage or even the term "heathen" hardly describes the indigenous Indians of the Pacific Northwest. These Native Americans received the first American intruders openly and generously. At the hour of Governor Stevens' arrival the Indians exercised great restraint and forbearance in the face of an edict that was to end their traditional way of life. Instead of being bitter, this Indian chief even accepted some of the blame for their demise as a people. The American government was willing to negotiate treaties with the Indians and pay them for their land. In light of the prevailing mores of the hour an argument could be made that this may have been the only solution available to the American government. The indigenous Indians were not culturally ready to live and compete with the white nation supplanting them.

Seattle continued, "Youth is impulsive. When our young men grow angry at some real or imaginary wrong, and disfigure their faces with black paint, it denotes their hearts are black, and that they are often cruel and relentless, and our old men and old women are unable to restrain them. Thus it has ever been. Thus it was when the white man first began to push our forefathers westward. But let us hope that the hostilities between us may never return. We have everything to lose and nothing to gain. Revenge by young men is considered gain, even at the cost of their own lives. But old men who stay at home in times of war, and mothers who have sons to lose know better." (Nerburn, p. 70,71)

Chief Seattle had converted to the Catholic faith through the ministry of French Catholic missionaries He had been taught the Catholic virtue of forgiveness. The dilemma for Chief Seattle was the American government also represented the Catholic faith, at least to these Indians. The Indians did not differentiate between the Catholic and Christian faith. Nor did the Indians differentiate between either the Christian and Catholic faith and the American government.

"Our good father at Washington-for I presume he is now our father as well as yours, since King George has moved his boundaries further north-our great and good father, I say sends us word that if we do as he desires, he will protect us. His brave warriors will be to us a bristling wall of strength, and his wonderful ships of war will fill our harbors so that our ancient enemies far to the northward-the Hadeas and the Tshimshian-will cease to frighten our women, children and old men. Then in reality will he be our father and we his children. But can that ever be? Your God is not our God. Your God loves your people and hates mine. He folds His strong protecting arms lovingly about the white man and leads him by the hand as a father leads his infant son. But He has forsaken His red children-if they are really his." (Nerburn, p. 71)

We have arrived at the one of the central issues of this research. Chief Seattle lamented that the God of the white man did not love and protect the red man. If the Oregon Territory was indeed under the shadow of the Almighty, then did the Almighty favor the 'manifest destiny' of the white race to usurp the red race within the confines of the Pacific Northwest? One of the biblical definitions of the Almighty is that God has no favorites. According to God's word, "There is neither Jew nor Greek, there is neither bond nor free, there is neither male nor female: for ye are all one in Christ Jesus" (Galations, 4:28) The Indians, from Chief Seattle to Chief Joseph saw the American government and Christianity as one. They saw the 'Great White

Chief,' the President of the United States, as the supreme representative of the Christian faith. Therefore they saw the policy of the American government as the policy of God toward their people. In the Indian culture the Indian chief did represent their religion.

"Our God, the Great Spirit, seems also to have forsaken us. Your God makes your people wax strong every day. Soon they will fill the land. Our people are ebbing away like a rapidly receding tide that will never return. The white man's God cannot love our people or He would protect them. They seem to be orphans who can look nowhere for help. How can we be brothers? How can your God become our God and renew our prosperity and awaken in us dreams of returning greatness?" (Nerburn, p. 71,72)

Chief Seattle was a great friend of the first white settlers in the Puget Sound. He protected these early pioneers and in turn they named the great city of Seattle after this Duwamish chief. When Seattle died he was buried in a Catholic ceremony with Catholic rituals. Although this chief apparently sustained his Catholic heritage the questions he identifies are central to the thesis of the research. If the Oregon Territory was under the shadow of the Almighty, as the thesis of this research contends, why did not the Almighty protect the Indian race from the onslaught of white civilization? This was the very question that Chief Joseph and Chief Seattle were asking. If the Almighty God of the Americans was the same 'Great Spirit Chief' of the Native American Indians, then why were the Indians dying and the whites prospering? According to Chief Seattle 'the white man's God cannot love our people or He would protect them.'

The answer to this dilemma is found in the bible in Hosea four, verse six. "My people are destroyed for lack of knowledge." According to God's word all nations belong to God and all peoples, tribes and kindred are loved by God. The knowledge that had been denied to the indigenous Indians of the Pacific Northwest was the great truth of the Gospel message of the Bible. "For God so loved the world, that he gave his only begotten Son, that whosoever believeth in him should not perish, but have eternal life." (John 3:16) The Indians saw God and his Son Jesus Christ as a white God and a white son. They did not understand that the Almighty God of the bible was not a white God. They did not understand that the Almighty God of the bible was the same 'Great Spirit God' of the Indians that created all nations and all tribes and kindred of every color. They did not understand this truth in part because it was miss-represented by some of the missionaries. This confusion was accentuated by the Protestant/Catholic rift previously documented.

The confusion the Indian peoples experienced when they considered the blessing they saw over the white race and the rejection they felt from the 'Great Spirit that had forsaken them' must be examined in greater detail because the resolution to this dilemma is at the very heart of this research. It is common for all peoples to equate God's blessing with success and God's rejection with failure. In the Christian paradigm in issues of theology the opposite is true. The Almighty God of the bible so loved the world, (all kindreds, tribes and peoples) that He sent his only begotten Son to die for the composite sins of mankind. In other words God rejected his only begotten Son, and sacrificed his beloved to be a once and for all time sin sacrifice that all mankind could be reconciled back to the Father, i.e. the 'Great Spirit Chief.' The Christian faith demands understanding of opposites. In the Christian faith to win you must first be willing to lose. To live you must first be willing to die. To be accepted you must first be willing to be rejected. To gain eternal life the Christian must be willing to give up his worldly life. These are difficult spiritual concepts to teach within homogenous cultural groups. To teach these spiritual truths across cultural boundaries required great commitment, dedication and sacrifice few individuals were willing to give. For that reason we shall examine this process and the theological premises of the first Protestant missionaries in the next chapter.

Chief Seattle asked one of the essential question of this document. 'How can your God become our God and renew our prosperity and awaken in us dreams of returning greatness?' The purpose of the first waves of Protestant missionaries was to accomplish this goal. The watershed issue in the Oregon Territory was the Whitman Massacre not because this massacre led to the statehood of Oregon but more so because the massacre effectively ended the positive impact of the Protestant ministry to the Native American Indians of the Pacific Northwest. The Protestant missionaries were forced from all the Columbian plateau Indians including for the purposes of this research the Cayuse and Nez Perce at the most critical hour in their history. These Protestant missionaries came both to bring the truth of the message of liberty and freedom in Christ and the keys to prosperity in White mans civilization. The Indian nations had no white advocate to ensure justice and liberty in the new process of treaty negotiations. Chief Seattle expressed these grievances in his speech.

"If we have a common heavenly father He must be partial-or he came to his white children. We never saw him. He gave you laws but had no word for His red children whose teeming multitudes once filled this vast continent as stars fill the firmament. No we are two separate distinct races with separate destinies. There is little in common between us." (Nerburn, p. 72)

The Protestant missionaries that took their grievances to the Supreme Court in 1831 on behalf of the Cherokee nation ultimately prevailed only to have President Andrew Jackson refuse to honor the edict of the Supreme Court of the land. Things had changed since 1831. There had been a Civil War over the issue of slavery. There were no lands left in the west to relocate the American Indians. The Supreme Court had ruled the indigenous American tribes were sovereign nations and could negotiate as sovereign nations with the American governors. In this case Seattle was right. The two nations were soon to become separate distinct races with separate destinies. The separate destiny of the indigenous American Indian in the Pacific Northwest on reservations would be a tragedy in the beginning for the Indians. The laws God gave the forefathers of the American revolution were for the benefit of all tribes and peoples, not just white Americans. The early Protestant missionaries came to share these laws at the request of the Indians of the Pacific Northwest. The two races had the most important realities of life in common. They shared the same forests, the same rivers, the same land, the same natural resources, and the same common destiny. Whatever would become of America in the future would equally impact both races and both nations. "The ashes of our ancestors are sacred, and their resting place is hallowed ground. You wander far from the graves of your ancestors, and seemingly without regret. Your religion was written upon tablets of stone by the iron finger of your God so that you could not forget. The red man could never comprehend nor remember it." (Nerburn, p. 72)

The Indian nations saw the Americans as numerous as the grass of the valley because the Almighty had blessed the American Republic as no nation since possibly Israel. The message of the Protestant missionaries to the Indians was that the Creator would bless them in response to their willingness to live their lives according to the precepts of the Ten Commandments. The great shame of the American manifest destiny was that the nation began to believe God would bless them whether they obeyed the covenant or not. The Cherokee nation in the south accepted the teachings of the Protestant missionaries and the covenants of the Bible including the Ten Commandments; nevertheless, they were forced to abdicate their land to white southern plantation owners. This is one of the reasons some of the Indian nations began to believe the Christian God was a white god only and Jesus Christ was his white son.

Chief Seattle spoke of the fundamental Indian ancestral belief system. "Our religion is the traditions of our ancestors – the dreams of our old men, given them in the solemn hours of night by the Great Spirit, and the visions of our sachems - and is written in the hearts of our people. Your dead cease to love you and the land of their nativity as soon as they pass the portals of the tomb and wander beyond the stars. They are soon forgotten and never return. Our dead never forget the beautiful world that gave them being. They still love its verdant valleys, its murmuring rivers, it magnificent mountain sequestered vales and verdant-lined lakes and bays, and ever yearn in tender fond affection over the lonely hearted living, and often return from the Great beyond to visit, guide, console and comfort them." (Nerburn, p. 60)

The Native American ancestral religion taught the dead could return in the form of spirits to guide and console the living. The Indians did not believe the white race respected the earth and in particular the burial grounds in the manner the Native Americans did. Chief Joseph had a stronger Protestant Christian based faith. He believed the Great Spirit Chief who ruled from above would hold all men accountable for their individual actions. Chief Joseph, in contrast to Chief Seattle, believed the white race and the red race were one, "brothers of one father and one mother, with one sky above us and one government for all." (Nerburn, p. 60)

Chief Seattle concluded his epic speech with one final exhortation. "Day and night cannot dwell together. The red man has ever fled the approach of the white man, as the morning mist flees before the morning sun. However, your proposition seems fair and I think that my people will accept it and will retire to the reservation you offer them....Then we will dwell in peace, for the words of the Great White Chief seem to be the words of nature speaking to my people out of dense darkness. It matters little where we pass the remnant of our days. They will not be many. The Indians' night promises to be dark. Not a single star of hope hovers above his horizon. Sad-voiced winds moan in the distance. Grim fate seems to be on the red man's trail, and wherever he goes he will hear the approaching footsteps of his fell destroyer and prepare stolidly to meet his doom, as does the wounded doe that hears the approaching footsteps of the hunter. A few more moons, a few more winters – and not one of the descendants of the mighty hosts that once moved over this broad land or lived in happy homes, protected by the Great Spirit, will remain to mourn over the graves of a people once more powerful and hopeful than yours. But why should I mourn at the untimely fate of my people? Tribe follows tribe, and nation follows nation, like the waves of the sea. It is the order of nature, and regret is useless. Your time of decay may be distant, but it surely will come. For even the white man whose God talked with him as friend to friend, cannot be exempt from the common destiny. We may be brothers after all. We shall see." (Nerburn, pp. 73, 74)

Chief Seattle lamented the destruction of his race, yet he warned the victors not to be haughty. Certainly historical documents have illustrated that the Creator talked with the forefathers of the American Republic as he talked intimately with the great patriarch Abraham, the friend of God. Chief Seattle concluded his exhortation with these final words. "Let him be just and deal kindly with my people. For the dead are not powerless. Dead did I say? There is no death. Only a change of worlds." (Nerburn, p. 76)

This research has documented how the Nez Perce were lied to and cheated by the American government and white settlers. This is where the term "Indian giver" came from. Fortunately not all treaties turned out so one-sided.

Chapter 29

The Bridge Between the Protestant Almighty and the Indian Great Spirit Chief

By the end of the first decade of the nineteenth century the great democratic experiment of the American Republic, grounded in the idealism of liberty, justice and freedom for all, was in decline. The future of the nation was threatened by greed for land and material wealth and oppression in the form of the institution of slavery and Indian injustice. The emerging nation turned away from its rich religious heritage of equality for all and embraced a new spirit of independence from all authority. Into this spiritual void, zealous Protestant evangelical preachers began calling American citizens back to a personal relationship with the God of their fathers. The leading evangelist of the hour, Charles G. Finney, led over 500,000 Americans into a personal commitment to God. Finney became the lightning rod that the Almighty used to bring America back to its commitment to liberty and justice for all. Under his leadership Oberlin College became the first university in the land to award degrees to women and blacks. His college was the hub of the Underground Railroad, which secretly brought slaves to freedom. Finney helped form the Benevolent Empire that turned America into a thriving beehive of volunteer societies that would battle the multiple injustices of the emerging nation. These volunteer societies energized and revolutionized the church in America and the result was a spiritual explosion that made the emerging Republic the greatest Christian nation in the world.

The Second Great Awakening shook the ground America stood on. The Methodist Church, aflame with the missionary zeal of Finney, sent out scores of itinerant circuit horseback preachers. The Baptist Church established a lay ministry evangelistic outreach that swept across the frontier. Protestant churches including the Congregationalists, Disciples of Christ, Presbyterian, and Episcopal helped form a Christian ethos for the emerging nation. It was at this time in response to slavery, prison abuse, intemperance, and the Indian removal policy that spiritual revival began to break out across the entire land, making America the wonder of the world. The Second Great Awakening started the great evangelical movement that birthed the American Board of Missions in 1810, the American Bible Society in 1816, the American Sunday School Movement in 1817, and the American Home Mission Society in 1826. The Protestant missionary outreach to the American Indians was birthed through this Second Great Awakening.

Protestant evangelicalism of the nineteenth century was the dominant force shaping and inspiring the American people for both social reform and missionary expansion. It was these Protestant mission boards that sent missionaries to the American Indians. What kind of men and women answered this call to dedicate their lives to live among the so-called heathen indigenous American Indians? We have already documented the commitment of Marcus and Narcissa Whitman and Henry and Eliza Spalding. We also documented their largely unsuccessful efforts to enlist support for the mission to the Oregon Territory. In light of the missionary zeal of the hour, it was perplexing that so few answered the call to the last great frontier in the West.

A Protestant missionary manual of 1840 illustrated the requirements for this life in the unknown wilderness of the West. "In no other service are deep piety, genuine personal holiness, and singleness of purpose in the service of Christ more indispensably required." (Coleman, p, 22) At the time of the Whitman massacre new missionary candidates were exhorted: "The work to which you have given yourself, and to which we trust you are called of God, will demand your whole time and energies…untiring effort, incessant vigilance, great self-denial, much patience and forbearance, and above all, great zeal for God and love to souls. It is a work for which you must permanently walk by faith, looking for your reward not here—in the approbation of men or the gratitude of those for whom you labor." (Coleman, pp. 22, 23) These missionaries were required to attain both undergraduate degrees and seminary degrees when few Americans chose a college-required profession. These missionaries had to be physically strong, academically bright, and spiritually gentle in order to learn and appreciate the indigenous Indian culture and language. In short, these Protestant missionaries were the finest sons of the Republic the nation had to offer and unfortunately there were not many to go around.

Any ray of hope for the emerging Republic's Indian policy fell by default into the hands of these Protestant missionaries. By the end of the Civil War most of the Indian nations of America had moved onto reservations. Chief Joseph lamented, "could an animal grow fat tied to a post?" Many Indian nations were forced to go on the warpath in an attempt to survive American injustice. By 1871 Congress was forced to abolish the land removal/treaty pretense and admit the Indians were essentially now wards of the state. President Grant initiated the so-called "peace policy" toward the Native Americans. The historical record revealed the only American institution to deal effectively and constructively with the Indians was the Protestant missionary network. Unfortunately, even many of these zealous missionaries often attempted to convert the Indian to the white man's Christianity and the American way of life without learning and appreciating Native American culture. Often that meant American dress, haircuts, and manners that further separated the Native Americans from their heritage and way of life. The American government virtually threw its hands into the air when the ill-conceived land removal policy of Andrew Jackson became a national embarrassment.

The government turned to the church for deliverance for the downtrodden American Indians. Chief Joseph became a lightning rod of embarrassment to the proud nation. Helen Hunt Jackson's book *A Century of Dishonor* came out in 1881, further prodding the nation to repentance. Unfortunately, the proud nation had so bungled the handling of the Native Americans that no program or act of Congress could fix the problem. The Board of Indian Commissioners was established in 1869 and for six decades the Protestant churches worked with this board to provide the only viable and positive ray of hope to the original American citizens now locked in prison reservations. The New Deal under Franklin D. Roosevelt represented the first true change in spirit toward the Native American Indians. The foundation of a national effort to allow the Native American spirit to rise again began in 1934 with the New Deal.

We shall examine this new wave of hope in the next chapter, especially as it relates to the Native American Indians of the Columbia Plateau in the Pacific Northwest. This new wave of liberty and justice was the vision of missionaries like Marcus and Narcissa Whitman and the prayer of Chief Joseph. For the new wave of liberty and justice to bear real fruit for the Native American Indians there had to be a recognition that the Almighty God of the Bible and the Great Spirit Chief were in principle the same God.

The Protestant vision and hope for the American Indian to survive and better yet prosper in white man's culture was a massive challenge. Chief Seattle did not see his people making that quantum leap. Chief Joseph knew his people must change and adapt or they would not survive in the white man's world. The Protestant missionaries Marcus and Narcissa Whitman knew that the Columbia Plateau Indians must adapt to white man's culture if they were to sustain their way of living with the advent of American laws and mores. After the Whitman massacre and the expulsion of the Protestant missionaries, the Indians of the Oregon Territory were left to fend for themselves. The dismal failure of the forced Indian reservation policy caused the American government to throw up its hands in despair hoping the church would somehow clean up the mess. Some of the missionary organizations attempted to make the American Indians look, act and feel like white American Christians and that didn't work either. Once again the problem was rooted in scripture: "My people are destroyed for lack of knowledge."

The Native American culture was unique. The Indian men were accustomed to providing for their families and culture by hunting and fishing. The Indians were semi-nomadic and relished their freedom and liberty to come and go as they pleased. To cultivate the land was women's work. The very fact that Whitman and Spalding were able to teach some of the Cayuse braves to cultivate the land was a monumental accomplishment. The woman's place of food gathering on root and berry expeditions also ended. In actual fact the Indians didn't know what to do with each other, particularly in regards to the husband and wife relationship, in these foreign-mandated Indian reservations.

A new wave of Protestant missionaries was sent to the Indians of the Pacific Northwest and they were in varying degrees instrumental in helping the indigenous American Indians accomplish a monumental mores switch. Presbyterian publications detail the "degraded position of women in every heathen land." (Coleman, p. 94) If there was one horse the male would ride and the woman would walk carrying her children. By 1888 Nez Perce missionary Kate McBeth noted the Kamiah Indian women were "no longer man's servant but his equal." (Coleman, p. 94) The Presbyterian missionaries to the Nez Perce taught the arts of American life including sewing, washing, cooking and nurturing children to the girls and cultivating, farming and working at simple trades for the boys. Some may claim these practices amounted to an ethnocentric white Christian indoctrination, but the cold reality of the hour was that some of the Native American cultural practices had to be changed. The cruelty of such practices as female infanticide and suttee (burning of widows on the husbands' cremation fire) had to be ended if the American Indians were to survive.

The cry of Chief Joseph was liberty, freedom and equality. He eloquently implored the American government to treat his people with equality. Chief Seattle ended his speech with "let him be just and deal kindly with my people." (Nerburn, p. 76) Disappointingly, the American policy toward the indigenous peoples of the nation was fraught with injustice. Fortunately, the fundamental standard of the American Protestant missionary movement to the Indians of the West was a vehement denunciation of racism at an hour when the majority of American people to some degree justified racism. Many of America's founding fathers abdicated to racism in regard to slavery. The Protestant missionary organizations worked diligently to change this racist mindset. Their stated goal for the Native Americans was to see them "placed on a footing of perfect civil and social equality with the surrounding white population." (Coleman, p. 142) Walter Lowrie, secretary of the Baptist Foreign Missions, represented the attitude of these missionaries. He believed with education the Indian could "know as much as the white man, read God's own book, read the books of the white man…and in short to be equal to the white man in all respects." (Coleman, p. 141)

Many Protestant missionaries and conscientious Catholic priests and nuns ministered fairly and diligently toward the Native American peoples to prepare them to one day prosper in white man's civilization. The American Indians were confused at first because they believed the Great Spirit Chief would speak to them and protect them under the authority of the white man's Great Chief (President). When they witnessed the white man prosper and the Great Chief and his ambassadors lie to them, they began to believe the white man's God favored the white man and could not be trusted. The elder Chief Joseph renounced his Christianity when the white man lied to him regarding treaty promises. Confusion about the white man's God has never been fully rectified for the Native American Indian nations. Once again the scripture exhortation rings true: "My people are destroyed for lack of knowledge." (Hosea 4:6)

Chapter 30

The Confederated Tribes of the Umatilla, Walla Walla and Cayuse and the Peace Treaty of 1855

From the very first contact between the Indians and Caucasians in the Pacific Northwest, the pioneer explorers, fur trappers, missionaries and settlers developed a harmonious relationship with the indigenous Columbia Plateau tribes. This research has documented this historically unique merging of two races from white men's records. The Native Americans felt the same way. The Confederated Tribes of the Umatilla documented, "The trappers were much impressed by the native religion in the area and found no conflict between Christianity and Native religion." (Confederated Tribes of the Umatilla (CTUIR) website, history, part 2, p. 2) The American Indians of the Columbia Plateau honored a creator God (Great Spirit Chief) that ruled from above, and these tribes received the teachings of Christianity with receptive hearts. Those receptive hearts began to close when the white settlers began to encroach upon their land, and more so when the white man did not honor or respect the treaties they had agreed to.

After the Whitman massacre, the Cayuse nation came under great duress. The Nez Perce captured the five Cayuse chiefs responsible for the killing and they were tried and hanged by the Oregon provisional government. The Columbia Plateau tribes were decimated by the measles and diphtheria epidemic of 1847 and after that hour the Protestant missionaries were no longer present to nurture and advocate for positive measures toward merger into white man's civilization. Under the nurturing hand of the Protestant missionaries the Indians had been cultivating the ground near the Whitman mission and selling their produce to the wagon train emigrants for years. With Dr. Whitman as their advocate, the Columbia Plateau Indians would have been well placed to negotiate a most favorable land allocation with the encroaching white government. After the Whitmans and their Presbyterian associates were murdered and all the Protestant missionaries of the Oregon Territory were ordered away from their missionary posts, there was no Christian advocate to ensure justice for these Indians.

The Donation Land Act of 1850 further agitated an already pressure-packed situation. The American government was encouraging its citizens to move to the Oregon Territory without first extinguishing Indian claims to the land. The munificence and good will carefully fostered by the Lewis and Clark Expedition, the first fur traders, and the missionaries had been reciprocated with benevolence and tolerance by the Columbia Plateau Indians for nearly fifty years. That carefully constructed, wonderfully weaved merger of the two

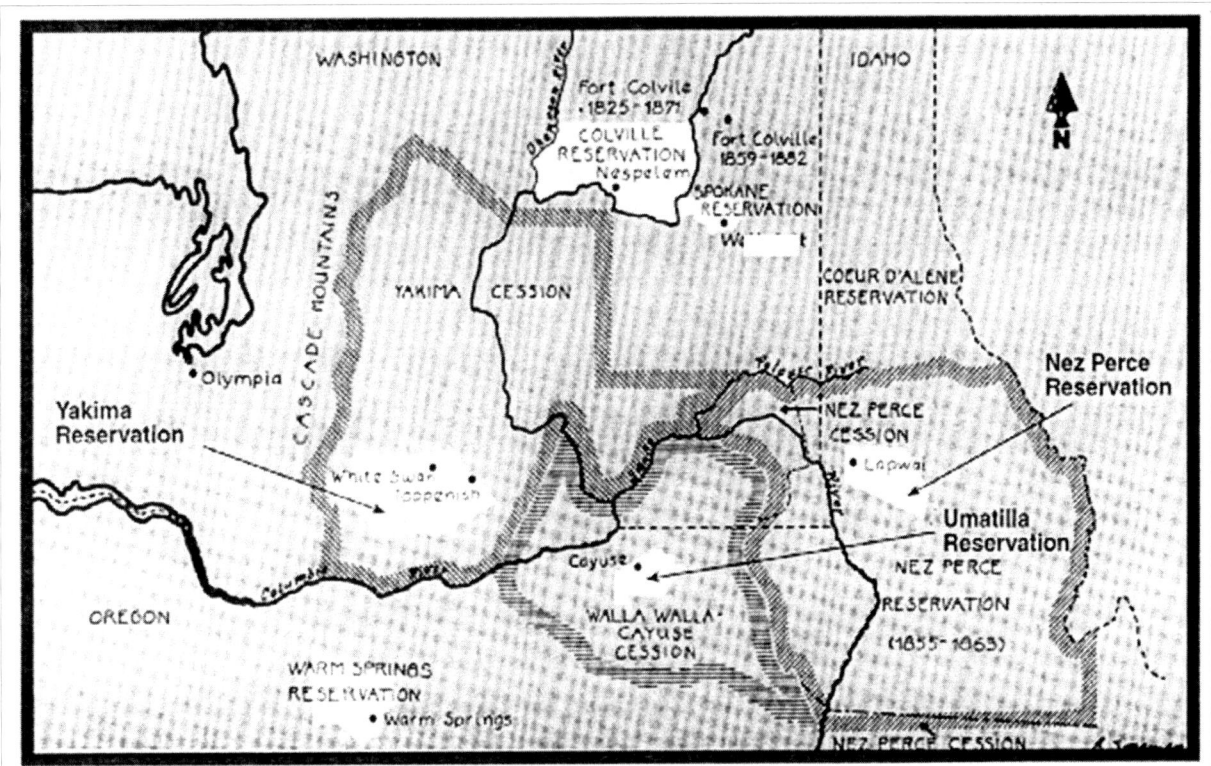

Map of Indian Reservations 1855

races was shattered by the Whitman massacre. Few historical heritages in western civilization can be found to replicate the uplifting meshing of the white and red races as exemplified in the Pacific Northwest between 1837 and 1847.

    The Donation Land Act created an unstable arena of distrust between the races and made Eastern Oregon a tenuous place for white settlers to even traverse through. By 1854 the nervous American pioneer settlers pressured the government to authorize negotiations in order to purchase Indian lands and establish reservations so the white settlers could have security in the territory. At this time Governor Isaac Stevens of the Washington Territory and Superintendent of Indian Affairs for the Oregon Territory Joel Palmer approached the combined Columbia Plateau Indians near the Whitmans' missionary station at Waiilatpu. Stevens had authority from the President of the United States to settle Indian and foreign claims, conduct rapid surveys, establish educational and transportation opportunities, and provide military protection.

    Governor Stevens attempted to place the Umatilla, Walla Walla and Cayuse tribes on the Yakima Indian Reservation. The tribal chiefs stood firm and successfully negotiated the land of the Umatilla River watershed for their permanent home. These three tribes ceded 6.4 million acres of the Oregon Territory to the United States but reserved the rights for fishing, hunting, gathering foods and medicine and pasturing livestock in perpetuity. These tribes reserved 510,000 acres for their homeland, a homeland guaranteed by the American government.

    The land deeded to these Columbia Plateau Indians was largely secluded from the path of western immigration. The Indian tribes along the banks of the Columbia River were removed by force when necessary. The United States government agreed in the treaty to move the Oregon Trail south of the Reservation to avoid conflicts between Indians and American settlers. Congress ratified the treaty on March

8, 1859. By the time of treaty ratification those tribes that resisted the treaty process had been defeated by the armed forces of the American government. The reservation Indians were required to lay down their guns and ammunition, making them vulnerable to the raids of the Shoshoneans. Once the Columbia Plateau Indians ceded their land to the American government they were required to move onto their designated reservation. Those Indians who refused to cooperate were moved by force, sometimes by the white settlers, onto reservations.

The Indians on the reservation were not safe from encroachment especially from white settlers. The Indians had to trust the American government's Indian Department to give them protection from horse thieves, whisky peddlers and white womanizers. The transition to reservation life was a most agonizing situation for the Native Americans. These Indians had roamed freely for centuries throughout the Columbia Plateau. The Blue Mountains was their playground. The rivers and tributaries of the Columbia River were their lifeblood. Their horses ran free throughout the lush foothills of those magnificent mountains. Their traditional food source was now on lands they were forced to cede to the Americans. Even the reservation choice was difficult because whatever choice they made would separate them from allied tribes and bands that the Indians previously visited and lived with at will.

They were no longer free men. Instead of relying on age-old methods of semi-nomadic living they were now required to learn what they termed the Christian work ethic and the new concept of self-sufficiency common in white man's culture. These Columbia Native American tribes were now at the mercy of white man's law and justice. The Native American Indians believed the culture they were learning was based on Christianity, but in reality their Christian advocates had been murdered and forced to flee the Columbia Plateau and the government made sure the Protestant missionaries did not return for over two decades. The Christian culture and work ethic the Indians learned had nothing to do with Christianity, as no Protestants were allowed to oversee this ministry in the beginning. What happened to the faith, the Christian way of life, of the Cayuse/Columbia Plateau Indians that had been taught by the Whitmans and their fellow missionaries? Did these Native Americans continue in their Christian faith and manner as taught by the missionaries? This research will study that question in the next chapter.

This was a dark hour for the Columbia Plateau Indians. Indian agents were assigned to oversee educating and civilizing the Indians. Conflicts arose because these agents did not understand Native American culture, especially when these agents did not go through the tribal chiefs and headmen and directly supervised the Indians. The Jesuit missionaries continued to teach their Catholic traditions under the leadership of Father Brouillet, the same Jesuit priest who carried out the orders that led to the Whitman massacre. It was not long until Indians of school age were required to cut their hair, wear uniforms, and submit to strict discipline. The children were not allowed to speak their own language. The Indian agents believed they were doing what was best for the Indian children, preparing them for white man's civilization.

In 1849 the Bureau of Indian Affairs was transferred to the Department of the Interior. This policy led to political appointees. Often these Indian agents were appointed as political favors and the appointees had little to no knowledge or conviction for the job. The Indians on all the reservations of America languished during the dark hour of the Civil War. The Indians were called to fight for both the North and South and suffered higher casualties, percentage wise, than any other ethnic group in the Union. The Cherokee nation was nearly wiped out during the Civil War. The Bureau of Indian Affairs was in shambles after two decades.

In 1869 President Grant's "Peace Policy" initiated an Indian program where missionary boards provided agents to manage the reservations. The government allowed the Quaker, Protestant and Catholic denominations of the victorious North to choose agents who oversaw the teaching of denominational distinctives at respective reservations. The Indians had no choice in the denomination that ministered their reservation. Unfortunately, both the Catholics and Protestants saw few if any cultural values worth preserving in the Indian groups they ministered to and sought to convert the Indians to their respective faiths. The government of the United States financed the schools and ministry activities of these denominations for nearly a decade until controversy forced the government to start its own schools in 1878. By 1899 the United States Congress ended all sectarian school funding. By this time the damage had been done and by the end of the century the grand reservation experiment was a dismal, pathetic failure.

The policy of the United States government toward the American Indian was bathed in compromise, deception and greed from the beginning. Jeremiah Evarts, a Christian lawyer and secretary of the American Missionary Board, warned Andrew Jackson and the nation of the injustice of the Indian removal and reservation policy in the very beginning. He argued that if America did not manifest moral courage and equality toward the Native American Indians the soul of the nation would be compromised. By the end of the century the soul of America was compromised and the Indian reservations were in disarray.

The Confederated Tribes of the Umatilla fortunately fared better than most Indian reservations. These tribes had not been displaced to the extent of most of the other reservation Indians. The Catholic and Protestant heritage of the first missionaries acted as a foundation to at least give these tribes direction. Father Adolph Vermeersh, a Belgian Jesuit priest, replaced Father Brouillet and moved St. Anne's from Umatilla to a Pendleton campus in 1865. In 1883 St. Anne's was moved again to its present site below Emigrant Hill. A Catholic church was built at this location in 1884 called St. Joseph's. The Catholic Sisters of Mercy operated a boarding school at this site for four years until it was moved to its present location of Pendleton. A Protestant mission was established at Tutuilla, six miles East of Pendleton, in 1882 under the leadership of a young Nez Perce missionary by the name of James Hayes. Hayes was student of Sue McBeth in Lapwai, Idaho. Hayes was a zealous preacher, said to have ministered at one time or other to every Indian tribe of the Northwest Country. The Presbyterian Church at Tutuilla was the direct continuation of the early faith of the Nez Perce warriors that sought the Book of God a half century before. The Tutuilla Presbyterian Church sustained the Christian faith of the Nez Perce-Cayuse Indians taught by the Presbyterian missionaries. These Columbia Plateau Native Americans held firm to their faith in God after the massacre of the white missionaries.

The Confederated Tribes of the Umatilla had a choice of religion, something most reservations did not have. Unfortunately, the schism caused by the Whitman massacre would not be resolved in the 19th century or even in the 20th century. When the government started their own school in 1889, they restricted religious instruction as well as traditional native ceremonies, dancing, songs, language, arts and crafts. The Jesuits continued their ministry until 1961 when the Baker Diocese took over and built a new St. Andrew's church dedicated in 1964. The Presbyterian ministry at Tutuilla (the first Christian church in the Pacific Northwest) will be chronicled in the next chapter.

The reservation lands were under attack from the beginning. It did not take long for white settlers to discover the agricultural value of the rich Blue Mountain foothills. Fortunately for the Indians, no gold of merit was discovered in the Umatilla River watershed. By the late 1860s public meetings were held to discuss ways to open lands to the public that had been deeded to the confederated Indians. The white settlers had successfully forced the government to rescind the treaty of 1855 with the Nez Perce in 1863. The confederated tribes of the Umatilla had reserved 510,000 acres but by the time it was surveyed their reservation had been whittled down to 245,000 acres. The remaining Indian lands were under constant pressure from the white settlers. The commissioner of Indian Affairs for the Umatilla Reservation documented these tensions in 1878: "The rapid settling of that portion of the state has surrounded the reservation with white farming population, who have already run across it a telegraph-line and several roads. The route of the Blue Mountains and Columbia River Railroad line transverses the southern portion, and the junction of the road with a proposed branch line is to fall within reservation boundaries. This valuable tract is occupied by only 1,000 Indians, who cultivate between two and three thousand acres, and use of so much of the remainder of their lands as is required to furnish range for their 22,000 head of stock." (CTUIR history part 2)

The American Indians had no rights as citizens of the United States at this time. The commissioner of Indian Affairs was the designated government representative for the Indians. At this time, well over a decade since the Civil War, black or mulatto colored human beings were not allowed to reside in the state of Oregon. The growing land needs of the early Oregon pioneers motivated them to urge Congress to transgress the treaty rights of the Confederated Umatilla tribes. The city of Pendleton was settled on land deeded to the Confederated Tribes of the Umatilla. The Indian agent documented the concerns of the Confederated Tribes. "For several years past the citizens of Oregon have made persistent efforts to have these lands open to settlement, and several bills to that effect have been introduced in Congress. This desire, which gains strength yearly, is well known to the Indians, and begets a feeling of restlessness and uncertainty decidedly unfavorable to their progress in civilization." (CTUIR, pt. 2 www.umatilla.nsa.us/salmonpolicy.html)

Tribal members of the Cayuse joined forces with Chief Joseph in his historic flight in 1877. Most of the Cayuse warriors were either killed or never returned to their homeland on the Umatilla Reservation. At this juncture the population of the three tribes was 1,000 Indians. The fact they still had 22,000 horses and livestock illustrated their relative prosperity, especially in comparison to reservations in other parts of the nation. The foothills of the Blue Mountains continued to be a lush pasture with year-round grazing and grass resources without limit. The Confederated Tribes had made a relatively good deal with the American government, making them the envy of white Oregonians who came to Eastern Oregon.

The Confederated Tribes of the Umatilla had good reason to feel uncertain regarding their future. Two Acts of Congress were about to change their lives. In 1885 the Slater Allotment Act established the prototype for sale of "surplus" Indian lands. Of course there were no surplus Indian lands. In 1887 Congress passed the Dawes Act that essentially broke up the Indian reservations. The Congress of the United States essentially argued that the Indian reservation policy was a failure and the answer was to assimilate the Indian into American society and culture. To facilitate this new policy the Indians would be given individual title to their own land from the reservation. Proponents of the Dawes Act argued that the Indians should have the same right of personal possession of his own land as any other American citizen or immigrant. Many well-meaning, pro-Indian Americans supported this policy. Once again, God's people, the American Indians, were destroyed for lack of knowledge on the part of those who purported to help them. The Dawes Act destroyed traditional native culture. The American Indians were a communal society not comfortable with the so-called individual Christian work ethic. The goal of the Dawes Act was to assimilate the Indian people into white society. The impact of full implementation of the Dawes Acts on Indian culture, religion, tradition, leadership and government would have a devastating impact on their way of life. The following illustration shows Alice Fletcher, a government agent, helping Chief Joseph choose land for his own family farm.

It should come as no surprise that the result of the Dawes Act was demoralizing for the American Indian. By the time the Act was rescinded in 1934 the American Indians had lost 90 million acres of reservation land. The Umatilla Reservation was reduced from 245,699 acres to 158,000 acres. Greed and avarice ruled as the Dawes Act opened Indian lands to the white public. The Indians did not understand tax laws and many lost their land. Others sold their land because they could not afford to farm it. Nearly 100,000 acres of the Umatilla Reservation was allotted to non-Indians.

Even without the devastation of the Dawes Act, the Umatilla Reservation was being sliced up by avarice and deception. The Oregon Trail was not moved south away from the reservation as required by the 1855 treaty. In addition the Indians claimed the boundary of the reservation was mis-surveyed and the town of Pendleton was allocated 640 acres of reservation land without Indian approval. To the present hour the city of Pendleton rests on land deeded to the Confederated Tribes of the Umatilla Indians.

Chief Joseph with Dawes Act government agent Alice Fletcher and interpreter

The most devastating encroachment on the Umatilla Reservation was the railroad. The American government allowed the railroad to slice through the heart of the reservation without regard to the cultural and environmental concerns of the Confederated Umatilla tribes. Article 10 of the 1855 treaty allowed the creation of roads, easements, and right-of-way for "public purposes." The powerful thundering steel locomotives roaring through the reservation must have felt like a dagger through the hearts of these powerless Native Americans. The government provided lucrative subsidies for the railroad to plow through the Indian land without regard to the Umatilla River or any of its tributaries. Legislation from the American Congress continued to provide railroad land grants and allotment acts that enhanced non-Indian interests. The Umatilla Indians were feeling the raw power of America's manifest destiny up close and personal. The railroad would only be a precursor to a more dangerous train, the train of material capitalism powered by politically manipulated courts that allowed non-Indians to gain ownership of reservation land.

The treaty of 1855 had given the Umatilla Indians a wonderful piece of real estate. The challenge of the twentieth century for the beleaguered Native Americans would be to hold on to what was left of their heritage. A number of Congressional Acts enacted at the beginning of the 20th century worked to allow non-Indians to gain Indian land. The Leasing Act of 1891, the Heirship Act of 1902, the Burke Act of 1906 and the Wheeler Howard Act all expedited further removal of Indian lands from the reservation.

By the time the American government finally corrected the injustice of these laws with the Indian Reorganization Act of 1934 it was a wonder the Umatilla Reservation still existed. By the hour of the Great Depression beginning on Black Tuesday, Oct 29, 1929 the condition of American Indian Reservations was deplorable. The remaining American Indians were impoverished and the Native American civilization was dying. The moral heart of the nation has been seared with greed and avarice. A mighty judgment from the hand of the Almighty, the Great Spirit Chief of the American Indians, humbled the nation of manifest destiny and demonstrated that divine providence was no longer blessing the maturing but now tainted Republic. It was no coincidence that the Miriam Report, a comprehensive study of post-Congressional Acts and their devastating impact on the Indian nations of America, was released at the same time that God judged the nation with the Great Depression.

On August 22, 1787 the great American revolutionary statesman and father of the Bill of Rights, George Mason from the colony of Virginia, rose from his Constitutional Convention seat to proclaim the great principal of national accountability. "Every master of slaves is born a petty tyrant. They bring the judgment of heaven upon a country. As nations cannot be rewarded or punished in the next world, they must be in this. By an inevitable chain of causes and effects, Providence punishes national sins, by national calamities." (Federer, p. 423)

The greed, oppression, inequality and injustice that fueled slavery led to the tragic bloodbath of the Civil War that spilled the blood of nearly 600,000 American lives. George Mason's prophecy proved correct about national judgment. Providence punished America for the injustice of slavery. In the same manner Jeremiah Evarts, under the pen name of William Penn, warned the American nation of national calamity if the injustice and oppression manifest by the American government upon the American Indian was not repented of and corrected. By the end of the third decade of the 20th century in America the Red race had nearly been exterminated. The indigenous American Indian people were largely locked on reservations. They were desperately poor, out of work, discouraged, physically broken and disheartened. They had been cheated out of ninety percent of the reservation land given to them in multiple treaties and there was no champion on the horizon to give them hope.

In most reservations they were reduced to beggars, mocked as alcoholics and scorned as Americans. Chief Seattle had warned the American Republic: "Your time of decay may be distant, but it will surely come. For even the white man, whose God talked with him as friend with friend, cannot be exempt from the common destiny....Let him be just and deal kindly with my people. For the dead are not powerless." (Nerburn, p. 76) Chief Joseph echoed a similar refrain. "When the white man treats the Indian as they treat each other, then we will have no more wars. We shall all be alike, brothers of one father and one mother, with one sky above us and one government for all. Then the Great Spirit Chief who rules above will smile upon the land, and send rain to wash out the bloody spots made by brothers' hands from the face of the earth. For this time the Indian race are waiting and praying." (Nerburn, p. 61)

Indeed, God did see the oppression and injustice of the American nation upon the Indians. The Great Spirit Chief of the Indians did hear the prayer of the Indian nations. The prophet Daniel had warned Nebuchadnezzar, the great king of the Babylonian empire, to "break off thy sins by righteousness, and thine iniquities by showing mercy to the poor" (Daniel 4:27), or his kingdom would be removed from him. King Nebuchadnezzar learned what all nations must learn: "till thou know that the most High ruleth in the kingdom of men, and giveth it to whomsoever he will." (Daniel 4:25) God saw the great depression of his Indian nations. In response, God brought a great depression upon the nation that had forsaken its covenant with the Almighty.

The Great Depression hit America and the world like a thunderbolt. Almost overnight the nation went from riches to rags. The American Indians locked up on Indian reservations were unemployed. By the end of the third decade of the 1900s unemployment went from 3% to 25% for the American people. By 1932, 55% of the work force in America lost their jobs. The reservation incarcerated American Indians had little to trade and few partners to trade with. By 1930 worldwide trade dropped 62%. Industrial production dropped 36% in America. As the economy of the Native Americans had collapsed, so did the nation's banking system, causing a frightening wave of panic that touched every household in the nation. As the Native Americans endured generations of drought mostly on reservations that lacked cold clean water, drought struck America, creating the dust bowls of the Bible belt. As the American Indians had suffered for generations, now the whole nation suffered. As the American Indians had fallen into depression, the entire nation was gripped with the Great Depression. America and much of the world was brought to its knees. New policies and national corrections were the order of the day. The nation indeed repented of many of its errant ways. For the American Indian the Great Depression was the beginning of hope. The Indian Restoration Act of 1934 was the first installment of the answer to the prayer of Chief Joseph and fellow chiefs of all the Indian nations of America.

American forefather George Mason was prophetic. The Almighty does reward and judge nations in this life. Those peoples and nations that oppressed a downtrodden people, such as the American Indian, would one day be judged. In like manner those people and powers that blessed the American Indian would be rewarded.

The first sentence of the Miriam Report stated: "An overwhelming majority of Indians are poor, even extremely poor, and they are not adjusted to the economic and social system of the dominant white civilization." (www.skc.edu/netbook/of-1ra.htm) The Indian Restoration Act of 1934 was the beginning of revival for the indigenous Native American peoples of America. This Act corrected four decades of the injustice meted out upon the Indian peoples. The Act established and sustained tribal governments, it ended the sale of Indian lands, it provided a viable plan for tribal economic growth, it established preferential hiring for Indians in the BIA (Bureau of Indian Affairs) and it assisted the tribes in their endeavor to maintain traditional culture.

The Umatilla Tribal Council voted two to one to accept the provisions of the Indian Reorganization Act. The Confederated Tribes now had a blueprint and the authority to finally control their own future in white man's civilization. Still, independence and prosperity would not come easily. The BIA still governed tribal affairs. Nevertheless, the Tribal Council was slowly gaining the confidence necessary to govern their own nation. It was a process of necessity because they lacked the knowledge and authority to correct the multiple cancers that were destroying their native way of life. For instance, the encroachment on their reservation and procedures such as abusive logging practices, over-grazing and unwise irrigation practices had ended the salmon run on the Umatilla River by 1914.

In 1947 a committee of tribal members was authorized by the Tribal Council to research ways to establish self-government. That historic day arrived in 1949 when the Constitution and By-Laws of the Confederated Tribes of the Umatilla Reservation were ratified. By the middle of the twentieth century, nearly one hundred years after the historic peace treaty of 1855, the Columbia Plateau Indians of the Umatilla Reservation had the authority and power to govern themselves as a sovereign nation within the American Republic. The needs of the Indians were great and the grievances regarding the trespasses of the treaty of 1855 were colossal; nevertheless, the Indians finally had the promise of liberty and freedom guaranteed by the Protestant Reformation and the Constitution of the United States of America. The Constitution of the Confederated Tribes established the power and authority for these Native American Indians to determine their own destiny.

The stirring advances of the Native American Indians of the Pacific Northwest in the latter portion of the 20th century were accentuated with the addition of the gaming industry. The impact of the gambling industry on Native American culture has yet to be assessed. Nevertheless, the Nez Perce warriors who sought the written Word of God sowed the seeds of self-government. The ministry of the Presbyterian missionaries led by the Whitmans and the Spaldings further nurtured the seeds of the faith. Those seeds of faith in God would not perish after the massacre of the Protestant missionaries at Walla Walla, for they were sown in good soil. An unpublished manuscript written by J. M. Cornelison, the white missionary who would continue the work of the Whitmans a half-century after their deaths was prophetically titled *The Seed of the Martyrs*. We shall examine this manuscript in the next chapter.

Chapter 31

The Tutuilla Presbyterian Church

One of the significant issues yet to be documented by historians was the question of what happened to the church and ministry to the Cayuse and Columbia Plateau Indians established by Marcus and Narcissa Whitman after they were martyred. The Confederated Tribes of the Umatilla recently discovered an unpublished manuscript written in 1957 by Dr. J. M. Cornelison, minister of the Tutuilla Presbyterian Church and missionary to the Umatilla Indian Reservation from 1899 to 1942. The original manuscript is under the care of the Confederated Tribes at the Tamastslikt Cultural Institute near Pendleton. Dr. Cornelison, in a manuscript he called *The Seed of the Martyrs*,

Major Lee Moorehouse photograph of the Tutuilla Church in 1900.

documented the history and growth of the Cayuse Native American church initiated by the Whitmans in 1837. Dr. Cornelison was the first white minister to be commissioned by the Presbyterian Church to minister and live among the Umatilla, Walla Walla, and Cayuse Indians since the massacre at WAI-I-LAT-PU in 1847.

This research has previously documented that the United States government prohibited missionaries from ministering to the Indians after the Whitman massacre until after the peace accord of 1855. Spalding was allowed to return to Lapwai in 1858 but the American government forced Spalding to leave his mission at Lapwai once again in 1863. The advent and severity of the Civil War further compromised Protestant missionary momentum to the Columbia Plateau Native Americans. Nevertheless, Spalding did return once again to the Nez Perce with Miss Sue McBeth, an ardent Bible teacher, whom we have previously documented. Under the teaching of McBeth many Nez Perce men became zealous ministers of the Gospel and Dr. Cornelison documented these men "soon began to give part time evangelistic services among the Cayuse and Umatilla Indians in what later became Oregon and on the Umatilla Reservation." (Cornelison, *The Seed of the Martyrs*, p. 2) Cornelison documented the old Presbytery of Idaho initiated by the Spaldings included Baker, Union and Umatilla counties of eastern Oregon. The Presbytery of Idaho in 1882 sent a committee of three ministers to reorganize the church among the Umatilla and Cayuse Indians. "The

Committee of Presbytery consisted of Rev. G. L. Deffenbaugh, who had been a Missionary among the Nez Perce and spoke their language and two Indian Ministers, Rev. William Wheeler and Rev. Robert Williams. This re-organization was affected in the home of Win-Nanpts-Noot (or Elijah Lowrie)." (Cornelison, p. 2)

The Cayuse and associated Columbia Plateau Native Americans sustained their Christian faith for 37 years until the Protestant ministry established by the Whitmans was reestablished and reorganized in 1882. Dr. Cornelison lamented the fact that the Presbyterian Church U.S.A. allowed the ministry initiated by the great Presbyterian missionaries to languish for such an extended period of time. In 1935 the General Assembly of the Presbyterian Church listed the church of WAI-I-LAT-PU as "Organized August 18, 1838. Dissolved by Massacre November 29, 1847." (Cornelison, p. 3) Dr. Cornelison disputed the assumption the church at WAI-I-LAT-PU dissolved in 1847. "It is true that the White leaders of that day were cut down and massacred shamefully; but the WAI-I-LAT-PU Congregation or Church and all the Church members were not massacred, not the Christian Indians. Of course they were intimidated and maybe threatened if they had tried publicly to rehabilitate such an organization. But I came to know these Indian people intimately and to speak their language and eventually to know their hearts and minds "inside," as the Indians are want to express their feelings of some one near and dear to them. And these are the things I came to know. Things no hasty investigator would ever come to know. In the first place, just a few of the leading Indians instigated and perpetuated the Massacre. Some took no part in it and branded it as an act of Cowards. And the Christian altar fires were kept burning in many of the homes and hearts of the Indians during those long days and years from November 29th 1847 to June 17th 1882." (Cornelison, p. 3)

Dr. Cornelison was the first white missionary to minister and live among the Umatilla and Cayuse after the death of the Marcus and Narcissa Whitman and their fellow Protestant missionaries. He lived with the Cayuse and Umatilla Indians for 43 years, dedicating his life to the ministry birthed in part by the Whitmans. The Nez Perce nation actually birthed the first Christian Church in the Pacific Northwest when they sent the four warriors seeking the Book of Heaven in 1831. No other individual would be able to document the result of the Whitman mission with the authority of Dr. Cornelison. Those who cherish the history of Oregon and Umatilla County are fortunate

Major Lee Moorehouse photograph of Cayuse Indian Christian converts from the ministry of Marcus and Narcissa Whitman

that he left an unpublished manuscript and furthermore blessed that the Confederated Tribes of the Umatilla have established a wise stewardship for this manuscript. Dr. Cornelison documented the foundation of the Cayuse Columbia Plateau Native American church in his book. "The charter members of this reorganized Church now called Tutuilla were the children of those Indians formerly affiliated with the older WAI-I-LAT-PU Church." (Cornelison, p. 4)

According to Dr. Cornelison, the Christian church established by Marcus and Narcissa Whitman never died. The Cayuse and Umatilla Indians sustained their faith in Christ after the massacre of the missionaries and they taught the fundamentals of their faith in God to their children and maintained a family altar. Dr. Cornelison further documented, "one person, at least, a charter member, Sarah Minthorn (or IPNA-

TSO-LA-TALKT, her Indian name, which translated means, "She restrains herself"), was a pupil of Mrs. Whitman's school at the time of the Massacre. She was about fifteen years old at the time. Later Sarah became one of the four wives of Chief Yellow Hawk. She became a lifelong member of the reorganized church (Tutuilla); and attended the church for 26 years. Nine of those 26 years were after I had arrived to become Missionary on the Umatilla Reservation. So I say that Sarah Minthorn definitely ties the two churches together historically." (Cornelison, p. 4)

Dr. Cornelison's manuscript is supported by a picture of the Cayuse converts of the Whitmans taken by Major Lee Moorhouse. "This old woman remembers well her teachers and can sing English hymns and recite bits of scripture in English and yet cannot talk a word of the language. She has a book which Mrs. Whitman gave her and which she treasures dear as her life." (Steven L. Grafe, "Peoples of the Plateau, the Indian Photographs of Lee Moorehouse," University of Oklahoma Press, Norman, Oklahoma, 2005, p. 142.)

This research has carefully documented the facts that the Whitman's were loved and respected by the Cayuse Indians. Sarah Minthorn treasured a book from Narcissa Whitman because she treasured the ministry of the Protestant missionaries. Historians and museums including the Whitman Mission and the Confederated Tribes of the Umatilla Tamastslikt Cultural Institute do not present the Protestant missionaries in an historical context consistent with the witness of Sarah Minthorn and other Cayuse Christian converts.

Dr. Cornelison made no reference to the issue of polygamy represented by the fact Sarah Minthorn was one of four wives of Chief Yellow Hawk. There is no reference to indicate Sarah remained one of Yellow Hawk's four wives after she became a member of the Tutuilla Presbyterian Church. The teaching of the Nez Perce missionaries from Lapwai did not allow polygamy, so to be a member of the Tutuilla Presbyterian Church would have required adherence to marriage between one man and one woman.

Sarah Minthorn was buried at the Tutuilla cemetery, and on her tombstone was inscribed "Sarah Minthorn died 1908 (IPNA-TSO-LA-TALKT) last pupil of Dr. Marcus Whitman's School 1836-1847)." (Cornelison, p. 5) The very fact that Sarah Minthorn had "the last pupil of Dr. Whitman" written on her tombstone demonstrated her veneration for the martyred Christian missionary and the primary significance of their ministry in her life.

Dr. Cornelison has documented the Presbyterian Church birthed by Marcus and Narcissa Whitman became the Tutuilla Presbyterian Church near Pendleton, Oregon. This church would be the oldest continuous Christian Church in the Pacific Northwest. The Methodist Church established by Jason Lee at Oregon City in 1840 has been acknowledged by historians as the oldest Protestant congregation in Oregon and second only to the Catholic Church in St. Paul, Oregon, also birthed in 1840. These historical dates are based on buildings that still exist to this day. Marcus Whitman came to the Pacific Northwest in 1835, a year after the great Methodist missionary Jason Lee; however, Lee's first mission to the Indians was abandoned in 1838 because the Indians either died of white man's diseases or left the church. Both Protestant ministries, as well as the Catholic mission at St. Andrews, continue to have a positive impact on the heritage of Oregon to the present hour.

The primary place of the Tutuilla Church, a fundamentally Native American Church, as the oldest continuous Protestant or Catholic church in the Christian history of the Pacific Northwest, has been documented in Dr. Cornelison's unpublished manuscript. The church established by the Whitmans may not have met in a building that stands to the present hour; nevertheless, the ministry birthed by the Nez Perce Indians and nurtured by the Whitmans continues to the present hour in the Pacific Northwest in the Tutuilla Presbyterian Church.

This research has previously documented the prominent position of Stickus, the Cayuse Christian disciple of Marcus Whitman who led the first immigrant wagon train across the Blue Mountains in 1841.

Historians have failed to apply any distinction to Stickus or his heritage, and his name and legacy would be lost to our heritage were it not for the unpublished manuscript of Dr. Cornelison. Cornclison wrote regarding Stickus (ISH-TICK-KUS), "His grandchildren were all Christians. One of them, Mr. James Kash Kash, eventually united with the Tutuilla Church and served that Church as a faithful Elder many years. And his great grandchild, the son of James Kash Kash, is at this time an Elder of the Tutuilla Church. His name is Sam Kash Kash and Sam Kash Kash was the Elder commissioner from the Tutuilla Church and Presbytery of Eastern Oregon to the General Assembly of the Presbyterian Church U.S.A…" (Cornelison, p. 8)

Dr. Cornelison spent much time with Sarah Minthorn, learning about the Whitmans and their impact on the Cayuse Indians. "Many times visiting with her, I have heard her tell of the WAI-I-LAT-PU Mission and of what they did and what they learned there. Though she had forgotten all of her English language, she could and would sing in her quavering voice some song in English that Mrs. Whitman had taught them. She could repeat (and did the same rapidly), the whole alphabet—A.B.C.D.—and never forget to end by saying 'and so forth.' Thus showing that Mrs. Whitman was a careful teacher and never forgot any detail." (Cornelison, p. 6)

Sarah Minthorn was not the only link to the Whitmans at the Tutuilla Church when Dr. Cornelison arrived. Phillip Minthorn was a small child at the hour of the Whitman massacre. As a child he took his father's name PEE-TIN-MOX-MOX (Yellow Hawk); however, when he became a Christian and was baptized with his mother and half-brother they adopted the name Minthorn in honor of a prominent government doctor by the name of Minthorn at the reservation at that time. Phillip remembered his father speaking to the perpetrators of the massacre long before he was able to understand the terrible consequences. "Go cowards and kill your best friend, I will have no part in it." (Cornelison, p. 7) This testimony was consistent with the testimony of the white survivors of the massacre who witnessed the Cayuse Indians crying after they murdered the Whitmans and their fellow missionaries. Phillip Minthorn also recalled to Dr. Cornelison the Christian faith of his parents taught to them by the Whitmans. "…one of his earliest memories was his father and mother gathering all the family together to sing and pray in a worshipping service. He early perceived that these were not the chants and incantations used in many camps and festive occasions, and in cases of sickness by the Medicine men to Worship and call in the help of their WEE-WE-UE-KIN to cure the sick. Later his parents explained to him that these songs and this service had been taught to them by Dr. and Mrs. Whitman." (Cornelison, p. 8) The Christian teachings of the Whitmans had to survive in the hearts and spirits of the Cayuse Indians for over three decades until Nez Perce missionaries were sent to minister to them. This research has previously documented these Columbia Plateau Native Americans worshipped a creator God they called the Great Spirit long before the Whitmans came.

Phillip Minthorn recounted to Dr. Cornelison the dreadful time for the Cayuse after the massacre. He was a very young boy when the whole tribe, already decimated by the white man's epidemic, was forced to flee their traditional hunting grounds. Nearly half of the Cayuse tribe had perished in the epidemic. Not one family would be spared the sorrow of grieving the loss of their loved ones. In addition, their teachers and their father in the Christian faith had been slain by members of their own dwindling nation. Before they had opportunity to grasp the enormous consequences of the Whitman massacre they were forced to flee before the wrath of the approaching American volunteer army. To add insult to their grievous losses, their own kindred people, the Nez Perce, would capture the five Cayuse chiefs responsible for the slaying. Many historians have written that some if not all of the Cayuse Indian chiefs were innocent of the multiple crimes of murder at the Whitman massacre. The survivors of the massacre were brought to Oregon City to identify the Native Americans guilty of the killings. These survivors knew the Cayuse chiefs well. "Lorinda

Chapman, Elizabeth and Catherine (Sager), and other survivors appeared as witnesses against the Indians." (Helm, p. 80)

The Whitman massacre caused the United States to extend protection over the Oregon Territory and ultimately led to the statehood of Oregon in 1859. In contrast, the massacre was devastating to the Cayuse nation. The War Chief Teloukaite who took a prominent role in the massacre later recanted lamenting, "I have killed my best friend." (Helm, p. 60) Those Cayuse who took up arms to resist the American volunteers were soon dispatched. Tom McKay shot Chief Grey Eagle through the heart and Chief Five Crows was severely wounded by Charlie McKay. The Cayuse nation was forced into the mountains until the Nez Perce apprehended the five chiefs who took part in the massacre.

Most historians have assumed the Christian faith of the Cayuse Indians died at the Whitman massacre. This Cayuse/Columbia Plateau nation was not an ordinary people. They had been chosen by the Almighty to be imparted with the faith of the Book of Heaven and nothing or nobody could dislodge their faith from their hearts. Not the painful death of their precious children or parents or siblings in the violent measles epidemic brought by the white men. Not the violent death of their beloved ministers. Not the loss of their tradition homeland. Not even the threats of death if they continued with their Christian faith. When Joel Palmer helped the Cayuse move onto the reservation after the treaty of 1855 he wrote, on "Sunday morning, Chief Stickus rang his bell and 45 Cayuse met with him in worship. At the station of Mr. Spalding, 1,000 Nez Perce met with Chief Timothy for worship." (Helm, p. 81) The Cayuse have rightfully earned their place as the First Christian Church of the Pacific Northwest at Tutuilla and the Nez Perce warriors who sought the Book of Heaven birthed the first Protestant ministry in the Pacific Northwest.

Phillip Minthorn not only became an elder at the Tutuilla Church but he became the driving force to bring a Presbyterian minister who would learn the native language and live among his people. The Rev. James Hayes was a zealous Nez Perce missionary evangelist who spent two years at the Pendleton church and gave the church a strong foundation. The Tutuilla Church needed that boost because, with the exception of Hayes, from 1882 until the approaching new century the church existed with a haphazard supply of ministers. Phillip Minthorn went before the Presbytery of Eastern Oregon and requested that the board secure a young minister to become their own missionary and live among them. Fortunately, or more probably providentially, the lady superintendent of the Indian Boarding School on the reservation, an ardent Episcopalian, issued the following proclamation at the same time. "If the Presbyterian Church U.S.A. does not intend to secure a missionary to labor on the Umatilla Indian reservation, I would like to have our bishop secure an Episcopal Minister to be such a missionary." (Cornelison, p. 10) This was no endeavor for a Native American without courage, because securing a Presbyterian missionary from the Presbyterian Seminary meant bringing a white minister to live once again with the Cayuse/Columbia Plateau Indians. The last white ministers to accomplish that feat were the Whitmans, and the wounds from that confrontation between the forces of light and the forces of darkness have not healed to this very day. Phillip Minthorn was no ordinary man and without his undaunted courage Dr. Cornelison would never have been commissioned nor survived 43 years at Tutuilla.

The Nez Perce warriors risked their lives to secure the Book of Heaven. Phillip Minthorn risked his reputation and his place of honor among his people to bring a white minister to the reservation. According to Dr. Cornelison, "Elder Phillip Minthorn stood firmly, almost alone at times; a characteristic not too common among Indians; for they, like some white people, love to go with the crowd. He stood firm in his faithfulness to the Presbytery, to the Missionary, and to his own ideals of the Christian life and way. How many times! Has my almost bleeding, but never discouraged heart, been comforted by his kind words, advice and smile. One could always put his hand on the son of Yellow Hawk knowing exactly where he stood." (Cornelison, p. 11)

At this point in the story it is necessary to introduce Etta Conner Scott, a present member of the Tutuilla Presbyterian Church. At the age of eight during the Second World War, Etta remembered the words of her father Gilbert Conner, son of Presbyterian missionary E. J. Conner, regarding the Nez Perce warriors sent to find the Book of Heaven. E. J. Conner was ordained by the Tutuilla Presbyterian Church in 1907. He recounted to his oldest son Gilbert the oral heritage of two of the first Nez Perce Indian warriors seeking the written Word of God. "Their names were Swan Necklace and Rabbit Skin Leggings." (Etta Conner Scott, interview Nov. 1, 2007) Etta Conner Scott's great grandfather was Chief Joseph's younger brother, Ollokot. Ollokot was one of the great warriors of the Nez Perce's storied retreat to Canada. Ollokot was killed in the last battle at Bear Paw. Ollokot's daughter survived that retreat and married a white mountain-man named Conner. His son E. J. Conner attended seminary before his ordination, while his wife Sarah attended to their growing family. Their eldest son Gilbert Edward was Etta Conner Scott's father.

The great great granddaughter of Ollokot, brother of Chief Joseph, would become the director of Tamastslikt Cultural Institute, Bobbie Conner. The granddaughter of Phillip Minthorn, Malissa Minthorn, would in large part, as director of the library at Tamastslikt Cultural Institute, be responsible for Dr. Cornelison's unpublished manuscript being available to the public. God's Word declares, "Blessed is the man that feareth the Lord, that delighteth greatly in his commandments. His seed shall be mighty upon the earth: the generation of the upright shall be blessed." (Psalm 112:1, 2) The blessings of E. J. Conner and Phillip Minthorn rest upon their seed, and it is no coincidence that the Tamastslikt Cultural Institute has been blessed with such providential leadership at a most crucial hour in the history of the Confederated Tribes of the Umatilla Indian Reservation. The Whitmans and their ministry associates may have been martyred; nevertheless, "many of them who were the direct seed of the hero who was stricken down at WAI-I-LAT-PU who 'being dead yet speaketh.'" (Cornelison, p. 12) Marcus and Narcissa Whitman may have been martyred, yet their spirit lives on through the lives of the Native Americans at the Tutuilla Presbyterian Church.

Dr. J. M. Cornelison was a blessing from God to the heritage of the Oregon Territory. This man of God was a living testimony that Oregon remained under the shadow of the Almighty. Dr. Cornelison, like Dr. Marcus Whitman, was not just some country doctor who went to minister among the Indians because nobody else would have him. Dr. Cornelison was the best the San Francisco Theological Seminary had to offer at the turn of the 20th century. To Dr. W. S. Holt, the Synodical Executive sent from Oregon to find the Man of God for the Tutuilla Church, Cornelison was a very young man, just 21 and still green behind the ears. Cornelison had graduated from Central University College in Richmond, Virginia in 1896. He was only 19 years old when he entered Danville Theological Seminary. He completed his theological degree at San Francisco theological seminary before he turned 22, which was a most impressive accomplishment for the hour. When Dr. Holt realized Cornelison's age he said, "You are rather young to take up such a responsible job." (Cornelison, p. 47). Hebrew Professor Dr. Thomas F. Day came to Cornelison's defense. "Well, Dr. Holt, this young man expects to be older."(Cornelison, p. 48)

Dr. Holt was not deterred. He knew this was not just any assignment. After all, the charge to the Tutuilla Church would be the daunting task of following in no less a man's footsteps than the legendary Marcus Whitman. "I would like to have four or five letters from people who knew you as a boy, who knew your parents. These people could be your Sunday School teachers, your boyhood Pastors. Then I want a letter from each of your college Professors; and a letter from each of the Professors of the Danville Theo. Sem. and a letter from each of the Professors of the San Francisco Theo. Seminary. Let them tell of your standing as a Student, your student habits and especially your knowledge of Languages." (Cornelison, p. 48)

Why would a young man of J. M. Cornelison's talent, education and drive want to go to the wilderness of Eastern Oregon to live with the Native Americans? Didn't those same Indians kill their last white missionary? Cornelison knew full well the history and heritage of the Presbyterian missionary ministers who went before him and the Indian nations they sacrificed their lives to serve. Dr. Holt informed the young Rev. Cornelison the request of the Native Americans from Tutuilla. "Some of the descendents of these same people who are now Christians have come to the Presbytery and are asking for a young man to come among them to learn their language, to be their Missionary and to teach them and lead them in all the ways of the Christian life!!!" (Cornelison, pp. 45, 46)

"That was like a bolt of lightning that shot into my heart and soul and when I returned to my room and alone and on my knees, I said to my Savior, 'All my life training, and Education and Experience, has fitted me for just such a life work. And I have been guided and brought here to hear such a message. If I am the young man for the place and the right man, 'Here I am, send me.''" (Cornelison p. 46) The Almighty had chosen the man for the Umatilla Indian Reservation in honor of Phillip Minthorn's call on behalf of the Cayuse and Columbia Plateau Native Americans. The scripture that Cornelison was referring to can be found in Isaiah Chapter 6, verse 8. "And I heard the voice of the Lord, saying Whom shall I send, and who will go for us? Then said I, here am I; send me."

The secret of Dr. Cornelison's long and fruitful tenure with the Native Americans of the Confederated Tribes of the Umatilla was his willingness to become one with his soon-to-be-beloved friends. His first sermon as a 23-year-old man was preached in the Native American language with no interpreter. Cornelison wrote of those years. "Some years later those people never thought of me as a White man; but thought of me as that Indian Minister. Here is a Story, Yes, a true Story, to prove that point. About that time I was asked by the Presbytery to supply one of our Vacant Churches not far from Tutuilla. I arranged for the Pastor of the Pendleton Church to Preach that P.M. Service at Tutuilla for me, so it would not be without a Service. One of the older women spoke of that service to my wife, who had not been able to attend it and said, 'We had a White man preach to us today.' I had always thought of myself as a White man, but I was no longer a White man to these Indian people. I had so identified myself with them, was growing up with them. And, as they would say in their beautiful idioms, I came to know their hearts 'inside' (EMIT-Kinikai), and I spoke their language in more ways than with my tongue. And my thoughts and Prayers and my work were always with and for them." (Cornelison, p. 78)

Major Lee Moorehouse photograph of Dr. Cornelison

For the next four decades the Native Americans of the Confederated Tribes of the Umatilla were ministered to by Dr. Cornelison. The fruit of that ministry continues to the present hour; however, once again the Tutuilla Church has experienced an 18-year period of trial and tribulation beginning in 1989, with no minister to tend to the flock.

At this point in the narrative it is necessary to introduce the next major instrument for the hand of God for the Tutuilla Church, Jack Schut. Jack's real name was Yacoub Alayan, son of Meyouf Alayan, the Muktar (Chief in the TransJordan State in Palestine before the edict to reestablish Israel in 1948) who administered (in a position similar to that of mayor) Jerusalem. Jack's mother died at birth and a wet nurse at a Jerusalem orphanage nursed him with his twin brother. The American orphanage was evacuated when hostilities began in Jerusalem in late 1948. Dorothy Schut, the Assembly of God missionary, took Jack and his brother away using the government vehicle and license supplied by Jack's father. Jack's family was a powerful clan that owned large parcels of land between East Jerusalem and the Dead Sea, some thirty miles. Jack's brother died in America. Jack took the name of the Assembly of God missionaries who took him from his family and was raised in the Pacific Northwest. Jack's father Meyouf sought to find Jack the rest of his life but never realized that his son's name had been changed from Yacoub Alayan to Jack Schut. In time he did discover Jack's family but tragically he was told Jack had become a juvenile delinquent and had died in Oklahoma. Meyouf died the night he was told that lie. Many say he died of a broken heart.

Jack grew up in the Assembly of God church but grew disenchanted with the church in large part because of the infidelity of his adopted mother. As he grew up he distinguished himself in virtually every endeavor he set his heart to pursue. Immediately after graduation from Eastern Oregon State University in La Grande, Oregon (1969 with a dual degree in Education and General Studies) Jack was hired to be the Director of the Court under the Circuit Judge in La Grande. In this position he oversaw the Juvenile Court and was the Law Enforcement Administrator for ten Eastern Oregon counties. In 1979 Jack was hired by Eastern Oregon State University to administer a number of positions including Director of the Eastern Oregon Foundation, Director of the Alumni, Director of Public Relations, and Assistant to the President. He worked for the university for ten years. At the same time Jack began an exporting business called Alayan International in 1980 that eventually established offices in London, Tokyo, Taipei, Seoul, and branch offices in Malaysia, Germany and Denmark. Jack's business ventures were aided in large part by the confidence government leaders had in his integrity and keen business intuition. Governor Victor Atiyeh included Jack on his inaugural trip to Japan to encourage business on the Pacific Rim. In 1998 Jack established a consulting venture in the Guangdong province of China.

In 2007, Jack was called of God to minister to the Presbyterian Church at Tutuilla after an 18-year period of spiritual languishing. Jack must have sensed the hand of God upon his life because he completed a three-year course on Lay Pastor Training through the Presbyterian Church just prior to his call to the Tutuilla Church. This course was under the authority of the Presbyterian Seminary at Austin, Texas, the San Francisco Theological Seminary, and Dubuque Seminary in Iowa. Jack married an equally talented and industrious wife, Terrel, who had a distinguished career in her own right at Eastern Oregon State University working up to the position of Director of Admission and Records. The unique needs of the First Christian Church of the Pacific Northwest required at this hour the exceptional gifts and faith that Terrel and Jack Schut could provide. The commitment of this Christian couple would be best illustrated by the fact the Presbytery could not fund this full-time position at this time and therefore only sought a marginal commitment of one Sunday a month. Jack and his wife accepted the position to be full-time ministers despite the fact there would be no salary attached to the ministry.

A member of the Tutuilla Church, Walla Walla Chief Bill Burke, posed a question to Jack when he arrived: "What will you do when your ministry fails at Tutuilla?" The Schuts were not Native American. They had no financial support. The Tutuilla Church building was terribly run down, with few parishioners and little hope for the future. Schut responded, "We shall not fail, because if the Native American people do not support us then we shall jack the Tutuilla Church onto wheels and move it to Tamastslikt to become a museum relic for the public to view." Seventy-one people attended the Tutuilla Church on Sunday Nov. 11, 2007 and most fittingly E. J. Conner was honored in celebration of his ordination one hundred years ago. Once again the seeds of the first Nez Perce warriors and the Whitman missionaries would bear fruit at Tutuilla.

Chapter 32

Happy Canyon

Happy Canyon was a vision in the mind of Roy Raley at the same time the vision of the Tutuilla Presbyterian Church was blossoming. Roy Raley was son of a wagon train immigrant who came to Pendleton along the Oregon Trail in 1862. Raley was the epitome of the best of the Oregon pioneer forefathers of the Wild West. Roy Raley was the positive hope of America's manifest destiny in its correct manifestation. Roy Raley and Pendleton, at the foothills of the Oregon Trail where the American pioneers and the American Indians met, were a perfect match. Raley was born in 1880, the same year the city of Pendleton was incorporated. He grew up to be the city's leading citizen. He became a living example of everything the new Republic had to offer in the romanticized West. In one man Raley was a lawyer, a legislator, a cattleman, a banker, a surveyor, an Indian fighter, a sportsman, a businessman, and a Pendleton spokesman and author of community celebrations. At that time it was a mark of pride to be called an Indian fighter. He became the author and father of the Pendleton Round Up and Happy Canyon. The Rodeo became world famous but it was the creation of Happy Canyon where Raley birthed his greatest masterpiece. Roy Raley was central to the plans of the Almighty because he recognized the foremost position of the Native American Indians in America as well as Pendleton's heritage. Happy Canyon was Raley's vision to illustrate the unique and historic relationship between the two races of the West.

Roy Raley

In the beginning Raley called Happy Canyon the "Pageant of the West, An Outdoor Dramatic Production Symbolizing the History and Development of the Great West." Raley knew and respected the local Indian leaders and in turn they trusted him. The result was a dramatic recreation of the Wild West beginning with the civilization of the Native American Indians before the advent of white men. In historical truth the "wild west" was at least in part a "Happy Canyon," where Native American Indians and white frontiersmen, explorers, trappers, missionaries and settlers lived and intermingled in relative peace for nearly half a century until the advent of the Whitman massacre. The first time Lewis and Clark met the Columbia Plateau Indians they ate, fellowshipped and slept in the same camp. The first missionaries had the same experience the very first time they met these Columbia Plateau Indians who had sought the "white man's Book of Heaven."

This is not to suggest the Oregon Territory was a blissful utopia where no evil ever marred the scene. Nevertheless, Raley's vision of Happy Canyon was not unrealistic. Roy Raley's Happy Canyon established a reenactment of that unity between the Indians and the white civilization that existed before the Whitman massacre. The merging of the two civilizations to create the Happy Canyon pageant has endured for nearly a century, making the heritage of Pendleton unique in western culture. The heart and soul of the great west, manifesting the unique relationship between the Native American Indian and the white emigrant pioneers, has made Pendleton, Oregon the heart of the so-called "wild west." At this yearly event and Round Up celebration, Indians from all the tribes of the Columbia Plateau return to commemorate their culture with singing, dancing, tribal rituals, and native dress and artifacts.

Happy Canyon and the Pendleton Round Up gave many of the Columbia Plateau Indians hope. In this arena and at this community event the Indians were treated as equals, at least by Oregonians of Roy Raley's pedigree. The result has been a unique heritage uncommon in the West. The city of Pendleton and the Confederated Tribes of the Umatilla began working and growing together thanks in no small part to the Indian leaders who supported the pageant in the beginning. This is not to suggest that all Indians of the Confederated Tribes of the reservation supported Happy Canyon. Nor did all Oregonians of Eastern Oregon share Raley's vision and unity with the Columbia Plateau Indians. A significant number of Indians refused to partake in the pageant because they believed they were being exploited. They objected to the paternalistic representation that stereotyped their culture and history.

Many of these Indians objected for spiritual and religious reasons. At this time in American history the touring Wild Bill Cody exhibitions exploited the Indians and many Confederated tribesmen believed Happy Canyon would be the same. This schism, to some extent, still exists in the Indian community regarding the Pendleton Round Up and Happy Canyon. To the non-supportive Indians Happy Canyon does not exist. Once again the roots of this schism can be traced to the Whitman massacre and subsequent unjust treatment. The massacre separated the Cayuse and Columbia Plateau Indians from their Protestant Christian heritage as presented by the Whitmans. Many of the Native Americans of faith (Protestant, Catholic or ancestral) on the reservation refused to take part in the Round Up pageantry because they believed they were being exploited and their faith was being undermined.

One of the central purposes of this research has been to document historical truth to bring healing to the schisms that have divided and undermined both races in their relationship with each other. According to the Bible, there is only one God. Whether He is called Creator, Almighty or Great Spirit Chief does not matter. He is the same God. There is only one begotten Son, Jesus Christ. Whether He is White, Red or Black is of no consequence because in truth He is all three. He is the same God to all races. The Indians who joined the Happy Canyon celebration have been encouraged and honored over the years. Those Indians who refused to partake have forced the white Pendleton community to address issues over unequal treatment and exploitation that nearly caused the Indians to pull out of the Round Up celebration in the late 1990s.

One of the most inspiring examples of celebrating the racial victory of Pendleton's Round Up was the story of Jackson Sundown. Jackson Sundown was a Nez Perce warrior who rode with Chief Joseph during his historic flight. Jackson Sundown was a nephew of the great Chief. As a teenager, he was in charge of the Nez Perce ponies, the ones the U.S. cavalry could not keep up with even when the riders were children and old women. He escaped with White Bird to Canada and lived with Sitting Bull for two years. When he made his way back into the United States he remained free and continued to raise and breed Appaloosa horses. By the time the Pendleton Round Up began, Sundown was already revered among the Indians for his prowess with horses. You could say he was the Satchel Page of American Indians. (Satchel Page was a great American black baseball player who lived before Blacks broke the racial prejudice barrier in baseball.) By the time rodeos became a western tradition Sundown was already fifty years old. Today a few rodeo performers compete into their fifties, but virtually never in the rough stock categories. Sundown was so good that even in his advanced age other riders would back out if they found out he was entered in a rodeo competition. The great thing about many western rodeos was there was no racial barrier for competitors. At the age of 53 Sundown came out of retirement for one last rodeo in Pendleton, but only because his sculptor paid his entry fee.

"As Sundown eased onto Angel's back for his final ride, the blindfold was removed from Angel. Angel tried to whirl and leap to throw Sundown off. All Sundown's years as a child in the Wallowa's riding and his career in Montana as a horseman and his rodeo experience showed that day. It was said that Sundown became one with that horse. As Angel tried one last attempt at throwing Sundown off, Sundown fanned his hat at the horse. Jackson Sundown, Waaya-Tonah-Toesits-Kahn was the 1916 World Champion Bronc Rider." (www.nezperce.org/History/JacksonSundown.htm)

The Pendleton Round Up and Happy Canyon broke through racial prejudices common in America and Oregon at that hour. It was not only the Pendleton rodeo that allowed all races to compete, but Pendleton was unique because of Happy Canyon. It was not until 1946 that a man of color was allowed to break the racial barrier and play professional baseball. After Jackie Robinson's triumphant entry into American professional sports it was not long until African-Americans were competing and, in the case of basketball, dominating professional sports in America. In 1911, by Oregon law still in the state statutes, a Black man was not even allowed to live in Oregon let alone compete against whites. The Pendleton Round Up did not adhere to the racial prejudices of the hour. A Black cowboy by the name of George Fletcher made the finals of the first Pendleton Round Up Saddle Bronc Finals.

Major Lee Moorehouse photograph of Jackson Sundown at Pendleton Round Up in 1916

The first Saddle Bronc final was historic because none of the finalists were white American cowboys. Jackson Sundown was a native Indian America, John Spain was a European American and George Fletcher was an African-American. Although Indians and Blacks were allowed to compete that did not mean they would automatically receive a fair decision from the white American judges of the day. Sundown's horse was interfered with by one of the judge's horses but he was not allowed a re-ride. John Spain made a good ride but the crowd claimed he fouled by touching the horse with his free hand. George Fletcher made a good ride, bringing the crowd to its feet; however, the judges required Fletcher to ride again. Again Fletcher brought the crowd to its feet with another outstanding ride. Nevertheless, the judges awarded the championship to Spain. Sheriff Til Taylor was so angry at the judges' decision that he took an offering from the crowd and presented it to Fletcher, making him the people's champion.

The very fact that Jackson Sundown and George Fletcher were allowed to compete against whites was historic. The beginning of the 20th century was still the dark ages of racial prejudice throughout the world. It was unheard of at this time for Blacks or Indians to be allowed to compete on an equal playing field against whites in America or most anyplace in the world. At this time in Oregon, Blacks, Indians, Chinese, women and any other foreign race were not allowed to vote. The Exclusion law that denied Blacks the right to live in Oregon, own property or a business was not deleted until 1926 and universal voting rights were not passed in Oregon until 1927. The ban on interracial marriage was not repelled until 1940. The Pendleton Round Up broke the racial barrier three and a half decades before baseball allowed a black man to compete against whites.

Major Lee Moorehouse photograph of George Fletcher at Pendleton Round Up in 1915

In historical perspective, despite failings and inconsistencies, the Pendleton Round Up and Happy Canyon have been a healthy example of racial equality and America's great western heritage. These yearly celebrations merged the two cultures victoriously together and the Pendleton Round Up has never excluded any contestant based on color. Even women were allowed on rough stock until a lady bronc rider was killed. In truth the great pageant in Pendleton has been historically and strategically placed as has no community in America, with the potential to accomplish even greater cultural and spiritual victories.

There is another side of Pendleton that must be documented. Pendleton from the get-go developed a reputation as the gambling, bootlegging, maverick capital of the west, a reputation that the city proudly and unashamedly honors. The Pendleton Underground Tour meticulously and vividly brings to life the "cozy room" bordellos, the Chinese-built underground tunnels, the opium dens, the illegal gambling rooms and the wild life of Pendleton's past heritage. This maverick spirit pervades the culture and heritage of the community. Fortunately there remains a positive element to the liberal spirit that brought bordellos and opium to Pendleton. That spirit comes alive every Round Up season to permeate the community with gayity, celebration and civic pride. Roy Raley and Happy Canyon have best exemplified this positive spirit.

Unfortunately, the dark side to the maverick spirit gives license to those that would take advantage of the liberty won by our forefathers. The dark side of the maverick spirit in Pendleton has worked as a leaven to the present hour to thwart calls for integrity in many public arenas, from athletics to government. This should come as no surprise since Pendleton's heritage heralded the place of prostitution, gambling, bootlegging and the Chinese slave trade. The maverick heritage of Pendleton must be tempered with discernment, integrity and humility for Pendleton to attain the lofty title as the true center of the West as envisioned by Roy Raley. Pendleton must embrace the spiritual foundation and accomplishments of the Columbia Plateau Indians and the Presbyterian missionaries and subsequent Catholic priests and integrate their heritage of faith with the heritage of Roy Raley before the lofty title of the center of the true West can be bestowed.

The maverick spirit of the pioneer settlers of the west changed the landscape in terms of owning and cultivating the land. The Native Americans controlled the Blue Mountains but they never lived in those mountains during the harsh winters. The hearty pioneer knew no such boundaries. Once the Indians had been forced to abdicate their territory and settle on government-mandated reservations, the mighty Blue Mountains and their lush foothills were awaiting their next suitors. The Oregon immigrant men, women and children who would attempt to pioneer living in the Blue Mountains would be sorely challenged. The Indians never lived in these mountains during the harsh winters for good reason, always migrating to warmer, more hospitable terrain. These pioneers would not have that luxury. They would have to be very hardy to take dominion over this prized possession. No tribe or race or people had ever established their heritage by possessing these rugged and formidable mountains through the winter months. Undaunted mountain men and free trappers had endured these mountains in the winter, but no white women had ever-established homes and families there. Would the intrepid Americans be the first?

Chapter 33

Matteson School House Pioneers

The original pioneers of the Blue Mountains faced a most daunting task. The best farmlands had already been parceled out. Unfortunately, greed and a compromised code of integrity ruled the hour of pre-twentieth century Oregon as the opening of vast tracts of land allowed unscrupulous land speculators to drive up prices and lock up public and Indian lands for the profit of a few. The original purpose of this book was to tell the story of the pioneers of the Matteson School in the Blue Mountains of Morrow County. It has taken thirty-two chapters and nearly four hundred years of documented research to reach the point where the story was originally meant to begin. It was necessary to establish this groundwork so the reader could understand the incredible heritage of the Oregon Territory and the part the Blue Mountains played in that heritage. Unfortunately, the passion of telling this story has changed the emphasis and only one short chapter can be allotted to the incredible pioneers who tamed the mighty Blue Mountains.

Truly, if space allowed, these mountains could tell a more poignant story of God's sovereignty and omniscience, especially as the Indians first merged and related with the white man in these Blue Mountains. These Native Americans and the pioneers who followed them helped establish the foundation for the blessing that all Oregonians richly enjoy. To adequately tell their story would require another book. Others have already accomplished this task, much better than this author could ever attempt to duplicate. Rick Steber, from Prineville, Oregon, has dedicated much of his life to honoring the pioneer forefathers of Old Oregon and I would refer those who wish to know more about Oregon's pioneer heritage to read some of his work. For the purposes of this research I will turn to the original purpose of this study and focus on one group of original pioneers of the Blue Mountains in Morrow County, in particular those pioneers who sent their children to the Matteson School House beginning in the late 1880s.

In the preface of this document I shared that a twenty-first century visitor would never know there had been a civilization living in the Blue Mountains based on the present condition of what is left of a once magnificent forest. It has been said if mankind does not learn from the mistakes of past history and heritage then mankind is doomed to repeat the same mistakes. One of the most exciting purposes of this book has been to document the vigor and courage and persistence of some of the original pioneers of the Blue Mountains of Morrow County. For the purposes of this research their story must represent the story of countless other Pacific Northwest pioneers who shared their fate, endured their hardships, and spent their vigor and left their fortunes and possessions on the ground as only a few succeeded in carving out their heritage as sons of the pioneers of Oregon.

It was only after the excitement of the gold mines of California and the last tracts of Willamette Valley homesteads were exhausted that some Oregon pioneers remembered the lush foothills of the Blue

Mountains of Eastern Oregon. The first Eastern Oregon pioneer, George Vinson, came to Butter Creek and Morrow County before the peace treaty with the Indians. The first pioneers homesteaded the lush valleys and foothills of the Blue Mountains. Once all the prime agricultural lands were homesteaded, the next waves of pioneers staked out their heritage in the more difficult terrain of the Blue Mountains. To homestead a section of land a man had to file his intention to live on his claim and make improvements on it. It usually took about five years to prove progress and obtain a deed to the land. The government established every thirty-sixth section of a township for a school. This land was sold by the government for the schools at $2.50 an acre to the early settlers.

The first Oregon homesteaders under Black Butte (later to be named Madison Butte, a misspelling of Matteson) built the Lone Pine School House before the turn of the 20th century, some twenty miles south of Heppner. They were indicative of the courageous pioneers who won the West. These pioneers were the first to live in the Blue Mountains through the harsh winters and therefore the description of their character as hardy would be an understatement.

Lone Pine School House that burned down circa 1918.

When the cold fall winds began to bring the first snowfalls pushing the deer toward the foothills the Black Butte pioneers began hunkering down for the winter. Wood supplies had to be carefully stored, the hay supplies had to be secured for the livestock and horses and the canned vegetables had to be fully secured in the root cellars, for those pioneers fortunate enough to have built one. The winters would get very nasty, with snow piled over the fences for the duration of the long winter from early November through March. Homesteads dotted the forested draws around the schoolhouse, first named Lone Pine and later renamed Matteson. The schoolhouse would be the gathering house for the dances, pie socials, spelling bees, and social meetings that drew the early pioneers together. These pioneers were a hardy lot. They had come to Oregon to exercise their liberty and freedom: freedom to raise a family, carve out a place they could call their own and make a mark in this world that only Oregon could provide. They were drawn together to this most formidable environment by their courage, their faith and their endurance because this Blue Mountain forest terrain was some of the last land left for the taking in Oregon.

Near the turn of the century these pioneer homesteaders built a community church on a prairie above Jug Creek. Jug Creek was at the bottom of Thorn Creek canyon, deep in the forest nearly two miles below the Matteson Schoolhouse. Over two hundred pioneer family members would attend this non-denominational Bible-believing church. The pioneers would need all the encouragement that their faith in God could provide because life in the Blue Mountains in the winter would not be easy.

Some of these early pioneers attempted to carve out a living raising wheat and barley on the foothills bordering the forests to the north. Horses were the only source of power for tilling the ground. Each pioneer had the laborious and painstaking task of working his plow behind three horses. He had to hand-cast the seed usually from the back of a democrat wagon. Few pioneers could afford threshing machines and many had to pay traveling crews to harvest their crops. Each farmer had to be his own blacksmith. Some of the early Black Butte pioneers attempted to make a living mining the veins of coal they discovered in Black Butte.

The industry and perseverance of first pioneers of Black Butte, the Matteson family, was amazing. The four Matteson brothers, Robert, Albert, Edger and Ben by the sheer strength of picks and shovels bore a tunnel into Black Butte a mile long, wide enough to drive a team of horses, in an attempt to strike a rich vein of coal. It is difficult to imagine the faith and persistence that would have allowed these men to accomplish this task. All the labor had to be accomplished by the strength of their backs, with no machines or equipment save the dirty sweat at the hard end of a pick and a shovel. The four Matteson brothers worked mainly in the winter months for nearly two decades from 1880 to 1897 but no quality veins of coal were discovered. By the turn of the 20th century the Matteson's corporate strength and resources were exhausted and still no reliable vein of coal, the black fuel of energy and source of heat for the hour. Amazingly the Matteson's once again channeled their remaining energy and began boring a tunnel fifteen miles east on a mountain to be fittingly called Coal Mine Hill. Unfortunately the Matteson brothers fared no better with this endeavor.

A much more prosperous endeavor turned out to be harvesting the rich and magnificent tall Ponderosa pine, Tamarack and Douglas fir conifers that grew in abundance in these mountains. Sawmills began to spring up on streambeds throughout the forest. The Black Butte pioneers started Reeds mill on Thorn Creek, Hopman's mill at Three Rock, and Parkers mill on the nearby drainage of Board Creek, which soon became a thriving mountain community. The pioneer loggers only felled the select trees whose massive trunks were free of limbs well up these monoliths that reached to the skies. Stagecoaches ferried goods and mail from the mountain homesteads north to Heppner and south to Monument. Horse-drawn wagons ferried the milled lumber primarily to Heppner. Once again the reader can only marvel at the strength of these early pioneer lumbermen. Everything was accomplished by hand and with horses. These men with the assistance of their trusted and hardy horses could accomplish tasks that were Herculean.

The pioneer Black Butte homesteaders did without those commodities they could not produce. By necessity these families were large, sometimes up to a dozen children, but rarely did that many children survive. The pioneer family was an economic as well as a social unit because infant mortality was high and epidemics took a terrible toll. These Oregonians had to depend on careful preparation and their neighbors in times of trouble. Most of the homesteads were a crude "box" type construction framed with 2" x 4"s and finished with 1" x 12" with 4" battens from local sawmills. Cooking was accomplished on heavy cast-iron, wood-burning stoves. Every family made their own butter and cheese and kept their provisions cool in cellars in the summer. All pioneer families raised chickens, sheep, cows, horses and vegetable gardens. Some had turkeys and hogs as well. Washing was accomplished with washboards and hung out to dry, usually on a line. There was no such thing as indoor plumbing or bathrooms. Evening reading and entertainment was made possible by the ever-faithful kerosene lamp.

The hardy homesteaders of Black Butte would endure the hardships and rigors of the Blue Mountains for over half a century. They carved out a heritage that only the shadow of the Almighty could have made possible. These pioneers were a God-fearing, patriotic, and hardworking lot. They were fiercely independent and when the hour of prohibition came upon the land they became very proficient in making and bootlegging moonshine. In 1920 the United States government banned the sale, manufacture and transportation of alcohol for consumption as mandated by the Eighteenth Amendment. Prohibition changed the cultural landscape of America, however the law had a conversely positive impact on the Black Butte pioneers and for that matter most of the mountaineers and pioneers of the Blue Mountains. Mountain stills and bootlegging moonshine became the primary income for most of the mountaineers of the Blue Mountains. The Matteson brothers finally found an industry wherein they could prosper without breaking their backs.

Bill Lowe, an early sheepherder and bootlegger during the Prohibition era, recalled the temper of the time in an interview in 2002 at the age of 102. "Pert near every spring had a still. I would put a five-gallon barrel on each side of the mule and one between the forks. I would cover the barrels with a canvas and an axe and a shovel and come down through Heppner. I had one mule that was a bad one. If a stranger came near I'd say you'd better look out that guy will get you. If a stranger came too close he'd get four feet in the face. I packed many a gallon of moonshine past Sheriff Bauman's nose and he never knew it. My best customer was Dr. McMurdo. I ran moonshine for the Matteson's." (Bill Lowe, videotaped interview, Oct. 31, 02)

Bill Lowe came to Morrow County in 1913 at the age of 14. He was drafted to fight in the British Army in WWI where he lost all his teeth to mustard poisoning. He also lost the love of his life to mustard gas and thereafter never married. When he returned to America he spent most of his life in the Blue Mountains as a sheepherder and camp tender. He recalled many a party at the Matteson School House and Parkers mill where you "had to have a bottle of moonshine to be welcomed." (Lowe, 2002 interview)

Every Fourth of July these pioneers would celebrate America's independence at Three Rock between Parkers Mill and the School House. Ethel Moore Knighten, one of the early pioneers, remembered one of the Three Rock Fourth of July celebrations near the turn of the 20th century. "Dad would build a dance floor and move the piano (a Kimball) for the dances. The Hoskins family lived near there at the road intersection towards Parkers Mill and Rock Creek and on to Hardman. At one of the celebrations, I remember there was a boxing ring set up. Dad took me to watch the fights. We got up near the ropes so I could see. My, what a bloody fight! One was Jake Dexter and I think the other was Clarence Bauman. I was made so nauseous by the blood but I couldn't get out of the crowd. I never went back to watch another boxing match in all my life." (Personal letter from Ethel Moore Knighten) Clarence Bauman made quite a name for himself boxing and wrestling in these holiday events. He would parlay his fame into a storied career as Sheriff of Morrow County for four decades beginning during the romanticized hour of Prohibition and the 'roaring twenties' in America in 1928.

How did the Blue Mountain pioneers avoid the strict penalties and prison time for making and bootlegging moonshine? "They out fooled the law every time they came up there. Every time a stranger came into the mountains everybody within twenty miles knew it. They had a watchman and he put out signals. One man, one rag. Two men, two rags high in the tree. He thought he was alone but he wasn't. He never made a step without someone knowing it." (Lowe, Interview 2002) One must remember there was one road through the Blue Mountains at that time and even after the first Model Ts entered the picture there was only a single road to Ukiah and another to Monument. Even after Prohibition there was only one road, the old Ridge Road, to the John Day River between Monument and Ukiah until the Forest Service and logging industry opened up the Blue Mountains building a maze of roads beginning in the 1960's.

How did the pioneer woman endure this harsh mountain environment? It was one thing for a man to take on the Blue Mountains, but what about the courage and fortitude of the pioneer woman of that era. According one of those pioneer women, Lois Winchester "women didn't drink during prohibition." (Lois Winchester, video taped interview, Nov. 13, 02). Lois's family homesteaded the Reed place below Matteson Butte. A typical day for a pioneer mother would include cooking three meals a day and washing the dishes by hand after the water had been carried from the creek or spring. Bread was kneaded and set to rise and the cow would be milked for butter to be churned. The animals needed to be fed and cared for. All the clothes had to be sewed, even the underwear. Wool had to be washed and carded to spin for yarn and for bats for comforters. On school days children needed to be dressed for the trip to the Lone Pine School House and lunches had to be prepared. The Blue Mountain pioneer mothers had to be doctor and nurse for her children as well as be prepared to help deliver neighbor babies. No wonder these women didn't drink. After a days worth of chores required for survival there was no time or energy left for moonshine.

Despite the hardships of the hour the hardy pioneers of Black Butte and the Blue Mountains of Oregon were not deprived. These pioneer families learned how to survive in an environment that no other man, tribe or peoples before or since has been able to accomplish. The few living survivors of Black Butte, now known as the Matteson Butte homesteaders, long for those good old days in comparison to the hectic pace of modern life where families hardly do anything together anymore. Dorothy Matteson Scott, one of the last survivors of the Matteson School House, would glow every time she would reminisce about those days. This study will return for a vicarious moment for a winter's sleigh ride with Dorothy Matteson Scott as the sundown of the last days of the pioneer families of Matteson Butte was about form a sunset over Mount Hood never to be seen again except in the heart of pioneer homesteaders. Let us ride with Dorothy on a horse-drawn buggy on a winter's sleigh ride across the winter wonderland under Black Butte.

The snow glistened as the moon gave direction for the horse-drawn sleigh as Lewis Cason furiously drove the team up, up and up the heavily forested draw toward the Matteson School House. Little Katy and Dorothy huddled in the back of the sleigh gleefully wrapped in a blanket of straw. Lewis always drove the horses relentlessly. The girls didn't care. The sleigh bells clashed against the leather harness, piercing the cold winter's silence as the sled flew across the sea of snow. Soon the uneven cadence of the sleigh bells would give way to distant melodies pulsating from the Matteson School House. Roy Quackenbush was a master of the banjo, Bert and Geneve Corben worked their guitars and the Botts family played the mandolin and violin. It was Christmas and all the pioneers of the Blue Mountains under Matteson Butte would soon be robustly joining together in celebration of an era never to be known again. The sounds of laughter, dancing, and foot stomping, heart-soaring mountain music would soon be reverberating across the snow-capped forest, drowning the cries of the coyote.

Alas, the hardships of the Great Depression and the preparations for America's advent into the Second World War proved too great an obstacle for even these seasoned pioneer homesteaders. One by one the Matteson Butte pioneers began to abandon their homesteads and head for the city, in most cases Heppner, for work and a better life. It appeared after the fact they just got up one day and left. Many of them left their possessions; lock, stock and barrel. If it were not for the festering ruins of the rusting farming equipment and the ruins of a ransacked homestead, a 21st century visitor would never know there was once a hearty civilization that somehow survived over half a century in these Blue Mountains south of Heppner. Most of the original homesteads have been burned or vandalized, leaving no witness of the spirit and grit of that Blue Mountain pioneer heritage. The towering conifer forests of Ponderosa pine, Douglas fir, and Tamarack have mostly been hewed down by abusive logging practices. A motley high plateau desert remains. The once secluded forest no longer supports and protects sheltered springs that once fed streams that produced spawning gravel beds for steelhead and salmon. In like manner the remaining elk and deer that once provided sustenance for the pioneers have been largely forced to find new and untarnished habitat and to survive.

What lesson must the first generation of the 21st century garner from the heritage of the only pioneer Oregonians or peoples of any race to live year round within the Blue Mountains? They knew they had to depend upon one another to survive. They not only had to know their neighbors, they had to depend on their neighbors. They had to learn to get along with each other despite their differences. If they were going to have a church or a school they were going to have to build it and support it together. They had to work together to survive. They had to play together. They had to worship together. These pioneers knew if they abused the forest they would no longer be able to depend on the streams for trout, steelhead or salmon. They knew if they over-logged the forest they would ruin the aquifers that fed the springs they depended on for water. They knew if they abused the forest they would drive away the elk and deer they depended on for sustenance. These pioneers survived throughout the Blue Mountains for half a century, producing one of the great pioneer epics in the history of Oregon.

Floyd Jones ran cattle on the homesteads the Matteson Butte Pioneers were forced to abandon for twenty years from the late 1940's. He watched the homesteads deteriorate with many burned to the ground. He witnessed the abuse of the forests with abusive logging practices. He observed the streams that once provided spawning ground for salmon and steelhead dry up in late summer because the forest aquifers had been damaged and destroyed. He lamented the process of consolidation of the lands of the original pioneers into large ranches and subsequently closed to the public for fee hunting operations.

"I started hunting in 1926. We were allowed two bucks per season in the beginning. Elk season did not begin until 1938 after Rocky Mountain Elk were brought in from Yellowstone Park. The roads that the Forest Service built changed everything. I quit hunting over twenty years ago (1982). Fee hunting is killing us. I think it is a disgrace. It's a dirty shame that the kids have nowhere to go." (Floyd Jones, videotaped interview, Nov. 26, 02)

The only building that stands today, as a reminder of that heritage, is the Matteson Butte School House. That building remains as part of the heritage of the pioneers that once graced the forested draws and meadows under Matteson Butte. My father, L.E. Dick Jr. and his dear friend Bill Barrett purchased the Matteson School House in 1948 and they passed the heritage on to my wife and I. The pioneer heritage of the Matteson Butte School House and the memory of the first homesteaders will stand as long as my children and children's children are willing to sustain the Matteson School House as a testament to those pioneers and their dauntless courage for values that are largely missing in twenty-first century culture.

My father was a businessman of who demonstrated great courage and conviction in the face of formidable obstacles. He lost many valuable Standard Oil clients because he served on the school board for two decades during the era of consolidation. He also lost many business accounts when he stood against abusive logging practices as president of the Heppner Chamber of Commerce in 1972. He and his father L. E. Sr. carried many farmers through the great depression and subsequent recessions with oil and petroleum to sustain their livelihood. He warned the Heppner community that excessive National Forest road building, abusive logging practices, mismanagement of big game resources would ultimately undermine the economy and historical heritage of Heppner and other Eastern Oregon communities. "Roads created by the Forest Service and the logging industry have changed hunting. The Game Commission has been forced to reduce hunting seasons, reduce hunting opportunities, and reduce the numbers and types of animals that can be hunted. Fewer areas to hunt and shortened seasons will result in a reduction in the number of hunters. Less hunters means less income for the local merchants. Fee hunting has changed where the public can hunt and allows only those that can afford the price the opportunity to hunt. Many areas previously open to the public are now being financially subsidized by fee hunting and in most cases this income is more than the land can produce yet the land is still taxed under the agricultural exemption. These fee hunting operations should be taxed according to how the land is being used." (Ed Dick, videotaped interview, Nov. 26, 02)

This story and research will remain a testament to the spirit and courage and faith of these early pioneers. The Cayuse Indians roamed this land under Matteson Butte but these Oregon pioneers possessed the land. This book is written in honor of these hardy pioneers, because it is their story that inspired this research. May the lessons of their heritage be fastened around the heart of all Oregonians who cherish the same values.

Children at Matteson School House circa 1920.

Chapter 34

Irish Catholics Discover Eastern Oregon

This research of Oregon has documented the impact of the Protestant missionaries and their contention with the Jesuit Fathers. One of the abiding principles of this book has been the pursuit of truth instead of championing one faith or heritage at the expense of another faith. The impact of Catholicism on the first Protestant missionaries has been extensively documented. What about subsequent waves of Irish Catholics? Would these Irish immigrants bring the sectarian heritage that continued to foment division in Ireland or would these immigrants be fleeing not only from English oppression but from religious prejudice as well? Many of these Irish emigrants would be drawn to Oregon, in particular Eastern Oregon, and that migration turned out to be a marriage made in heaven.

Leaving their precious homeland in Ireland was not a joyful occasion for these pilgrims. The trip was soon to be labeled the "American Wake" because virtually all of the early emigrants would never see their families and homeland again. Many of the pioneer emigrants never reached the shores of America, dying on ships so wretched and crowded they were soon known as the "coffin ships." Those Irish who did survive the cooking pan of the Atlantic jumped into the fire of prejudice on the eastern seaboard of America. One Irish emigrant wrote home: "My master is a great tyrant, he treats me as badly as if I was a common Irishman. Our position in America is one of shame and poverty." (www.kinsella.org/history/histira.htm, "Irish Immigrants in America during the 19th century," p. 1) The Irish knew how to fight and they soon developed a reputation, especially with their fists. They stuck together especially in the large cities of the east and their indomitable spirit led one major newspaper to write, "The Irish have become more Americanized than the Americans." (Irish Immigrants in America, p. 1) The Irish arrived at the hour of destiny for America because the burgeoning nation was desperate for willing workers to build railroads, canals, bridges and new cities. A common expression for the railroad workers of the hour was "an Irishman was buried under every tie." (Irish Immigrants in America, p. 1) The hour would come when many an American would boast of having some Irish blood, but in the beginning even the black servants called the Irish "white nigger." (Irish Immigrants in America, p. 1) A song of the times called "No Irish Need Apply" illustrated the plight of the early emigrants.

"I'm a dacint boy, just landed from the town of Ballyfad:
I want a situation: yis, I sant it mighty bad.
I saw a place advertised. It's the thing for me says I:
But the dirty spalpeen ended with: No Irish need apply.
Whoo! says I; but that's an insult, though to get the place I'll try,

So, I wint to see the blagger with: No Irish need apply.

I started off to find the house, I got it mighty soon;
There I found the ould chap saited: he was reading the TRIBUNE.
I told him what I came for, whin he in a rage did fly:
No! says he, you are a Paddy, and no Irish need apply!
Tain I felt my dander rising, and I'd like to black his eye-
To tell an Irish Gintleman: No Irish need apply!

I couldn't stand it longer: so, a hoult of him I took,
And I gave him such a welting as he'd get at Donnybrook.
He hollered: Millia murther! and to get away did try,
And swore he'd never write again: No Irish need apply.
He made a big apology; I bid him thin goodbye,
Saying: Whin next you want a bating, add: No Irish need apply!

Sure, I've heard that in America its always in the plan
That an Irishman is just as good as any other man;
A home and hospitality they never will deny
The stranger here, or ever say: No Irish need apply.
But some black sheep are in the flock: a dirty lot, say I;
A dacint man will never write: No Irish need apply!

Sure Paddy's heart is in his hand, as all the world does know,
His praties and his whiskey he will share with friend or foe;
His door is always open to the stranger passing by;
He never thinks of saying: None but Irish may apply,
And, in Columbia's history, his name is ranking high;
Tain, the Divil take the knaves that write: No Irish need apply!

Ould Ireland on the battle-field a lasting fame had made;
We all have heard of Meagher's men, and Corcoran's brigade.
Though fools may float and bigots rave, and fanatics man cry,
Yet when they want good fighting-men, the Irish may apply,
And when for freedom and the right they raise the battle-cry,
Then the Rebel ranks begin to think: No Irish need apply."
    (Wikipedia.org/wiki/Irish_American p. 5)

As America approached the latter portion of the 19th century Catholics were regularly barred from most fraternal organizations. Even labor unions excluded Catholic immigrants. Father Michael J. McGivey was an Irish American priest who determined to establish a mutual benefit society to support the Catholic immigrants in New Haven, Connecticut. In 1882 he established the first order of the Sons of Columbus, later to be named the Knights of Columbus. Father McGivey chose to name the order after Christopher Columbus because the famous explorer was a pious and zealous Catholic Christian instrumental in America's foundation. The order developed a strong conservative Christian heritage and soon spread across America and the world to include over 14,000 world councils that have distributed billions of dollars in benevolent giving across the globe.

The positive impact of the Irish Catholics in America must be emphasized in this faith-driven history of the West because the initial force of the Jesuit fathers in the Oregon Territory led to the violence of the Whitman massacre and over half a century of religious sectarianism. At the turn of the 21st century it has been the Catholic Church with the support of the Knights of Columbus that has led the way for a restoration of many of the conservative values of the Christian faith. An honest unbiased interpretation of history has a way of turning the table. The villain can become the hero as each new generation takes the stage to either restore or tear down the spiritual values of the founding fathers. The persecution of the Irish Catholics in the Old World and in America, primarily in the 19th century, produced an iron faith of integrity in the growing Republic. The faith of the Irish Catholics developed into conservative advocacy for marriage and the sanctity of life. This conviction for the sanctity of life supported protecting the life of a baby from conception when the courts of America ruled in favor of abortion in 1973. The sanctity of life was based on honoring biblical scriptures and Papal proclamations that also protected the value of marriage between one man and one woman. Certainly not every Irish Catholic held these values, but as a people of faith the Catholics have led the battle for the sanctity of life and marriage in America. The Irish American values came to the surface as the culture of America became more liberal and humanistic, particularly in the latter portion of the 20th century.

The rich rolling hills of Eastern Oregon were nothing less than the Promised Land for the Irish immigrants fleeing the potato famine and subsequent poverty beginning in mid-nineteenth century England. The Irish immigrants endured persecution and poverty in the homeland and America as well which encouraged many to seek a fresh start in the uncharted wilderness of the West. One of the foremost of these Irish immigrants was John S. Kilkenny, born in County Leitrim, Ireland on May 14, 1870. John Kilkenny arrived in Umatilla, Oregon on the Short Line in May 1890. Why Eastern Oregon?

> "Blue are the mountains of Morrow,
> Green are its valleys and hills.
> Lofty its peaks, and grassy its plains,
> Its winters mean blizzards and chills.
> Then come the springs and summers,
> With sunshine and flowers galore.
> The livestock are fat and the wheat fields are brown,
> Thank God for abundance and more."
> (Kilkenny, John S., "*Shamrocks and Shepherds:
> The Irish of Morrow County*," Glass-Dahlstrom Printers, June 1969)

These Irish immigrants were seeking the same liberty and freedom that brought the first wave of Native Americans to the Pacific Northwest. This love of liberty and freedom was the promise that induced scores of pioneers to put their fortunes in a covered wagon and risk their lives and families to find a better life.

What impact would these bold Irish Catholics have on the emerging heritage of Eastern Oregon? This research has documented the negative impact of the Jesuit/Catholic Counter-Reformation and its impact on the Whitman mission. In like manner this research has documented the devastating impact of American manifest destiny imperialism on Native American culture. Would the new wave of Irish immigrants to Oregon bring religious prejudices that had birthed sectarian bitterness and warfare in Europe for centuries?

The first Irish immigrants to Eastern Oregon were few in number but their impact resonated throughout the Pacific Northwest. John S. Kilkenny established an empire that stretched into Montana and he marketed his sheep in transit all the way to Chicago. One would expect to find in these Irish immigrants at least a root core of religious sectarianism found in the native homeland, especially now that many ruled in the new sheep empires of the west. The first Irish immigrants were mainly Catholic; however, Kilkenny documents a substantial number were Protestant, and "religious intolerance was nonexistent." (Kilkenny, p. 15)

John S. Kilkenny

These Irish immigrants had tasted the fruit of religious bitterness and apparently they were determined to build their heritage in Oregon based upon religious tolerance and freedom. It appears once again the hand of the Almighty had drawn a peculiar people from Ireland to Eastern Oregon to develop a civilization based on the constraints and the spirit of tolerance and liberty found in the Book of Heaven. For instance, "Both Catholic and non-Catholics alike contributed the labor, materials, and money for the construction, in 1887, of the first Catholic Church in Heppner." (Kilkenny, p. 15) This is not to imply that only Irish Catholics molded the destiny of Morrow County. Some of the greatest contributors of the first Catholic Church in Heppner were Protestants. Henry Heppner, the father of the city of Heppner, was a Jewish merchant and a significant contributor toward the first Catholic Church as well. According to Kilkenny it was not until the mid 1920s and the immergence of the Ku Klux Klan that the community became conscious that there was such a thing as variance in religious beliefs.

Very little has been written about the unity between Protestantism, Catholicism and Judaism in Eastern Oregon as evidenced in Morrow County at this hour. There continues to abide in Eastern Oregon today a spirit of unity of one faith, one Bible and one community, and may this book encourage that unity. Attending a St. Patrick's Day celebration in Heppner, Oregon in the spring is the best way to experience the impact of the Irish in Morrow County. It is said this little celebration is the closest one can come to Ireland in spirit and terrain. The example of the first immigrants to Morrow County, led by the Irish Catholics, was illustrative of the virtue of religious tolerance, grace and justice. John F. Kilkenny leaves the reader with one final impression of the Irish of Eastern Oregon. "Is there a nation on the face of the earth whose history has not recorded the valor, the courage, the music, the social grace, the humor, the intellectual brilliance, and the drinking ability and inability, of this race of happy warriors whose wars were merry and whose songs were sad." (Kilkenny, p. 5)

Chapter 35

The Emergence of the Confederated Tribes of the Umatilla

By 1950 the Confederated Tribes of the Umatilla were governing themselves. They now had a Constitution and By-Laws and for the first time since the treaty of 1855 they could chart their own course. What would the Indians do with the restoration of their precious liberty that had taken nearly one hundred years to be reinstated? The greatest issue of the hour was the development of massive dams on the Columbia River that established hydroelectric power that unfortunately compromised the salmon runs and covered historic Celilo Falls with water. The Confederated Tribes of the Umatilla received $4,198,000 from the government to compensate for the loss of fishing sites. The Confederated Tribes allocated these funds to all enrolled tribe members in per capita payments and nothing was realized for future generations. The Umatilla Tribes continued to seek compensation for ceded lands and in 1969 once again the United States government rewarded the Umatilla Confederated Tribes and once again the tribe voted to give per capita payments to all enrolled members and only $200,000 was set aside for future scholarships. A significant, yet minority, faction of the Confederated Tribes of the Umatilla objected to the per capita allotments and these tribal board members were recalled. They became known as the anti-per capita faction. It wasn't long until the Confederated Tribes were broke and disorganized and the anti-per capita factions mobilized and picked up the loose ends and broken pieces of the Indian heritage and once again reestablished self-government.

This was a dark hour for self-government for the Umatilla Confederated Tribes. The community was wracked with alcoholism, housing was dismal and there were no salmon returning to the Umatilla watershed. The Confederated Tribes had been fully compensated for loss of their lands and they had logged significant portions of their forest reserves. The anti-per capita tribal board members who had been recalled in 1968 for their uncompromising stand for their heritage were restored to prominence and once again self-government began to prosper. These tribal leaders exercised diligence and justice and initiated the slow process of establishing policies of fiscal and social well being on the reservation. In due season, U.S government dollars became available through federal grants and the Education Assistance Act of 1974. As with all government grants there were strings attached that, at least in part, compromised tribal plans and priorities. Nonetheless, the governing council persevered with a long-range plan of tribal self-government that has given precedence to the restoration of the Native American cultural and environmental birthright. The Confederated Tribes were saved by the integrity of courageous leaders who would not compromise their heritage for short-term financial inducements.

It took a few decades for the Confederated Tribes of the Umatilla to figure out white man's politics. In every arena of social, economic and political affairs there was a learning curve for the Indians to master. By 1992 the Board of Directors wisely established the position of Executive Director to administer tribal programs. At the turn of the last decade of the twentieth century a series of providentially inspired opportunities impressively gave occasion for economic developments to spur a revival. The flagship of this revival has been led by Wildhorse Casino near Pendleton. The Casino has become a destination resort complete with a 100-room hotel, 18-hole golf course and the Tamastslikt Cultural Institute. The result has been stunning. The Confederated Tribes of the Umatilla are now the largest employer in Umatilla County. The Tribes' operating budget has grown from nothing in 1970 to $97 million in 2003. The number of tribal employees has grown from zero in 1970 to 1,110 in 2003. The primary source of the Confederated Tribes' new-found affluence has been the gambling casino, but the Confederated Tribes have learned from their past mistakes. The present leadership of the Tribe has managed its economic resources and treaty rights for the benefit of ancestral heritage and to a degree the common heritage of all Oregonians. Not all Oregonians would agree with the last statement, especially in light of some of the sovereign rights all Indians enjoy with regard to hunting and fishing that other Oregonians do not. Nevertheless, the Confederated Tribes through their newly achieved affluence and political power have restored the salmon run to the Umatilla River. This research will examine this issue later. The Tribes' position as the number one employer in the county has given the Native Americans a tremendous source of economic and political power never known before under the American government.

How would the Tribes wield their rapidly emerging power? The most resounding answer to this question can be found in the establishment of a most aggressive Department of Natural Resources. This department has developed into a vehicle for the tribe to work with land managers in all political arenas of American government to protect and enhance natural and cultural resources. The Tribes learned their lesson about giving away their economic blessings as per-capita allocations. Now they use their financial power in large part to enhance their heritage and restore the damage to the natural resources caused by decades of abusive and short-sighted land use practices countenanced by the U.S. government.

The most important and successful objective of the tribe to date has been the restoration of the salmon run in the Umatilla, extinct since the 1920s. The central core of the Indian civilization before the white man came was respect and sustainability of the natural habitat. The salmon were essential to the Indian culture and religion. Since the advent of white men and their industrial culture, the native salmon runs began to increasingly face the real prospect of extinction in America. In the white culture, some powerful interests believe the salmon cannot stand in the way of progress. To the Indian, "salmon are only a small symptom of a dying ecosystem. It is the Columbia Basin and the Pacific Ocean that are endangered. The salmon are telling us that the mountains, valleys, plains, rivers, and ocean are all sick. Many other species now face extinction." (www.umatilla.nsn.us/salmonpolicy.html, Salmon policy, p.1)

The Native American Indians believe if the salmon cannot survive it will only be a matter of time until one by one every indigenous living natural resource will perish, including mankind in the end. The Oregon Territory had not been pressed with this focus of vision since the hour of John McLoughlin and Marcus Whitman and more recently Governor Tom McCall.

The Native American Indians believed they had the answer to the dilemma facing all Oregonians. They believed there was an answer to save the salmon and enhance the economy of the Pacific Northwest at the same time. The history of the West documented in this book demonstrates that the American Indians have often been central to God's master plan for America, especially in the Pacific Northwest. "I know all the fowls of the mountains; and the wild beasts of the field are mine." (Psalms, 50:10, 11) According to the

Bible God gave mankind dominion over the fish of the sea, the fowl of the air and the beasts of the field and the Almighty will ultimately hold man accountable for stewardship of His creation. At the turn of the 21st century the Native Americans of the Columbia Plateau have gained tremendous political and financial power. Will the Confederated Tribes continue to honor and cherish the creation of the Creator or will power and money corrupt even the original stewards of God's creation in the Pacific Northwest?

The critical issue facing the vast arena of the original Oregon Territory was the same issue facing most nation states of the world at the turn of the 21st century: *water*. To the Native Americans of the Pacific Northwest, "Water is one of our most sacred gifts from the Creator, and is a essential part of our religion. Water is the lifeblood in the veins of the Pacific Northwest. Without good clean flowing water, nothing will survive." (Salmon policy, p. 3) The Columbia Plateau Indians have historically acknowledged the Creator and respected his creation. When the first white men discovered the Pacific Northwest they found a natural paradise the Indians had systematically cultivated for centuries. Captain William Clark wrote, "This multitude of fish is almost inconceivable. The water is so clear that they can be seen at the depth of fifteen or twenty feet." (Salmon policy, p. 2) The magnificent forests of the region had been groomed with centuries of Indian burning practices that left massive conifers with little under-brush and flowing quantities of berries and native plant species readily harvested by the Native Americans. The Indians saw the bountiful runs of salmon and steelhead as gifts from the Creator and their culture honored and nurtured that gift.

The battle over the future of the salmon runs in the Pacific Northwest continues to stand at the fulcrum of this document. The issue of water will dominate the economic and political culture of Oregon for the next century and perhaps for as long as civilization remains in the Pacific Northwest. All wildlife and human life on the planet requires a natural flow of clean, non-polluted water. All food crops also require adequate water. Salmon represent fish that require clean cool water, in contrast to those fish that live in warm water. The two hundred plus living species of the forests of the region require clean non-polluted water as well. The ancient lands of Oregon have been blessed with a rich array of vast quantities of pure cold aquifers flowing into the mighty Columbia River. When the first white men arrived in the Pacific Northwest all the tributaries of the Columbia River were teeming with massive runs of salmon and steelhead, and over sixty species of wildlife flourished in mountain forests that provided a reservoir for the cool aquifers that released their pure waters especially when these wildlife species needed the water the most, in the heat of the summer.

The Native Americans have exhorted their fellow Oregonians to be stewards of creation. "The water itself is sick. Grazing, timber, mining, agricultural and recreational practices in tributaries are drastically changing and damaging the health of the rivers." (Salmon policy, p. 4) Abusive logging, grazing and mining practices have altered the streams, riparian areas and forests of the Blue Mountains.

Can water be sick? Viktor Schauberger, the extraordinary Austrian natural scientist, inventor and philosopher warned that a bottle of water would become more valuable than a bottle of wine in 1920. He was ridiculed at the time. Schauberger warned that the destruction of the world's forests would ruin the vitality of water. In 1928 he wrote, "What can be said about the forest and its life? Unfortunately, my task is to write about its death. It is vital to alert those men who are still in a position to save dying forests from the hands of those who have no feeling for, or awareness of Nature. When a man dies the bells toll. When a forest dies and with it a whole people perishes, not a finger is lifted. It is known that for the death of a people the death of a forest has preceded it." (Alexandersson, Alex, Living Water, Viktor Schauberger and the Secrets of Natural Energy, Gateway Books, Bath, Utah, 1990, p.70,71).

Schauberger taught that scientifically water was a "living substance which is born and develops-normally to change into higher forms of energy-but can, with incorrect treatment, also die." (Alexandersson, p.54) The Native American understood this principle. Schauberger explained the reason why water is alive. "Good mountain spring water differs from atmospheric (rain) water by its suspended matter. Besides the dissolved salts, mountain spring water contains a relatively high content of gases in both free and fixed form as carbonic acid. The gases absorbed in a good mountain spring consist of 96 per cent carbon matter. By carbon matter in this context is meant all carbon matter known to the analytical chemist, all elements and their compounds, all metals and minerals: in other words, all matter with the exception of oxygen and hydrogen.

Atmospheric water (rain water, condensed water, distilled water or water exposed to a strong current of air and intensive light) as for instance surface water, contains a relative high content of oxygen, almost no or limited salt content, no or only a small amount of free and fixed carbonic acid and a gas content absorbed from the air consisting of oxygen which is dissolved in physical form. There are different ways in which the suspended matter is carried in solution in water. And just as the chemical composition of the solution can vary, so can the type of solution indicate the kind of energy that is at work in the water. Accordingly we differentiate water which contains a high percentage of energy derived from carbon matter, from water which exhibits a high percentage of energy derived from oxygen." (Alexandersson, p. 59)

Schauberger's life and research testified that healthy forests that produced living water were essential for the health of mankind and all living creatures. Alexandersson's book documented in this research is essential reading for those that wish to pursue the subject in greater depth.

In the previous chapter we documented the destruction of the lush forest between the Matteson School House and Matteson Butte after the pioneers left, caused by abusive logging practices. The forest springs and bogs had permanently dried up, the mountain streams (once flowing with steelhead and salmon) hardly flowed in late summer, and the massive Douglas fir, Ponderosa pine, Tamarack and associated conifers were harvested with no regard for the ecosystem of the forest or future generations. Largely malformed, diseased and mistletoe forests remain. In addition, the wildlife have been forced to seek new habitat to replace the largely sterile high mountain plateau that remains in this area and many of the privately owned forest lands of the Pacific Northwest. Large herds of elk have been forced away from the national forests and over-logged private timberlands onto large ranges of private ranch lands where these animals find sanctuary. Most of these Blue Mountain foothill ranches in the area near the Matteson School House now lock up their land to the general public and sell the right to hunt big-game animals through a legislatively protected business called fee hunting. We will research this issue later.

When the Native American Indians of the Confederated Tribes of the Umatilla ceded over 6.4 million acres to the American people they reserved the right to hunt and fish on the ceded land. In essence they ceded their land to the American government and agreed to move on to reservations with the promise that their heritage of the Blue Mountains and the water and timber it provided, especially for salmon, would be protected.

By the turn of the twentieth century the forests of America east of the Mississippi were exhausted of marketable lumber. By the sheer force of brute strength and horses, "some 300 billion board feet of lumber were moved to the market from the western forests during the 90-year pioneer period." (Williams, p. 22) Once the forests of the east were gone the forests of the Pacific Northwest, ceded by the Indians, were coveted and relentlessly harvested with "profligate waste by careless or uncaring loggers, by unthrifty sawmill techniques, by spoiled consumers, by preventable forest fires." (Williams, p. 217) Conservation was unheard of at this time and clear-cutting vast tracts of forest and moving to the next virgin stand of timber was standard procedure.

Fortunately men of conscience and vision began to speak out and initiate action to save the forests of the west. In the forefront of this wave of conservationism were John Audubon, John Muir, George

Grinnell, Gifford Pinchot and Theodore Roosevelt. These men actually coined the word conservation in 1907 to mean, "the interrelationship and sustained-yield use of forest, soils, waters, fish, wildlife, minerals, and all other natural resources." (Trefethen, James B., *An American Crusade for Wildlife*, Winchester Press, 1975, p. 126) Grinnell went on to form the magazine *Field and Stream*. Muir founded the Sierra Club. Pinchot became the first director of the U.S. Forest Service. Theodore Roosevelt became president of the United States and under his administration the government set aside vast tracks of national forests to be preserved for the American people in perpetuity. "Lumbermen could use the reserves, but under strictly controlled conditions." (Williams, p. 220) The Native Americans of the Columbia plateau had white men of kindred spirits that honored the creator and the fabulous creation of the natural resources of the west.

Gifford Pinchot had studied forestry in Europe since there was no such school in America. Pinchot returned from Europe and put into practice as director of America's forest reserves a management tool he called selective logging. The U.S. Congress defined the purpose of the national forests under Pinchot's selective logging guideline: "No public forest shall be established except to improve and protect the forest within the reservations…and to furnish a continuous supply of timber for the use and necessities of the citizens of the United States." (Williams, p. 220)

Not only had the U.S. government under President Roosevelt honored the treaty rights of the Native American Indians, they had also established a visionary policy whereby the national forests could be logged in perpetuity without harming the wildlife habitat or the aquifers that fed the mountain streams. The concept of multiple use and sustained yield of forest resources without waste became the theme of the national forests of America. Timber resources became the most valuable commodity of the Pacific Northwest at this time. The timber industry provided homes for the prospering American economy and jobs for a thriving work force in the new states of the Oregon Territory.

Certainly the Native American peoples did not share in this prosperity in the beginning, but the conservation policy that required selective logging, sustainable harvesting and multiple use of the forest was consistent with Native American cultural ideals. The vision and foresight of the early American conservationists sustained magnificent forests, pure cold aquifers and abundant fisheries and wildlife. The question of the hour was: Would succeeding generations share the values of the founding American conservationists? The answer can be found in the definition of industrial progress.

One of the main differences between the white and red nations has been the definition of industry. To the European-Caucasian people industry has historically meant utilizing a resource to its maximum potential by developing or inventing tools or methodology to accomplish that purpose. For example, the American Caucasian race observed the Columbia River and saw an untapped energy potential and in time built massive concrete dams to harness the hydroelectric power. These massive dams also tamed the mighty Columbia and facilitated cargo trade. To the white civilization this was industrial progress.

To the Indian peoples, industry meant utilizing a resource to its maximum potential without changing or damaging the resource. To the Indians these dams have produced a series of stagnant lakes that have severely hindered the clean flow of cold water necessary for salmon and steelhead. Cargo can ply up and down the Columbia River but the reversed timing of in-stream flows severely damaged salmon runs and propagated salmon predators such as squawfish that thrived in the warmer water. White man's progress to the American Indian has polluted the rivers, reduced the flow of cool clean water from the tributaries and turned the Columbia River into a series of warm water lakes.

In like manner the American Caucasian race defined progress in terms of inventions that facilitate power and production such as nuclear power, paper mills, chemical fertilizers, herbicides, and pesticides that increase food production and have enhanced the quality of life for all. Unfortunately, in the Pacific

Northwest increased food production and the production of industry and power has forced the Columbia River to become the final dumping ground for millions of gallons of toxic chemicals, radioactive nuclear wastes, and dioxins from paper factories and pollutants from industrial factories. These wastes have accumulated in the Columbia River estuary, and the fish and fowl of the river system have ingested these toxins to the detriment of the entire food chain, in particular human beings. This research will document the pollution of the Columbia River estuary and the Native American response in Chapter 37.

The question of the hour in the American west is the issue of industrial progress. Is the survival of the salmon vital to the survival of civilization in the Pacific Northwest? Steve Eldrige, general manager of the Umatilla Electric Coop, responded emphatically in the negative at a conference in early 2006. "One-third of its power rate (Bonneville Power) support salmon restoration costs, which translates into 20% of a UEC customer's rate. Summer spills to aid fish represented the loss of millions in power revenues for the region, and there is no proof they didn't hurt as much as they helped the fish." (McCune, Hal, "Salmon Meeting Shows Complexity of Challenge," *East Oregonian*, Feb. 22, 2006) The primary issue that drives power companies and industrial companies is the requirements of man, not fish. In the eyes of those who are responsible for sustaining industrial progress, salmon must not stand in the way of the needs of mankind. Accordingly, the chief of the fish management of the Army Corps of Engineers has commissioned and funded studies that prove "survival of adult salmon through the eight lower Columbia and Snake dams is about 98%." (McCune, Feb. 22, 2006)

To the historical Native American culture, industry and progress must be consistent with sustaining and conserving the natural environment. The ecomomic emergence of the Confederated Tribes of the Umatilla has helped establish a political power base to ensure that Native American cultural ideals are not destroyed by the needs of industrial and agricultural power. The tribes continue to advocate for healthy aquifers that produce cool, flowing streams manifesting healthy runs of salmon and steelhead. Over twenty years ago the Confederated Tribes of the Umatilla shut down salmon fishing altogether in the Columbia tributaries and they claimed their mainstream harvest lasts only a few days. According to these Indians "salmon are being destroyed for economic profit by hydropower, irrigation, timber and grazing interests." (Salmon policy, p.6)

In the twentieth century, especially after the Second World War, the needs of progress in the United States required rapid growth in industrial power. The Columbia River was dammed to create hydroelectric power. The baby boom generation was facilitated by increased production and inventions in every arena that by necessity produced a stream of chemical pollution that ultimately flowed into the mighty Columbia River. The once crystal clear and mighty river of the west became a series of lakes, replete with elevated water temperatures and dangerous levels of industrial pollution. Chain saws and later hydraulic clippers and technologically advanced saw mills made quick work of the existing private forestland that sustained and protected many of the aquifers of the Columbia River. When these aquifers dried up, the cold clean water necessary for the streambeds for spawning steelhead and salmon was severely compromised. As the private forest acres were consumed, the definition of multiple-use national forests came under great pressure to be redefined to allow for much higher harvest levels on the national forests. The issue according to those who favored the industrial progress was jobs, timber revenues, grazing rights, land rights and with no government interference. Those who favored conservation of America's national forests were labeled preservationists who would lock up land vital for progress and jobs.

By the late 1960s progressively larger and larger timber harvests were being taken off the national forests of America based on a new definition of the Multiple-Use Sustained Yield Act of 1960. By 1976 the National Forest Management Act (NFMA) established a new game plan to log the national forests of

America according to an environmental impact statement that had to go through a review process. The logging industry, in concert with the Forest Service, favored this new process to open the door to clear-cut the national forests of America and replace them with forest plantations. The Forest Service was required by law to manage the national forests for the benefit of the American people in perpetuity. Under redefinition of multiple-use laws the Forest Service was allowed to sell the American people timber complete with road building contracts with no profit to the American people save a portion of the timber receipts that were returned to the counties for school funds.

The Knutson-Vandenburg Act (K-V) was passed to promote reforestation, which allowed the Forest Service to keep all the profits of a timber sale. The Knutson-Vandenburg Act opened a pandora's box, which gave forest managers a big incentive to run up restoration costs. The 1976 Congress gave these Forest Service managers the additional discretion to use these K-V funds (up to $200 million) for other purposes. To obtain the K-V funds for reforestation the national forests had to be clear-cut. In no time the Forest Service became the agent to sell the forests of America at no profit for the American people (below cost timber sales) and pay timber companies to build roads (further destroying the forests of America) at taxpayer expense. The timber companies and the Forest Service prospered at taxpayer expense and the National Forests of the west were harvested indiscriminately. Local city and government officials did not expose the flawed system because they did not want to jeopardize their shared timber revenues that were allocated by law to the county for schools. The result was the forests of the west were harvested with no foresight for future generations and no stewardship toward the needs of wildlife and fisheries. The aquifers, vital to the quality and quantity of water necessary for steelhead and salmon runs and agricultural needs, were compromised and in some cases destroyed, never to be replenished. The Confederated Tribes were slow to understand the depth of the destruction of forest aquifers at an hour their political voice could have stopped or at least curtailed the rampant clear-cutting of the forests east of the Cascades.

The result of the Forest Service clear-cut policy was a removal of multiple generations of America's national forest for nearly two decades, from 1970 to 1990. There was no place in this Forest Service bureaucracy for conservationists. The habitat of the multiple species of wildlife was decimated in forests throughout America, primarly in the west. Mountain soils were compacted, riparian areas were destroyed, streambeds were silted in, soil and water temperatures increased and mature forest conifer stands were removed. Some of these forests would not be harvested again for a century in the arid portions of the Pacific Northwest. In Idaho and Montana the Forest Service administered 22 national forests, all of which lost money between 1979 and 1984. In the Heppner Unit of the National Forest the Forest Service increased timber harvest three-fold from 1978 to 1987. The policy of the Forest Service, driven by Knutsen-Vandenburg funds, was turning the forests into plantation farms created by man.

The Indians must have feared this would happen to their ancient forests. They must have feared in the name of progress some elements of the white race would attempt to cut down the natural forests of the Blue Mountains and attempt to remake them in their own image as tree plantations. Fortunately men and women of courage and integrity in Eastern Oregon stood up for the forest against the timber industry and Forest Service and exposed this clear-cutting scheme.

In Heppner, area local game biologist Glen Ward produced a document called "A Critical Review of the Predicted Results From the Wickiup Timber Sale Environmental Analysis Report" in 1980 that exposed the Forest Service clear-cutting scheme. Lexington conservationist Beryl Stillman lost his job at the Kinzua saw mill in Heppner because of his vocal stand against the blatant abuse of timber management policies and wildlife resources. The author of this research produced a film in 1988 called "National Forests for Nobody" that was carried on local television in Heppner exposing the disingenuous policies of the Forest

Service. In 1988 a local retired businessman, L. E. Dick (my father), warned that the current Forest Service timber harvest plan would put the local sawmill out of timber within a decade and would severely undermine the local economy. Kinzua Resources closed its doors permanently eight years later. Dick, as president of the local Chamber of Commerce, had unsuccessfully exhorted the city to support conservation forest practices in 1972 at great expense to his business. At that time Heppner had five grocery stores and five gas stations supported in large part by the multi-revenues of the forest including logging, recreation, hunting and tourist dollars. In 2009, after two decades of abusive logging practices beginning in the '70s, Heppner has one gas station and one grocery store and battles to sustain its population base.

In Milton-Freewater the city council went on record January 27, 1988: "in opposition to the U.S. Forest Service draft plan to allow logging in drainage areas that feed into the North and South forks of the Walla River." (*East Oregonian*, Jan. 28, 1988) Herb Saager, a twenty-year council member, warned, "today in the late summer, flows are near to nothing from the North Fork (Walla Walla River) watershed, although they once had been excellent. Through their (Forest Service) doing, clear-cutting the entire area, it virtually ruined that fork of the river." (*Oregonian*, Feb. 29, 1988)

The Oregon Natural Resource Council, a grass-roots environmental organization, filed 226 appeals to thwart the timber harvest policies of the Forest Service. In response, pro-timber harvest Oregon Congressman Bob Smith denounced the "economic terrorism" of the Council. "I'm angry and deeply disappointed with the Council's use of reckless legal tactics in its attempt to stop the resale of federal timber stands returned under the terms of federal timber contract relief." (*East Oregonian*, March 3, 1988) In these sales the timber companies defaulted on their contracts. In other words they refused to pay for the timber they purchased from the Forest Service until they were granted a better deal.

By the close of the twentieth century the forests of the west were in serious trouble. The salmon as well as the two hundred forest species that comprised a healthy and symbiotic ecosystem were all dependent on the magnificent majestic conifer trees that made up a forest. The Forest Service practice of clear-cutting America's national treasures to claim Knutson-Vandenburg funds for reforestation undermined the vitality of the forests of the west. Unfortunately the Confederated Tribes of the Umatilla did little to use their emerging political and economic clout to protect the forest of the west.

Gifford Pinchot was a visionary. A forest can be selectively logged and that same forest, complete with the aquifers, wildlife habitat and a diverse and multiple species ecosystem, could still remain intact. The needs of industry and progress will always require the harvest of the mature trees of the forest to sustain the multiple needs of western civilization. The forests of the west were not damaged or compromised by selective logging, but rather by abusive and indiscriminate logging practices, in particular clear-cut logging in arid forests. In major areas of the Blue Mountains it takes up to a century to produce a mature conifer tree (12 inches at breast height).

This research has documented that the American Indians did have allies that respected the Creator and were willing to be wise stewards of God's creation. The American conservation movement was modeled in the same reverential respect toward nature that the American Indians exhibited for centuries before the advent of white men. The Congressional mandate to conserve and sustain the national forests of America was upheld by multiple acts of Congress every time greed and avarice attempted to mine America's greatest treasures. The Organic Act required timber to be sold for not less than the appraised value. The Antiquities and Historic Preservation Act required protection of cultural sites. The Clean Water Act and Safe Drinking Water Amendments required the Forest Service to protect water quality. The Endangered Species Act required the Forest Service to attempt to recover the population of plants and animals that were considered threatened or endangered. This research has already documented the Multiple-Use Sustained-Yield Act requiring all national forests to be utilized in a manner that guaranteed sustained yield and met the needs of the American people in perpetuity. This research has also documented the impact of the National Forest Management Act that required an environmental impact analysis in order to protect the environment from abusive logging practices.

The Supreme Court under John Marshall in 1830 discovered they could rule but if the executive branch was not willing to enforce the law there was nothing they could do. The Clean Water Act of 1960 stated: "It is the National Goal…that wherever attainable, an interim goal of water quality which provides for the protection and propagation of fish…be achieved by July 1, 1983." (Clean Water Act, 33 USC 125d (a)) The written policy of the American Indians has demonstrated their desire to consult and work with the American people in order to conserve and sustain our mutual natural resources. The Salmon Policy of the Confederated Tribes of the Umatilla Reservation exhorts negotiation and cooperation. "Our economies can co-exist. Instead, non-Indians have taken not only the resources we gave them, but also the resources we specifically reserved to ourselves. As a result, their economies have thrived, while ours has been driven to extinction." (Salmon Policy, p. 3)

The Confederated Tribes have documented how the construction of the Hells Canyon Dam on the Snake River has caused the total extinction of the anadromous (fish that go from river to ocean and back to the river) fish of the entire Powder, Burnt, Owyhee and Malheur watersheds. The Tribes also point out salmon are on the verge of extinction in the Grande Ronde, Yakima, Imnaha and Tucannon watersheds. The Salmon runs are so low in these watersheds the Indians cannot fish these rivers. "Already, the Snake River Coho, the Wallowa Lake Sockeye, the Walla Walla Chinook, and the Grande Ronde lamprey are extinct, among others." (Salmon Policy, p. 3).

The mountain forests of America are the reservoirs for the most essential and precious commodity known to man, water. In addition to the air we breathe, water is every nation's greatest resource. There is a finite limit to the amount of water and there is no constant formula for how it will be delivered to any region. No land in any continent in the world has been blessed by the Almighty with such an abundant quantity and quality of water as the Pacific Northwest of America. The Columbia River and its magnificent tributaries are living flowing proof of that providential blessing. The most magnificent salmon runs in the history of the world have occurred in the tributaries of the Columbia River.

All rivers begin in the protected aquifers of the highlands and mountains of a watershed. Like the anadromous fish the water works its way to the ocean and back again to the mountain reservoirs. In like manner all underground streams also begin at the top of the watershed. When the aquifers of the watershed are undermined and in some cases destroyed the water is no longer kept cool and stored in mountain reservoirs but rather runs off, usually eroding the landscape. In like manner the underground wells are also diminished, especially during the dry hot portions of late summer when human and agricultural water demands are high.

The issue of salmon restoration will only grow in intensity in the new century. A team of congressmen and stakeholders toured the Pacific Northwest in 2008 in search of solutions. The divergent views on salmon recovery illustrate the difficulty of resolving this issue. Will Anderson, chief of fish management for the Army Corps of Engineers in Portland, claims, "survival of adult salmon through the eight lower Columbia and Snake dams is about 98 percent." (McCune, Feb. 22, 2006) The Confederated Tribes of the Umatilla claim the lower Columbia and Snake River dams and reservoirs "kill an estimated 77-96% of migrating juvenile salmon and an estimated 37-61% of migrating adults." (Salmon Policy, p. 14) The Tribes believe that the extremely warm conditions of the water in the reservoirs also cause disease, stress and death as well.

The Confederated Tribes have developed a plan to restore the salmon and they have demonstrated in the Umatilla River (next chapter) that their plan works. The emerging economic and political power of the Confederated Tribes has given them a platform to demonstrate some impressive results. The Tribes' philosophy for salmon recovery in streams now devoid of anadromous fish requires "gravel to gravel" management. Hatcheries are used to reintroduce salmon into their habitat from which they will reproduce naturally if the water quality and quantity of the watershed has been restored. According to the Indians and conservationists, the most important resource of a forest is water. To sustain and protect the mountain reservoirs requires that the forests are managed with sound conservation practices and all stakeholders abide by fair and equitable rules for water distribution that leave enough water for a safe progression of anadromous fish. Indians and conservationists believe if the fish can survive then mankind will survive also. If the anadromous fish prosper, mankind will prosper as well.

Perhaps the most controversial issue to face the Pacific Northwest is the Tribes' position on removal or modification of Columbia and Snake River dams. The precise Indian policy is: "We support the staged, strategic modification or removal of dams, such as the lower four Snake River Dams and the John Day Dam, coincident with development of a New Energy Plan for the region and implementation of aggressive energy conservation programs." (Salmon Policy, p. 15) According to the Confederated Tribes the removal of these dams would restore the mighty Columbia River, at least in part. This policy would restore salmon runs in the entire Columbia Plateau watersheds. In concert with forest restoration the area would be invigorated with greater water quality and quantity, restored salmon and steelhead runs, increased agricultural water resources, enhanced recreation values and a revived tourist economy.

Unfortunately the removal of any of the Columbia River dams would severely damage multiple industries that have improved the quality of life in the Pacific Northwest including barge traffic and hydroelectric production. The staged modification or removal of any Columbia River dam would cause a significant hydroelectric depletion of energy, and the Tribes and their supporters would need to provide some viable alternatives in addition to an aggressive energy conservation program. In addition, the removal of any Columbia River dam would end barge and tourist vessels that have become essential to the economy of the Pacific Northwest. Certainly there is unlimited potential for both wind and solar energy in the region, but it would be difficult to replace the commerce on the river the dams have provided.

A significant issue facing the region in relation to the Native American Indians is a lack of knowledge and understanding. Many Oregonians have little understanding of the culture and heritage of the American Indians. One of the great purposes of this research is to restore the vision and hope of the original Oregonians and provide non Indians an understanding of Indian culture. Tourism and recreation are two of the greatest economies of the future. A cooperative team approach between the American and Indian nations could produce an exciting new hour of cooperation and industry. Healthy, clean, unpolluted, flowing, cold water is the greatest potential resource of the Pacific Northwest. Hunting, fishing, recreation, hiking, and increased water for agriculture are just a few of the benefits of restoring the health of the Columbia River and its tributaries. Diligent and reasonable statesmen can find a way to sustain the hydroelectric power and commerce of the Columbia River and at the same time enhance the flow of clean, cold, unpolluted water through the entire system. That vision will remain one of the most important purposes of this research.

Sadly, even the Native Americans have not always demonstrated the courage or conviction to confront some of the most dangerous threats to the survival of salmon, especially pollution. This research will examine this issue in the Chapter 37. The American Indians have become one of the most powerful political players in the battle for the natural resources of the Pacific Northwest. The question of the hour is, will they use their newfound economic and political prowess with conviction and integrity to restore the ecosystem of the Columbia River basin? Never have the treasures of Old Oregon needed their stewardship more than now.

The issue of pollution of the Columbia River in its tributaries is one of the most grievous dilemmas facing Old Oregon. This is not ordinary pollution. This research will document the mostly hidden controversy over pouring millions of tons of known carcinogens into the waterways and airways of the Columbia River basin in the next few chapters. The problem is the public has little knowledge or understanding of the depth of the crisis. The question that remains to be answered is, why have the Confederated Tribes allowed the well-documented pollution of the Columbia River to continue virtually unabated without confronting the United States government, the Army, or state regulatory agencies like the Oregon DEQ (Dept. of Environmental Quality) and EQC (Environmental Quality Commission)? Certainly the tribes have the economic savvy and political power to begin the process of restoration of the health of the waterways of the region in spite of the powerful political powers that oppose their vision.

This research will examine the record of the Confederated Tribes of the Umatilla on resurrecting the Umatilla River before examining the larger issue of pollution. The resurrection of the Umatilla River is one of the marvels of the 20th century in Old Oregon. The Native Americans have developed the skill, knowledge and patience to successfully negotiate huge projects for the benefit of all stakeholders in the region. The cooperation and negotiation that spurred the resurrection of the Umatilla River can serve as a template for future obstacles between the two nations. The Umatilla River can serve as an example for the changes and adjustments that can be made on both sides in order to restore and sustain our common heritage.

CHAPTER 36

THE RESURRECTION OF THE UMATILLA RIVER

In the late 1970s, as the Confederated Tribes were establishing the foundation of self-rule, they made a strategic decision to restore salmon to the Umatilla River. Not one salmon had returned to its ancestral home in half a century, but the Tribes envisioned their river teeming with anadromous fish once again. To accomplish this monumental task the Tribes would need some miracles. Every year irrigators along the Umatilla River would suck the river dry of precious water to water their crops. The Tribes could sue the irrigators under reserved treaty rights or they could negotiate using the Treaty of 1855 as a fulcrum to build alliances. The Columbia Plateau Indians of the Pacific Northwest have always been a pragmatic, deliberating culture that historically had sought diplomatic solutions in the face of hostility. The strategic battle to resurrect the Umatilla River would be a classic example of the Tribes' ability to exercise political savvy to restore their natural heritage.

Fortunately, the Tribes had powerful allies among non-Indian conservationist legislators who shared their vision. The Northwest Power Act of 1980 established the Northwest Power Planning Council (NPP), the ideal vehicle for the Tribes to express and implement their vision to restore salmon runs to the region. The NPP Council was "charged with creating a program that would restore salmon runs crippled by the hydropower system." (Shelley, Christopher, The Resurrection of a River, www.ccrh.org/comm/river/docs/ubasin.htm, p. 1) Not only did the Tribes have a vehicle to express and implement their vision for salmon recovery, they also now had potential financing from the Bonneville Power Administration. The Tribes were encouraged by the Oregon Department of Fish and Wildlife to create a master plan to restore the ecosystem of the Umatilla River. "Tribal biologists would use small hatcheries to artificially spawn some salmon for brood stock, but they would allow many of the strongest salmon to remain in the river, to swim upstream into the tributaries and spawn naturally. Fish managers would use hatcheries to jump start salmon runs, but they would rely on a 'gravel to gravel' strategy to propagate most of the salmon in the basin." (Shelley, p. 2)

The Tribes now had a vision and the vehicle and technology to implement the plan. There was still one major hurdle. This hurdle was more than a hurdle, more like a mountain that had to be picked up and thrown into the sea. For most of the twentieth century the Umatilla River had been virtually emptied during the summer by irrigators. The United States Bureau of Reclamation had instigated projects that caused the desert regions of the Columbia Plateau to blossom with agricultural produce. The major salmon rivers of the Columbia basin—the Umatilla, the Imnaha, the Grande Ronde, the Wallowa, the Walla Walla and the Tucanna—became tools of irrigation at the expense of anadromous fish. The Umatilla River was severely undermined, in part by abusive grazing and logging practices, but more significantly by irrigation demands that virtually drained the river dry in the summer. All the money and technology in the world could not bring back the salmon if there was not enough water flowing in the river during the critical times of salmon and steelhead runs.

The Tribes contracted biologist Ed Chaney to meet with the Umatilla River irrigators to express the Indians' need for water for anadromous fish. The Tribes wanted the irrigators to know that the Umatilla River would one day flow with runs of salmon with their help or without their help. The Tribes charged Chaney with the mission of restoring salmon to the Umatilla River, at any cost. Chaney met with Umatilla county irrigators in Stanfield in 1982 to initiate a dialogue for salmon restoration. In 1983 the Bureau of Reclamation conducted an in-stream flow analysis that determined huge pumps could draw water from the Columbia River above McNary Dam to meet irrigators' needs through a series of water channels instead of the Umatilla River. The Umatilla River restoration program could not be facilitated by Columbia River water pumped into the Umatilla River because these waters would confuse migrating anadromous fish.

There were two major obstacles to this plan. The cost of pumping Columbia River water into the irrigation viaducts of the Umatilla basin would be enormous. Who would pay this expense? The second obstacle was that the irrigation districts—Hermiston, Stanfield, Westland, and West Extension—were not willing to negotiate without an increase in irrigation water. Bill Porfily, manager of the Westland Irrigation District, expressed the irrigation districts' position. "The irrigation districts want to get something more from the project than a guarantee of the status quo. If they get no further benefit from the project then the districts might as well allow the tribal litigation to run its course." (Shelley, p. 3) The support of the irrigators was essential to the Tribes in order to lobby for the project with Congress. The Tribes refused to compromise their position and the irrigators wisely yielded their unreasonable demands and joined the Umatilla Basin Project Steering Committee.

Time became a motivating factor once the Tribes released the first salmon in 1982. These salmon could not return up the Umatilla River until the cold clean waters could be saved from irrigation by the pumped water from the Columbia. Two powerful allies joined hands with the Tribes: Oregon Senator Mark Hatfield and Oregon Governor Neil Goldschmidt. Visionary non-Indian Oregonians hailed the Umatilla Basin Project as "right for the environment" (Shelley, p. 4) and Governor Goldschmidt called the project "morally essential." (Shelley, p. 4)

This research has documented how God had allowed the American people to discover the mighty Columbia River with the trust that ultimately the American people would be wise stewards of the environment. Restoring the salmon runs was indeed a moral issue that was right for the Pacific Northwest. In 1987 Senator Mark Hatfield fulfilled a century-old promise to the Columbia Plateau Indians and sponsored Senate Bill 1613, creating the Umatilla Basin Project. The unlikely alliance of farmers and Indians was on the verge of restoring salmon runs to the Umatilla River without impeding irrigation needs. The precedent this alliance would establish could be used as a blueprint to restore salmon runs across the entire Columbia basin and fulfill the hope and dream of the Native American for their ancestral homeland. That dream, first spoken of by Chief Joseph, had enemies and they quickly acted in an attempt to kill Senate Bill 1613.

Bonneville Power's chief customer was the Pacific Northwest Utilities Conference Committee that included the aluminum factories, paper mills, and private and public utilities. In March 1987 this Committee sent out a flyer to its constituents warning that the Umatilla Basin Project would obligate Bonneville "to provide free pumping for fish." (Shelley, p. 4) What the Committee of industries and utilities feared was a precedent whereby Bonneville Power would pay for damage done to salmon streams caused by irrigation. In truth these companies feared they would be saddled with the bill for pumping Columbia River water to ensure salmon runs. The fact these industries did not want brought to the surface was that the aluminum and paper factories had poured tens of thousands of gallons of dioxins, heavy metals and chemical pollutants into the Columbia River for decades, sickening and killing anadromous fish and all other sorts of wildlife species.

These industries should have been shut down by the government, or at the very least forced to abide by the Clean Water Act of 1960. These polluting industries have continued to exercise their political and financial power to pour contaminants into the waters of the Pacific Northwest to the present hour. This research will examine how these industrial companies have been able to pollute without regulation in the next chapter. The companies that polluted the Columbia River should have been required to foot the bill for salmon restoration. Fortunately, Congress refused to buckle to the threats of industry and public and private utilities and passed the Umatilla Basin Act in 1988. The anadromous fish would have water and for the first time in over half a century salmon and steelhead would once again flow up and down the Umatilla River.

The victory of the Confederated Tribes of the Umatilla River "marked an important shift in the struggle to re-allocate western resources according to values other than extraction. In a mere eight years, the Umatilla Tribes had succeeded in making environmental and cultural concerns integral parts of discussion…" (Shelley, p. 4) For the first time since the advent of non-Indians into the Oregon Territory the Native American value of stewardship of the environment was elevated to a level playing field with the white civilization's principle of industrial progress. The irrigators, statesmen and Indians had successfully allocated essential resources, in this case water, on the basis of what Governor Goldschmidt called the principle of what was "morally right." Instead of extracting resources from the environment, for the first time essential resources were being reintroduced into the environment. Instead of the dominant principle of mining wealth with no regard for the environment, essential resources were protected and conserved.

The precedent was monumental. The Confederated Tribes proved that their natural resource heritage in the Pacific Northwest could be restored through cooperation and mediation. For the first time the Confederated Tribes had elevated the value of stewardship of God's creation on equal footing to industrial progress. However, before the Tribes and irrigators could relish their monumental victory, another deadly threat to the alliance was unleashed by an environmental organization.

WaterWatch was an environmental organization concerned with water flows and irrigation practices. WaterWatch had been monitoring the illegal practice of "waterspreading" for decades. Waterspreading was the unlawful sale of the irrigation districts' unused irrigation water that by statute was required to be left in the river. In 1991 WaterWatch initiated litigation exposing "illegal water marketing activities." (Shelley, p. 5) WaterWatch essentially exposed the source of the problem for water in the Pacific Northwest. The U.S. government had "promised the river twice: to the irrigators between 1904 and 1924 and to American Indians in the Treaty of 1855." (Shelley, p. 5)

The fallout from WaterWatch's litigation threatened to undermine nearly a decade of careful negotiations. The Tribes were caught in the crossfire between the irrigators they were in alliance with and the environmental organization they supported in principle. This dilemma threatened to topple the whole Umatilla Basin Project. "The tribes certainly did not condone the irrigators districts' illegal water practices, but neither did they want to anger or alienate their partners and jeopardize their larger goals." (Shelley, p. 5) The issue to the Indians was elementary: save the salmon run. Their skillful biologist, Ed Chaney, illustrated the great strength of the Confederated Tribes: their uncompromising position to restore their heritage with the salmon runs and their ability to negotiate to reach that goal. Chaney addressed the issue with these words: "Contrary to what the good folks at Oregon Water Watch [sic] think, the tribe should not have to wait more decades for fulfillment of its treaty reserved rights to fish until the state, BR and irrigators can get around to cleaning up their water-use act." (Shelley, p. 5) The Tribes were instrumental in jumpstarting negotiations that proceeded with all stakeholders, and the Umatilla Basin Act passed in

Congress in 1992 releasing $48 million to begin the process of restoration of the salmon runs on the Umatilla River.

In 1994 the first salmon runs returned to the cool clean flowing summer waters of the Umatilla River. An unlikely alliance of irrigators, environmentalists, politicians, statesmen, and Indians forged a blueprint for a new era in the Pacific Northwest. By 1998 the return of over 2,000 salmon initiated the first sport season on the Umatilla River in history. Every stakeholder benefited by the alliance that brought anadromous fish back into the Umatilla River. The sports fishing industry was not the only industry that profited by the return of anadromous fish in the Umatilla. The tourist and recreation industry in eastern Oregon received a boost by the restoration of salmon in the river as well. Recreation activities brought dollars into the community, but more important than dollars was the spiritual and cultural boost that anadromous fish brought to the region.

Quality of life cannot be measured in dollars and cents. Quality of life was what brought the first American pioneer settlers into the Oregon Territory. These courageous pioneers desired a fresh start where they could prosper, and to many of the first pioneers it was the clean and cold flowing waters, alive with natural resources, that brought them to Oregon. Restored salmon runs required cold clean flowing water, the essence of life for all living species. If the salmon could survive, then a multitude of associated wildlife species could prosper as well. Salmon were only a small part of the equation, in terms of restoring the whole forest ecosystem. To the Indians the salmon were the essential piece to restoring their cultural heritage. To these Confederated Tribes, salmon represented the heart of their religion. The Great Spirit Chief gave the Indians salmon and their lifestyle depended on consistent returns of these anadromous fish to their ancestral homelands deep in the rivers and streams of the Blue Mountains.

Salmon are not the only species that requires cold clean flowing water. All living species require clean, unpolluted water to live. The source of most cold clean flowing water is the forest reservoir. The Indians have been exhorting their non-Indian brethren to restore the mountain forests and habitat for decades. The Confederated Tribes proved through the restoration of the Umatilla River that the wonderful natural resources of the Pacific Northwest could produce blessings and prosperity through conservation instead of extraction. Logging, mining, grazing, and irrigation policies of extraction without regard for the environment have done great damage to the heritage of all Oregonians of the entire Pacific Northwest.

The Indians believe they have a vision and a plan to restore the ecosystem of the entire Pacific Northwest and they are willing to negotiate with all stakeholders to achieve this purpose. They have established their vision on the Umatilla River with conviction, integrity, cooperation and perseverance. They have demonstrated a positive vision for the future for all Oregonians of the Pacific Northwest—restored aquifers that produce cool, clean, flowing water. Will the Confederated Tribes exercise the integrity to use the political power and financial blessings pouring into their coffers to restore the polluted and languishing Columbia River in the manner in which they restored the Umatilla? This research will study that question in the next chapter.

It was the Columbia River, the fabled Northwest Passage, the great mariner nations of the world were all seeking to discover and claim. It was this great river of the west that gave Oregon its name. It was this great river that was the lifeblood of communication and civilization in the Pacific Northwest since the beginning of recorded history. How flows this mighty river after a century and a half of white man's rule? What would the nation that won the greatest sweepstakes of all time do with its great prize? Would the Confederated Tribes succumb to political pressure and financial enticements to compromise their stewardship values or would they stand firm and exercise moral courage against the polluters of the Columbia?

Chapter 37

The Destruction of the Columbia River: The Fabled Northwest Passage

In 2006 the Fish and Wildlife Oregon Sports Fishing Regulations handbook issued a fish advisory warning that some Oregon waters have contaminants that are harmful to human health. According to the Oregon Fish and Wildlife Department the lower portion (from Hanford) of the Columbia River was contaminated with PCBs, dioxins and pesticides in all resident species. Thirteen other streams, reservoirs, sloughs, and harbors have also tested so high in contaminants that consumption of fish should either be avoided or carefully limited. Not all Oregon streams, rivers and reservoirs have been tested so there was no documentation to determine the spread of contamination of Oregon waters. The Environmental Protection Agency has conducted extensive studies on the Columbia River and its tributaries as well that "confirm the need for regulatory agencies to continue to pursue rigorous controls on environmental pollutants and remove those pollutants which have been dispersed into our ecosystem." (EPA, 910-R-02-006, 1996-98, p. E-8)

How have the once pure waters of the Columbia River and its tributaries become so infested with toxic chemicals? Did not the Clean Water Act of 1960 ensure clean water for all Oregonians? How could a massive powerful river such as the Columbia, one of the most powerful rivers in the world, become so polluted? The Native Americans of the Pacific Northwest have depended on the Columbia River and its vast watershed for their food, culture and religion for centuries. They entrusted their ancestral heritage on the Columbia River and the life this great river provides for all living things into the hands of the American government. Let us examine this mighty river at the beginning of the 21st century; a river bestowed from time immemorial by the Almighty with cold crystal clear waters, crystal clear waters in which Lewis and Clark two hundred years ago viewed salmon as deep as twenty feet.

Presently thirteen pulp mills and multiple municipal and industrial polluters release 1,048,853 tons of carcinogens into the Columbia River every year according to the U.S. Environmental Protection Agency. (www.Columbiariverkeeper.org river facts) According to the research of Columbia River Keepers this astounding poisoning of the Columbia River has been documented to be a "decrease of 95% in the past twelve years." (Columbiariverkeeper) The American government's need for industrial progress has changed the landscape in the Pacific Northwest with the authority of political power controlling the policy of ecology and environment health.

Neither the state of Oregon nor that of Washington assumed responsibility for the water quality of the Columbia River until a grassroots citizens' group called Columbia River United in 1989 forced the two states to establish the Bi-State Water Quality Commission. The results of the testing of the Columbia River for water quality since this commission was established have been astounding. The initial sediment testing "showed safe reference levels were exceeded for arsenic, cadmium, chromium, copper, iron, mercury, nickel, silver, and zinc." (Columbiariverkeeper) Because the Columbia River was not monitored for pollutants prior to the Bi-State Commission, 281,600 tons of mercury was dumped into the river between 1940 and 1980. It is no wonder the Oregon Game Commission has been forced to issue a health advisory against eating the fish in the Columbia River.

The cancer rates along the lower Columbia River, especially along the Columbia River between Hermiston and the Tri Cities in Washington, are some of the highest in America. (See www.downwinders.com) The rivers and streams of the Columbia Basin have been poisoned with industrial pollutants, nuclear waste, fertilizers and pesticides since 1940 and the resultant diseases caused by the deadly carcinogens have never been documented by any government agency or study. The dioxins and furans that are being released into the water by the pulp mills and into the environment by the Chemical Weapons Incineration near Hermiston are some of the most toxic carcinogens ever tested. These toxins cause cancer, immune suppression, endocrine disruption, and debilitating autoimmune sicknesses because the human body has no natural defense system against these man-made poisons. The heavy metals released into the atmosphere by the Umatilla Chemical Incinerator and the industrial and municipal pollution released into the Columbia River and its tributaries are equally damaging to the health and heritage of the peoples of the Columbia Basin. Arsenic causes lung and heart disease. Lead poisons the central nervous system and harms multiple systems of the body, manifesting itself in headaches and autoimmune diseases. Mercury damages the internal organs, making a person irritable, sluggish and susceptible to disease. Cadmium causes prostate, lung and kidney cancer plus myriad associated diseases. Excessive doses of copper, iron, nickel, silver and zinc cause innumerable physical disorders depending upon the individual and his or her relative genetic weaknesses.

In addition, Columbia River waters test high in over twenty pesticides; nevertheless, the state and federal government have yet to test or regulate the level of pesticides or herbicides based on a standard reference level for water contamination. In addition to the incessant and persistent hazards of pesticides, herbicides, and carcinogenic toxins and heavy metals working their way into the once magnificent Columbia, a much greater evil has been silently leaching its way ominously into the mighty river near a little village called Hanford since 1943.

In 1943, Hanford was a quiet city near the Columbia River in eastern Washington. Hanford was blessed because of its ideal proximity to the rich natural resources of the area and the mighty Columbia River. The top secret Manhattan Project, which produced the first atomic bomb that destroyed Hiroshima and Nagasaki, would change everything for Hanford and the heritage of the Pacific Northwest. Hanford was the perfect location for this secret project, because of its secluded position with an unlimited supply of cold clean water. The twelve hundred inhabitants of Hanford were uprooted and moved without explanation and the hunting and fishing rights of the Indians were ended, cold turkey.

A force of fifty one thousand workers turned Hanford into the largest plutonium producer in the world, virtually overnight. Within two decades the Columbia River turned from the cleanest purest river in the world to the most toxically radioactive polluted river on the planet. "By 1960 more radiation had been released to the river than released by Chernobyl…(turning the Pacific Northwest into) the most grossly contaminated area of North America, possibly the world." (Columbiariverkeepers.org, Hanford) In a deliberate effort to conceal the extent of the toxic pollution, the two states and the U.S. government have yet to establish reference levels for radionclide (plutonium, cesium) concentrations in the Columbia River. The greatest threat to the Columbia River for the future generations of mankind and all living species will be the radiation threat from the stored waste of the Hanford plutonium production reactors still leaking into the Columbia River.

This ominously menacing radioactive toxic hazard, buried at Hanford near the banks of the Columbia River, has no proven technology for safe storage or removal. Fifty-three million gallons of radioactive waste has been stored in tanks that are slowly disintegrating. The government had no technology to dispose of the radioactive waste when the plutonium was produced. The government still has no technology to dispose of this carcinogenic cesspool over sixty five years later. The current plan is to attempt to turn the radioactive waste into glass through a vitrification process and bury the residue within Yucca Mountain in Nevada. The clean up of Hanford is estimated at $100 billion, to be financed by the next multiple generations of Americans. In addition, the government has plans to bring countless tons of the rest of the nation's radioactive waste to Hanford over the objection of the citizens of Washington. Catholic Pope John Paul II, at the conclusion of the 20th century, declared, "Today the dramatic threat of ecological breakdown is teaching us the extent of which greed and selfishness—both individual and collective—are contrary to the order of creation, an order which is characterized by mutual interdependence." (Columbiariverkeeper.org/theorg.htm) The American nation produced a radioactive monster that now terrorizes the "manifest destiny" of countless generations of future citizens in the Pacific Northwest.

The desecration of the mighty Columbia River in the twentieth century has been stunning. The anadromous fish, native fish and the American Indians were not the only living beings threatened by the ecological breakdown of the Columbia River system that has been occurring with little resistance for much of the past century. Silently, with countless forewarnings ignored, dark menacing clouds of destruction are now ominously threatening the precious water of the region, undermining the future health and culture of the American people of the Pacific Northwest.

The remote seclusion of Eastern Oregon did not only attract attention for the mass production of plutonium for nuclear power. The U.S. military determined, after the Second World War, that the secluded desert sands of Umatilla County next to the Columbia River would be the perfect place to store a significant portion of the nation's chemical nerve agents. The only impediment to this plan was potential local resistance so, like Hanford, the citizens of Eastern Oregon were not told of the true nature of the potential catastrophic danger of nerve agents. When the news of nerve gas finally was exposed in 1970 the community leaders were deceived into supporting local storage. In fact, the local civic leaders in Hermiston were so misled they clamored for the war gas in the beginning. These civic leaders lobbied the government to have the nation's entire nerve agent supply stored in Umatilla County. They believed industrial progress would bring jobs and financial benefits for the region. Fortunately, Oregon Governor Tom McCall thwarted the Hermiston civic leaders' call for all the nation's war gas. By the time the nerve agents began to leak two generations later, civic leaders were once again deceived by the Army's plan to incinerate the toxic nerve agents, rockets and propellants included.

The threat to the atmosphere, the food chain and the Columbia River and its tributaries caused by incinerating these agents was exposed by the public and watchdog organizations. Nevertheless, the Army and the Oregon DEQ (whom the Army fully funded) used virtually unlimited taxpayer funds to sell the incineration project to the public. The impact on global warming of the chemical incinerator has never been evaluated even by environmentalists. The Environment Protection Agency (EPA) warned against the carcinogenic dangers of incineration early in the process but the local civic leaders and politicians were already committed to the Army's chosen method of disposal so the required public meetings were held only to meet government requirements. The EPA in the beginning warned, "Sampling and analytical techniques for incineration emissions are so limited that the vast majority of chemicals have not been characterized. Forty to 99 per cent of the total mass of chemicals remain unidentified, posing thoroughly unpredictable threats to health and the environment....Incinerators that burn commercial hazardous wastes emit thousands of different chemicals, including heavy metals, unburned wastes and products of incomplete combustion, no matter what technology is used." (EPA, Standards, Hazardous Waste Incinerators, 1990)

The warnings were issued in vain. The Army wined and dined the Eastern Oregon area civic leaders and spent millions of dollars of taxpayer funds to convince the public that incineration was the only proven technology capable of removing the dangerous nerve agents. To put a little more pressure on the public, the Army claimed the chemical agents were dangerously close to auto-exploding. The specter of a decade or more of incineration-caused air pollution over the already polluted Columbia River basin should have caused some public scrutiny, but since the airborne carcinogens were silent and untraceable killers the warnings fell on deaf ears.

The Army skillfully, yet disingenuously, argued that no other technology could safely destroy the deadly nerve agent. Half of the eight chemical agent stockpile sites in America did not swallow the smoothly packaged Army propaganda. Four sites wisely chose closed-loop neutralization technology to destroy the chemical agent at no risk to the public or environment. Sadly, the Pacific Northwest did not have that opportunity. The Army and a select few community civic leaders, in particular Hermiston Major Jerry Harkenrider, determined in advance that the chemical agent stored in the Pacific Northwest would be incinerated. That meant the dioxins, furans, heavy metals, PCBs, and hexachlorobenzene would be released into the dry Eastern Oregon air and ultimately bio-accumulate in the environment and magnify up the food chain. For the first time in America the known carcinogens of incineration would be purposely released into a rich agricultural ecosystem to potentially biomagnificate up the food chain with no proven testing system in place to protect the public. Even the army admitted that 94 percent of the total organic emissions were unknown. "Knowledge of their true 'toxicity' is a source of uncertainty." (DEQ Information Session, Hermiston, Oregon, May 29, 2008)

The Department of Environmental Quality, the agency charged to oversee the project, was funded by the U. S. Army, so no objective, unbiased regulatory agency was commissioned to protect the public. The Army was required by the permit to submit a risk assessment protocol to the DEQ before live agent was to be incinerated. The Army failed to provide COPC (compound of potential concern) emission rates and COPC toxicity and transport data, essential for protection of the public. By the time the project was set to begin in 2004 the Army did not have a single risk assessment employee on staff. Despite the clear violations of the permit the DEQ gave approval for incineration to commence. The EQC (Environmental Quality Commission) quickly followed suit. There is evidence that rare forms of cancer are occurring at alarming rates in the fall-out area of the chemical incinerator since nerve agent incineration began. Unfortunately, there is no statistical evidence to prove the cancer rates have accelerated because the Army, the DEQ, and local public officials have thwarted every effort to establish a baseline of cancer diagnosis in order to determine whether toxins from incineration were causing cancer in the fallout area. Many studies have demonstrated that women in particular are susceptible to developing autoimmune diseases caused by dioxins, furans, PCBs and heavy metals.

Most of the carcinogenic toxins of incineration would eventually work their way into the Umatilla and Columbia River systems. The voice of the Confederated Tribes, the ancient stewards of creation and the strongest advocates for clean waters for the migrating salmon, was strangely silent. The stewards of the Columbia River had the political power to require the government and the Army to establishing stringent guidelines to protect the public and environment from carcinogens being released into the Columbia River and its tributaries. The Tribes were the only stakeholders with the political power to protect the delicate habitat of the basin. In October 2006 the department of science of the Confederated Tribes of the Umatilla did present risk assessment results to the DEQ and Army that indicated significant potential for cancer risk above the RAWP (Risk Assessment Work Plan) threshold. Unfortunately, the warning was too little and too late and no action was taken to protect the public.

The DEQ-approved human health risk model was unbalanced from the beginning to favor incineration. The model assumed every person in the area of incineration was young and healthy with no health issues and no known toxins in their systems. Furthermore, the flawed model only considered the effect of one carcinogenic toxin at a time and did not include the impact of the synergistic effect of multiple carcinogenic toxins that have been released from the incinerator. The Confederated Tribes remain the best hope to stop the poisoning of the environment by incineration and the pollution of the Columbia River, but with the exception of the Nez Perce they have demonstrated little conviction to contend with or confront the polluters of the Columbia basin.

The reader may well understand why most citizens of the Columbia River basin refuse to swim or eat fish, with the exception of steelhead and salmon, from the Columbia River. The miracle of the story is that any salmon have survived the environmental toxin minefield they must face to make it home to their spawning grounds. The multiple lethal toxins, whether they are radionclides, dioxins, heavy metals or pesticides in the water, have made the corridor between Hanford and the Umatilla Army depot the most contaminated area in America. The Native Americans continue to preach that the greatest threat to the anadromous fish are the fourteen cement hydroelectric dams these fish must traverse to reach their spawning grounds. Certainly these dams impede anadromous fish and quench the ability of the rivers to cleanse through healthy currents. Nevertheless, these dams create hydroelectric power for the public and provide a healthy cargo trade industry. It is accurate to say the dams have changed the historic flow of the two rivers and caused the temperature of the Columbia River to routinely exceed 68 degrees, which is the maximum temperature anadromous fish can stand. In addition, the warm waters allow trash fish that feed on the young salmonoids to prosper and proliferate. Nevertheless, the greatest danger to the salmon (and human beings) are the multiple government, municipal and Army polluting industries, not the hydroelectric dams.

The question of the hour in the Pacific Northwest is: Should the salmon be saved, and if so at what cost? The Native Americans and those who would attempt to restore the ecosystem of the Columbia River and the Pacific Northwest would argue that to save the salmon is to save humanity. If the salmon cannot survive, then ultimately man will not survive either. Many Americans who advocate a restoration of the ecosystem of the Pacific Northwest would agree with the Indians that the four Snake River dams should be removed to restore the health of the entire region. The Indians also believe the dams of the Columbia could be retrofitted or operationally changed to allow more free-flowing water. The Indians and conservationists are striving for a restoration of the Columbia River tributary habitat to include changes in logging and grazing practices that restore aquifers and cool water temperature and quality.

The problem does not end with the Columbia River. The salmon fishing season from Oregon to Point Sur, south of San Francisco, faced the prospect of the largest closure ever in March 2006. The problem was not salmon fishing but rather the destruction of salmon watersheds. "Fishermen, whose livelihoods are at risk, said the problem in the Klamath isn't fishing harvests, it's a sick river." (*East Oregonian*, "Federal Fish Managers Advise Closure of Salmon Fishing," March 8, 2006) The State of Oregon and the stakeholders of the Klamath River have allowed the Klamath River to be so desecrated with grazing, logging and irrigation abuse that a healthy run of anadromous fish cannot survive. "…The estimated value of the salmon business in California alone (stood) at $150 million." (*East Oregonian*, March 8, 2006)

On May 2, 2008 salmon fishing was banned along the entire Pacific Coast for the first time in 160 years. The primary cause of the demise of the Pacific Coast salmon run was the absolute demise of the Sacramento River due to persistent environmental abuse and poisoning of the river with toxins and unhealthy irrigation and logging practices. The warning had been sounded for decades but nobody listened. Unless there is a great awakening in the Pacific Northwest, Old Oregon is about to face some dire choices. The next chapter will examine why the pollution of the Pacific Northwest continues and enumerate the steps necessary to restore clean and pure water to the watersheds of the west.

No stakeholder has more power and influence in the battle to restore the Columbia River and tributaries than the sovereign Native American tribes. It is difficult to understand why the Confederated Tribes of the Columbia River have not taken a more active part in cleaning up the Columbia River. Many of the major rivers of Oregon, especially the mighty Columbia River, are so polluted that the water is not potable, the fish are not edible and the waters are not fit to swim in. The question that begs to be offered is why the Confederated Tribes have not used their immense political clout to demand that the polluters stop poisoning the precious waters of the Pacific Northwest. The Native Americans from the beginning of recorded history have been the stewards of God's creation. Never has their voice been more desperately needed to stop the carnage on the increasingly fragile natural resources of the Pacific Northwest. Without cool clean flowing water, all life will soon be in peril. Nobody knows that truth better than the Native American people.

CHAPTER 38

GIVE THEREFORE THY SERVANT A DISCERNING HEART

God appeared to King Solomon and said, "Ask what I shall give thee." (I Kings 3:5b) Solomon responded, "Give therefore thy servant an understanding heart to judge thy people, that I may discern between good and bad." (I Kings 3:9a)

Why have the Confederated Tribes failed to exercise their political and economic power to confront the devastating effects of pollution of the Columbia River? This is one of the most perplexing questions this research has been grappling with. The Native Americans have been the stewards of the Columbia River and the salmon since the beginning of recorded history. Why has the collective voice of the Confederated Tribes been largely silent in response to the horrific impact of pollution in the Columbia River?

In the spring of 2008 the Confederated Tribes of the Yakima, Warm Springs and Umatilla made a deal with the federal government to back off on a key lawsuit to protect fisheries in return for $900 million. Before this "deal" the state of Oregon had been allied with the Tribes in demanding more help for fisheries. "Environmental and Oregon officials said the deal fails to help endangered fish past the dams that kill them or address removal of Snake River dams that risk throwing more dollars at a problem that has swallowed billions without restoring endangered fish." (Milstein, Michael, "Tribes and Feds Seal 900 million Deal for Fisheries," *Oregonian*, April 8, 2008) According to Oregon Governor Ted Kulongoski, "I firmly believe this agreement doesn't go far enough to restore our salmon runs." (Milstein, April 8, 2008) The spokesman for the Confederated Tribes, Charles Hudson, responded to the concerns of the state and environmentalists: "There's a lot of political pragmatism in this agreement." (Milstein, April 8, 2008)

Based on the research of this book, one potential and highly logical reason the Native Americans of the Yakima, Warm Springs and Umatilla tribes have not pressed the polluting industries, be they industrial, governmental, municipal or Army, is because they have compromised their moral position as stewards of God's creation for money. It would be a tragedy for all citizens of the west if financial inducements are the reason for the Confederated Tribes' support of this nine hundred million dollar deal. The support of the Native Americans has given the federal government the moral high ground in the battle over the multiple resources of the Columbia River. One major problem remains for the Federal government. The Nez Perce, the great friends of the American people, have refused to sign on to this lucrative agreement.

"Once again the Nez Perce Tribe has made a courageous decision for wild salmon and steelhead,' said (Idaho Rivers United Director) Bill Sedivy. "I hope they will continue to hold the line under what must be incredible pressure from BPA, so they can fully participate in all the legal and scientific discussions about real salmon recovery." (Barker, Rocky, "Columbia Tribes give up call for breaching dams," *Idaho Statesman*, April, 8, 2008) A reader in response to this article illustrates the temper of the public response to the $900 million Indian pay-off from a blog. "If a nickel of each dollar that is eventually spent goes to something that will actually benefit salmoids I'll be amazed. There will be lots more research, development of crazy expensive contraptions on dams and reservoirs that don't work, more poorly run hatcheries to produce feed for cormorants and pike minnows, more funding for bio-cowboys to chase and wrangle sea lions that can't be shot." (Blog from Barker article, *Idaho Statesman*, April 8, 2008)

With the exception of protests from organizations like Columbia River Keepers and the Nez Perce Indians, the multiple polluters of the Columbia River have a virtual free hand to continue dumping their toxic waste into the atmosphere and waterways of the great northwest. The state of Oregon has yet to sign on to the Columbia River deal; however, the environmental oversight of the Oregon DEQ and EQC on the Columbia River has been negligible even under two decades of Democrat governor control.

Is there hope for the American West? One of the great purposes of this research has been to provide knowledge and discernment of the history of the lands of Old Oregon in order to give understanding to restore the cultural, natural resource and spiritual heritage of the Pacific Northwest. The land and the heritage of all Oregonians will continue to languish until these injustices are rectified. Once again men and women of integrity and conviction must stand up for justice. Native Americans need to return to the convictions and courage of their forefathers and use their treaty rights to develop the natural resources of the Pacific Northwest for the benefit of all citizens. If the forests and rivers are restored to their former state and pro-conservation select logging practices are reestablished in the arid mountain lands, the natural resources of the area will begin to heal. The Indians have a plan to restore the water, river, forest, salmon and big game resources to the Pacific Northwest. The $900 million buy-off illustrates that their leaders may lack the moral conviction and courage to implement this plan.

There is hope, but without couragous integrity and knowledge of the problem nothing is going to change. Every landowner, irrigator, sportsman, Indian tribesman, hunter, farmer, and citizen must be willing to cooperate to work together to heal the land and restore the heritage bequeathed by the Creator to all citizens of the West. Despite the Columbia River buy off there are still wise and courageous Native American leaders in addition to the Nez Perce that have not compromised and still adhere to the principles of Chief Joseph that all men are still accountable to the Great Spirit who created them.

It is time for these men and women of conviction to take a stand because there are many dangerous dilemmas facing the citizens of the Pacific Northwest that by fate continue to occupy the same real estate in the lands of Old Oregon. Most of the issues that divide Oregonians are issues of contention over land or more specifically how the land is used and cared for. The question before all Oregonians of any race has always been an issue of stewardship. The Native Americans claim treaty rights that allowed them to hunt and fish on not only their reservation lands but also ceded lands. The Indian nations of the Pacific Northwest believe the American government has a responsibility to sustain and conserve the habitat that protects the fish and game of the Columbia River basin. These treaty rights are a matter of public record and have been upheld by the courts of the American government. Conservationists, sportsmen and hunters have joined forces with the Indians in this disagreement defined as "a conflict between the Public Trust Doctrine and private rights." (McAllister, Tom, "Fee Hunting on Private Lands Is Hot Issue for Next Legislature," *Oregonian*, Nov. 17, 1987) The issue boils down to the controversy over hunting/fishing rights and stewardship of the natural resources of the Pacific Northwest.

The pressure point of this conflict evolves around three issues: salmon fishing, hunting rights and water rights. This research has documented the controversy regarding the salmon issue and water rights; however, the hunting rights issue is another can of worms and continues to fester in the Pacific Northwest. The destruction of the habitat of the mountain riparian areas and the national forests of the west has forced big-game animals, particularly deer and elk, to seek refuge on large privately owned ranches. The loss of national forest habitat has forced the game commissions of the Pacific Northwest to reduce the quantity and quality of big-game hunting opportunities. All stakeholders agree that the big-game animals belong to the American people. Unfortunately, America's big-game animals have been increasingly forced to find shelter on secluded ranges owned by private landowners. The result has been the growth of a private "fee hunting" enterprise that further locks the American people away from the big-game animals that are essential to their hunting heritage. The Indian peoples, because of treaty rights, have been able to sustain their hunting heritage in the midst of declining forests and wildlife habitat. In essence, the hunting regulations established by the government do not pertain to the American Indians. Their treaty rights allow them to hunt and fish most of the year. In contrast, non-Indian Oregonians must draw a hunting tag through a lottery system to hunt in designated areas for a very short period of time, usually five to ten days for elk and deer. The Indians can hunt over half the year throughout the ceded lands with few restrictions. The result has caused much resentment and ill will between the Indians and non-Indian Oregonians. A separate but more contentious issue over hunting rights pits landowners against non-Indian sportsmen over the issue of fee hunting.

"What we have got is a bunch of different players that are all good people who represent different viewpoints, and they basically hate each other." (McAllister, *Oregonian*, Nov. 17, 1987) Hate might be too strong a word, but the distrust between the players, especially the sportsman hunter and the private fee hunting operation, continues to fester in the first decade of the 21st century. "The result is what in economics is called a negative sum effect." (McAllister, *Oregonian*, Nov. 17, 1987) If the non-Indian Oregonians were not being squeezed so hard by the loss of national forest habitat and shortened hunting and fishing opportunities they would be more tolerant of Native American treaty hunting and fishing rights. What the West needs for the future will be governors and legislatures that exercise the wisdom of Solomon. Decades of mis- management of the forests of the Pacific Northwest toward the end of the 20th century has caused a "negative sum effect" on the entire region that has damaged wildlife, salmon, hunting, and water quality and aquifer quantity. Unfortunately, the Native Americans have not used their position of leverage to protect the natural resource habitat essential for deer and elk for the benefit of all the stakeholders. The Native Americans have an essential position of privilege based on the treaty of 1855. The Native American position of privilege requires responsibility and accountability to all Oregonians to protect the common heritage, and the leadership of the Native Americans has yet to support that high calling.

The American Indians historically did not claim individual property rights. They believed the land belonged to the Creator, so how could man claim to own what only God had created? The Indians have since learned if they are to survive in white man's civilization they must express, defend and exert land treaty rights. The question of the hour that must be resolved to counter the negative sum effect of the present statis quo will be the equitable distribution of water, hunting and fishing opportunities for all stakeholders and Oregonians.

If private landowners are to be allowed to exercise private ownership rights for fee hunting, then the rights and liberty of all Oregonians must be considered since the big-game animals belong to all citizens of the land. This research has already examined the economic impact of abusive logging practices in the Heppner district of the Blue Mountains. The Kinzua mill at Heppner went out of business because the timber industry was harvesting and milling logs faster than the forests could sustain the resource. The degradation of the forest resources and habitat caused the big-game hunting seasons to be shortened and forced large elk herds and to a lesser extent deer populations to leave the national forest and hastened the advent of fee hunting enterprises. At the dawn of the 21st century most of the private landowners bordering the national forests have closed their lands to the public for hunting. The economic impact of closing the lands of the foothills of the Blue Mountains has significantly limited the economic boost that hunting season brought to the local communities, especially Heppner, Oregon. The large numbers of big-game and bird hunters stopped coming because there were significantly fewer places left to hunt. The Blue Mountain gateway city of Heppner went from five gas stations and five grocery stores in 1970 to one grocery store and one gas station by the turn of the 21st century. The new fee hunting enterprises have wined and dined their wealthy clients however the merchants of the community have realized little income.

This research is not intended as a criticism of the landholders that have restored their economic base with fee hunting. Some owners, like John Orville Kilkenny of Heppner, grandson of John S. Kilkenny previously documented in chapter 34, have wisely used government incentives and programs to greatly enhance and protect riparian areas to produce excellent pheasant hunting opportunities. Kilkenny in particular has been a leader in developing similar areas for the public. It will require leadership from visionary men like John O. Kilkenny for the citizens of the Pacific Northwest to follow if the tide is to be turned for the restoration of America's wildlife heritage in the Pacific Northwest. The issue for the private landowner remains the question of property rights. The ranchers of the west are facing increased production costs with greater government restrictions on their land without corresponding increases in their profit. Big-game herds have moved on to their land and use their pasture, damaging their property and often their alfalfa, with marginal restitution from the government. These issues have given the large landowners a position of leverage through the state legislatures. Unfortunately, the fee hunting industry has taken advantage of the problem to gain special rights and privileges not available to the rest of the citizens of the west.

At present in Oregon, landowners are allowed to lease their land to the government to obtain CRP (Conservation Reserve Program) tax dollars. In turn, landowners are allowed by statute to charge hunters to hunt big-game animals on their land. Justice dictates the land leased to the government and taxed at an agricultural rate should not be used at the discretion of the landowner for a purpose other than agriculture for personal profit. The powerful pro-fee hunting landowners' lobby in the Oregon legislature has been allowed to skew the law to allow lands used for recreational hunting purposes to be taxed as farm deferral, then leased for CRP public tax dollars and then sold again to the rich for private hunting clubs. In Morrow County, in the Heppner district of the foothills of the Umatilla Forest, the farm deferral tax amounts to .15 cents per acre. In addition, ranch lands that exercise fee hunting enterprises sell at three times the value of comparable ranch lands. This present policy, based on exploiting the American people's big-game animals, allows a small minority of private landowners who have assumed the position of a privileged aristocracy to have a monopoly over the big-game resources of the west. The negative sum effect of fee hunting robs the county and community of tax dollars that should be levied for recreational activities and it robs the hunting heritage of American citizens. The laws must be changed to reflect justice and equality or injustice will continue to undermine the common natural resource heritage of all Oregonians.

Under the oppression of limited opportunities to hunt and fish the non-Indian and non-landowner Oregonians have become increasingly resentful of private landowners receiving preferential treatment by the Oregon legislature. In addition, these same non-Indian Oregonians are becoming more resentful of American Indians who are allowed by treaty to hunt for more than half of the year with few restrictions. Once again the stewards of the Pacific Northwest need the wisdom of Solomon to resolve this dilemma. The answer to the dilemma must be found in the source of the problem. The American Indians are not the source of the problem even though they have not been willing to help mediate the injustice in the present system by using their political clout to press for greater environment safeguards. One solution would be to tax agricultural lands that are used for hunting clubs for the elite at a recreational tax rate and distribute the funds to protect and enhance water, forests, fish, and big game resources. If the habitat of the national forests was protected from abusive and shortsighted logging, grazing and mining practices, America's natural resource heritage could be protected. Another solution would be to implement the forest and salmon policy of the Confederated Tribes of the Umatilla Indians. That would require some political action on the part of the Tribes to stop the pollution of our rivers and cooperation with non-Indian Americans to help restore the health of our forests.

In the final analysis King Solomon had to turn to God for the wisdom necessary to discern between good and evil. The affluence and wealth of Solomon's kingdom turned even his heart away from God and then the king no longer was concerned with the welfare of his kingdom or had the integrity to govern righteously. The same thing appears on the surfaces to have happened to the Native Americans. Nine hundred million dollars is a lot of money. Political pragmatism will not restore the waterways of the Columbia River or the natural resources of Old Oregon. Without wise impartial stewardship and judgments based on wisdom the breaches between non-Native American Oregonians and Native American Oregonians will never heal. Without men of vision like John O. Kilkenny the breach between the Oregonian landowner and the Oregonian sportsman will never heal.

God has a plan for Old Oregon. That plan has not changed since the beginning of recorded history in the Pacific Northwest. The Almighty did not blind the eyes and hearts of three centuries of mariners to the mighty Columbia River only to have the present generation of Oregonians ignore his providential works of grace. The Almighty did not peacefully and victoriously merge together the white man with the red man in the beginning only to see their relationship fail due to deceit and guile. It was the Almighty's plan from creation that mankind would cherish and exercise stewardship over his dominion. The American Indians under allegiance to the Great Spirit Chief exercised, for the most part, wise and careful stewardship over the manifest resources of the Pacific Northwest from their beginning. In less than two centuries the American culture has consumed much of the vast resources of the region with little regard for stewardship of the gifts of the Creator. The days of wine and roses are over. One question remains: Will the American people wake up before it is too late?

Chapter 39

A Controversy With the Inhabitants of the Land

"Hear ye the word of the Lord, ye children of Israel: for the Lord hath a controversy with the inhabitants of the land, because there is no truth, nor mercy, nor knowledge of God in the land. By swearing, and lying, and killing, and stealing, and committing adultery, they break out and blood toucheth blood. Therefore shall the land mourn, and every one that dwelleth therein shall languish, with the beasts of the field, and with the fowls of heaven; yea, the fishes of the sea shall be taken away." (Hosea 4:1-3)

The words of the prophet Hosea speak resoundingly to the peoples of the Pacific Northwest. When truth, mercy and the knowledge of God are compromised evil abounds and the people, the wildlife and the fisheries languish. Hosea speaks directly to America and the Pacific Northwest as the first decade of the 21st century draws to a close.

This research has documented how God, the Creator of the universe, whether He is called the Great Spirit Chief or the Lord Almighty, kept the land of the Oregon Territory under the shadow of His providence from the beginning of recorded history. The indigenous American Indians of the region were a spiritual people that honored a creator God they knew intimately and evidenced that relationship by their respect of the creation. To these Native Americans their heritage was predicated upon their relationship with their Creator. When the indigenous Indians heard of the white man's Book of Heaven they sought this book.

The central place and prominence of the Protestant missionaries in bringing the truth of God's word and purpose to the Oregon Territory has been fully documented in this study. This research has also documented the desecration of the culture and heritage of the American Indians and the natural resources of the region. God had preserved the great Pacific Northwest for the American peoples and this research has sadly documented how American civilization has in many ways dishonored and spoiled this magnificent heritage. Now the Almighty God of the Book of Heaven has a controversy with the inhabitants of the land because "there is no truth, nor mercy, nor knowledge of God in the land."

The state of Oregon has become one of the most liberal, anti-God states in America. Oregon was allowing legal abortions before the practice of killing babies before they could be born was legalized in America in 1973. In 2007 the Oregon legislature enacted laws legalizing gay marriage in defiance of the 2004 vote of the people that amended the Constitution to declare marriage to be a sacred union between one man and one woman. In 2007 the governor of Oregon, 14 county clerks and a federal judge nullified the vote of the citizens of Oregon and provided marriage benefits and rights to gay couples and a new radical gender law that threatened the liberty of all Christians in the state. Efforts to use the initiative process to seek redress by allowing the citizens of the state to vote on these two oppressive laws were denied by the government. Thousands of petitions were thrown out, allowing the state of Oregon to assert the petitioners were a few hundred petitions short. For eight weeks during the months of May and June 2008 the Oregon Supreme Court refused to act on a second petition initiative, once again denying the citizens of Oregon the opportunity to vote on the same two oppressive laws. Democracy requires the vote and the support of the people and that is no longer the case in Oregon. Judges presently rule in the state of Oregon thwarting the democratic voice of the people as represented by voting initiatives that have been overruled by the judiciary.

The state of Oregon has become one of the most godless states in the world. The deceit and tyranny of the government has caused the land to mourn and the once proud culture of the "Sons of Oregon" to languish. The spiritual heritage of the land and people of America and, for the purposes of this research, the Pacific Northwest, has been undermined because a lack of knowledge. The Church of Jesus Christ has a sacred responsibility to sustain a moral compass. According to the Bible, "judgment must begin at the house of God." (I Peter 4:17) Judgment must begin at the house of God because the church of God has been entrusted with the Book of Heaven to proclaim and minister the truth of God's word. The lack of knowledge of God's word that has caused the spiritual demise of the Pacific Northwest would never have occurred had the church remained true to its calling. The church of Jesus Christ has historically been a spiritual barometer to guide and sustain America's moral foundation, the cornerstone of the nation's vitality. The Protestant faith, in large part, has lost its moral fiber and has become bound to pastors and ministries that do not extend their voice beyond the four walls of the church. Instead of reaching out across denominational distinctives to unite to mend America and Oregon's crumbling spiritual heritage the present Protestant Church in many cases appears to view other denominations as competition for dollars and followers. In addition, most Protestant denominations have lost their courage to take a public stand against the powerful onslaught of humanism in the form of homosexuality, promiscuity, abortion and toleration of deeds and actions prohibited by the Bible.

Fortunately, the Catholic Church has risen up at this hour to lead the charge to restore a moral standard, particularly in the focal battle issues of marriage, abortion and the responsibility of the church to take a public stand, politically and morally. In Eastern Oregon Father Bailey Clemens of St. Marys Catholic Church in Pendleton has taken a uniquivicable public stand for marriage between one man and one woman and the sanctity of life beginning at conception. In the Nov. 2, 08 edition of the East Oregonian a front-page picture illustrates a picture of the Pendleton Catholic church taking a stand for pro-life. Pope Benedict XVI has called abortion "an intrinsic evil" – "an aggression against society itself." (Kathy Aney, East Oregonian, Nov. 2, 08 p.2). According to Father Clemens, "No evil is proportionate to the number of children killed by abortion. There have been 50 million abortions in the U.S. since the beginning of Roe vs. Wade." (East Oregonian, Nov. 2, 08 p. 2) Father Clemens has written a book called *Imaginations Gone Wild* available on line from his church web site as an E Book. Father Clemens powerful book exposes the root causes of the destruction of America's moral foundation.

Reverend Michael Fitzpatrick of St. Andrews Mission near Pendleton is another postive example of the Catholic leadership in Eastern Oregon. Rev. Fitzpatrick has faithfully served the Native American mission for over two decades. Reverend Fitzpatrick's ministry presently extends throughout the Pacific Northwest to Native Americans, Catholics and Bible believing Christians and is particularly significant to the purposes of this research because Reverend Fitzpatrick is a Jesuit Priest. Reverend Michael Fitzpatrick illustrates the danger of labeling any person or ministry according to historical actions in the past. Churches, societies, organizations and governments change over time. It is not fair to judge any church, organization or government according to the spurious deeds of the past if the harmful and negative standards and principles have been repudiated. The Protestant, Catholic and Jesuit ministries will probably never agree in all areas of Christian theology, nevertheless it is essential for the common spiritual heritage of Old Oregon for these historical ministries to join together in the areas they agree, especially in the battle for the sanctity of biblical marriage and the sanctity of human life from conception.

Fortunately many Protestant churches have not compromised and are joining the Catholic Church in this historical battle. The history of the rich spiritual heritage of the church in the Pacific Northwest contained in this research can provide insights and knowledge necessary for the church to gain vision and courage to once again battle for the soul of America. The victorious vision for Old Oregon must be coupled with faith and fortitude to turn the tide of darkness in order to restore a moral compass and stewardship for God's creation.

In many ways the Columbia River represents the state of the church of Jesus Christ in the Pacific Northwest. The river is sick and no longer flows with cool clean water. The Columbia River has been central to the Oregon Territory, Native American culture and history, and the heart and soul of the Pacific Northwest from the creation of the universe. It was the magnetism of the fabled Northwest Passage, the mighty Columbia River that drew the multiple mariner nations of the world to the Pacific Northwest. When the white race discovered the Columbia River they found a mighty river flowing with crystal clear and clean water teeming with vibrant fish of all sorts. The tributaries of the Columbia River were rich with beaver and the forests sustained elk, deer, sheep, bear, cougar, mountain goats, wild turkeys and over 60 wildlife species, all prospering under the stewardship of the Columbia Plateau Indians. The Columbia River represents the church of Jesus Christ in the Pacific Northwest. The church has become polluted by the ways of the world. The church has become lukewarm and stagnant like the Columbia River because the spirit of God has been stifled and resisted. Bold moves must be taken to restore both the Columbia River and the church of Jesus Christ in the Pacific Northwest or both will eventually become so polluted nothing will be able to sustain life within their confines.

This research has documented the sins of our fathers that allowed the Indians to be disgraced and abused by the American culture. This research has also documented the positive changes that are working to regenerate the Native American culture at the turn of the 21st century. Nevertheless, the Columbia River still languishes and the water remains sick. This sickness cannot be blamed on past generations because the deceit that is destroying the Columbia River and causing the forest reservoirs to dry up continues unabated to the present hour. The Lord has a controversy with the inhabitants of the land because the present generation continues to allow His creation to be desecrated. That includes all Oregonians, including Native Americans.

One of the primary reasons the Lord has a controversy with the inhabitants of the land is because the Christian church in the Pacific Northwest as a whole has not accepted the biblical mandate for evangelizing the lost or taking a stand to restore moral standards or the responsibility of stewardship for God's creation. That is the central reason the church is so weak and the Pacific Northwest is one of the most un-churched areas in America. Paul Otto, associate professor of history at George Fox University, succinctly and correctly expressed this position. "Christ's work is not to save us so we can escape to heaven. His work is to forgive our sins, renewing us and freeing us from sin's corrupting power, so that we can go about our task ordained at creation: to oversee, care for, and develop that creation: to flourish as human beings, creating human culture that brings honor and glory to the maker of all things." (Otto, Paul, "The Biblical Mandate for Social Justice," *George Fox Journal*, Spring, Vol. 2, Number 1, 2006) The work of the first Protestant missionaries exalted winning souls to Christ, honored without compromise God's word, and worked with the Native Americans cooperatively to oversee God's creation.

Lawmakers attempted to exercise stewardship of the vast natural resources of the American Republic during the 20th century. The Clean Water Act of 1960 led to the establishment of state and federal agencies to protect the environment. In Oregon the Department of Environmental Quality (DEQ) was established to protect the quality of the state's water and air. Unfortunately no laws will govern a people that are not willing to honor the rule of law or live under the moral precepts of the Bible. Unless the Christian faith is willing to present the statutes and precepts of the Almighty beyond the four walls of the church there will be no constraints on the people to require righteous laws to be enforced. There are presently thirteen pulp mills and multiple municipal and industrial facilities that must meet DEQ standards for clean water for the purpose of protecting the Columbia River as well as all Oregon rivers. Despite these safeguards the Oregon Fish and Wildlife Department has issued an advisory, warning sportsmen and Indians that virtually all tested Oregon rivers and reservoirs are so contaminated with pollutants that the fish are largely inedible. What happened? It is one thing to legislate wise laws. It is quite another thing to enforce them.

In 2005, "The state's environment agency is moving to let factories and plants pour dirtier water into Oregon Rivers, in a change paid for partly by one of the industries that would benefit from the looser rules." (Milstein, Michael, *Oregonian*, Oct. 31, 2005) The Northwest Pulp and Paper Association, an alliance of 13 paper mills on the Columbia River, committed $120,000 to the DEQ to "expedite or enhance a regulatory process." (Milstein, Oct. 31, 2005) Because of shrinking state budgets the Oregon Legislature has allowed the DEQ to receive up to two-thirds of its budget from the same industries it has commissioned to protect the environment from. The new DEQ rules allow reduced standards that tolerate murkier waters that will make smaller streams twice as cloudy. According to the DEQ, now largely funded by the polluting industries, "current rules are more rigid than necessary to protect salmon, drinking water and other uses dependent on clean water….Fish adjust to natural changes in rivers, and the new rules keep cloudiness to levels fish can handle." (Milstein, Oct. 31, 2005)

If the state agency established to protect the quality of the environment is largely funded by the polluting industries, who is left to protect the quality of the water and air in the Pacific Northwest? The director of the DEQ in Oregon, Stephanie Hallock, has become an advocate of procuring additional funds from polluting companies even though it means further contaminating Oregon's water. DEQ policies require that the agency accept no outside funds that would "result in an apparent or actual conflict of interest" (Milstein, Oct. 31, 2005) Nevertheless, Director Hallock would only stop using polluters' resources if "the perception raised is that it's not acceptable to the public…" (Milstein, Oct. 31, 2005) Environment advocates warn that fish cannot tolerate pollutants allowed by the DEQ at present and there is no evidence that DEQ would enforce a weaker standard that the agency is presently advocating. The DEQ under the leadership of director Hallock (no longer with the DEQ) has no problem with the cloudier waters as long as the money keeps pouring in from companies that make money contaminating Oregon waters.

The Lord has a controversy with the inhabitants of the land because there is no truth or righteousness in regard to stewardship of His creation from the agencies charged to protect Oregon's resources. The salmon will never be restored if the states of the west continue to allow industry to pollute and contaminate the once pure and clean waters. The salmon season has been closed off the coast of the entire Pacific Northwest in 2008. The primary reasons for the decline of the salmon runs has been 1)the demise of many of the watersheds of the Pacific Northwest, 2)the pollution of the rivers and 3)too many dams that reduce the rivers to largely stagnant lakes. The first two problems are fixable. The purpose of this research is to document the knowledge necessary for the public and the Christian and Catholic churches to speak out and demand changes in the agencies like the Oregon DEQ. Under Stephanie Hallock's leadership the Oregon DEQ has become an agency that financially benefits by partnering with polluters that desecrate Oregon waters.

In like manner the Oregon DEQ has partnered with the U.S. Army to fund studies and environmental protection policies that are allowing the Army to burn highly toxic chemical agents that are flooding the environment with invisible carcinogenic toxins. These toxins will magnify and multiply up the food chain and inevitably work their way into the streams and contaminate water for fish, birds and ultimately humans.

One would think the DEQ and Stephanie Hallock would be defensive when they are challenged regarding their failure to protect the environment. This research has documented the degree the DEQ in Oregon has developed into a purely political organization with little to no concern for protection of the environment or stewardship of Oregon's resources. Hallock makes no apology for the solely political purposes of her organization. "The environmental and national resources agenda for the state of Oregon is directed by the governor....We propose things, but that's the way the system works....All DEQ rules must be approved by the Environmental Quality Commission (EQC), which is appointed by the governor." (Duin, Steve, "EQ is no advocate for environment," *Oregonian*, Nov. 1, 2005)

In actual practice the EQC rarely if ever overrules the DEQ. The two commissions work together passing responsibility for blame to each other when the heat is applied so neither organization is ever held responsible for the present dismal state of the environment. The governor appoints politically correct individuals who have demonstrated by word and deed they will not rock the boat, particularly when it comes to procuring more industrial or Army dollars for the state's coffers. Therefore the DEQ bureaucracy elevates pragmatists like Stephanie Hallock who work with industrial polluters and the U.S. Army to promote economic and political policies that turn a blind eye toward the desecration of the environment. Meanwhile the governor of the State of Oregon, Ted Kulongoski, controls the whole process and speaks words of comfort to the public so the money continues to flow into the state as the pollution flows into the water. All the while the governor says all the ecologically correct things. "I'm talking about protecting our air, water and land resources from the ravages of industrial pollution and unbridled development. I'm talking about protecting our old-growth forests....And I'm talking about protecting our traditional fishing and farming communities." (Duin, Nov. 1, 2005)

Indeed, the Lord does have a controversy with the inhabitants of the land. Lies, deceit and guile rule the day when it comes to stewardship of the wonderful resources God bequeathed to the Oregonians who would rule this vast domain. Will the present generation of Oregonians stand with their Native American brethren and restore justice and integrity in the land or will the land continue to mourn and the health of the people continue to languish because the knowledge and mercy of God faileth? Will the Christian and Catholic churches rise to the high calling of biblical social and ecological justice found in the example of Jesus Christ himself? The inhabitants of the land of the Pacific Northwest are in the valley of decision and the hour of crisis ominously approaches.

The lands and people of Old Oregon are in trouble. Most of the rivers are polluted and the Columbia River is so sick some of the fish are largely uneatable, but that is only a symptom of the greater problem. There is little movement in the church or in the environmental associations to heal the breaches. The Native American confederated tribes, the great stewards of God's creation, have the political power but lack the conviction and commitment to press the regulatory agencies, the Army and the American government to end the indiscriminate poisoning of the waterways of the mighty Columbia River. The purpose of this research has been to provide knowledge so the citizens of Old Oregon could "see things that were previously undetectable with (their) natural eyes." (Otis, p. 81) The Protestant Church has not responded because it lacks the knowledge of how God has blessed our common heritage through the sacrifice of men and women of faith who understood God's plan for Old Oregon. It is time for the church and the citizens of Oregon to awaken from their slumber. The freedom and liberty the citizens now enjoy in the great Pacific Northwest is not a right but rather a responsibility. Liberty is something that must be purchased. Most peoples and nations of the world do not know the meaning of liberty or enjoy the fruits of freedom and there is nothing that promises our present liberty and freedom will remain. The Republic of America has moved dangerously close to the precipice that divides freedom and liberty from oppression and ruin.

One of the primary purposes of this research is to uncover the truth in order to wake up Americans. America is in the process of removing all the righteous standards from our land including the Bible, the Ten Commandments and prayer. If the church continues to be silent in the face of this attack against the word of God there will be no knowledge of God left in the country. Newspaper reporters and editors no longer advocate a righteous standard or moral compass because they are controlled by the religion of liberal humanism that disdains the righteous standards of the word of God. Without a moral populace, or an unbiased press, or an uncompromising and courageous church, there are no safeguards to protect America's heritage and culture. The result will be chaos and erosion of liberty and that is what America is experiencing at the end of first decade of the 21st century.

God is calling for a restoration of the Christian message brought by the original missionaries who came to bring liberty, truth and the hope of eternal life through Jesus Christ. God is calling for men and women of faith with the same courage and convictions that brought the Nez Perce warriors to St. Louis and Jason Lee and the Whitmans and Spaldings to the Pacific Northwest. The greatest need of the hour is a "great awakening" in the land of the original Oregon Territory. The problem in Oregon today is a moral issue and God has commissioned the church to speak to the Republic regarding the stewardship of His creation. God is calling for a revival in the Bible-believing evangelical Protestant and spirit-filled Catholic churches to restore the vision of the Sons of the Republic for the lands of Old Oregon. God is calling for Native Americans to rise up and honor the faith of their fathers that would not compromise their heritage for white man's dollars. For want of a better term let us call this revival the "Third Great Awakening." Christianity in the Pacific Northwest is anemic, one of the most un-churched areas in America. Less than five percent of the citizens of the Pacific Northwest attend church services regularly. When the church of Jesus Christ begins to speak God's truth concerning the real and pressing issues of the hour the church will have a new awakening. One of the purposes of this book is to foster that spiritual awakening.

Chapter 40

The Third Great Awakening

The purpose of this research is to awaken the people of Old Oregon and all peoples that love liberty. The "Third Great Awakening" must begin with repentance. "If my people, which are called by my name, shall humble themselves, and pray, and seek my face, and turn from their wicked ways; then will I hear from heaven, and will forgive their sin, and will heal their land." (II Chronicles 7:14) The documented history of the Oregon Territory uncovered by the research of this study illustrates the need for repentance. All the major players including the Native American Indians, the Protestant Church and the American government have failed to execute justice and integrity in the lands of Old Oegon. All have failed to honor God's word in relationship to stewardship of God's creation. The Lord has a controversy with all the inhabitants of the land and that includes the author and all citizens of America, especially those living in the Pacific Northwest.

The God of America's forefathers, the Great Spirit Chief of the American Indians, will hear our prayer if the church and people collectively humble themselves and seek His face and turn from our wicked ways. The Pacific Northwest desperately needs a Third Great Awakening. May the present generation of Oregonians have the courage of Marcus Whitman to plunge into the roaring Colorado River and take on the moral and political challenges that threaten their liberty and freedom and undermine their faith in God. For this purpose this book is written.

The lands and people of the Old Oregon Territory have a great part to play in the final drama to conclude the present age in America and in the world. The respective governments and churches in the Pacific Northwest have not been faithful with the charge to bring justice and liberty and equality to the lands and peoples of the region. In like manner the government of the United States of America has failed in the sacred charge of sustaining the moral precepts of the founding fathers as well. The American government and people have been blessed with the righteous and godly biblical standards of their forefathers. Nevertheless, this nation at the turn of the 21st century, has turned away from God's righteous standards and permitted and/or supported corruption, perversion, immorality, materialism in excess, abortion, homosexuality, and compromise of our most cherished national values. According to the warnings of our forefathers there must come a time of judgment to cleanse the land of the sins the present generation condones, supports and practices. According to biblical scripture those sons of the Republic who keep their faith in God will endure this time of severe national chastisement brought about by apostasy, immorality and abandonment of Bible-grounded faith. According to the knowledge revealed in this research the lands of the Old Oregon Territory will play a major role in this end-time drama, a drama in which the last chapter began on September 11, 2001.

This research of the history of the Old Oregon Territory has documented the multiple reasons why the land languishes; however, the parameters of this study have not examined the greater sins of America as the nation enters into the 21st century mired in conflict in the Middle East. A great hour of peril confronts the American Republic in the form of worldwide economic collapse, Islamic fundamentalism, international terrorist cell groups, aggressive Communist regimes around the world and an antagonistic anti-American European Commonwealth. America, the shining light of liberty and freedom for the whole world, does not have a single faithful ally in the world today, with the possible exceptions of Australia and England. Indeed, today in the Pacific Northwest as in all of America, adultery, militant homosexuality, pornography, and abortion are ravaging America. The government-sanctioned practice of abortion has spilled the blood of over 50 million innocent American babies. To add insult to God, Oregon was the first state in the union to legalize assisted suicide. How tragic that martyred Protestant missionaries in Oregon would pay with their blood for a state that would one day sanction and legalize the culture of death through assisted suicide and abortion. America has many enemies abroad but the greatest threat to America is developing from within. Politicians that do not know or uphold the principles of the Constitution or the values of our founding fathers are in the process of taking over all three branches of the government of the United States as this book goes to press. The liberal press and media of the country is orchestrating the political coup of the American government to change the face of America from the vision and purpose of the founding fathers.

The collapse of the American government is happening by design. In America today over half of marriages of the land end in divorce and adultery is a primary cause, and there is little statistical difference between the church and the world. The name of the God of our fathers, the God of Abraham, Isaac and Jacob, has been systematically erased from the land. Public prayer has been banned from our schools and government institutions. "In God we trust" has been erased from our sacred institutions by judicial decree. Homosexuality in the form of same-sex marriage is slowly by judicial edict, against the will of the people, becoming enshrined into the humanistic standard of the new American morality. The hour is upon America where those men and women of God who speak out against the biblical sins of the nation will be persecuted and ultimately imprisoned.

The Book of Revelation warns the world, the church and America of judgment for those nations, tribes, peoples and churches that turn away from the Almighty God of the Bible. A greater judgment awaits those nations and peoples and religious sects that openly contend against the God of creation as revealed through the Bible and his only begotten Son, Jesus Christ. The final and most important purpose of *Old Oregon, Under the Shadow of the Almighty* is to prepare God's people for the hour of tribulation spoken of by Daniel the prophet and articulated by Jesus Christ in Matthew chapter twenty-four. "For nation shall rise against nation, and kingdom against kingdom, and there shall be famines, and pestilences, and earthquakes, in divers places." (Matthew 24:7)

This research has recorded the hand of the Almighty over the great land of the Oregon Territory for over five centuries. The citizens and the churches of the Pacific Northwest have not lived up to the sacred charge of honoring the statutes and precepts of the Almighty nor have they exercised a faithful stewardship of God's creation, especially when compared to the original stewardship of the Native Americans. The church of Jesus Christ in the Pacific Northwest has not lived up to the high calling of the original Nez Perce warriors, or the Protestant missionaries, in particular Jason Lee, Marcus and Narcissa Whitman and Henry and Eliza Spalding. Fortunately, the purposes of God are not dependent on the works of man. In spite of the failing and compromise of man, God still has a divine purpose for His heritage in the Pacific Northwest. The greatest founding father of America, George Washington, was given a prophecy regarding the hour that is fast approaching America and the world. This great man of God was given a vision of hope when his beleaguered and ragged army was approaching despair in the winter of 1777 at Valley Forge. This vision will give the reader a greater understanding of the high calling for all Americans and in particular, for the purposes of this research, those Americans who live in the lands of the original Oregon Territory. This vision and prophecy in the words of America's greatest patriot George Washington was taught to American students for over a century and a half after his death. At the greatest hour of America's peril the vision needs to be opened once again to the American people.

"This afternoon, as I was sitting at this table engaged in preparing a dispatch, something seemed to disturb me. Looking up, I beheld standing opposite me a singular beautiful female. So astonished was I, for I had given strict orders not to be disturbed, that it was some moments before I found language to inquire the cause of her presence. A second, a third and even a fourth time did I repeat my question, but received no answer from my mysterious visitor except a slight rising of her eyes.

By this time I felt strange sensations spreading through me. I would have risen but the riveted gaze of the being before me rendered volition impossible. I assayed once more to address her, but my tongue had become useless, as though it had become paralyzed.

A new influence mysterious, potent, irresistible, took hold of me. All I could do was to gaze steadily, vacantly at my unknown visitor. Gradually the surrounding atmosphere seemed as if it had become filled with sensations, and luminous. Everything about me seemed to rarify, the mysterious visitor herself becoming more airy and yet more distinct to my sight than before. I now began to feel as one dying, or rather to experience the sensations that I have sometimes imagined accompany dissolution. I did not think, I did not reason, I did not move; all were impossible. I was only conscious of gazing fixedly, vacantly at my companion." (Grady, John, "George Washington's Vision and Prophecy for America," Benton, Tennessee, pp. 10-11)

George Washington and his haggard army had support from less than five percent of the colonists at the hour of the great revolution. Nobody, save the most fervent and faithful in his exhausted army, believed the American revolutionaries had even the faintest hope of defeating the mightiest army in the world at that time. Washington's poorly equipped army had not even been able to engage the mighty British as the fierce winter of 1777 reduced the Americans to the brink of surrender. The Almighty God of the Bible sent an angelic visitor to encourage Washington, his troops and those patriots who would follow in his footsteps. Only the angelic visitor from God could have known that America would one-day stretch from sea to shining sea. Certainly the angelic vision inspired Washington and his troops to maintain their faith and sustain the battle to bring liberty to the land.

"Presently I heard a voice saying, 'Son of the Republic, look and learn,' while at the same time my visitor extended her arm eastwardly. I now beheld a heavy white vapor at some distance rising fold upon fold. This gradually dissipated, and I looked upon a strange scene. Before me spread out in one vast plain all the countries of the world – Europe, Asia, Africa and America. I saw rolling and tossing between Europe and America the billows of the Atlantic, and between Asia and America lay the Pacific.

'Son of the Republic,' said the same mysterious voice as before, 'look and learn.' At that moment I beheld a dark shadowy being like an angel, standing, or rather floating in mid-air, between Europe and America. Dipping water out of the ocean in the hollow of each hand, he sprinkled some upon America with his right hand, while with his left hand he cast some on Europe. Immediately a cloud rose from these countries, and joined in mid-ocean. For a while it remained stationary, and then moved slowly westward, until it enveloped America in its murky folds. Sharp flashes of lightning gleamed through it at intervals, and I heard the smothered groans and cries of the American people.

A second time the angel dipped water from the ocean, and sprinkled it out as before. The dark cloud was then drawn back to the ocean, in whose heaving billows it sank from view. A third time I heard the mysterious voice saying, 'Son of the Republic, look and learn.' I cast my eyes upon America and beheld villages and towns and cities springing up one after another until the whole land from the Atlantic to the Pacific was dotted with them." (Grady, "Washington's Prophecy," pp.11-12)

The angelic visitor had given George Washington and his freezing army a prophetic vision of victory over the mighty British army. In essence, all George Washington and his valiant troops had to do was believe and never give up and God would defeat the British. Those who have studied the Revolutionary War will confirm that is exactly what happened. Through a series of bold exploits by Washington and his army and miracles from the Almighty, the poorly funded and equipped American revolutionaries defeated the mighty British and won independence.

"Again, I heard the mysterious voice say, 'Son of the Republic, the end of the century cometh, look and learn.' At this the dark shadowy angel turned his face southward, and from Africa I saw an ill-omened specter approach our land. It flitted slowly over every town and city of the latter. The inhabitants presently set themselves in battle array against each other. As I continued looking I saw a bright angel, on whose brow rested a crown of light, on which was traced the word 'Union,' bearing the American flag which he placed between the divided nation, and said, 'Remember ye are brethren.' Instantly, the inhabitants, casting from them their weapons, became friends once more, and united around the National Standard." (Grady, "Washington's Prophecy," pp. 12-13)

The American Republic had endured less than a century when the second great peril of the angel's prophecy for America struck the land. The Civil War was one of the bloodiest wars ever fought in the history of mankind, yet the nation reconciled almost miraculously at the conclusion of the war and united under the national standard of one nation under God once again.

George Washington's prophecy was taught to American students for over a century and a half until a powerful wave of anti-God, anti-prayer and anti-Bible liberal politicians, judges, educators and newspapers began to overpower the slumbering compromising church in the mid-twentieth century. At the hour of the greatest peril to the American Republic the voice of Washington's prophetic warning had been censored. How could this wave of liberal humanistic and secular voices overpower the might of the church of Jesus Christ and America's Christian heritage? Two hundred years of blood-won national spiritual victories including the Declaration of Independence and the Constitution had made America the great land of liberty and freedom for the entire world to emulate. What happened to those cherished ideals that made America great? The church of Jesus Christ has been deceived from within. The liberal, humanistic and secular teachings of the world infiltrated the seminaries of the great churches of America and soon the authority and inspiration of the word of God was reduced to the interpretation of man through the theologians of the seminaries of the hour. Instead of the word of God scrutinizing the believer, the seminaries of the land scrutinized and redefined the word of God according to higher forms of biblical criticism. The result was that the church of Jesus Christ in America began to compromise the great biblical mandates that protected America and made the nation the shining light of liberty and freedom for the whole world.

Never in the history of the gospel of Jesus Christ has the church in America been more prosperous or successful. Mega churches with thousands of members have been birthed throughout the land. The prosperity of the church in America has never been equaled in history. Television evangelists and ministries have multiplied and magnified across the land ministering to millions and millions of believers. The evangelical movement was the heart of the conservative Republican Party in America at the turn of the 21st century. The church of Jesus Christ has never experienced such material and numerical success, manifesting magnificent cathedrals and outreach ministries across the land. In the face of the exponential growth of the church of Jesus Christ there has been an equally exponential growth in American society of the biblical sins of the hour: abortion, homosexuality, divorce, pornography, drug abuse and a national movement to erase the name of God and the authority of the Bible from America's heritage. How could the power of the church and the forces of evil co-exist with so little conflict?

The Apostle John wrote about this church in the book of Revelation. "I know thy works, that thou art neither cold nor hot: I would that thou wert cold or hot. So then because thou art lukewarm, and neither cold nor hot, I will spew thee out of my mouth. Because thou sayest, I am rich, and increased with goods and have need of nothing; and knowest not that thou art wretched, and miserable, and poor and naked: I counsel thee to buy of me gold tried in the fire, that thou mayest be rich; and white raiment, that thou mayest be clothed, and that the shame of thy nakedness do not appear; and anoint thine eyes with eye salve, that thou mayest see. As many as I love, I rebuke and chasten: be zealous therefore, and repent." (Rev. 3: 15-19)

God's word warns that "the time is come that judgment must begin at the house of God." (I Peter 4:17) The present dismal moral state of America illustrates that the Christian heritage of the founding fathers has been compromised. The church of Jesus Christ has compromised the word of God and therefore the judgment that is coming to America will begin at the house of God. "Many pastors have destroyed my vineyard, they have trodden my portion under foot, they have made my pleasant portion a desolate wilderness…the whole land is desolate because no man layeth it to his heart." (Jeremiah 12: 10,11b)

New York pastor and author David Wilkerson warned America in 1998 in a book titled, *America's Last Call* that America was on the brink of financial holocaust. "What ails our American society? How can our whole nation party, dance, drink and be saturated with entertainment, while thousands of babies are being aborted? What kind of disease has so blinded our nation that the President could veto a bill outlawing doctors from sucking out the brains of babies just weeks before they are born?" (Wilkerson, David, "America's Last Call," Wilkerson Trust Publications, Lindale Texas, 1998, p. 36)

God is warning America through prophets like David Wilkerson and America's first President George Washington that a time of great judgement is about to strike the nation. The first act of the judgement from God will be a collapse of the financial system similar to the Great Depression. The stock market will stagger like a drunken sailor and the banking system will crumble because graft and corruption have become the standard in the land instead of moral and financial integrity based on the word of God. The warnings of the prophets have fallen on deaf ears in America, in the same manner the warnings of the prophets fell on deaf ear in Israel before the Babylonian captivity. The prophet Jeremiah spoke over 2500 years ago of a similar hour in Israel. "A wonderful and horrible thing is committed in the land. The prophets prophesy falsely, and the priests bear rule by their means; and my people love to have it so." (Jeremiah 5: 30,31)

Jesus warned in Matthew 24 of an hour of suffering and tribulation such as the world had never experienced before. Wilkerson warns that America's rebellion against God has crossed the line and financial collapse is only the beginning of sorrows.

George Washington's prophetic vision for America confirms the warning of this book and pastor Wilkerson. "And again I heard the mysterious voice saying, 'Son of the Republic, look and learn.' At this the dark shadowy angel placed a trumpet in his mouth, and blew three distinct blasts; and taking water from the ocean, he sprinkled it upon Europe, Asia, and Africa. Then my eyes beheld a fearful scene: from each of these countries arose a thick, black cloud that was soon joined into one. Throughout this mass there gleamed a dark red light by which I saw hordes of armed men, who by moving with the cloud, marched by land and sailed by sea to America. Our country was enveloped in this volume of cloud, and I saw those vast armies devastate the whole country and burn the villages, towns, and cities that I beheld springing up." (Grady, Washington's Prophecy, p. 13)

Americans have a false sense of security. For the most part the citizens of America believe they are invincible because they believe they are the most powerful nation in the world and God will bless America no matter what America does. The thought of civil war, cities going up in flames, mortal conflict, pestilence, stores without food and civil chaos are unthinkable to a nation that has known only blessing and prosperity. Most Americans believe God will continue blessing America even as the nation removes the word of God and statutes of God from every national standard in government, education and society. The citizens of the greatest Republic in the world have come to believe that America is special. No matter what happens in the world the nations superior armaments and technology will somehow save the day. The idea that America will be held responsible for the blood of innocent aborted babies does not register on the collective heart and soul of the American people. The culture of American society near the close of the first decade of the 21st century will no longer tolerate the proclamation of the Word of God by any of his prophets warning them they must repent or judgment will fall across the land. Nevertheless the citizens of the Republic still claim to be a Christian nation in hope that a form of godliness will protect them in case the prophets warning may come to pass.

Fortunately there is still in America a remnant of believers that have not bowed to the modern gods of baal. These believers mourn at the fallen condition of the once God fearing Republic. These men and women have not compromised their souls to the seduction of America and they continue to stand against the manifest sins of the nation. As the nation grows darker and evil upon evil and deceit upon deception multiplies across the land these saints of God will grow brighter and stronger as the return of the Lord Jesus Christ draws nearer.

"My ears listened to the thundering of the cannon, clashing of swords, and the shouts and cries of millions in mortal combat, I heard again the mysterious voice saying, 'Son of the Republic, look and learn,' When the voice ceased, the dark shadowy angel placed his trumpet once more to his mouth, and blew a long and fearful blast. Instantly a light as of a thousand suns shone down from above me, and pierced and broke into fragments the dark cloud, which enveloped America. At the same moment the angel upon whose head still shone the word Union, and who bore our national flag in one hand and sword in the other, descended from the heavens attended by legions of white spirits. These immediately joined the inhabitants of America, who I perceived were well nigh overcome, but who immediately taking courage again, closed up their broken ranks and renewed the battle." (Grady, "Washington's Prophecy," p. 13)

The ruthless forces of Islam, armies of terror and death that live by the sword, are rising throughout the world and are posed to strike against America and Israel. The borders of America, once protected by the word of God, are presently essentially undefended. The prophet Ezekiel wrote over twenty-five hundred years ago that a massive anti-God coalition of Muslim and Communist forces would merge together to form a mighty army to come against Israel at the end of the age. The ancient prophet documented the Communist and Muslim nations by name in the 38th and 39th chapters of Ezekiel. The angelic visitor showed Washington that these armies would come against America from Asia, Europe and Africa. The book of Ezekiel names the nations from Asia to come against America: Tubal (38:2), Meshech (38:2,3), Rosh (38:2), Togarmah ((38:6) and Gog (38: 1-2, 14-16, 18 and 39:1, 11). The nations to come against Israel from Africa were Sheba (38:13), Dedan 38:13), Cush (38:5) and Put (38:5). The nations to come against Israel from Europe were Tarshish (38:13) and Gomer (38:6). These same nations that will come against Israel will come against America as well as long as America remains as Israel's greatest defender.

America has been deceived from within because America has forgotten its Almighty Father, the author of the Republics long and glorious years of liberty. Americas defense of Israel may end when Barack Obama is elected President of the United States. The real identity of Barack Obama has been hidden from the American people by the liberal press and media. Again Hosea's warning, "My people are destroyed for lack of knowledge," is directed at the American people. When a blessed nation forgets their God they have historically inherited a ruler that opens the gates to destruction. In Washington's vision it was ruthless nations from Europe, Asia and Africa coming against America.

It may appear confusing that Islam and Communism would one day merge, but in actual fact the relationship began at the beginning of Lenin's Bolshevik revolution. "In the early days of the Bolshevik struggle, many native leaders in Central Asia, the Caucasus, and other Muslim areas looked favorably upon Lenin's revolution. They saw it not so much as the beginning of a new socialist era but as the end of Russian imperialist domination….As the Communist Party is fighting this same imperialism in Russia and abroad, we must accept Soviet Power." (Broxup, Marie Bennigsen, "Comrade Muslims!" *The Wilson Quarterly*, Summer 1992, pp. 39-40)

The dark red light of Washington's vision most certainly reveals the armies of communism that rule in Asia and Africa today. Russia (Gog) has never been more despotic and dangerous than under the ruthless regime of Vladimir Putin. Even Europe, the nation states that America saved from Hitler's Nazi oppression, has turned against America. This change in Europe has occurred because the nation states of the European Commonwealth are no longer Protestant but are rather secular godless states consistent with atheistic communism. The question that arises is, how can godless communism form a marriage with the "total submission to Allah" theocracy of Islam? This question cuts to the heart of the final purpose for the lands of the Oregon Territory. The vision that God gave George Washington for America was intended also for the sons of the Republic of the present hour. The vision that God gave the prophet Ezekiel was intended mainly for the Christian believers of the present hour. Sadly, many Christians of the present hour do not believe or take heed of biblical prophecy. The usual excuse of Christians of the present age is "we are not to know day of the hour." In addition, Christians of the present hour have been seduced to believe they will be delivered from the wars and destruction prophesied in the Bible by a secret pre-tribulation rapture. According to this "rapture deception" God is going to remove all Christians (especially American Christians) from the earth so they will not have to suffer during the terrible hour of warfare and destruction prophesied to encompass the whole world. Fortunately Christians in Islamic, Communist and nations ruled by dictatorships have already experienced tribulation without being saved by such a 'rapture' and have not been deceived by this American religious false teaching.

America has few allies left in the world and none with the power to come to her defense. In light of the fact that America has systematically removed the allegiance of God from the land, the providential protection afforded to the nation from the beginning, to whom will America turn in the nation's greatest hour of need? Godless communism and theocratic Islam will form a merger because they are politically, ideologically and economically linked for the common purpose of the destruction of Israel and America. According to the Book of Revelation the armies from Europe, Asia and Africa will be ruled by a "seven headed beast with ten horns." (Rev. 13:1) According to the Gospel of Matthew (24:15) this beast will rule the world from Jerusalem. The prophet John articulated the power and authority of this end-time ruler known as the "Antichrist."

"And he causeth all, both small and great, rich and poor, free and bond, to receive a mark in their right hand or in their forehead. And no man might buy or sell save he that had the mark or the name of the beast, or the number of his name." (Rev. 13: 16,17)

The world financial system is spinning out of control. This financial collapse is happening by satanic design according to the word of God. The ancient prophets of the bible all wrote about an end time economic system that would be solved with the mark of the beast. American Christians have been deceived to believe that they will be saved from this evil system by a secret pre-tribulation 'rapture' and therefore the church in America and many places in the world has been deceived by this American teaching and has made virtually no preparation to endure the hour of trouble coming to the world.

There can be little argument against the proposition that America as a nation deserves the judgment that the Bible forewarns. Even the foremost American evangelist spokesman of the age, Billy Graham, once proclaimed, "If God does not judge America he must apologize to Sodom and Gomorrah." The Bible foretells the horrific battle whereby the forces of good under the power and authority of Christ will be arrayed against the forces of evil under the godless authority of the Antichrist. The book of Revelation reveals in panoramic and spell binding wonder the climactic events of the end of the age where one third of the world's population dies through warfare, pestilence, starvation and natural disasters.

The purpose of *Old Oregon, Under the Shadow of the Almighty* is consistent with George Washington's prophecy and the Book of Revelation. The common purpose of the Bible, George Washington's prophecy and this book is to bring a message of hope in spite of the judgment facing the world. The Sons of the Republic in Washington's vision were not defeated nor did they give up. They took courage, closed up their broken ranks and renewed the battle. The Book of Revelation is a message of hope to all who trust in God and have the faith and courage to never give up and overcome against all adversity. The message of *Old Oregon, Under the Shadow of the Almighty* is a similar message of hope. Jesus Christ promised victory and blessing to all Christians of every church and of every age that refused to give up and refused to compromise their faith. (See Revelation Chaps. 2 and 3) The purpose of this history of America and the Oregon Territory is to bring that same hope. There is a reason why God in his sovereignty shielded the Pacific Northwest from every foreign power that attempted to rule this vast domain. In the twelfth chapter of the book of Revelation the true church of God is given "two wings of a great eagle, that she might fly into the wilderness, into her place, where she is nourished for a time, and times, and half a time, from the face of the serpent." (Rev.12:14)

The Almighty God of creation has always protected his people "under His shadow" in times of great duress and tribulation. God uses the earth to help his people. In Rev. 12:16, "the earth helped the woman (the true church), and the earth opened her mouth, and swallowed up the flood which the dragon cast out of his mouth." God will once again use the earth to help his people throughout the world in the time the Bible terms the hour of tribulation (see Daniel 9: 24-27 and Matthew 24) soon to grip all mankind. Washington's vision accentuates that same hope for America. "Again, amid the fearful noise of conflict, I heard the mysterious voice saying, 'Son of the Republic, look and learn.' As the voice ceased, the shadowy angel for the last time dipped water from the ocean and sprinkled it upon America. Instantly the dark cloud rolled back, together with the armies it had brought, leaving the inhabitants of the land victorious!

Then once more I beheld the villages, towns, and cities springing up where I had seen them before, with the bright angel, planted the azure standard he had brought in the midst of them, cried with a loud voice: "While the stars remain, and the heavens send down dew upon the earth, so long shall the Union last." And taking from his brow the crown on which blazoned the word 'Union,' he placed it upon the Standard while the people, kneeling down, said, "Amen."

The scene instantly began to fade and dissolve, and I at last saw nothing but the rising, curling vapor I at first beheld. This also disappearing, I found myself once more gazing upon the mysterious visitor, who in the small voice I had heard before, said, "Son of the Republic, what you have seen is thus interpreted:

Three great perils will come upon the Republic. The most fearful is the third, but in this greatest conflict the whole world united shall not prevail against her. Let every child of the Republic learn to live for his God, his land and the Union." With these words the vision vanished, and I started from my seat and felt that I had seen a vision wherein had been shown to me the birth, progress, and destiny of the United States." (Grady, "Washington's Prophecy," p. 14)

Never in the history of America has there been an hour when the whole world could be allied against the nation, until the present hour. The Protestant Reformation is over. There is arguably only one Protestant, God-fearing nation left in the world and that nation, the United States of America (Australia could be considered the only exception), is presently enduring a great crisis of confusion and compromise. Even in America the forces of liberalism/atheism are beginning to triumph over the truth of biblical Protestantism. It is fitting that the Almighty is using the Catholic Church to bring the Protestant Church back to its spiritual roots.

America was experiencing another great hour of compromise at the turn of the nineteenth century. Great men and women of God under the leadership of Charles Finney spoke against the compromise of the hour and the nation repented and turned once again to Jesus Christ and forgiveness based on his sacrifice on the cross two thousand years ago. God is calling for another great awakening, and Christian leaders like David Wilkerson and James Dobson are calling the nation to repent and turn away from compromise and the great national sins of the hour. Do you know Jesus Christ as your Lord and Savior? Jesus died on the cross to pay the price for the sin of every human being to ever live on the earth. The purpose of this history of Oregon is to tell the story of salvation through Jesus Christ. All those that yield their hearts to Christ and repent of their sin will live forever with Christ in heaven. The only hope for the hour of tribulation about to enflame the world is reconciliation with God through Jesus Christ, his only Son. As the father of the Republic prophesied, "Let every child of the Republic learn to live for his God, his land and the Union."

The message of this book is the same message as that of Washington's prophecy. The true Sons of the Republic must put their hope and trust in the God of their fathers, the Lord Jesus Christ, and learn to live for Him. To live for God means to live for our country and our families as well. God has given the Sons of the Republic of the Old Oregon Territory one of the greatest natural resource heritages known to the world. The Sons of the Republic of the Old Oregon Territory must learn to understand and cherish the treasure that God has given them and see the vision of hope and refuge this land represents in the hour that is upon America. May the true church and the true Sons of the Republic rise to the challenge and merge together under obedience of Christ the King and finish the high calling for America and for Old Oregon. May the true church prepare physically, spiritually and emotionally for the tribulation that is coming to America and the world. Most importantly, may this research inspire and motivate the true church and the faithful Sons of the Republic to serve our sovereign God with all their heart, all their soul, all their strength and all their might.

Amen.

BIBLIOGRAPHY

BOOKS

King James Bible, Thompson Chain Reference.
Letter From the Secretary of Defense, Ye Galleon Press, Fairfield, Washington, 1903.

Ahlstrom, Sydney, *A Religious History of the American People,* Vol. I, Doubleday and Co., Garden City, New York, 1975.
Alexandersson, Olaf, *Living Water, Viktor Schauber and the Secrets of Natural Energy,* Gateway Books, Bath, Utah, 1990.
Bourne, Edward G., *Essays in Historical Criticism*, Charles Scriber's Sons, London, New York, New York, 1901.
Brown, John, A. & Ruby, Robert H., *The Cayuse Indians; Imperial Tribesmen of Oregon*, University of Oklahoma Press, Norman, OK, 1989.
Burgess, John W., *The American Historical Series, 1817-1853*, Charles Scribner and Sons, New York, NY, 1897.
Cannon, Miles, *Waiilatpu*, Capital News Publisher, Boise, ID, 1915.
Chiniquy, Father, *Fifty Years in the Church of Rome*, Toronto Willard Tract Depository, Toronto, Canada, 1887.
Coleman, Michael C., *Presbyterian Missionary Attitudes Toward American Indians, 1837-1897*, University Press of Mississippi, Jackson, Miss. and London, England, 1985.
Converse, George, L., *A Military History of the Columbia Valley*, Pioneer Press Books, Walla Walla, Washington, 1988.
Cornelison, J. M., *The Seed of the Martyrs* (unpublished manuscript), Tamastslikt Cultural Institute, Pendleton, Oregon, 1957.
Cross, Francis E. & Parkin, Charles M. Jr., *Captain Gray in the Pacific Northwest*, Maverick Productions, Bend, Oregon, 1987.
Curtis, George Ticknor, *The Life of Daniel Webster*, Vol. II, S. Appleton and Co. Publishers, New York, NY, 1870.
Dowling, John, *History of Romanism*, Edward Walker, New York, New York, 1845.
Drury, Clifford, *Marcus and Narcissa Whitman and the Opening of Old Oregon*, Vol. I & II, Arthur H. Clark Company, Glendale, CA, 1973.
Drury, Clifford, *Where Wagons Could Go*, University of Nebraska Press, Lincoln, Nebraska, 1997.
Farnham, Thomas D., *History of Oregon Territory*, New York, NY, New World Press, 1844.
Federer, William J., *America's God and Country*, Amerisearch, Inc. St. Louis, MO, 1999.
Forbush, William, ed., *Fox's Book of Martyrs*, Zondervan Publishing House, Grand Rapids, Michigan, 1926.
Garraghan, Gilbert, *The Jesuits of Middle United States*, Vol. I and II, Loyola University Press, Chicago, Ill. 1984.
Grady, John, *George Washington's Vision and Prophecy for America*, American Christian Church, Benton, TN.
Grafe, Steven L., *Peoples of the Plateau, The Indian Photographs of Lee Moorehouse,* University of Oklahoma, Norman, Oklahoma, 2005.
Gray, W. H., *A History of Oregon*, H. H. Bancroft and Company, Portland, Oregon, 1870.
Halley, Henry, H., *Halley's Bible Handbook*, Zondervan Publishing House, Grand Rapids, Mich., 1962.

Helm, Myra Sager, *Lorinda Bewley and the Whitman Massacre*, Metropolitan Press, Portland, Oregon, 1951.
Kilkenny, John F., *Shamrocks and Shepherds: The Irish of Morrow County*, Glass-Dahlstrom Printers, 1969.
Lansing, Isaac J., *Romanism and the Republic*, Arnold Publishing Co., Boston, Mass., 1890.
Lansing, Robert B., *Juggernaut: The Whitman Massacre*, Ninth Judicial Circuit Historical Society, 1993.
Limerick, Patricia N., *The Legacy of Conquest, The Unbroken Past of the American West*, Norton, New York, 1987.
Lyman, Horace, *History of Oregon: The Growth of an American State*, Vols. I, II, III, IV, New York, NY, North Pacific Publishing Society, 1903.
Marshall, Peter, & Manuel, David, *From Sea to Shining Sea*, Fleming H. Revell, Grand Rapids, Michigan, 1986.
McLuhan, L. C., *Touch the Earth*, Pocket Book Publisher, New York, NY, 1972.
Morgan, Dale L., *Jedediah Smith and the Opening of the West*, University of Nebraska Press, Lincoln, Nebraska, 1953.
Mowry, William A., *Marcus Whitman*, Silver Burditt and Co., New York, NY, 1901.
Nerburn, Kent, ed., *The Wisdom of the Great Chiefs*, New Classic Wisdom Collection, San Rafael, Ca., 1994.
Nixon, Oliver W., *How Marcus Whitman Saved America,* Star Publishing Company, 1895.
Otis, George Jr., *Informed Intercession*, Renew Books, Ventura, Calif., 1999.
Parson, William, *History of Umatilla and Morrow County*, W. H. Lever, 1902.
Phelps, Eric Jon, *Vatican Assassins*, Halcyon United Services, Tehachapi, Ca., 2001.
Ross, Alexander, *Adventure of the First Settlers on the Oregon or Columbia River*, Oregon State University Press, Corvallis, Oregon, 2000.
Sager, Catherine, *The Whitman Massacre*, Ye Galleon Press, Fairfield, Washington, 1986.
Sager, Catherine, Sager, Elizabeth, & Sager, Matilda, *The Whitman Massacre of 1847*, Ye Galleon Press, Fairfield, Washington, 1986.
Schwantes, Carlos Arnoldo, *The Pacific Northwest, An Interpretive History*, Nebraska Press, Lincoln, Neb. and London, England, 1996.
Semlyen, Michael de, *All Roads Lead to Rome?*, Dorchester House Publisher, Norwich, England, 1993.
Steber, Rick, *Where Rolls the Oregon*, Bear Wallow Publishing Company, Union, Oregon, 1985.
Trefethen, James, B., *An American Crusade for Wildlife*, Winchester Press, Alexandria, VA, 1975.
Victor, Francis, *Early Indian Wars of Oregon*, Frank Baker State Printer, Salem, OR, 1894.
Wilkerson, David, *America's Last Call,* Wilkerson Trust Publications, Lindale Texas, 1998
Williams, Richard R., *The Loggers*, Time Life Books, Alexandria, Virginia, 1976.
Whitman, Narcissa, *The Letters of Narcissa Whitman*, Ye Galleon Press, Fairfield, Washington, 2002.

NEWSPAPER ARTICLES AND MAGAZINES

Aney, Kathy, "Church Pushes Pro-Life Stance," *East Oregonian,* November, 2, 08.
Associated Press, "Branding Oregon," *Oregonian*, January, 25, 2004.
Associated Press, "Federal Fish Managers Advise Closure of Salmon Fishing," *East Oregonian*, March 8, 2006.
Confederated Umatilla Journal, January 2005.
Barker, Rocky, "Columbia Tribes Give Up Call for Breaching Dams," *Idaho Statesman*, April 8, 2008.
Broxup, Marie Bennigsen, "Comrade Muslims," *The Wilson Quarterly*, Summer 1992.
Duin, Steve, "EQ Is No Advocate for the Environment," *Oregonian*, Nov. 1, 2005.
East Oregonian, "Federal Fish Managers Advise Closure of Salmon Fishing," March 8, 2006.
Gransbery, Jim, "Nez Perce War of 1877, Valley Pause," *Billings Gazette*, August 5, 2002.
Gransbery, Jim, "Nez Perce War of 1877, Camp Attacked," *Billings Gazette*, August 12, 2002.
McAllister, Tom, "Fee Hunting on Private Lands Is Hot Issue for Next Legislature," *Oregonian*, Nov. 17, 1987.
McCune, Hal, "Salmon Meeting Shows Complexity of Challenge," *East Oregonian*, Feb. 22, 2006.
Milstein, Michael, "Murkier Waters Flow With New Rules," *Oregonian*, Oct. 31, 2005.
Otto, Paul, "The Biblical Mandate for Social Justice," *George Fox Journal*, Spring, Vol. 2, Number 1, 2006.
Ruby, Robert H., "The 1847 Whitman Massacre," *Confederated Umatilla Journal*, Vol. IX, Issue 1, January 2005.

Thackeray, Lorna, "Campaign Casts a Shadow on Career," *Billings Gazette*, July 28, 2002.
Thackeray, Lorna, "Nez Perce War of 1877, No Happy Ending," *Billings Gazette*, Oct. 2007.
Thackeray, Lorna, "Nez Perce War of 1877, Turning North," *Billings Gazette*, Sept. 16, 2002.
Thackeray, Lorna, "Siege and Surrender at Bear Paw," *Billings Gazette*, Sept. 30, 2002.
Woodward, Tim, "Nimiipuu: The Story of the Nez Perce," *Idaho Statesman*, September 2005.

INTERNET SOURCES

http://bluebook.state.or.us/cultural/history/history14.htm Indian Wars
http://en.wikipedia.org/wiki/Council_of_Trent Fourth Session, 1546
www.columbiariverkeepers.org
www.crh.org/comm/river/docs/ubasin.htm Shelley, Christopher, THE RESURRECTION OF A RIVER
www.dfw.state.or.us OREGON SPORTS FISHING 2006 REGULATIONS
www.downwinders.com
www.nezperce.org/History/JacksonSundown.htm
www.reformed.org/books/fox/fox_martyrs.html Fox' Book of Martyrs, Forbush, Byron
www.salemhistory.net/peoplejason_lee
www.ski.edu/netbok/of-ra.htm
www.umatilla.nsn.su/hist2.html CTUIR History and Culture
www.umatilla.nsn.us/salmonpolicy.html CTUIR Salmon Policy

CONGRESSIONAL REPORTS

Brouillet, Rev. J. B. A., "Protestantism in Oregon," 35TH Congress, Ex. Doc. No. 38.
Browne, Ross J., "Causes of the Late Indian War in Oregon and Washington Territories," 35th Congress Ex. Doc. No. 38.
Spalding, Rev. Henry, "Letter for the Secretary of the Interior," 41st Congress, Ex. Doc. No. 37.

PERSONAL LETTERS OWNED AND DOCUMENTED BY AUTHOR

Ethel Moore Knighten (deceased)
George Moore (deceased)

CONGRESSIONAL LAWS AND STANDARDS

Clean Water Act, 33 USC 125d 1960.
Environmental Protection Agency, Standards, Hazardous Waste Incinerators, 1990.
Environmental Protection Agency, 910-R-02-006, 1996-98.

INDEX

A

Abernathy, Governor George, 135, 155
Accolti, Father, 159
Adams, John Quincy, 47
Adams, Samuel, 190
Age of Discovery, xi, 1-3, 9, 10, 12-14, 25, 28
Anderson, Will, 247
Appaloosa, 188, 225
Applegate, Jesse, 91
Ashburton Treaty, 79, 80
Astor, John Jacob, 23, 33, 34, 52
Aztec, 4, 5

B

Baranoff, Alexander, 11
Barrows, Rev. William, 79, 96
Bauman, Clarence, 231
Bear Paw Mountain, 185, 187
Beecher, Lyman, 189
Bering, Vitus, 11
Bi-State Commission, 255
Black Butte, 229, 230, 232
Black Pope, 111, 113, 120, 125, 135
Black Robes, 134
Bonneville, Captain Benjamin, 40, 42
Book of Heaven, 45, 47-52, 59, 103, 104, 109, 140, 154, 170, 179, 215, 218, 219, 224, 238, 265, 266
Boone, Daniel, 35
Boston men, 23, 34, 64
Bridger, Jim, 55
Brobdingnag, xi, 8
Brouillet, Father, vi, xvi, 121, 122, 132-139, 141-144, 146-153, 155-157, 161, 162, 208, 209
Brouillet, Vicar General, xvi, 132, 134-136, 141, 143, 149
Brown, Dr. John, 98
Browne, J. Ross, xvi, 127, 142, 143, 145, 146, 161
Bryant, William Cullen, 26
Burke Act, 211
Burke, Chief Bill, 221

C

Calvin, John, 46
Catholic Counter Reformation, xiii, xiv, 64, 65, 68, 74, 89, 95, 106-108, 110, 119, 120, 135, 141, 142, 152
Catholic Ladder, 118-120
Catlin, George, 50
Cason, Lewis, 232
Cayuse, vi, vii, xii, xv-xix, 18-23, 28, 35, 40-43, 47, 50-52, 69, 71-74, 83, 87, 88, 93, 98-106, 108, 112, 114-116, 118-123, 126-129, 131-142, 144-153, 155, 158-161, 163-166, 175, 200, 204, 206-210, 214-218, 220, 224, 233, 281
Cayuse Wars, 142, 160, 161
Chapman, Mr., 179
Charles II, 38
Cherokee, xviii, 192-194, 200, 208
Chinook, 17, 18, 33, 247
Choctaw, 192, 194
Christian Advocate, 50, 206
Clark, George Rogers, 162
Clark, Ramsey, 35
Clark, William, 28, 32, 48-50, 241
Clean Water Act, 246, 247, 252, 254, 268, 283
Clemens, Father Bailey, 266
Columbia Rediviva, 14, 15
Columbia Plateau Indians, 12, 13, 16-19, 45, 36, 41-45, 47-50, 59, 60, 76, 80, 98-111, 115, 118, 132, 137, 140, 141, 160, 163, 165, 170, 179, 196, 204, 206-208, 213, 214, 218, 224, 226, 241, 250, 251, 267
Columbia River, v, vi, ix, xi-xiii, xvi-xxi, 1-3, 9-11, 13-20, 22-25, 31-43, 45, 47-50, 55, 59, 60, 63, 64, 70, 73-76, 80, 82, 83, 86-88, 90, 93, 94, 98-104, 106-113, 115, 118, 119, 131, 132, 137, 138, 140-142, 152, 158-161, 163-166, 169, 170, 173, 179-181, 189, 196, 197, 203, 204, 206-210, 213-215, 217, 218, 220, 224, 226, 239-241, 243, 244, 247-261, 264, 267-269, 281, 282

Columbus, Christopher, 4, 236
Confederated Tribes of the Umatilla, vi, xviii-xx, 101, 108,
    140, 157, 206, 209-211, 213, 215, 216, 219, 220, 224,
    239, 240, 242, 244, 246, 247, 249, 252, 258, 264
Conner, Bobby, 219
Conner, E. J., 219
Cook, Captain James, xii-14, 29
Cooley, Chief William, 194
Corben, Geneve, 232
Cornelison, Dr. J. M., xviii, 49, 219
Cornelison, xviii, xix, 49, 213-220, 281
Coronado, Francisco, 7
Cortés, Hernán, 4
Council of Trent, 46, 65, 110, 111
Counter Reformation, xiii, xiv, 46, 64, 65, 68, 74, 89, 95,
    106-110, 119, 120, 135, 141, 142, 152, 155
Craig, William, 147
Crockett, Davy, 195
Cumberland and United Presbyterian Churches, 154

D

Daste, Father, 21
Dawes Act, 210, 211
Day, John, 20, 35, 36, 165, 231, 248
De Aguilar, Martin, xi, 9
De Heceta, Don Bruno, 3, 12, 15
De Maldonado, Lorenzo Ferrer, 8
DEQ, xx, 268, 269
De Smet, Father Peter, 99
Desoto, Hernando, 4, 7
Deffenbaugh, George, 170
Delamater, Dr. John, 54, 55
Demers, Father, 111, 112
Department of Environmental Quality (DEQ), xx, 268, 269
Dick, Ed, ix, 233
Donation Land Act, 166, 196, 206, 207
Dorion, Pierre, 35
Drake, Sir Francis, 9
Drury, Dr. Clifford, 54, 67, 88, 91, 97, 103, 132

E

Eells, Dr. Cushing, 81
Eldrige, Steve, 244
Emerson, Ralph Waldo, 195
Endangered Species Act, 246
Environmental Protection Agency, 254, 283
Environmental Quality Commission (EQC), 269
Evan, Hon. Elwood, 95
Evarts, Jeremiah, 209, 212
Exclusion Law, 226

F

Finlay, Nicholas, 144
Finney, Charles G., 202
Five Crows, 135, 136, 218
Five Wounds, 181, 183
Flathead Indians, xiii, 21
Flatheads, 159
Fletcher, Alice, 210, 211
Fletcher, George, 225, 226
Fontenelle, Lucien, 55
Fort Boise, 42, 60, 61, 92, 93
Fort Hall, 42, 60, 76, 90-93, 126, 127
Fort Nez Perce, 42
Fort Santa Fe, 76

G

Geronimo, 178, 183
Gibbon, Colonel John, 184
Gibbon, General, 184
Gilliam, Colonel, 133
Grant, Captain, 92, 93
Gray, Captain Robert, xi, 3, 14, 15
Gray, H. H., 96, 99
Gray, William Henry (W. W.), 55, 56, 59, 61, 64, 94, 96
Green, Jerome, 184
Greene, Secretary, 75, 90, 98, 99, 102, 107, 111, 115
Greenhow, Robert, 8, 37
Griffin, Rev. J. S., 142
Grinnell, George, 243

H

Hale, Dr. Edward, 79
Hallock, Stephanie, 268, 269
Hanford, xx, 254-256, 258
Happy Canyon, vi, xix, 223-226
Harkenrider, Jerry, 257
Hart, Senator Thomas, 61
Hayes, President Rutherford, 189
Hayes, Rev. James, 218
Heceta, Don Bruno de, 3, 12
Heirship Act, 211
Holt, Dr. W. S., 219
Howard, General Oliver, 176-182, 188
Hudson's Bay Company, v, xiii, xiv, 34, 37-39, 42, 43, 47-49,
    52, 53, 57, 59-64, 69, 72, 82, 92, 131, 132, 137, 144,
    146, 152, 154, 157, 158, 160, 164, 165
Huss, Dr. John, 45

I

Indian Removal Act, 193, 194
Indian Restoration Act, xviii, 212, 213

J

Jackson, President Andrew, xviii, 36, 189, 190, 192, 193, 197, 200, 203, 209
Jefferson, Thomas, xii, 14, 26-30, 32, 33, 39, 61
Jesuits, xiv, xvi, 46, 65-68, 88, 89, 95, 99, 100, 104, 107, 108, 110-113, 116, 118, 122, 123, 125, 127, 134, 136, 137, 142-144, 149, 151, 152, 157-161, 163-165, 167, 209, 281
Joint Occupation Treaty, 37, 54, 63, 88, 125
Joseph, Chief, xvii, 22, 166-181, 183-192, 194, 195, 198, 199, 201, 203-205, 210-213, 219, 224, 251, 261
Joset, Father, 151, 158

K

Kash Kash, James, 217
Kash Kash, Sam, 217
Kilkenny, John F., viii, 238
Kilkenny, John O., 263, 264
Kilkenny, John S., 237, 238, 263
King Charles II, 38
King George III, xii, 26, 46, 64
King George men, 23, 34, 38, 39
King Louis XVI, 14
Knox, John, 46
Knutson-Vandenburg Act, 245

L

Lady Washington, 14
Lane, Governor, 158
Lapwai, xiv, xv, 21, 65, 95, 161, 168, 173, 175, 176, 178, 179, 187-189, 209, 214, 216
Lawyer, 62, 172, 173, 209, 223
Leasing Act, 211
Ledyard, John, xii, 14, 29
Lee, Jason, 52, 53, 89, 111, 216, 270, 272
Lewis and Clark, xii, xx, 7, 11, 18, 21, 22, 26, 29-33, 35, 39, 43, 48, 50, 118, 140, 164, 165, 171, 206, 224, 254

Lewis, Joe, 122, 125-128, 146, 151
Lewis, Meriwether, 28, 30, 32
Lincoln, Abraham, vii, viii, 10
Linn, Senator Lewis, 83

Lock, Michael, 8
Looking Glass, 178, 181, 183, 185, 186, 188
Lorinda Bewley, 128, 133-136, 282
Louisiana Territory, 14, 25, 27
Lovejoy, Asa, 76, 81
Lowrie, Walter 204
Loyola, Ignatius, xiv, 65, 67
Lyman, Horace, 10, 14, 48, 111

M

Macbeth, Kate, 21
Mackenzie, Alexander, xii, 26, 27
Magellan, Ferdinand, 4
Manhattan Project, 255
Manifest Destiny, vi, xvii, 25, 27, 28, 33, 47, 82, 84, 86, 164, 190, 192, 193, 195, 197, 200, 211, 223, 238
Marshall, William, 96, 157
Mason, George, 211, 213
Matteson School House, ii, vi, vii, ix, xix, 228, 231-234, 242
McBean, Captain William, 122, 131-133, 158
McDougal, Duncan, 33
McGivey, Father Michael J., 236
McKay, Thomas, 60
McKinley, President William, 189
McLeod, John L., 60
McLoughlin, Chief Factor, 42, 53, 58, 122
McLoughlin, Dr. John, 39, 52, 60, 63, 64
Meares, Captain John, 13
Meek, Helen Mar, 99, 121
Meek, Joseph, 196
Miles, General, 185-190
Miller, William, 88
Minthorn, Phillip, 217-219
Minthorn, Sarah, 215-217
Miriam Report, 211, 213
Monroe, President James, 47
Moorehouse, Major Lee, 181, 214, 215, 220, 225, 226
Mowry, William A., 94
Muir, John, 242
Multiple-Use Sustained Yield Act, 244

N

Napoleon, 25, 27, 117, 157
National Forest Management Act, 244, 247
Nez Perce, vi, xii, xiii, xvii, xix, 18, 20-23, 35, 42, 43, 48, 49, 52, 54, 55, 57, 59, 62, 69, 72, 99, 103, 104, 126, 136, 137, 139, 140, 145, 147, 148, 151, 156, 157, 160, 161, 163-192, 194, 195, 197, 200, 201, 204, 206, 209, 213-219, 222, 224, 258, 260, 261, 270, 272, 283
Nixon, O. W., 96

Northwest Company, 63
Northwest Fur Company, 38, 39
Northwest Passage, v, vi, xi, xx, 1, 3, 8, 9, 11-13, 15, 16, 24, 26, 29, 253, 254, 267
Northwest Power Act, 250

O

Obama, Barack, 277
Ogden, Peter Skeen, 39
Ollokot, 181, 185, 186, 219
Oregon Christian Church, 154
Oregon Conference Methodist Episcopal Church, 154
Oregon Congregational Association, 154
Oregon Presbytery of the Old School, 154
Organic Act, 196, 246
Osbourne, 128-132
Osbourne, Josiah, 128
Otto, Paul, 267

P

Palmer, Joel, 148, 155, 158, 166, 197, 207, 218
Parker, Rev. Samuel, 55
Penn, William, 212
Peter the Great, 11
Pinchot, Gifford, 243, 246
Pinkham, Allen ,140
Pittman, Anna Maria, 53
Pizarro, Francisco, 4
Pleasant Butte Baptist Church, 154, 155, 164, 165
Polk, President James, 196
Pollen, J. H., 10
Pope Benedict XVI, 266
Pope Gregory XVI, 110
Pope John Paul II, 256
Porfily, Bill, 251
Professor John W. Burgess, 93
Protestant Reformation, xiii, xiv, 5, 6, 10, 39, 44-47, 64, 65, 74, 76, 85, 94, 95, 97, 107-110, 119, 120, 123, 141-143, 145, 154, 161, 172, 213, 279
Protestantism in Oregon, 132, 139, 140, 143, 163

Q

Quackenbush, Roy, 232
Queen Elizabeth I, 9

R

Rainbow, 181, 183
Raley, Roy, xix, 223, 226, 227
Rogers, Mr., 117, 128, 149
Romanism, vi, xvii, 65, 67, 68, 97, 110, 111, 113, 115, 118, 125, 154, 155, 157, 161, 163, 281, 282
Roothaan, General John, 111
Roothaan, General, xvi, 107, 120, 135, 146
Ruby, Dr. Robert, 98, 108, 135, 137, 138

S

Saager, Herb, 246
Sacajawea, 32
Saffrons, Dr. Henry, 131
Sager, Catherine, 105, 110, 116-121, 123, 134, 157
Sager, Elizabeth, 128
Sager, Francis, 123
Sahaptin, 18-21
Sails, Mr., 133, 134
Schut, Jack, 221
Scott, Etta Conner, 219
Seattle, Chief, xviii, 197-201, 204, 212
Seminole, 192-194
Shakespeare, William, 9
Shaw, Captain, 105, 146
Shining Mountains, 14, 26
Sitting Bull, 178, 183, 185, 187, 188, 224
Slater Allotment Act, 210
Smith, Alex , 156
Smith, Frederick, 197
Smith, Jedediah S., 64
Snake Indians, 19, 35, 42
Sonneck, Vera, 136, 140
Spain, John, 225
Spalding, Eliza, xv, 54, 57, 58, 60, 93, 113, 118, 134, 143, 163, 164, 166, 170, 171, 178, 203, 272
Spalding, Henry, 72, 74, 82, 96, 102, 103, 122, 126, 127, 130, 131, 135, 136, 138, 140-142, 145-148, 151, 155, 156, 161, 162, 166, 171
Spanish Armada, 10
Steber, Rick, 228
Steller, Georg, 11
Stickus, xv, 93, 122, 123, 133, 216-218
Stillman, Beryl, 245
Straits of Anian, 3, 8, 9
Straits of Fuca, 13
Stuart, Robert, 35, 41
Sturgis, General, 185
Sundown, Jackson, 224-226
Swan Necklace, 219

T

Tamastslikt Cultural Institute, 216, 219, 240, 281
Tamayhas, 128
Tamuscky, 122, 128
Tartar, 18
Taylor, Sheriff Til, 226
Tchirikof, Alexei, 11
Teloukaite, Chief, 128, 218
Third Great Awakening, vi, xxi, 271
Thompson, Lucy, 53
Thurston, Hon. S. R., 155, 157
Too-hool-hool-suit, 176, 177, 179-181, 185, 186
Toupin, John, 146, 147
Treaty of 1855, vi, xvii, xviii, 108, 167, 177, 206, 209, 211, 213, 218, 239, 250, 252, 262
Tutuilla Church, 214, 216-222
Tutuilla Presbyterian Church, vi, xviii, 49, 209, 214, 216, 219, 223
Tyler, President John, xv, 82, 87

U

Umatilla Basin Project, 251, 252
Umatilla River, vi, 35, 36, 41, 121, 207, 209, 211, 213, 240, 248-253

V

Van Buren, President Martin, 195
Vancouver, Captain George, xi, 15
Vermeersh, Father Adolph, 209
Voyage of Discovery, 3, 13, 14, 22, 28-32, 36

W

Waiilatpu, 70, 74, 87, 93, 95, 99, 100, 104-107, 112, 115, 118, 123, 125, 127, 128, 131, 133, 135, 138, 144-146, 149, 150, 152, 207, 281
Waiilatpus, 19
Walker, Elkanah, 71, 75
Walker, William, 48, 49
Wallowa, xvii, 167, 172-180, 182, 247, 250
Ward, Glen, 245
Washington, George, ix, 272-275, 277
WaterWatch, 252
Watkuese, 21, 22
Webster, Daniel, xv, 61, 81, 82, 113, 281
Wheeler Howard Act, 211
Wheeler, Rev. William, 215
White Bird, 178, 180, 185-188, 224
White, Elijah, 53
Whitman, Marcus, ii, xv, xviii, 23, 48, 53-57, 61, 64, 71, 72, 74-76, 81, 84-86, 91, 93-97, 100, 101, 103, 104, 109, 112, 113, 127, 148, 149, 161, 162, 216, 219, 240, 271, 282
Whitman, Narcissa, xiv, 23, 54, 56-58, 60, 65, 73, 74, 97, 98, 100, 102, 105, 106, 112, 113, 123, 128, 143, 148, 175, 203, 204, 214-216, 219, 272, 281, 282
Whitman, Perrin, 92, 99, 131
Wilkerson, David, 275, 279
Williams, Ezekiel, 33, 35
Williams, Robert, 215
Wycliffe, John, 45, 76
Wyeth, Nathaniel, 52, 60

Y

Yelleppit, Chief, 22
Yellow Hawk, 216, 217, 219
Yellow Wolf, 185, 188
Young, John, 147

Z

Zwingli, Huldrych, 46

About the Author

Stuart Dick graduated from Eastern Oregon State University in 1970 with a dual degree in history and education. He did graduate work in anthropology at Oregon State University and completed his Master of Divinity degree from George Fox Evangelical Seminary in 1982. Dick worked as a secondary school teacher and coach and later as a youth minister and Pastor in a number of Evangelical churches. He is an elder and serves on the board of Pendleton Faith Center Foursquare Church and owns and operates a construction company in Pendleton. His first book, *Outback to Asia,* was released in 2002. Dick's wife, Julie, is a Registered Nurse. They have five children and eight grandchildren.